Freya Stark (1893–1993), 'the poet of travel', was the doyenne of Middle East travel writers and one of the most courageous and adventurous women travellers of her generation. She travelled extensively throughout Syria, Palestine, Lebanon, Iran, Iraq and Southern Arabia, where she became the first western woman to travel through the Hadhramaut. Usually alone, she ventured to places few Europeans had visited. Her travels earned her the title of Dame and huge public acclaim. Her many, now classic, books include *Traveller's Prelude*, *Ionia*, *The Southern Gates of Arabia*, *Alexander's Path*, *Dust in the Lion's Paw*, *East is West* and *Valleys of the Assassins*.

To all lovers of Peace, this book is dedicated.

'So the final end achieved by this work will be, to gain knowledge of what was the condition of each people after all had been crushed and had come under the dominion of Rome, until the disturbed and troubled time that afterwards ensued.'

(Polybius: *Histories*, III.410)

D0988607

'It's hard to think of a writer in the travel game who most closely demonstrates the merits of Flaubert's three rules for good writing: clarity, clarity and finally clarity. Re-reading her now, her restrained powers of description shine as brightly as they ever did, and they will continue to shine until the next Ice Age... Her books are more relevant than ever. Besides sheer enjoyment, one should read her for a fresh perspective on the intractable issues dogging Christian-Muslim relations. She was able to see both sides and what she found was similarity, not difference. The greatest woman traveller of the 20th century? I think so.'   Sara Wheeler, *The Times*

'It was rare to leave her company without feeling that the world was somehow larger and more promising. Her life was something of a work of art...The books in which she recorded her journeys were seductively individual...Nomad and social lioness, public servant and private essayist, emotional victim and mythmaker.'   Colin Thubron, *New York Times*

'Few writers have the capacity to do with words what Fabergé could do with gems – to fashion them, without violating their quality. It is this extraordinary talent which sets Freya Stark apart from her fellow craftsman in the construction of books on travel.'   *The Daily Telegraph*

'Freya Stark remains unexcelled as an interpreter of brief encounters in wild regions against the backdrop of history.'   *The Observer*

'One of the finest travel writers of the 20th century.'   *The New Yorker*

'A Middle East traveler, an explorer and, above all, a writer, Freya Stark has, with an incomparably clear eye, looked toward the horizon of the past without ever losing sight of the present. Her books are route plans of a perceptive intelligence, traversing time and space with ease.'
Saudi Aramco World

Tauris Parke Paperbacks is an imprint of I.B.Tauris. It is dedicated to publishing books in accessible paperback editions for the serious general reader within a wide range of categories, including biography, history, travel and the ancient world. The list includes select, critically acclaimed works of top quality writing by distinguished authors that continue to challenge, to inform and to inspire. These are books that possess those subtle but intrinsic elements that mark them out as something exceptional.

The Colophon of Tauris Parke Paperbacks is a representation of the ancient Egyptian ibis, sacred to the god Thoth, who was himself often depicted in the form of this most elegant of birds. Thoth was credited in antiquity as the scribe of the ancient Egyptian gods and as the inventor of writing and was associated with many aspects of wisdom and learning.

ROME ON THE EUPHRATES

The Story of a Frontier

Freya Stark

TPP

TAURIS PARKE
PAPERBACKS

New paperback edition published in 2012 by Tauris Parke Paperbacks
An imprint of I.B.Tauris and Co Ltd
6 Salem Road, London W2 4BU
175 Fifth Avenue, New York NY 10010
www.ibtauris.com

Distributed in the United States and Canada Exclusively by Palgrave Macmillan
175 Fifth Avenue, New York NY 10010

First published in 1966 by John Murray (Publishers) Limited

Copyright © John R. Murray, 1966, 2012

Cover image: 'Euphrates River, Turkey' © Braden von Bibra

ISBN: 978 1 84885 314 0

A full CIP record for this book is available from the British Library
A full CIP record is available from the Library of Congress

Library of Congress Catalog Card Number: available

Printed and bound in India by ScandBook AB

Contents

Illustrations

All photographs not otherwise acknowledged are by the author

Acknowledgements

My grateful thanks are due to Mr Peter Green in the first place, who read and advised me on my manuscript; to Mrs Alan Moorehead in the second, for expert disentangling of script; to Mrs Janet Berens, for devoted work on the background dates and to Mr G. Holland and his staff at the Royal Geographical Society for their habitual kindness in dealing with my maps. The care and help of the house of Murray, with a godson now added to its ranks, has been continued through so many years that one is in danger of taking it for granted. I should also like to remember Miss Knight and Miss Dowley at the British Consulate in Istanbul for their kind help with my typescript.

Preface

'The touch of Time is perhaps always unimaginable.'
(T. R. Glover; *C.A.H.,* X, p. 513.)

The writing of history is restricted by so many more obligations than most other literary forms, that a short explanation is allowable from one who, like myself, ventures upon it as a novice.

My argument is not an innovation. The facts it relies on are not controversial; they have been described and accepted piecemeal by most historians ancient and modern though they have never, so far as I know, been strung on a single thread to make a coherent whole: *the spotlight in this book is concentrated on one corner only of the vast Roman world and follows it through eight centuries of the development and failure of a single political idea.*

This produces novelty only by putting a series of recognised events into perspective; and the conclusion is possibly controversial, though the facts on which it is based are not. For this reason, because, that is, I was dealing with accepted facts, it has not been necessary to go into the many controversies on matters of detail with which the historian's path is strewn: the exact sites or dates of Lucullus' or Trajan's marches for instance were irrelevant to the trail I was following and it was therefore advisable to avoid a number of fascinating byeways. I have on the other

hand quoted a great deal from our most eminent historians, not out of
a want of confidence in my own conclusions, but out of regard for my
reader, who may like to feel that the thread with which my web is woven
has been spun by more authoritative hands than mine.

The difficulty has been to extract this thread from the huge and
general mass of the Greco-Roman world hastening through its plenitude
to its decline. In this welter, the fragments that relate to the lands of the
Euphrates are very scattered, and the problem has been to bridge the
gaps between them and tie them together into the cohesion to which
they belong.

To this a secondary problem is added. What reader is the book
written for? Does he belong to the dwindling few who remember their
Roman history? Or did he never get far beyond Antony and Actium? I
have given him a great many dates, having been so often exasperated
myself when rummaging through pages of text. For any statements I
think he might like to look into I have given references, not necessarily
to the best available authorities but to such as are sufficient to lead
on to further research. They are intended as a preliminary guide to
anyone anxious to follow a trail, and are not meant to supplement a
bibliography such as can be found in most of the general histories quoted.
My own bibliography is confined to general works and to such sources as
I have found available in translation, since I am unhappily unable to read
Greek.

I have assumed that the main lines of Roman history are known:
if not, the reader is advised to keep a handy little supplement manual
beside him.

The unavoidable use of names such as Armenia or Kurdistan –
countries now incorporated in Turkey, Iraq or Persia – has presented
some difficulty, and it is well to explain that the references to them
under their independent names are historical and have no modern
implication.

Another problem has been that of the ancient currency, which cannot
be modernised over so long a period (eight centuries) in any permanent
way. Values had decreased by about ten to fifty per cent under Trajan
and fifty per cent under Severus (T. Frank, IV.880,897), and a daily
wage in the third century was ten or fifteen times what it had been in the
first (T. Frank, IV.222). This author, Tenney Frank (1.352–3), gives

the following values for the end of the Republic:

$$\text{Talent} = \$1,250 = \pounds 358$$
$$\text{Denarius} = \$\tfrac{1}{5} = \pounds \tfrac{1}{18}$$
$$\text{Sestertius} = \$\tfrac{1}{20} = \pounds \tfrac{1}{72}$$
$$\text{As} = \tfrac{1}{32} \text{ of Imperial denarius}$$

I suggest these values as a rough guide for my reader, but have kept to the Latin figures in my text. Anyone in search of a more accurate translation will have to supplement this exchange rate with a computation of whatever the debasement of any particular date may be.

Apart from these tangible problems is the fear that a certain number of inaccuracies – minor I hope – may be lurking undetected in a work which has spread itself over three years through various copyings and in many places; in these circumstances one can only assure one's readers that one has sweated blood over the references, and hope for the best.

An advantage I have had in my work is perhaps a knowledge of the geography: I think there cannot be more than half a dozen places mentioned that I have not either visited or stayed in. With this background, which feeds and pleases the imagination, I spent three years of steady and absorbing study, and I should like to tell how the idea of the book first came.

I grew up near a frontier, and learned to trespass across it (and across a good many others) in my time: and the impediment which it produces in human intercourse has always seemed to me a historical monstrosity.

It becomes more monstrous when it saddles some otherwise prosperous artery, as in Mesopotamia, where an east-west horizontal of trade was ever cut at recurring intervals of history by a north-south vertical of war. The commercial stream flowed happily through the Lydians; was cut in the fifth century B.C. by the Athenians (at the sea); was reopened by Alexander; was cut by the Roman Republic and intermittently re-opened or cut by the Empire; reopened by the Arabs; was again intersected and destroyed in its remoter reaches by the Iron Curtain today. It is the perennially recurring diagram in the history of north-west Asia.

The great route of Asia is the oldest, the richest, the longest, the most persistent and most romantic of all the chequered streams of trade; and the benefits when it flows, and the catastrophes when it is interrupted, have been visible through all its vicissitudes, from the age of the Assyrians to our own. With China at one end and Europe at the other and Russia between them, the subject is as topical today as ever it was before: and the question of this book – *Why did the Romans fight along their rich Euphrates frontier?* – can just as easily be asked today.

One must notice that the frontier I illustrate – from the Black Sea along the Tigris-Euphrates valleys south into Iraq – is only one among many other and different kinds of boundaries: it is not, for instance, a frontier with the quite uncivilised who may have little to lose and much to gain by attack. What I am interested in is the frontier between two trading communities who gain *mutually* through traffic and lose through war; this was the situation of Rome and her south-eastern neighbour, as it is our situation today; and the fact that she spent eight centuries in almost unbroken warfare seems, with every effort at an impartial reading of the evidence, to have been one of her most cardinal mistakes.

I thought of this frequently during the last world-war, when desert boundaries were flattened out and tanks and aeroplanes poured up from Karachi to the Caucasus in one unhindered flood. But what decided me to study the question happened some eight years ago, one summer, along the Black Sea coast.

I was driving in a bus through Giresun, the ancient Cerasus – a notorious little town where Mithradates had his wives and sisters killed to save them from what was assumed to be worse than death. Lucullus brought the cherry thence to Europe, and Xenophon, passing through with his Ten Thousand and getting a very dubious welcome along the coast, discovered painted boys for sale in the market place, fattened with what I feel sure were not, as they say, chestnuts, but hazel nuts,[1] since they still clothe the hillsides today. Apart from their green glades and fountains, history has left no visible trace in the little place except a peaceful acropolis of rock shaded by plane trees, under which the ages drip as if their stones were sand. Capes curve away, with mountain ranges subsiding to flat stretches and hooks of sand between them. Beyond a Byzantine monastery island, fishing boats lie far out, as if their sea were to be for ever calm; they carry two sails at one end in the fashion of graffiti scratched on rocks by ancient sailors. Beside a pink and rather derelict Casino, a tomb to 'Osmana' brings one up to date, killed in Mustapha Kemal's war of 1922; and in the foreground, as if in a Pompeian painting, naked boys are splashing waist-high in a sea that lies pale and bodiless, cocooned in vagueness, lisping on porphyry and malachite pebbles, as if always the underworld came through, not fierce nor sad but dim.

This is Black Sea necromancy, for as a matter of fact Giresun is a go-ahead and prosperous little town with shops and a clean hotel, and a harbour then projected and now probably built. From my window I could watch the caiques come and go like dolphins, their ends high and their waists low under cargoes, which were easy to wade out to and unload with a ladder from the shore. They carried agreeable merchandise, amphorae glazed and unglazed, passed from hand to hand and stacked in a mound, or sheep herded in the shade till the moment came for their reluctant climbing of the ladder, while an easy leisure pervaded the beaches. Children played in and out of the water, and old men came to paint their boats for an hour or two, and covered them with strips of cotton against the sun, which shone full and blinding through the day, and threw a crimson column as it sank across the harbour. Then, if a motor-boat chugged out, pale turquoise feathers would flake from the wake and die in the sulphur-coloured water, where the young labourers came to wash off the dust of their day.

I was travelling westward and after a time took a bus from Giresun to Amisus, which is now Samsun, along the coast: and the bus, as it happened, was crowded with young recruits, who were being sent for some temporary alarm to Erzerum on the Russian border. Their friends and the whole of Giresun were seeing them off and it was a cheerful enough departure; they felt smart with their new hair-cuts and frayed shirts touchingly clean. The women waited in a little group by the roadside till the men's greetings were over, and presently, as the bus was starting, came forward in a sort of wave and pressed their packages of home-baked bread and other food on to their children or their grandchildren. They were old (for the young would scarcely come out in public) and were almost hidden by the cotton *chadurs* which they wear here, enveloping body and head and chin and forehead in broad magenta stripes; nothing but the hands and the eyes were left to see, but in those outstretched hands and longing eyes such love and sorrow, such timid uncomplaining hope, that I have never forgotten, and think of them, and see them as Euripides saw the Trojan Women, a background or chorus for the quarrelsome nature of man.

This accidental episode started my book and opened what has been to me a vital window on the past and present too.

*   *   *

It is perhaps no longer usual to think of history as something one can learn from, and yet the problem is exactly what it has always been. The stream of the east-west trade which could nourish the world is held up in exactly the same way. It must be useful to examine how the Romans dealt with it; how far and in what they succeeded, and how far and why they failed. I would be happy if my attempted interpretation might induce some more basic historian to investigate more thoroughly.

Meanwhile there is one point I would like to make, preventively, against such objectors as like to say that frontier wars are inevitable, they always have been and must always be. This overlooks a far older warfare that *has* been eradicated (more or less); and that is the family war. The old get in the way and the young are a menace, and yet they live together in amity on the whole, and usually draw the line at homicide. With this reflection, which when you come to think of it points to a remarkable triumph in human relations, we can turn to the arrival of the Romans in Asia.

I

The Battle of Magnesia

The Roman arrival in Asia is an accident, an aftermath and partly a consequence of the Carthaginian Wars – a product of the fear of Hannibal and of the aggressiveness not of Rome but of Macedonia. The riches of Asia were too remote to be coveted in Rome at this time; yet the rumour of them, purposely presented by interested Greek reporters, enhanced a picture which finally prodded the Romans into war. This chapter ends with the first view of that swift deterioration which soon followed a policy of war indemnities and plunder.

> 'The same motive impelled the British . . . to move onwards until they . . . reached the barrier of the Himalayas, and . . . to ask themselves wistfully whether even that frontier was sufficiently secure.' (Cromer: *Ancient & Modern Imperialism*, p. 29.)

> 'Between the beginning and end lies a space of fifty-three years, comprising a greater number of grave and momentous events than any period of equal length in the past.' (220–168 B.C.) (Polybius: *Histories*, III.i.6.)

The Roman Arrival in Asia

It is easy to drive from Smyrna inland by the Bel Kahve pass, under an acropolis which has been called Argiroessa. A piece or two of wall is left, invisible from below, and the Lydian Olympus is to the south. At a café nearby Atatürk stood in 1922 to watch the distant capture of Smyrna. Beyond the pass, a shaly cleft leads down to Magnesia (now Manisa) and the open valley of the Hermus.[1] History lies strewn about the whole area as if it were a half-uncovered battlefield of nations. By southern foothills, beyond Byzantine walls, a Hittite road winds towards Ephesus through pines and brambles, and shows one of those thick-set warriors, with bow and spear, carved on an elephant-grey cliff about 1280 B.C. – the century of Troy. North of Nif a windowed ruin is said to have imprisoned one of the Comneni; it, too, is built on older layers of which the bettercut stone shows through. As one is taken back from pause to pause into these ranges of time, one comes suddenly upon a nameless monument – a tomb carved out of the stratified hill itself, with walls and steps barely emergent from the embracing limestone – a house of death unskilled and unadorned and yet affecting because of the patient labour that made it, and because, like man himself, it is still only half divorced from its most ancient background of the rocks.

High on a promontory near by, the shapeless face of Niobe – a natural object – trickles with the springs that feed her tears; and below her, to east and west, the valley is shallow and relaxed under a golden decay of vineyards. The olives slope into its billowing light; the pines of Tmolus pencil its distant skyline with darkness; and its dip is so imperceptible and so extended that, but for the gentle gradient of the river, one would think of it less as a valley than a plain.

The battle between East and West was fought here in 189 B.C., and is known as the Battle of Magnesia. The demarcation line of Occident and Orient shifts, one may observe, continually, and will soon no doubt reach the borders of China; on this occasion the Romans overstepped it, defeating the Seleucid king Antiochus, fifth in descent from one of Alexander's generals. His realms extended from Babylonia to India, and it always surprises me that this collision, which opened Asia to the West and laid Alexander's world in ruins, should not be given its due importance among the decisive engagements of the world.

Battles should not be called decisive unless they alter history in a durable way, and few of them do so. Nations have been overrun and have worn down or shaken off their invaders; the broken armies have congregated again like sand, or the grand-children of soldiers have lived to turn the tide. The crusading centuries, the campaigns of Belisarius or Napoleon, have in their total account achieved less than peaceful trade and intercourse might have achieved without them; and it is doubtful if history in its eventual outlines would have been very different if Waterloo had taken an opposite turn.

Yet the aim of all art is to lead to a climax, and the art of war, which is no exception, sometimes brings fate to the plunging-point, and lets a single day at Hastings or Chaeronaea settle the affairs of England or the city-states of Greece. Then the variable world, with its hopes, possibilities and disappointments, its distances of infinite surprises, is condensed into something made definite for ever, as far as some tribe or nation is concerned.

This resolution of vagrant hopes, this condensation pressed to its essence and thrown with sublime or foolish confidence into a cauldron to prove the metal it is made of, is the lure and the enchantment of battle, distinct from the unfortunately inseparable squalor of war; and there is much to be said for whatever gives an accent to the brittleness of life we too easily forget. Under nuclear shadows, that must eliminate warfare if any sanity is left us, it may become one of our difficulties to notice the world's precariousness. The old-fashioned remedy was by fighting, and when there was no acceptable alternative, and before the atom bomb was invented, it was probably better in many cases to engage, though the bloodshed that punctuates a nation's decline makes dreary reading and is mostly mere confirmation of the inevitable. A good battle is therefore not to be risked except in the extremity of hope or fear; and some noticeable difference must appear when it is over. The first of these conditions was absent for Magnesia: no more reluctant or less necessary war was ever started. But the magnitude of the result was stupendous. The hellenistic supremacy of the Mediterranean was cut for ever; the Greek civilisation in Asia, so fragile and so recent, henceforth transformed itself in poverty and chaos; and most of the abstract things we live by, conquered but undefeated, were gradually carried by the Roman victors to the west.

All this was gathering when the two armies faced each other on a dark winter's morning on the left of the river Phrygius (modern Kum) that flows through Hermus into the Gulf of Smyrna.

The Battle (189 B.C.)

The battle opened with cavalry, the arm in which Alexander the Great
was never defeated, and if he had been commanding the day's success
would have been on the Macedonian side. Antiochus, a brave cavalryman
but a poor general, lost by chasing the squadrons of Roman horse too
far. He came back from partial victory to see his footmen butchered on
the ground and his army annihilated. It was the end of the Macedonian
phalanx, even as Chaeronaea had been that of the citizen armies of
Greece: and the plain, with its dead red vines, seems still to offer to the
imagination that expired splendour. For the phalanx had after all walked
across the breadth of Asia victorious, and the whole world of its day was
surprised by its defeat. 'Many Greeks', says Polybius, 'considered the
event as almost incredible, and many will still continue to wonder why
and how the phalanx comes to be conquered by troops armed in the
Roman fashion.'[2]

The Seleucid armies were the veterans and descendants of Alexander's
forces that had remained, after 323 B.C., under his general Seleucus
Nicator in Asia. In the first generation and again under Antiochus the
Third, they had garrisoned the world from Antioch to Bactria, and
made the traditions of their Macedonian home magnificent while keeping
them basically unaltered (as had all the Hellenistic armies). Their officers
dyed the original shallow broad-brimmed hat crimson, and embroidered
their cloaks and buskins with crimson and gold. The guardsmen's boots
were studded with gold nails and the cavalry's bits were gold; the
shields bronze or silver, or decorated with bronze or silver crescents.
Writers of that age confirm over and over again this military glow of the
Macedonians, gleaming in the pride of life with gilt armour and scarlet
coats; 'glittering in the sun as they marched down in their order, the
elephants with their castles, and the men in their purple, as their manner
was when they were going to give battle . . . '.[3]

'As these were taking their places they were followed from the camp
by the . . . phalanx called the Brazen Shields, so that the whole plain
seemed alive with the flashing of steel and the glistening of brass; and
the hills also with their shouts.'[4]

So Plutarch.

And 'the mountains glistened and shined like lamps of fire.'[5]

On the wings of these armies were the cavalry, the mountaineers 'girt for running', Cretans, Carians, Cilicians; the archers, the javelin men from Thrace with black tunics; slingers; naked Gauls from Galatia with wild hair and huge shields – and behind them a camp with four times their number of non-combatants inside it, for the ancient armies travelled with most of their possessions about them.[6] The elephants stood like towers near the front or between the sections into which the phalanx was divided; Indian for the Seleucids, African (and inferior) for the Ptolemies, their mahouts strewed red juice to break them to the sight of blood and dressed them with red housings for a battle; and behind their frontlets and crests they carried four men in a turret on their backs.[7]

In spite of prestige, the elephants must have been a frequent disappointment. They were useful to Hannibal as he walked them along a river bank and trampled his enemies at the crossing, though only one out of his thirty-seven survived the north Italian cold.[8] Generally they got frightened and ran in the wrong direction when a fight was on; and the African usually turned tail when pitted against the Indian. Yet the Romans feared them so much that they 'would never come down at all to meet the enemy on flat ground, so much did they dread a charge'[9]; and even in the fourth century A.D., Ammianus Marcellinus writes that 'nothing more terrible can be presented to the mind of man'.[10] The hellenistic armies loved and conferred military decorations upon them,[11] and 1,231 tusks were carried after Magnesia in Scipio's triumph[12]: when the bad days came and a Roman commissioner was sent to ham-string these great beasts in their stables, the Syrians of Latakia rose up and lynched him out of hand. This was in 162 B.C., twenty-seven years after Magnesia; in the meanwhile, during a century and a half before the Romans landed in Asia, elephants would open battles, 'putting forth their strength and meeting forehead to forehead', interlocking their trunks while the pikemen struck from their towers, till one beast or the other turned his flank and was gored by his enemy's tusks.[13]

Even less decisive on the hellenistic battlefield were the scythed chariots put out of commission at Magnesia by the king of Pergamon's order to shoot the horses. Cataphracts or heavy-armed cavalry were as yet scarcely noticeable, but important later, foreshadowing the armoured knight of Europe; Arabs, too, were there on camels, with long swords.

But the heart of the Seleucid warfare was the phalanx at the centre, like a hedgehog, or sectioned like a series of hedgehogs, sixteen or sometimes thirty-two deep, Greek or Macedonian in origin, immensely trained, immensely brave, immensely proud of its tradition, and doomed.

The historian Polybius gives the best possible account both of its strength and weakness, which came down to a matter of mobility. In the battle lost by Antiochus in Greece, the prelude to Magnesia, his phalanx was wedged in the pass of Thermopylae and held its own, until its mountain allies allowed the Romans under Cato to repeat history and cut in on it from the back.[14] Now, on the open plain by the Phrygius, its flanks, unprotected by cavalry, were defenceless. The Roman infantryman behind his long shield could move individually; the space of a yard allotted him on each side was double that allowed to the Macedonian, and in it he could wield his two-edged sword, which 'could both cut and thrust', and 'was strong enough to endure repeated blows'.[15] But face to face on even ground, when the phalanx charged against him with the accumulated depth of its ranks and the weight of its great spears, he had not a chance. 'Aemilius the Consul . . . often confessed . . . that he had never seen anything more terrible and dreadful than a Macedonian phalanx, although he had witnessed and directed as many battles as any man.'[16] Its spear, the sarissa, was twenty-one feet long, grasped in both hands and weighted with a pike at the near end, which could both do damage and served to keep it couched; it was carried horizontally by the first five ranks in a charge, so that 'each man of the first rank must have the point of five spears extending beyond him', a dark impenetrable wood impossible for any force, cavalry or infantry, to grapple. The eleven rear ranks on the other hand, though they would do what they could with a flank attack, were there mainly to add impetus to the charge, which was terrific and famous, and during which they would carry their spears 'slanting up in the air over the shoulders of those in front of them'. It was the impetus of these eleven ranks pressing towards the front, which was also stiffened by the horizontal spears, that made it impossible for the phalanx to turn once it had started.[17]

Polybius makes the point that the phalanx, invincible in a charge upon even ground, was not good for anything else, while the Roman was an all-purpose infantryman, adaptable in small groups or greater divisions.

His superiority had been recognised by Hannibal, who armed his troops in the Roman way with sword and lance, greaves, breastplate and shield. The battle of Magnesia however was won not by this infantry, but by Eumenes, the Greek king of Pergamon (197–159 B.C.), who charged with three thousand horsemen at the right moment against Antiochus' left wing while that commander was galloping along Phrygius' bank with his right. Sixteen thousand Macedonians, 'thirty-two deep, divided into ten sections with their elephants between them, were now unsupported by cavalry. They preserved the appearance of being about to charge, yet they did not advance, because they were foot soldiers and heavily armed, and saw that the enemy were mounted. Most of all they feared to relax their close formation, which they had not time to change. The Romans did not come to close quarters . . . they feared the discipline, the solidity, and the desperation of this veteran corps; but circled round them and assailed them with javelins and arrows, none of which missed their mark in the dense mass. After suffering severely in this way they yielded to necessity, and fell back step by step, with threats, in perfect order and still formidable to the Romans, who even then did not venture to close with them, but continued to circle round and round them, until the elephants . . . became excited and unmanageable, and the phalanx broke into disorderly flight. . . . '[18] It was a dark winter's day, with bad visibility in the dawn when the battle started, and a dampness that clung to the archers' bowstrings and the thongs of the javelins and weakened their aim.[19] When Antiochus rode back, thinking himself victorious, the clumps of poplars in the bare valley, so little changed, must have looked as if the spears of the phalanx were still vertical and undefeated, while the actual footmen lay in heaps – fifty thousand it was said – among the elephants and the dismembered chariots on the ground.

The Hellenistic King

Suspicious but not warlike embassies had led for over ten years to this final inexorable end; and a more than usually unmanageable deficiency in human foresight tied the knot which so much violence had to cut. The Diadochi, the Successors, had divided the empire of Alexander the Great between them, and after a century and a quarter these divisions in their main outline still survived. The Ptolemies were in

Egypt, the block of Asia Minor and the trade routes across the Euphrates were ruled by Antiochus III, the Seleucid king, while Philip V was in Macedon.

Antiochus held the greatest of these kingdoms; it secured the Asiatic bridge, and the commerce which that implied; and he had restored it to the height of its Levantine fame. He had visited, conquered, or pacified his subjects, from the uplands of Iran that supplied his cavalry, through Hyrcania where the Parthian future lay hidden, to Bactria, the most easterly home of the Greeks; and after six years of travel had returned as 'Great King' to Babylon, by the Persian Gulf and the eastern roadsteads of Arabia.

Antiochus had inherited his kingdom – the most lacerated realm in Asia – as a young man under twenty, and his aim seems to have been simply to restore it to its original rights and dimensions. He fought Ptolemy for the strip of Palestine and the Phoenician seaports, and lost; he defeated a revolt in Babylonia: he fought his kinsman Achaeus for the peninsula of Asia Minor and won: engaged on his six years' travel in the tenth year of his reign: returned with immense prestige and his eastern borderlands organised, to make another and this time successful effort for the re-acquisition of Palestine; and finally turned to the borders of Thrace, the outlying promontory of Europe, which the great founder of his dynasty had claimed. In all these proceedings he showed himself on the whole a reasonable and a moderate man, conciliatory where he felt he could be so without endangering the main purpose of his life, the Empire's restoration. He had joined with Philip V of Macedon in the spoliation of Egypt – but that was to obtain the coveted Palestine coast which his dynasty had owned. Ptolemy had been defeated; Philip in his turn was defeated by the Romans; and when the towns which Antiochus claimed remained vacant – without a protector either Egyptian, Macedonian or Roman – he had no particular misgivings in absorbing them. When he set about the fortifying of Lysimacheia in Thrace, he was very little interested in the affairs of the West.

Polybius, comparing his remoteness with the intimacy of Egypt, writes that 'there was not a single act of kindness of any practical value which the Achaeans had met with from the dynasty of Antiochus',[20] whose preoccupations lay along the axis of his two capitals – Antioch in the west, where stood Seleucus' palace and bridge which he completed, and the port of Seleucia; and the other Seleuceia in the east across the Tigris, in a land so wealthy that in the days of Herodotus, 'for four months of the year Babylon supports the king'.[21] Here ran the visible stream of the trade of Asia – coveted later by Parthians and Romans, Persians, Byzantines and Seljuks – the heritage which Antiochus had restored through thirty brave and persevering years. While busy with Lysimacheia, which dominated the Hellespont and completed the link with Europe, he probably scarcely noticed what serious enemies he was arousing: the island of Rhodes, paramount in the Aegean, whose trade in grain came largely from the Black Sea ports; and Pergamon, whose new kingdom was strong and influential between him and the northern coasts. This oversight lost him the war. As for the distant Romans, he was justifiably unaware of an impending collision for which there was no cause. His crossing to Thrace, which filled them with anxiety, was – he explained with uncomprehending sincerity and politeness – entirely on his own business: "'he was at a loss to know by what right they disputed his possession of the Asiatic towns. . . . He requested them not to trouble themselves at all about Asiatic affairs, for he himself did not go in the least out of his way to concern himself with Italy. He had crossed to Europe . . . to recover the . . . cities in Thrace, for he had a better title to their sovereignty than anyone else. . . . As for the Lysimacheians, who had been expelled from their homes by the Thracians, he was doing no injury to Rome in bringing them back and resettling them; for he did this not with the intention of doing violence to the Romans, but of providing a residence for his son Seleucus. And regarding the autonomy of the cities of Asia (for which Smyrna and Lampsacus had appealed to Rome) it was not proper for them to receive their liberty by order of the Romans, but by his own act of grace." When the two cities' envoys were called in . . . the king, taking it amiss that the dispute against him should seem to be submitted to a Roman tribunal, interrupted, saying: "Enough of that long harangue . . . our differences should be submitted to the Rhodians and not to the Romans.'"[22]

Antiochus told the truth in a straightforward way, treating the less civilised West as an old-fashioned landowner in England used to treat 'those damned radicals' emerging into power. The Romans disbelieved him from the first. Until their own emperors adopted it later, the complex and extremely personal dynastic foundation of the hellenistic monarchies was as unintelligible and antipathetic to them as most oriental arrangements have remained to the West ever since.[23] They looked at it through the windows of the Greeks in Hellas, who had a cliché about kings and magnified a power and wealth 'which could buy the Romans themselves – *ut ipsos emere Romanos posset'*.

Greek Autonomy

Philip V of Macedon had been defeated by Rome in the height of her Carthaginian struggle and his defeat was sealed by the proclamation of the liberties of Greece. Like many another liberation, this soon appeared to be little more than a glitter of words, but their influence was great, on the victors as well as on the cities. These heard the saga of autonomy proclaimed at the Isthmian, games of 196 B.C. and thought, in the shelter of their temples, of a golden age under the beneficence of Rome.

From the autonomy of the cities in Greece to that of the ancient Greek colonies in Asia Minor was but a step with no change of direction; Thrace and some towns on the western coast had been roughly seized by Philip in defiance of Greek custom; and in their age-old dream of independence such cities turned naturally to the new 'liberators' against the habitual but never popular domination of their 'kings'. It mattered little that they had usually been well used and their civic sensitiveness treated with as much respect as was convenient; they wanted more than the shadow of freedom.

In 197 B.C., Antiochus was sailing up the western coast of Asia Minor, receiving allegiance and besieging the recalcitrant Coracesium, which is now Alanya in its Seljuk walls and towers. The Rhodians met and told him in a not unfriendly way that he must remain south of the Chelidonian cape; the king had no wish to antagonise the great trading island; he described his innocuous errand in much the same terms as to the Roman envoys a little later – and promised to send an embassy to explain. The Rhodians, reassured by the news of Philip's defeat which had just reached them, let him sail by.

The king continued to regain his ancestral north. From Ephesus and Sardis, historic capitals old in his day, he repeopled Lysimacheia, 'calling back the citizens who had fled, redeeming those who had been sold as slaves, bringing in others, supplying them with cattle, sheep and iron for agricultural purposes, and omitting nothing that might contribute to its speedy completion as a stronghold.'[24] He was fulfilling the obligations of an hellenistic king.

The Romans, to whom Antiochus was little more than a myth, grew more and more uneasy. His alliance with Philip, a hollow affair devoted to the dismembering of the Ptolemaic possessions, they had looked upon as a threat to themselves; they were unaware that he was delighted to have his colleague attacked. After the Macedonian defeat, when the freedom of Greece was proclaimed at the Isthmian games, the king's ambassadors happened to be present and the Romans gave them a message 'as regards the Asiatic cities, to keep his hands off those which were autonomous . . . and to withdraw from those previously subject to Ptolemy and Philip which he had recently taken. At the same time they enjoined him not to cross to Europe with an army, for none of the Greeks were being any longer attacked.'

Antiochus was in Europe already, and Roman ambassadors hastened to Lysimacheia for the interview I have already described. What they said there may still be quoted, since it reveals the fear which, far more than the more advertised freedom of the cities, underlay their interference in Asia. 'Generally speaking', Polybius says, 'they wondered on what pretext the king had crossed to Europe with such large military and naval forces. For anyone must suppose that he was trying to put himself in the way of the Romans.'

A cold war, where fear creates the substance of its fear, went on through the following years. The golden hopes of Greece were crumbling and many discontents began to look for other liberators among the powers around them. Another interview with Rome, in 195 B.C., showed the fallacies inherent in words like freedom (we may remember self-determination as one of the trapwords of our time). 'I see', said the representative of Antiochus, 'that you employ the pretext of liberating Greek states, but . . . lay down one rule for Antiochus and yourselves follow another. For how are the people of Smyrna or Lampsacus more Greek than the men of Naples or Rhegium or Tarentum, from whom you exact tribute, from which you expect ships . . . ? Why do Syracuse and other Greek cities of Sicily receive every year a praetor with the imperium and the rods and axes? Assuredly you make no other assertion than that you have imposed these conditions upon cities that have

been conquered in battle. . . . The case is the same with Smyrna and
Lampsacus and the cities which are in Ionia or Aeolis. Conquered in
war by his forefathers . . . Antiochus restores them to their ancient status. Therefore I wish that he be answered on these points, if this is a
discussion based on equity and not a search for a pretext for war.'[25]

By this time the Romans were expecting invasion. Rumours threatened a Syrian landing in Sicily: a fleet of twenty vessels was sent, emer-
gency troops strengthened the garrisons of all the towns that faced the
Grecian coasts, and sixty thousand men were collected to cross the Adriatic in the spring. Persuaded by the restless and dissatisfied Aetolians,
led to count on the defection of cities and the help of Philip, Antiochus
was in Greece already. The king of Pergamon's brother came with the
news to Rome.

Character of Antiochus and Hannibal

There is a mouse-and-snake feeling as one watches the toils closing round
a perfectly unnecessary catastrophe which no amount of prudence can
avert. Antiochus had a good deal of prudence, apt to give way to
moments of carelessness, a sort of optimism of careful natures whose
imagination is not strong enough to look over their own fences into
the equally straightly-fenced lanes of other people. He was sentimental
too. All this, I think, one may read in the rare bronze that shows him
in the Louvre – an anxious, sensitive, civilised, extraordinarily modern
man, with reasonable eyes and a delicate wry mouth, and the ghost of
a smile that life has drowned. It is hard to re-erect the human figure
round the naked bones that history has saved: yet sentiment shows here
and there – in the life-long devotion to the family restoration; in the
absolute refusal of a man usually ready for compromise to come to any
agreement where this was infringed; in his dealings with Ptolemy after
the battle of Raphia, when easy terms were hindered by his refusal to
pardon a kinsman's rebellion – the crime against his family code. It
shows with the girl he fell in love with and married when he came, aged
fifty and a king, to Euboea, and called her by that island's name: for he
was returning from the passionately Greek exile of the communities of
the East to the lands of his tradition, and what man would give to the
woman he cared for the name of a land he did not love? This homeward

ANTIOCHUS III THE GREAT

THE PLAIN OF MAGNESIA FROM SARDIS ACROPOLIS

love, too tenuous to be noticed in the historians' pages, must still be counted as one of the tragedy's strands, drawing him to the West.

Sentiment, too, made him bury the bones of the soldiers that had lain for six years on the rocks of Cynoscephalae uncovered[26] after Philip of Macedon's final defeat there in 197 B.C. There again his imagination failed him; Philip's enmity to Rome was now swallowed in rancour against Antiochus, who brought him this last disgrace; and he opened the gates of Thrace to the Roman army. Unlike a Greek tragedy, where the chorus stands helpless round Necessity, the catastrophe of Magnesia was chiefly prepared by subsidiary characters; left to themselves, with no contrasting interest to pitch them one against the other, the chief protagonists might never have come near enough to grapple.

I incline to see Philip as Nemesis, unaware but none the less effective, bringing one figure after another into the orbit of the tragedy of Asia. He had begun by creating an anti-Macedonian bias till then wholly unknown in Rome,[27] which brought the senate into the Adriatic and then into Greece in 212 B.C. After that, it was not Philip alone, it may have been Antiochus who suggested the spoliation of Egypt, but it was Philip's brutal disregard of Greek conventions, his promiscuous attacks on cities free or unfree – Lysimacheia, Chalcedon, Abydus, Iasos, Thasos (enslaving its people) Cius (sacked and its population sold) – that enraged the Levant. Antiochus was tactful in his conquests and ended the Syrian victories by the wedding of his daughter to Ptolemy: he disliked, and lifted no finger to help, Philip in Asia Minor, while cities were attacked and the Rhodians betrayed. Iasos is so lost now and so quiet beside its grey walls that the tumult of those days can scarcely be imagined. Its siege provoked the friendly Rhodians to protest. Nothing less than the future of Rome was being built in these lost bights and small Aegean harbours – stone by stone by unconscious hands: in another long inlet now steeped in the same tranquillity, Bargylia was soon to be the first place in Asia 'freed' by Rome.

The Rhodians, watching Philip in the straits where their Black Sea trade always made them nervous, 'peace-loving though they were, decided to fight'.[28] They had been unfriendly with Pergamon, but the danger united them: and in the late summer of 201 B.C. these two governments sent envoys to Rome. Whatever persuasion they used, it was

cogent enough to make Rome accept it, and it seems a reasonable con-
jecture that they exaggerated the Seleucid-Macedonian alliance – hollow
as they must have known it to be – to spur the Senate to a 'preventive
war': allied with Philip, the great Antiochus would surely dispute the
West with Rome: he did not think of doing so, but he well might have:
the senate was instigated in the first place to an interest in Greece, and
thence spurred across the Hellespont as soon as Philip had been dealt
with. Envoys from Smyrna and Lampsacus asking for freedom were received with open arms, and Rome's 'phil-hellenic' policy was extended
to Asia. The needless enmity of Rhodes, the more unescapable one of
Pergamon, were to be paid off by one of the most calamitous wars ever
created out of an unexisting threat.

Antiochus continued to show himself unaware of these implications,
or of any aggressive plans. He rejected a scheme for invading Italy and
was convinced that, once home again in Asia after his Greek defeat,
matters could rest as they were: he 'was quite free from concern, . . . on
the ground that the Romans would not cross to Asia'[29]: the suggestor of
the invasion scheme was Hannibal, the only person who seems to have
been surprised that the Romans had not already arrived.

Philip not only brought the Romans into Greece, and indirectly
provoked Rhodians and Pergamese to entice them into Asia – he had
also been responsible for bringing the greatest of Rome's yet undefeated
enemies into the Levantine world: he had signed a treaty of alliance
with Hannibal in 215 B.C., 'in the presence of Zeus, Hera and Apollo:
in the presence of the Genius of Carthage, of Herakles and Iolaus: in the
presence of Ares, Triton and Poseidon: in the presence of the gods who
battle for us and of the Sun, Moon and Earth; in the presence of Rivers,
Lakes and Waters; in the presence of all the gods who possess Carthage:
in the presence of all the gods who possess Macedonia and the rest of
Greece: in the presence of all the gods of the army who preside over the
oath. . . . '[30]

In 202 B.C., Hannibal was defeated at Zama and, threatened by his
own people in Carthage, came to Macedonia. After Philip's defeat,
he made his way to the Seleucid court in Ephesus. He thus provided
Antiochus with a local habitation and a name of the most menacing sort on the Roman horizon; for 'of all that befell both nations,
Romans and Carthaginians', says Polybius, 'the cause was one man and

one mind – Hannibal . . . and he was likewise active in Greece and Illyria, threatening the Romans from these parts and keeping them alarmed and distracted by his understanding with Philip.'[31] Surrounded by his halo of darkness, he did in fact suggest the things the Romans dreaded, and Antiochus might easily have fought his war in Italy by Hannibal's advice. That he did not do so was attributed by the historians to jealousy or suspicion on the part of the Great King: but the evidence seems to show that Antiochus was not anxious for an all-out war; had he defeated the Romans in Greece he would probably have made easy terms – as he did in Bactria and Armenia, and with the young Ptolemy of Egypt – for his actions were remarkably true to their pattern all through his long and hitherto successful reign.

> *Pyrrhumque et ingentem cecidit*
> *Antiochum Hannibalemque dirum.*[32]

  One could be beguiled into studying the historical influence of *habit* – the power that inspires the bull's *querentia*, his place of imaginary safety in the bull-ring, or makes a man or woman marry a wife or husband as nearly alike as possible to the one they have just divorced. Hannibal and Scipio as well as Antiochus exhibit the habit of their lives in this story. Having fought in Italy, Hannibal wished to do so again. 'If I had been listened to', he says in 191 B.C., 'the Romans would not now be hearing that Chalcis in Euboea was captured, but that Etruria and the coasts of Liguria and Cisalpine Gaul were aflame with war and – what they dread beyond everything else – that Hannibal is in Italy.'[33] Scipio too, on his way to Asia, was drawn towards a repetition of his own life, a fight within the enemy's borders. He was not actually in command of the Roman forces, but acting as adviser to his brother, and 'well knew that the object of the war and the whole expedition was not to subdue the Aetolians but to conquer Antiochus and become masters of Asia . . . and had for long been eager to play a part in Asiatic affairs'.[34] As for Rome itself, a whole crowd of reflexes must have been stirred by every event overseas so soon after the Carthaginian war. 'The *patres* could not banish from their minds that a coalition had been conjured up against them.' When the news of their first naval victory in Asia reached them, they were relieved enough to order a nine days' holiday, for thanks to the gods.[35] Antiochus seemed dangerous 'partly because he had Hannibal to direct his operations'.[36]

*   *   *

Such was the long and varied panorama that led through the defeats in Greece to the coming of the Romans to Magnesia; and there were no great mistakes to look back to, apart from the want of tactics on the battle-field – Antiochus had taken no wrong direction in things he could have known. The gods were adverse. When the Romans crossed to Asia, he tried to fight them with his two navies; his Phoenicians under Hannibal were beaten off Antalya in the bay that is like an amphitheatre under Taurus; and his northern fleet missed a near victory, almost under his eyes, off Myonnesus, a naked headland near Teos. I once spent a night there and remember yellow flowers and a trickle of water among the rocks. The Roman fleet, pursuing some pirates, had moved to Teos and, by chance, altered their anchorage at the last moment from one of its two harbours to the other, to take in five thousand casks of wine. The coincidence saved them from an ambush in the night, and the battle of Myonnesus was turned into victory by the seamanship of the Rhodians, the best sailors of their age. Without command of the sea the Hellespont was not defensible (Constantine and Licinius discovered this nearly five hundred years later)[37]: Antiochus abandoned it – leaving, with the carelessness which appears so strangely in his methodical nature[38] – a quantity of stores in Lysimacheia. The Romans were helped by Philip through the defiles of Thrace, and reached the shore where the Rhodians ferried them across; and Eumenes of Pergamon prepared their reception 'in, as it were, a state of peace, with no one opposing them, without confusion, different ships seeking different ports'.[39] Antiochus was concentrating, as he had to do, on his land army – the only decision that was left him. Hellenistic kings were no believers in unconditional surrender; he had tried to offer a reasonable peace while events were in his favour but – in the not unfriendly silence of the Rhodians – had been foiled by Pergamon; and so the battle of Magnesia was prepared, and fought, and lost. The rancours engendered by Philip rose up again and again, like the ghost of Philippi, out of their unforgotten past.

So perhaps Antiochus thought, as he rode towards Sardis; or – being tired – thought not at all; or, perhaps, under the shock of emotion, lingered as we all do among memories made lenient by distance, post-poning what must be faced. About midnight, under the steep acropolis now half washed away, he must have remembered his youth, when he had waited below the beleaguered city and Achaeus, his rebel kinsman, was brought trapped and bound and cast like a bundle before him. He too had been made great, and had governed all Asia west of Taurus, and had revolted, and now, escaping, was led by two Cretans who betrayed him, guessing at his disguise as his friends helped him down the zig-zag path of the acropolis in the night. 'Antiochus, who had long been waiting the issue in a fever of excitement, had dismissed his usual suite and re-mained awake in his tent attended only by two or three of his bodyguard. When the Cretans entered and set down Achaeus on the ground, bound hand and foot, he remained speechless, and at last burst into tears . . . for Achaeus . . . had married the daughter of King Mithradates, and had been sovereign of all Asia on this side of the Taurus; and now when he was supposed by his own forces and those of the enemy to be secure in the strongest fortress in the world, he was actually sitting on the ground bound hand and foot and at the mercy of his enemies'; who did indeed decide to mutilate, behead and crucify him next day, for Antiochus was brought up in a tough school.

Yet 'he was not boastful in the season of his prosperity and being a man was prepared for anything' – easy-going in his dealings except when they endangered the re-establishment of his ancestral lands.[40] He had shown moderation in opposition to his own minister in the earliest years of his reign',[41] and Livy, who draws on Polybius, who had little knowledge of him or sympathy for him, speaks of his 'well-known clemency' in Greece.[42] He speaks also of the gentleness with which he treated Scipio's son, who had become his prisoner, whom he sent back to his sick father without ransom. 'If personal relations or mutual hospitality had existed between the king and the Scipios, the young man could not have been entertained with greater kindliness and generosity'[43] – a politic kindness perhaps, but one which, together with his courage, is apparent in many details of his life.

Antiochus has had, on the whole, a poor press – his strategy at the last unfairly criticised, his geniality – he would dance in the Macedonian manner at his military banquets – put down to drunkenness, and his care for his friends not remembered. He did not hand over Hannibal, whom the Romans asked for, and he interrupted his flight to pick up his own beautiful wife as he had already done once in Greece, and rode with her at 'about the fourth watch', from Sardis. He rode south, and sent ambassadors to accept the Roman conditions for peace; and died a few years later, obscurely, east of the Tigris, where the bravest years of his life belonged. Perhaps his trouble was that he lived too long? Polybius speaks of him as one who at first conceived great projects and possessed courage and capability but showed himself inferior to his former self as he advanced in life. There is no real comparison, but one cannot help wondering what the verdict might have been on Alexander the Great at fifty-four?

After Magnesia

At Dinar, which was then Apamea, tucked high and cold under the plateau of Anatolia, the peace was signed that brought this campaign to an end and opened, for Asia, the long intervention of Rome. Another fifty-five years passed before the senate undertook any government directly, but the whole of Asia Minor north of the Taurus was now closed to the Seleucid kings: the good recruiting grounds – Galatia, Greece, Macedonia – were forbidden: the elephants were handed to Pergamon: the fifty ships of Antiochus were burnt on the sandy flat shore of Patara.[44] Ten only were left him, to sail no farther than the Sarpedonian cape, and piracy soon revived in the Aegean.

Eumenes of Pergamon, inheriting most of the northern kingdom, quickly learnt how hard it is to trot in the shafts of a foreign power. Antiochus' ambassadors after Magnesia already found him unexpectedly friendly. A year after the battle, although it was he who had inspired the whole trouble of Lampsacus and Smyrna, the liberties of the Greek cities, as far as he was concerned, went by the board at once: 'This fine name of freedom and autonomy will', he said, 'entirely detach from me not only the cities about to be liberated, but those previously subject to me . . . and add them all to the Rhodian dominion.'[45] The Rhodians, partly but not entirely disinterested, spoke in a more lofty way: 'You went to war with Philip', they said to the Roman Fathers, 'and made every sacrifice for the sake of the liberty of Greece . . . and gained more glory than by the tribute you imposed on Carthage. For money is a possession common to all men, but what is good, glorious and praiseworthy belongs only to the gods and those men who are by nature nearest to them. The noblest of the tasks you accomplished was the liberation of the Greeks; if you now thus implement it your glorious record will be complete; but if you neglect to do so, that glory you have already gained will be diminished. . . . '[46]

Diminished it was, and Eumenes and the Rhodians were soon equally unpopular in Rome. The Rhodians lost their supremacy, financially undermined in one way and another, and particularly by the encouragement of Delos, which became the slave market of the Aegean and a great *entrepôt* for Italian and international traders: while the security of the sea, which Rhodes with the Seleucid kings had fostered, and the laws for seafarers which went by their name and which they had upheld, were all eclipsed through a century of chaos. As for Eumenes, landing in Brindisi twenty years or so after Magnesia, a quaestor met and asked him if he stood in need of any service from the senate: 'and in case there was nothing he wanted, he was to leave Italy as soon as possible'. The king 'remained perfectly silent after saying that he was in want of nothing'.[47] Hannibal died seven years after Magnesia in Bithynia, poisoned on an order from Flamininus, the liberator of Greece.

Such dust and ashes hit vanquished and victor alike. Few, very few, had seen the catastrophe coming – Hannibal probably, and the unknown ambassador eighteen years before Magnesia, who saw 'surely the beginning of terrible disaster to all the Greeks when the Romans get the war in Italy off their hands'.[48] A few years even earlier the Aetolian Agelaus of Naupactus (which was Lepanto, with a minute walled harbour now sheltering caiques and a stray tourist yacht or two in the gulf of Corinth), Agelaus, then, speaking before King Philip, said: 'It would be best of all if the Greeks never made war on each other, but regarded it as the highest favour in the gift of the gods could they speak ever with one heart and voice, and marching arm in arm like men fording a river, repel barbarian invaders and unite in preserving themselves and their cities. . . . For it is evident even to those of us who give but scanty attention to affairs of state, that whether the Carthaginians beat the Romans or the Romans the Carthaginians in this war, it is not in the least likely that the victors will be content with the sovereignty of Italy and Sicily, but they are sure to come here and extend their ambitions beyond the

bounds of justice. . . . If you desire a field of action, turn to the west',
he continued, giving a typically Aetolian piece of advice unfortunately
adopted by King Philip: 'For if once you wait for these clouds that loom
there to settle on Greece, I very much fear lest we may find these truces
and wars and games at which we now play, so rudely interrupted that
we shall be fain to pray to the gods to give us still the power of fighting
with each other and making peace when we will, the power, in a word,
of deciding our differences for ourselves.'[49]

'The power of deciding our differences for ourselves.' The cry comes
pathetically down the ages, echoed by all small peoples who ask only to
be troublesome and unhappy in their own way, and have found this their
Aetolian voice in one of the most trouble-giving and trouble-meeting
tribes of Greece. What Agelaus foresaw came true, and if anyone wishes
to follow the change – from that rapture of liberty with which the foxy-
faced Flamininus was greeted in Olympia, to the hatred of Rome that
the highlands of Asia were preparing – he can do no better than to read
the dawn of disillusion in Polybius, the friend of Rome.

Polybius was so engaging that one would have liked to marry him.
There is a Victorian touch in his admiration for Rome, the response of
the careless Levant to financial honesty, to 'Law and Order', to 'Business
is Business', to 'Time is Money' – 'so universal and so extreme is the
Roman exactitude about money as well as their desire to profit by every
moment of time.'[50] He says surprising things in view of their approaching
record in Asia: 'For no less strong than their approval of money-making
by respectable means is their condemnation of unscrupulous gain from
forbidden sources. A proof of this is that at Carthage candidates for office
practise open bribery, whereas at Rome death is the penalty for it: and
among the Greeks, apart from other things, members of the government,
if they are entrusted with no more than a talent, though they have ten
copyists and as many seals and twice as many witnesses, cannot keep
their faith; whereas among the Romans those who, as magistrates and
legates, are dealing with large sums of money, maintain correct conduct
just because they have pledged their faith by oath. . . .'[51]

The fierceness of their integrity is praised whether in the army or
in the execution of dishonest envoys, and the note of doubt is very
faint at first. In the Sicilian war, twenty-two years before Magnesia, 'the
Romans decided to transfer all these objects to their own city and leave

nothing behind. As to whether in doing so they acted rightly and in their own interest or the reverse, there is much to be said on both sides, but the more weighty arguments are in favour of their having been wrong and still being wrong.'[52] Less than a century was to pass before Roman corruption became a by-word in the East and the precarious hellenistic trading gave place to the simple economy of plunder. The next few chapters will study the extraordinarily rapid deterioration in the light of conquest – its capture and mutilation of the Asiatic trade.

Meanwhile Polybius is an oasis, civilised, truthful and delightful, and as his Greek is said to be poor, he is probably most enjoyable in translation. He gives a solid reason for the general welcome to the Romans in Asia – the freeing 'of this side of the Taurus from the fear of barbarians and the lawless violence of the (Galatian) Gauls'. But the critical note grows sharper: he notices the victors 'availing themselves of the mistakes of others to build up their own power . . . while appearing to confer benefits',[53] strengthening those who, no matter whether rightly or wrongly, appealed to Rome. . . .[54] It became patent to everyone that . . . they were displeased if all matters were not submitted to them and if all was not done in accordance with their decision.'[55]

A note of sadness and of disgust soon follows, 'for though the whole of Greece and her several parts had often met with mischance, yet to none of her former defeats can we more fittingly apply the name of disaster with all it signifies than to the events of my own time'.[56] Watching the obeisances of the king of Bithynia in the Roman senate, 'impossible to surpass in unmanliness, womanishness, and servility', he says witheringly that, as 'he showed himself to be utterly contemptible, he was therefore answered with kindness'.[57]

The Policy of the 'Weak Periphery'

Such, in very scanty outline, was the genesis and outcome of the battle of Magnesia, so that its claim to be one of the world's decisive battles seems to me very great. It ended, for two thousand years, the unifying dream of Alexander, which the Seleucid dynasty alone among the 'Successors' had, however imperfectly and perhaps unintentionally, prolonged; *they had kept the passage into farther Asia open as a bridge, which the Romans closed as a frontier.* The Greeks were always traders; under

their management, the Seleucid, Parthian or Sassanian caravans continued to transport goods from the plateaux of Central Asia to the West –
and would reach the Mediterranean whenever the uneconomic Roman
mind admitted a respite from war. This happened rarely, for the clearing away of all able and independent rulers from their outer kingdoms
gave a threatening complexion to the problems of Parthia, Armenia
and Iran, almost continually through the eight succeeding centuries that
finally brought Greek rule back to Byzantium and the Arabs to the
Mediterranean.

It is true that the Seleucids, like many another dynasty, were probably able to engineer their own ruin without any Roman help; it is
possible, perhaps probable, but not certain: Antiochus himself, and the
two generations that followed him, were strong and able men, with
no sign of particular decadence from the Macedonian toughness. The
peace of Apamea (189 B.C.), turned them from what they had been
before, stepping stones between Asia and the Mediterranean, into an
almost wholly oriental empire, with all its defects and dangers, and an
added Macedonian incompatibility for quiet family life. The Romans
meant to keep them weak and they succeeded; the weaknesses were
there, and Rome 'made them catastrophic . . . [58] she helped forward all
the processes that were ruining the political stability of the hellenistic
world . . . ' and welcomed the gradual disintegration of its kingdoms.
The exhaustion of Syria after Magnesia was Parthia's opportunity, and
many things went down which, in the next two centuries, Rome once
more tried laboriously to build: the interest in geography, the trade
links, the development of banking, the spread of coined money, the
roads with their postal services inherited from Persia, the economic
system, the beauty of cities which, like Pergamon or Antioch, had been
turned into the jewels of Asia by their rulers.

Other, more subtle values went underground only to reappear, after many centuries, in a more congenial atmosphere. Two leaders of
the Achaean League, before that also went under, expressed the only
policies possible to the defeated: 'I know too well', said Philopoemon
of Megalopolis, who had once fought against Rome, 'that the time will
come when the Greeks will be forced to yield complete obedience; but
do we wish this to be as near or as distant as possible? Surely as distant.'
But his colleague held that it was right for those, in whose power it lies

to do so, to aim at gaining honour, 'but those who are powerless must take refuge in the attainment of their interest'.[59]

This sad necessity the descendants of the Great King continued to comply with for over a century, yet never succeeded in allaying the implacable Roman fear until the end, when a last Antiochus 'entered Syria clandestinely and assumed the government with the consent of the people'; and Pompey, in 64 B.C., one hundred and twenty-five years after Magnesia, expelled him 'although he had done the Romans no wrong'.[60]

II

The Tax Collectors

The corruption of Roman official methods under the Republic is not yet strong enough to destroy the prosperity of the Asiatic provinces; yet signs of decline along the northern Black Sea coast begin to extend towards the Mithradatic wars.

> 'This system of credit and finance which operates at Rome in the Forum, is bound up in and depends on, capital invested in Asia.' (Cicero: *Lex Manilia*, 19.)

> 'Take pity on our pauperised "allies" – royalties reduced to their own skeletons with all their marrow sucked away.' (Juvenal: *Satires*, VIII.123.)

> *Wider still and wider*
> *May our bounds be set;*
> *God who made us mighty*
> *Make us mightier yet.*

Apart from the rashness of its theology, this greedy little poem is misleading. The good boundary has little to do with width: laid along the easiest line for holding, everything beyond is weakness; and the world is full of ruins like the crusader castles of Syria, which their defenders were too scanty to keep. While the Roman Republic's boundaries grew wider still and wider, few voices were raised – too late – in pleas for moderation.

There were slight scattered signs of trouble: the Roman aristocracy took little interest in commerce, and the cost of the armies had to be met by indemnities and booty[1]; and piracy and slavery were increasing hand in hand, although military roads, like the Via Egnatia across the Balkans,[2] had opened the Levant. The looting of the cities was already noticeable, though Flamininus had left no single Roman in Greece; but his ships sailed away freighted with works of art,[3] and the cities on Manlius' march of liberation after the defeat of Antiochus could obtain 'Roman friendship' only for cash. The diminished lands of the Seleucids were of course burdened with an immense indemnity, 'apart from what was taken for the various triumphs'.[4]

Yet in spite of all, a period of great prosperity set in for the towns of Asia Minor.

During her first decades in Asia, Rome had no thought of expansion. The native rulers still appeared supreme. The Seleucid king, and his son after him, kept their treaty with scrupulous care; the humiliation of the king of Pergamon did not extend to his brother and successor; the undermining of Rhodes went to no unbearable lengths; and Asia Minor as a whole was still rejoicing 'not so much at the defeat of Antiochus . . . as at their release from the terror of the barbarians',[5] the Gauls whom Manlius Vulso, the successor of the Scipios, routed in their Anatolian mountain forts.[6]

The kings of Pergamon, though they were half Paphlagonian, had become more Hellenic than the Hellenes, and their presence is still felt in the capital they beautified – the first great city of the Greeks to be built on the slope of a hill. One finds their traces in the clean elegance of its earlier walls latent under the magnificence of Rome, for whose coming their Hellenic patriotism had been so largely responsible. (Gladstone and Lloyd George were not the first phil-Hellenes through whom the Greeks have suffered.)

Left as the chief state in Asia Minor, sincerely Greek in feeling and scattering fine gifts, Pergamon seems to have tried to preserve a sort of economic unity in the hellenistic world. She guided the oriental trade into Greek harbours (her own), and spread across the Seleucid dominions a currency that was later continued by Rome. Cicero's brother, in 59 B.C., had his salary paid in Asiatic coin,[7] and this uniform currency was an outward sign of an East-West continuity, in a trade which the diminished Seleucids still shepherded from the steppes of Central Asia.

The coastal cities, Pergamene, or Pontic, or Bithynian, free, or royal, reached a zenith of prosperity in the later second century B.C.; or at least it was not obvious that the zenith was past. They combined the beauty of their buildings with the continuance of their quarrels; and while Rome was still busy with her own affairs, the hellenistic rhythm maintained its regulated chaos unhindered: Miletus organised games, hired mercenaries, fought with Priene and Magnesia, who also divided their incomes between architecture and war. Rhodes at her sea crossing[8] remained in spite of Roman coolness the queen of the Aegean – the commercial clearing house, especially for grain – the chief centre of banking in the Hellenic world – the only navy strong enough to face the pirates – and a city which the travellers of that day held to be more beautiful than any other. Supplies of corn now reached her from Carthage and Numidia as well as from the Black Sea, so lightening the perpetual hellenistic difficulties with food; and while the East-West trade and the enormously growing slave trade had largely gone to the Roman nursling, Delos,[9] the quays of Rhodes were still crowded with Anatolians and islanders, Alexandrians and Arabians and even the more intellectual Romans, though the city's proud exclusiveness seems often to have been little to their taste. Her aim too was 'without doubt the unity of the Greek world, at least in its economic aspect'[10]; and her sea-code was tacitly accepted as international maritime law and went on into the ages of Rome.

As for the Seleucid lands, which still spread westward from beyond the Tigris, they were possibly more productive than they were ever to be again.[11] The generic name of Syria covered all Aramaic-speaking country from Euphrates to the Egyptian border, and Posidonius of Apameia (c. 135–112 B.C.) is probably describing his own Orontes valley and the fertile crescent around it when he writes of people who 'because of the plenty which their land afforded were relieved of any distress regarding the necessaries of life'.[12] There is still a dim echo of their crafts and quickness in the *suqs*[13] of Aleppo and Damascus. In the Seleucid age, the discovery of blown glass which they eventually handed on to Venice had not yet been made, though it was only a generation or two away[14] – but their arts and their industries were flourishing, and the 'purple' of their sea-shells[15] was worth its weight in silver. Their enjoyment of life and leisure can be guessed under the disdainful and probably unjust words of Polybius as he watches King Antiochus IV in the shops of the goldsmiths, or the pomp of the display with which the king in Antioch paid back the snubs of Rome.

Even in Greece, so desperately battered, the first half century after the Macedonian wars is mentioned as a time of prosperity.[16] Eastern shipping, though it remained chiefly in the hands of the eastern peoples, rapidly fostered trade[17]; and perhaps the most beneficial result of the Roman aggression was the development of oriental commerce with the West. Greeks had been visiting Rome before: 'so great is the crowd of them that I see flocking here,' Polybius writes in his youth,[18] and mentions Roman embassies to Egypt for corn. Greek mercenaries served in the Carthaginian armies and the word generally used for banking[19] was Greek. With the opening of Asia, the current turned the other way. Business men, mostly Graeco-Italians from the south,[20] went out to settle; and in their comings and goings, about 150 B.C., the large palaces of Pompeii began to be built[21] with painted walls. The south Italian merchants, 'far from being exploiters and oppressors, . . . were the men who helped Greece to her feet again',[22] and soon spilled over into Asia. Their traffic was old in the Mediterranean. Many had fled from Italy to escape slavery during the Hannibal wars, and their historical function was to carry the trade route from its remote Asiatic sources one step farther to the west. The pendulum of history drips blood at every swing, and they were practically all massacred in 88 B.C. by Mithradates; but 'they brought capital when capital was needed', and after the hurricane of the Mithradatic wars, they gradually intermarried and identified themselves with the Greeks.[23] Meanwhile they built their depôts near the tall houses of Delos, and settled in all the western Asiatic cities on the great estuary of trade.[24]

The Class War

In 133 B.C. the kingdom of Pergamon was bequeathed to the Republic as a free-will gift by the last Attalid king, and the motive for this generosity has never been ascertained. A threat of social revolution may have had something to do with it, for the Graeco-Roman world was divided,

BIREJIK NEAR THE (ANCIENT) BRIDGE OF ZEUGMA

THE ROMAN BATHS AT PERGAMON

vertically by government and horizontally by class, like our own, and the
poor in the cities, worse treated than ours are, were often seething on
the verge of rebellion.[25] This horizontal cleavage must be remembered,
for it explains the frequency and the apparent suddenness of changes
that were racial merely by accident; circumstances rather than theory
produced the bias – the fact that the foreigner, the Greek and then the
Roman, lived in towns. Greeks or Macedonians had been the aristocracy
from the time of Alexander, and in much of western Asia Minor long
before, where kings and cities did their best to cherish people who could
supply their armies and provide an intelligent and reliable middle-class
to draw on. There was no actual barrier, except that of their civilisation
itself, to prevent a gradual fusion which did in fact eventually absorb and
submerge the Greek traditions: and when this happened, it produced no
animus against a way of life that continued to be imitated and admired.
The basic division remained as it always had been, nakedly between rich
and poor; the rich lived in towns and the greater number of the poor in
the country; and the gulf between townsman and countryman originated
or prolonged itself, as it continues to do in most of the eastern lands
today.[26]

In Asia Minor the country kept its religions, its village temples, its
sanctities and – in a great measure – its language: the Anatolian peasant
has come down little changed – and if one has seen him standing in
Ankara before the tomb of Atatürk in the square mausoleum, with
shabby clothes loose about him and open palms, and lips moving in a
fervour of prayer, it is because there for the first time in his long history
he has come upon the phenomenon of one of the great ones of this world
cherishing him as he is.

There were plenty of reasons in the ancient society to induce him
to seek for change; and there were parties in the cities also to stir him
up, together with the slaves with whom he felt more or less at one.
These slaves were required in Italy in increasing numbers by Rome's
new agricultural policy,[27] and were sent largely from the Anatolian
countryside, from Cappadocia and Bithynia, where the Roman slave-
dealer had begun to kidnap or buy them from the kings, long before
Mithradates. Laodike, Mithradates' sister, sent a present of thirty to
Delphi, and Roman literature soon after this time is full of Cappadocian
slaves. Bought for an average price of about 400 denarii,[28] they came

from the comparative freedom of their primitive life in Anatolia to the great estates in Italy, to be locked up at night in communal dungeons and thrown out when old to starve. A pint of oil per month, a peck of salt per year and ten amphorae of wine to those that were chained, and less food in the season when the figs were ripe, was Cato's recipe; with a short tunic, and a cloak and a good pair of wooden shoes every second year.[29] In Anatolia, by contrast, slaves were little used except for household service[30]; and while the coastal cities there were welcoming the Romans, the serfs of the countryside rose in fear. They were ready for any cry that would be called nationalist in our day; and popular rebellions − like that of Aristonicus which kept the Romans busy for three years in their new province of Pergamon[31] − or even the attacks of the Parthians or the wars of Mithradates, could always count on this support.[32] Mithradates had fifteen thousand slaves to whom he promised freedom, fighting in his army in Greece.[33]

Along this razor edge of oppression from abroad on the one hand and revolt from below on the other, the bourgeoisie which formed the backbone of the hellenistic cities had to move into the Roman age.[34] When the king of Pontus or anyone else began to stir up the poor, it was not surprising that the support given to him by the cities and their middle classes was far from unanimous. It was a strong, patriotic, and extremely rich middle class right into the first century B.C., when the Roman Republican administration finally completed its ruin. Until this happened, the names of wealthy men, their gifts of ships, of buildings, their help with food or money or oil for the gymnasiums, their exertions against the tax collectors, are gratefully written up in marble on structures which, during the second century in particular, they made more beautiful than ever they had been before. These were the people whom the fair-minded among Roman governors, the Scaevolae or Rufi or Servilii, found to support and help them, whom they gradually came to rely on and eventually copied − a hellenistic legacy − in the cities of the West; and it was they who had to pay for public works in the province of Asia when the Romans had taken possession, and the Pergamene treasure had been sent to finance Tiberius Gracchus in his Italian philanthropy.[35] According to Pliny, an end had been put 'to all moderation when the king's [of Pergamon] properties were auctioned off at Rome' after 133 B.C.

Roman Rule

Direct Roman rule was soon extended from Pergamon to Cilicia. The tax-gatherer followed, and the pressure was never lifted for any length of time until the Republic's end. The lower orders and the professional classes suffered most, since the well-to-do could make friends, obtain exemption from taxation, and sometimes make their voices heard in Rome – and while this increased the class distinction and the discontent of the poor, it also sometimes helped to lighten their share of the general load. Efforts for good government were made. In the long struggle which was now beginning between the orders, senatorial and equestrian, the aristocratic party was the kinder to the provincials on the whole, and the knights 'while gathering taxes in Asia, came into conflict with the senatorial proconsols who tried to protect the tax-payers'[36]; but the *Lex Sempronia* in 123 B.C. gave the Asiatic tithe to the proconsuls to collect, and 'the expansion of Roman equestrian business in the East dates from the passage of this law.'[37] The returns from Asia brought in about 10 million denarii a year apart from 10 per cent collection fees and whatever was superimposed, and the impossibility of rooting out corruption, the disgrace of Lucullus, the exile of P. Rutilius Rufus, reveal 'the knights at the zenith of their power'.[38]

'If we oppose them', Cicero wrote to his brother, 'we shall alienate from ourselves and from the commonwealth, an order that has deserved extremely well of us . . . ; and yet if we yield to them in everything, we shall be acquiescing in the utter ruin of those whose security, and indeed whose interests, we are bound to protect.'[39] How terrible the provincial load could be appears vividly enough in his letters during his short term as governor of Cilicia fifty years after its adoption as a province (in 101 B.C).

Cicero was loved as one of the few good administrators. 'Asia has given me an astonishing welcome,' he writes. 'My coming has cost no one a penny. I trust that my staff are cherishing my good name. . . . [40] I avoid opening the wounds that Appius has inflicted on the province, but they are patent and cannot be hidden. . . . [41] I need not mention his prefects, his staff and his legates, the acts of robbery, of rape and insult.'[42] Six days later, from the remoteness of Anatolia, he writes: 'groans and lamentations in the towns, and awful conduct of one [Brutus' father-in-law] who is some kind of savage beast rather than a man. All the people are, as you may suppose, tired of life. However, the poor towns are relieved that they have had to spend nothing on me, my legates or quaestor, or anyone. . . . '[43]

Other governors could say the same. M. Scaevola was recorded in far-away Olympia as the 'saviour and benefactor' of the Asiatic Greeks. His friend, Rutilius Rufus, after a notorious trial in Rome, found a refuge among the people he was falsely accused of having oppressed, and ended his life in Smyrna. But the virtuous Brutus was pocketing forty-eight per cent on his loans in Cyprus, through an agent 'who had been a prefect, and indeed had had some squadrons of cavalry, which he had used to beset the senate of Salamis in their own chambers, so that five members of the House died of starvation. . . . Brutus', Cicero writes, 'never told me that the money was his. . . . If he thinks that I ought to have allowed 48 per cent when throughout my province I have recognised only 12 . . . , if he complains of my refusal to give office to a business man . . . and is angry at the disbanding of his cavalry, well, I shall be sorry that he is angry with me, but I shall be far sorrier he is not the man I imagined he was.'[44,45]

Some years before his mission to Cilicia, Cicero prosecuted the Sicilian governorship of Verres and described abuses which, however oratorically presented, were such as could and did happen under any bad governor at a distance from Rome: and while the supreme court did what it could with such cases as reached it, one has an uneasy feeling that even the prosecution of Verres might have ended differently if the senate had not been interested in his condemnation. With every allowance made, the case is among the most damning in history, hardly even now to be read without shame for what a province might have to undergo if unlucky. Not lingering over the invective, it is worth while to observe a few of the *methods* by which a governor could grow rich when he had his praetorship 'so parcelled out as to feel he would do well if he might apply the profits of one year to increasing his own fortune, hand over those of his second year to his advocates and defenders, and reserve the whole of the great third year, the richest and most profitable of the three, for his judges. . . . With the courts as they are now, each governor carries off what will be enough to satisfy himself, his advocates and supporters, and his judges and their president; . . . [The provincials] feel they may meet the demands of a greedy man's cupidity, but cannot face those of a guilty man's acquittal.'[46]

Verres' earlier record was bad, for he had 'robbed the treasury and plundered Asia and Pamphylia'; had alienated the whole province of Asia by outrage and judicial murder in Lampsacus,[47] the city that had first called in the Romans; and in Miletus had stolen the best of the ten cruisers which formed part of the tribute collected to fight the Aegean pirates: having asked for it to escort him, and having reached the headland of Myndus that dips its gentle walled declivity among a shoal of islands, Verres 'ordered the marines and rowers to return on foot and sold that handsome cruiser to two residents of Miletus'.[48]

Cicero remembers 'standing among the people of Rome, and looking at the decorated Forum . . . a decoration splendid to the eye, but painful and melancholy to the heart and mind: I looked at the brilliant show that was made by your thefts, by the robbing of our provinces, by the spoliation of our friends and allies. Note that it was then, gentlemen, Verres received his chief encouragement to continue his misdeeds: he saw that the men who aimed at being called the masters of the courts were the servants of desire for such things. . . . And it was then that the allied and foreign people abandoned their last hope of prosperity and happiness; for a large number of persons from Asia and Achaia, who happened at the time to be in Rome serving on deputations, beheld in our Forum the revered images of their gods that had been carried away from their own sanctuaries, and recognising as well the other statues and works of art, some here and some there, would stand gazing at them with weeping eyes.'[49] The story of the officer entertaining Augustus may be remembered, who when asked whether the golden statue of Anaïtis carried off by Antony's troops from Media had stricken his captor with blindness, replied that the Emperor was at that moment eating his dinner off one of the Goddess' legs as he himself had been the robber.[50]

Depopulation

Aspice solitudines per multa milia sine habitatore desertas; has ira exhausit.[51]

In the mass and variety of the Sicilian evidence, the most interesting instances are those that deal with farmers and the collecting of their tithes. The depopulation of the countryside round all the Mediterranean, which is continuous from this time – 'the rapid decrease in the area of cultivated land . . . the increased difficulty of renting it, . . . and the abandoned property, when the owners fled from their houses and left their property behind them' – are pointed out by Rostovtzeff as main causes of decay in Egypt, in Greece and later in Rome[52]; and probably in other lands where the record has not survived. Reasons for this general and suicidal strike of the farmers appear not to be obtainable, but it is perhaps because historians are not usually farmers that they do not take it as an axiom that nothing except absolute starvation will wrench a peasant from his soil. I have argued with a townsman in Turkey about a village in the high rocks that was dying from want of water. 'They can come to the plains,' he said: 'There is no need to help them; all they need to do is to leave their village and come down: land is provided:' and although I pointed out that, once abandoned, no one ever again would be found to till those barren interstices of the rocks, no words of mine could make him see the calamity, when the peasant's life is made impossible on his own soil.

'When I arrived in Sicily,' Cicero declared, 'it had to my eyes the look we associate with countries that have been the seat of a cruel and protracted war. The fields and the hillsides that I had once seen green . . . I saw now devastated and deserted; the countryside seemed itself to feel the loss of the men who once tilled it . . . cornlands . . . for the most part so completely abandoned that we looked in vain not only for the cattle but for the proprietors who were once so numerous. The year before had dealt the farmers a staggering blow; this last year had ruined them altogether.'[53]

These things were brought about by the governor and the gover-nor's private court in collusion with the tithe collectors – 'a fearful and a terrible charge . . . the governor in league with the collectors,'[54] by whose agency the province had for three years been ravaged, so that 'throughout all the lands that are subject to the tithe, one-tenth of the harvests went as tribute to Rome, and all the rest as tribute to Gaius Verres'.[55]

'There is a man of Centuripa named Nympho. . . . Verres had caused a collector to state that Nympho had not made any return of the acreage he had under crop . . . and, Nympho having declared his readiness to defend himself before an impartial court,' Verres appointed his own staff and sentenced him before he had fairly taken his place ' . . . to pay all the corn he had on his threshing floors'. He not only deserted his farm, but fled from Sicily.[56]

'You perceive, gentlemen, how these collectors fell upon the farmer and like some great consuming fire swept through their fields; and not their fields only, but all their possessions: and not their property only, but all their rights as free men and citizens – when Verres was governor of Sicily.'[57]

After the tithe corn had been sold to the tax contractor, and in addition to the trouble with the tithes, bonuses had to be provided at far less than the current price,[58] and money payments which Verres could pocket were substituted for the corn which the cities were expected to sell to Rome.

'Having had the whole of the corn brought where he could deal with it, he would make the several cities pay him money, refusing to pass their corn, and sending to Rome from his own ill-gotten supplies. . . . You see, gentlemen, the type of robbery I thus unearthed. A governor whose duty it is to buy corn sells it instead, embezzling and walking off with all the money which it is his duty to pay to the various states.'[59]

I have quoted at length from these sad records because of the supreme interest of the problem of depopulation in the decline of Rome. It is, incidentally, a problem which faces modern governments such as Greece and Turkey today, whose capitals grow at the countryside's expense. The Verres trial shows the process in full swing.

'How, you may ask, can the truth of what I saw be recognised? Most clearly from the fact that . . . the tithe-paying lands of Sicily were deserted. . . . Not merely those who did stay on their land went on ploughing with far fewer yokes of oxen, but a great many well-to-do men, the active cultivators of extensive properties, abandoned their broad and fertile acres, and left their farms completely derelict. . . . And now please read the return of the number of farmers in the Leontini district when Verres arrived – eighty-four; now, in his third year, thirty-two. Fifty-two farmers, cast out in such a fashion that nobody so much as came in to take their places. . . . In the Mutyca district? . . . One hundred and eighty-seven. How many in the third year? Eighty-six. . . . The Herbita district had two hundred and fifty-two farmers in his first year, one hundred and twenty in his third; the Agyrium district two hundred and fifty, and now eighty.'[60]

When the next governor, Metellus, was to replace Verres, he wrote while still in Rome to the Sicilian communities, urging and entreating them to plough and sow their land and promising fairness.

'It is the letter from Metellus, gentlemen, that has grown all the corn we have had from Sicily this season. If he had not sent off that letter, in all the tithe-bearing areas of Sicily not one man would have turned one clod of soil. . . . And even so he could nowhere succeed in getting corn on the old scale; . . . for . . . a great many of the people had gone away, deserting not their cornfields only but the homes where they were born. . . . Metellus has all but given hostages to those farmers to guarantee his behaviour unlike that of Verres in every respect. But what is it, pray, over which he tells us he has taken such elaborate pains? – Read further: "That the surviving farmers should sow as much corn as possible." The *surviving* farmers? What does surviving mean? What horrible war or devastation do they survive that your successor, Verres, should make us feel that he has pulled together and inspired with fresh life, the *surviving* farmers ?'[61]

The good governors could do what they might in their short terms, but there is no safe remedy in a system that relies solely on virtue, and the records of innumerable crimes must have perished. Aquilius, a consular legate who had been accused but had bribed his judges, finally died under Mithradates by having liquid gold poured down his throat.

The distance from Rome, where alone an appeal could be lodged, must have greatly facilitated corruption; and the Roman support of the rich in Asia encouraged these too to oppress when chances came. The system of farming out the taxes is still adopted in Italy – or at any rate was so when I was young, for I remember a rather pleasant tax collector who had a gift for cutting flowers with a penknife out of sheets of thin cardboard, twisting their petals into a charming relief; we would spend an hour or two in this agreeable way while I watched him fascinated, instead of attending to the taxes, until he would go, leaving the bouquet with me, and imposed a very reasonable assessment when the moment came.

*   *   *

In spite of all, the riches of Asia stood up to their extortion. Anatolia was a more or less self-sufficing area[62] and the Roman portions covered only a small part of it; around them Seleucids, and northern kings, and the Ptolemies in Egypt, carried on a greater or lesser prosperity according to the amount of the eastern trade which they could capture. The Parthians had reached the Euphrates, and that – which is the main theme of my story – I will leave for a later chapter; the point to notice is that the caravans still travelled along the desert edge and the great trading centres of Babylonia remained as they were before. The cities were standing along the coast from Alexandria to Trebizond, – Tyre and Sidon and Latakia, Seleucia, Side, Telmessus (now Fethiye), Ephesus and Miletus and Smyrna – the currencies of East and West poured through them. Ephesus and Miletus were bridgeheads and centres of transport, enriched with many gifts by the last kings of Pergamon; and the southern coasts of the Propontic and Pontic seas also were studded with rich towns – Cyzicus, Chalcedon, Byzantium, Heraklea, Sinope, and Amisus (now Samsun). They guarded their independence in the shelter of Rome.

The Black Sea Coast

But the poor in the Roman provinces had little to lose by disorder, and the slaves had all to gain – and other exceptions to the general prosperity were the cities of the northern Black Sea coast. Their wealth came from their Scythian hinterland – pressed by the Sarmatians newly arriving from dim highlands of Central Asia – and itself now pressing south in turn; and through consequent famine and epidemics the Greek cities – Istrus, the Danubian trade terminus, and Olbia for instance – were in danger of being deserted altogether, and Lysamacheia, that had been the cause of so much trouble to Antiochus, was destroyed by a Thracian robber king about 145 B.C. Some capitalist anxious to be a dynast would come to their rescue, defending and perhaps betraying them with his own slaves and freedmen, or furnishing ships or food at his own expense. The riches of the grain trade kept them going, the export of fish, which was vital to the Greeks, and the opening of interior markets among tribes 'none of whom deserves the name of barbarian, for all could look back on a long evolution of civilised life'[63] of a Homeric kind. During the second century B.C. a Black Sea trade route to the East developed – a four days' wagon road across the Caucasus, and down the Cyrus river and round the Caspian,[64] to Oxus *through the hushed Chorasmian waste*. The trade north of the Caspian became important later, and Strabo describes 'large quantities of Indian wares brought to the Hyrcanian [Caspian] sea',[65] by tribes that 'could import on camels the Indian and Babylonian merchandise . . . and wore golden ornaments, owing to their wealth'.[66]

Strabo describes the Greeks of the Crimea rich again at the turn of the Christian era, with a thirty-fold yield of grain[67] round their city of Panticapaeum (modern Kertch). It was strategically placed at the entrance to the sea of Azof, and in the course of time was to give birth and baptism to the Russian Vladimir and to the idea of Holy Russia.[68] But meanwhile, pressed by the Sarmatians descending, with harbours and docks for about thirty ships, and villages around it, the harassed city sat under its Cimmerian acropolis, exporting native manufactures and furnishing wine and precarious Greek luxuries to the local kings.

The Tauric coast was rugged, and subject to furious storms, with hot summers and 'winters so cold that the horns of cattle are filed off, for this part of the animal is sensitive to cold . . . and bronze water jars burst and their contents freeze solid:' and the waterway of the Crimean strait was 'crossed by wagons on the ice, so that the general of Mithradates fought a naval battle in summer in the same strait and a cavalry engagement in winter'.[69]

Pressed and tormented throughout the second century, inhabited less and less by Greeks and more and more by Iranians, Scythians and Sarmatians, Panticapaeum and its neighbouring cities of the Bosporan kingdom applied at last for help to Mithradates on the southern coast: and straight and invisible as an arrow that shoots out of sight and drops from the sky on its objective, this remote cause led to the Roman wars.[70]

III

Mithradates

T he Mithradatic power based on the Black Sea trade became a
second victim of the Roman policy of the *weak periphery*. The trade
itself, draining the northern steppes as far as Mongolia, is to become
increasingly important to Rome as the strain of her luxury imports
through the Parthian and Arabian customs grows more severe: this
motive is still latent under the Republic, and nothing much appears on
the surface beyond greed of civil and military officers, uncontrolled by
any central economic vision.

> "While four years sufficed to defeat Pyrrhus, and thirteen to defeat Hannibal,
> Mithradates resisted for forty years.' (Florus: 1.xi.2.)

The Black Sea

The mists of the north have bewitched the Black, or Pontic, Sea. Beyond it
lay the Bosporan kingdom and at its western end the Symplegades opened
to the Amazon coast – merciless cliffs with dark patches streaked like
walnut leaves in autumn; and the eastern or Caucasian end was known
as the 'furthermost run for ships', where seventy tribes all spoke their
separate tongues. 'Thence people go to Amisus and Sinope, a sea voyage
of two or three days, since the shores are soft because of the outlets of
the rivers,'[1] which build small sombre beaches, blackish like a dream.

The water is shallow with flat rocks, and so little salt that rock-doves come to sip it; the foam is not crisp like the Aegean but greenish as old ivory, and loosely spangled; and the sun flecks it weakly, like flashes from rings. Even when the combed smooth sea is glossy, a threat is lurking as in Pyrrha's hair:

> *heu quotiens fidem*
> *mutatosque deos flebit et aspera*
> *nigris aequora ventis*
> *emirabitur insolens,*
>
> *qui nunc te fruitur credulus aurea,*
> *qui semper vacuam, semper amabilem*
> *sperat, nescius aurae*
> *fallacis*[2]

Even on a summer's day, when bands of turquoise lead these waters from shallow to deep, the land behind is hung with vapours. The sky is padded white, as if a cold sleeper were wrapped in his quilt inside it, and the houses that flourish with tiled roofs on the lower wooded reaches of the hills as Strabo describes them are cloudy white also, as is the drifting cirrus on the horizon's floor.

With the loss of all edges, nothing is quite what it seems. Anything might come out of the soft greyness; Slavonic dreams are across the water, and Medea is in Colchis with her spells; and if the Black Sea weather lifted, Prometheus would be hanging from the solitary Caucasus. One's fancy watches Mithradates, sacrificing his chariot and white horses to Poseidon in the sea.

Following him through the Roman history, I left Istanbul in the summer of 1956 in a handsome steamer that coasts from roadstead to roadstead (or port to port now, for harbours are being built). At Sinope (Sinop), a gaggle of geese swam half a mile to meet us and feed on what was thrown to them and swim home – a maritime behaviour that seemed to belong to the Hans Andersen atmosphere of eccentricity that creeps down from the north. And Sinope continued to be unexpected, for as I wandered to look at the walls that still surround it, a group of young men sitting through the afternoon at leisure in their public garden saw me interested and took me to their prison, which is built into the wall itself under two ancient Greek inscriptions, and contains a thousand murderers, they told me as we went along. It seemed a lot for only fifty thousand inhabitants, but they were gathered, I discovered, from all over Turkey, and sentenced for thirty years; and the women had a smaller prison, and only twenty-five years, since they had usually killed their husbands, which apparently made it more understandable. A windowless dungeon in the old wall showed nothing but an earthen floor and a privy and darkness; and here the new arrival would be kept for the first month of his sentence, 'so that when he comes out the ordinary prison life is paradise', they said. 'It is sensible,' said my guides in chorus; and perhaps it is; and the modern prison which was built beyond the wall seemed a friendly place where every sort of craft was practised by carpenters, shoemakers, tailors, weavers of cloth, knitters of socks, and embroiderers: from whom I chose a small bead purse to buy. The murderer was sent for to receive his money, a man so tall and heavy that he stooped; his huge hands might easily kill someone without disturbing the quiet and rather trustful expression of his face: and with those enormous and disastrous hands he had stitched my purse, passing his needle through the beads, and planning his design of two birds on a branch, with the Turkish flag above them and a star. I keep the little work of art to be reminded not only of Sinope, but of the ups and downs of life.

Sinope was one of the greater cities of the Black Sea shore, built, they thought, by an Argonaut and flourishing when Xenophon passed by with his Ten Thousand. It fell under a second siege of the Pontic kings, and became their residence on the coast – and here Mithradates V, the friend of Rome, was murdered in 121 B.C., and Mithradates VI, a young boy under his mother's regency, succeeded him. It stood for him later against the Romans as long as it could in a divided way, and 'fought them on the water not without success'. And at the end of the story, made a free city again under Pompey, it received the huge armour and buried with honour the body of its defeated king, conveyed across the sea.

The struggle with Mithradates finally carried the Romans beyond Euphrates to where the long fight between West and East, between western infantry and eastern cavalry, played itself out and the cavalry won. And the Romans reached this battlefield by way of the Black Sea shore.

THE SELJUK WALLS OF BAIBURT (MITHRADATES SINORIA?)
MITHRADATES EUPATOR

The Rise of Mithradates

Mithradates was not the first to think of managing the Black Sea trade with the help of its Greek cities and of the horse-breeding nations of the north. His grandfather, who had acquired Sinope, dreamed this dream, and so did the Bosporan dynasty before him.[3] One of the fourth century rulers at Panticapaeum attempted it and failed, but filled the tumuli of himself and his descendants on the hills around the city with beautiful objects of gold; and Mithradates, growing into manhood under his mother's hellenised government, and inheriting a diminished realm subservient to Rome, also escaped into the dream. The Scythian grain, which Rome had not yet begun to deal in directly, was to support the unification of the Pontic Greeks round one dynasty, 'a Greek sea-front and an oriental hinterland' with its oriental subjects and allies behind it. Mithradates therefore listened to the Black Sea cities' call for help, accepted the invitation from the northern shore, and began to build a Crimean kingdom in alliance with the equally go-ahead king Nicomedes II of Bithynia.

It had to be partnership or enmity as far as Bithynia was concerned, since that country controlled the straits of the Bosphorus, the door of the Pontic trade; and one may say to Mithradates' credit that he tried the friendly way first. The two kings dismembered Paphlagonia (on the coast between them) in a peacefully unscrupulous alliance, and occupied Galatia, bribing their way in Rome. Mithradates already held Lesser Armenia, Colchis and Trebizond – the eastern corner most valuable for mines – and the two gamblers now turned to Cappadocia, an agricultural land which had been hellenising itself quietly on their southern border under a king who unfortunately died. His dynamic Macedonian widow made away with five of her sons before the sixth killed her and married Mithradates' sister. He also then died, leaving one son only; and between this boy and the Cappadocian inheritance Nicomedes inserted himself by marrying the mother. The alliance between Pontus and Bithynia naturally split; Mithradates turned out the son of Nicomedes, Nicomedes III, and remained in sole possession of Cappadocia, apparently to the satisfaction of its inhabitants.

The ousted Nicomedes appealed to Rome, and the senate restored Paphlagonia and Cappadocia. Mithradates, not strong enough to oppose them, persuaded the king of Armenia on his eastern border to marry his daughter and recapture Cappadocia in his stead. But the senate again interfered, and sent Sulla – able but disastrous in Asia and at that time (92 B.C.) pro-praetor of Cilicia – to reinstate the Cappadocian king.

Rome had her hands so full of internal troubles that Mithradates was soon able to embroil himself once more both in Cappadocia and Bithynia: and when the Republic decided to re-establish the appearing and disappearing kings, he was again forced to acquiesce.

His peaceful answer disappointed the Roman commissioners, who had looked for a profitable campaign in Pontus. The country, untouched for generations, was very rich. Polybius describes it[4] as a wide and warlike land of horsemen, reaching as far as the Caspian and still under Persian rule, 'having been overlooked in the time of Alexander'; and Mithradates was held to be the wealthiest of the Asiatic kings.

War still paid. The Roman booty from the East after Antiochus is calculated at about 70 million denarii.[5] The fact that the home government now got less because the generals and their armies intercepted more, was an added encouragement to any army in the field, and Pompey's method of withdrawing a fifth of the plunder was soon to be considered normal.[6] (Manlius Vulso in 188 B.C. got one million pounds worth of gold from his 'liberating' expedition[7] which the senate, doing its best at a distance, qualified as a private piratical expedition – *privatum latrocinium* – of his own.) Even Cicero, writing about the invasion of Britain, remarks that 'there is not a scrap of silver in the island, nor any hope of booty except from slaves'.[8] However moderate the Republic's colonial theory in Rome, the policy of the army in the field may be summed up in Lord Kitchener's unhappy phrase, to 'loot like blazes'.

The Roman commissioners in Bithynia were therefore naturally anxious in this instance to secure the large sums which Nicomedes III owed to the generals and ambassadors for restoring him to power, 'together with other large sums which he borrowed on interest from the Romans in their suites',[9] all of which he seemed unlikely to disburse: so they spurred him on reluctantly to attack Mithradates' territory, where he met no resistance and collected enough money for his debts. 'Mithradates, although he had his forces in readiness, held his hand, as he wanted to have good and sufficient cause for war.'[10] He sent a protest to the senate against the illegal aggression, and a disregarded envoy to the commissioners, who advanced in three columns from south and west behind the unwilling king. They were defeated (88 B.C.) in two battles in the wheat-bearing country that rises to the Bithynian highlands, where the defenders' scythe-bearing chariots did real damage for the only time on record so far as I know.

Mithradates had kept away from his troops in the Persian fashion, but he now joined his army and passed from triumph to triumph over the old battlegrounds of Asia. He spent two gilded years in Pergamon enjoying the height of power, until plots thickened, and the city bourgeoisie turned away. Threatened and spurred like most dictators, he ventured into Greece as rashly as Antiochus had done before him, and Sulla repeated the earlier history by defeating him and crossing the Hellespont to impose a (temporary) peace in 84 B.C.

*   *   *

Mithradates had thought to put his seal on the rousing of Asia by a carefully planned massacre of eighty thousand Italians which blackened his reputation in one day (88 B.C.).[11] Yet it was not what most shocked his contemporaries. Dio remarks that 'the deed of Mithradates, deemed so terrible . . . was regarded as of slight importance in comparison with the number now massacred (by Sulla in Italy) and their manner of death'.[12] People were alive who remembered the destruction of unresisting Corinth in 146 B.C., and had heard of Carthage from whose ruin fifty thousand men and women were sold to slavery. They had heard of the Roman general in Epirus who gave secret orders for seventy cities to be sacked and one hundred and fifty thousand men to be enslaved in a single hour[13]; the shock of such triumphs of organisation had come to the hellenistic world with Roman methods long before. Nor do I believe it was necessarily the 'rabble' that got out of hand to commit these crimes. Rostovtzef is an optimist in thinking that the well-to-do 'could not possibly have had very strong feelings' against Roman business men who were not oppressors; for we are constantly suffering from strong feelings and seeing them roused in sudden waves without any real dislike behind them: a question like Cyprus presses like a whirlwind and leaves desolation, but passes temporary as a summer shadow over the granite features of geography and time; and there have been many turmoils in the Middle East in our day, and every one of them of any importance has been carefully and usually artificially organised. The heart of the matter was probably given by Sulla in his speech to the cruelly ruined – *'crudeliter direpta'* – province of Asia, which Mithradates had despoiled as he retired[14]:

'Now, after twenty-four years, during which you had attained to great prosperity and magnificence, public and private, you again became insolent through peace and luxury, and took the opportunity . . . some of you to call in Mithradates and others to join him when he came. Most infamous of all, you obeyed the order he gave to kill all the Italians in your communities, including women and children, in one day. . . . You have received some punishment for this crime from Mithradates himself, who broke faith with you and gave you your fill of rapine and slaughter, *redistributed your lands, cancelled debts, freed your slaves, appointed tyrants over some of you*, and committed robberies everywhere . . . so that you learned by comparison what kind of champion you had chosen instead of your former one.'[15]

Sulla, at odds with the rival government in Rome, was at this time all-powerful in the east with his army, and was talking to his supporters, the well-to-do; and there can be little doubt that what chiefly influenced these, both on his arrival and later, was Mithradates' subversive policy, as it would now be called, outlined in my italics, above. 'It was evident to all that in the cities the leading men and all the aristocracy were in favour of the Roman alliance . . . while the multitude and those whose affairs were not in the best condition desired a complete change.'[16] So Livy describes Greece, long before, and the same conditions continued in Asia Minor. Sulla's references to the Aristonicus revolt of 132 B.C. make this clear[17]: for it too began as a war of independence, and is then described by contemporaries as a fight of 'oppressed against oppressors, of country against city, of slaves and serfs against their masters . . . a struggle for life of the bourgeoisie of Asia Minor'.[18]

The people of Pergamon, Cicero says, 'these shoemakers and belt-makers, approved with their shouts the proposal which Mithradates said he wanted. . . . What trouble is it to inflame artisans and shopkeepers and all those dregs of the country, especially against a man who lately had the highest office? . . . How gladly those men to whom our symbols are hateful, our name bitter, to whom the pasture tax, the tithe, the port dues are death, how gladly they seize the chance for retaliation when it is offered.'[19]

There were not many well-to-do left in the cities that had renounced Rome, when Sulla had done: 'They mortgaged their theatres, their gymnasiums, their walls, their harbours, and every other scrap of public property . . . and the province of Asia had her fill of misery.'[20]

> *Sullanus bibit ensis et horrida tellus*
> *extulit in lucem nutritas sanguine fruges.*[21]

The Paradox of Change

As this book hopes to be the study of an historical mistake, one may add a note which seems relevant on the paradox of change – change that always defeats itself because it cannot stop: once admitted, one change produces the wish for another *ad infinitum* and it is Cronus eating his children. The opponents of change at the same time produce what they most wish to avoid, an almost identical result by explosion as it were, trying to bottle people up in what is abhorrent to nature – a *status quo*: the changers destroy because they are rootless, and the conservers keep because they fear: between them the transmitter, or transformer, alters if he can without destroying, and makes a habitable world, not overstraining. It is a mistake to think of extreme left and right as opposite when their results are so often the same: the true contrast is between either of them and the moderates, who, whether they belong to one side or the other, resemble each other in their effects and have, incidentally, been for many centuries the strength and fortune of policy in England – builders and not destroyers. This is why it seems to me that a choice between a *reasonable subverter* and an *adventurous conservative* is a matter of small importance, whereas the choice between these two and either extreme is full of risk and danger.

Mithradates, like most 'oppositions' in Greece or Asia, was out for radical change, and this helped him to get in but not to stay. The great free cities like Rhodes or Cyzicus he besieged in vain; they feared him from the first, and many of the others were evidently growing in opposition before his short swift spurt of glory was expended. The difference of calibre between him and Alexander is nowhere more apparent than in

their contrasting management, in very similar circumstances, of democracy in Ionia – although on their way down through Phrygia, they are
said to have lodged by chance at the self-same inn.[22]

The Northern War

Sulla used 'all the income of the treasury at pleasure',[23] exacted a
moderate indemnity from his enemy, and left Asia to attend to the
urgency of his own revolution in Rome; while Mithradates retired to
take up the restricted kingdom of his youth with no farther horizon than
the Pontic trade.

But Sulla had left behind him his legate Murena, who was out for
plunder with the best. Denying by a quibble the peace treaty's existence
because it had not been written down, he attacked Mithradates in Pontus,
and few facts in history more neatly illustrate the fable of the wolf in La
Fontaine: it is only the un-lamblike character of Mithradates in general
and the fact that Rome wrote the histories that has reversed the part of the
aggressor. At the beginning of the Italo-Abyssinian war, the Abyssinians
were accused of attacking (at Walwal) *one hundred miles within their own
border*[24]; the note is similar; and indeed the Republic and Mussolini
continually remind one of each other.

The Roman legate wintered in Cappadocia, which was to be for
centuries a centre for the legions, and then marched north from dry
cornland towards a greener country, until he reached Comana and
sacked the temple of the Mother of the Gods (83 B.C.).

This was among the oldest and holiest of sanctuaries, and the high
priest, a member of the royal family, ranked second in the realm to the
king. He owned the land and six thousand temple servants who could
not be sold, and the city, as Strabo describes it, was a 'notable emporium
for the Armenians', a religious domain typical of Anatolia. When the
processions in honour of the Goddess came around in their season, the
crowd assembled from far away, the people slashed themselves with
knives as I have seen them do in Iraq and Iran in the holy places, the
temple prostitutes gathered the money that the merchants and soldiers
squandered, and the city lived 'in luxury, all their property planted with
vines'.[25]

I travelled here in 1958, climbing from the Lycus (Kelkit) valley into a landscape of walnut trees and maize when the harvest was ending. Old men or children drove wooden threshers studded with spikes that split the ears of corn, and ox-carts with creaking axles carried the loads away. Tokat was in sight, under three crags of fortress – a quiet little town at a bend of the Green River (Yeshil Irmak) where the loud-speaker had not yet come to call prayers from the minarets and the citadel's covered stairways were older than Rome. The steep ascents were scattered with marble fragments; the market was still built in the Roman fashion, a tiled rectangle of roof sloping to an *impluvium*; and the charming museum was lined with turquoise tiles. A new boulevard to the bridge and old things crumbling behind it – baths, hospital, mausoleum, earth-coloured in decay: the security of mere continuity gave pleasure in a town where nothing seemed to be coming to a violent end.

The temple that once stood some seven miles away along the river is now a shallow ghost-mound by a modern barrage in the plain of ancient Dazimonitis rich with vines. The afternoon light enveloped its oblivion. A piece of marble cornice with lion spouts and dentils lay broken except for the name of Comana in Greek letters, found no doubt when the barrage was building by the Turkish engineers. Into this peaceful world, before the Muslim or Byzantine castles stood on their rocks, Murena entered; and Mithradates again protested to the senate in vain. When a second invasion threatened Sinope, his capital, the king fought. He defeated Murena's army and drove him to the west (82 B.C.) and orders came from Sulla to desist. Another pause, and the last chance of peace – and that a poor one – was destroyed by the dying Nicomedes, who followed the fashion of the time and bequeathed his kingdom of Bithynia to Rome (74 B.C.).

No one except his horse[26] seems to have regretted him, and his act handed over the door of the Bosphorus. With Sulla dead – he died in 78 B.C. – and the senate deaf to protests, the irreparable massacre of the eighty thousand Italians behind him, and a popular revolt in Bithynia luring him on, Mithradates prepared his forces. He gathered as many as he could of the city Greeks to help him, the only people of that day sufficiently expert to lead an army or a navy against Rome; and sent to the rebel Sertorius, who was fighting against Sulla's party in Spain, to ask for military advisers to train his army in Roman methods. But the useful moment had gone; Bithynia was declared a Roman province; and Lucullus, the friend of Sulla and among the best of all the Roman generals, was already on his way to take possession.

The king had a chance if the great cities stood by him – as those of Pontus did. But Rhodes, fearful of social change, had wrecked his prospects fifteen years before; and Cyzicus now closed its gates and harbour. It had been the first free town to resist the introduction of a garrison after Alexander, and the strength and independence of these northern cities was now once more to be proved by their formidable resistance on one side or another. Heraklea, entered by a trick of the king's admiral, snatched the chance to kill her tax collectors (the democrats no doubt getting the upper hand), and astonished the Romans by sustaining a two-years' war. The garrison in Sinope fought for the king of Pontus, and Amisus held out for him till it was burnt. But Cyzicus, out of touch of Black Sea problems and queen of the Marmara trading, resisted the concentrated efforts of the king.

A slight rise and drop is all a passing car will notice now as it enters the obliterated walls. From within their enclosure, across their bay, the starving people could see the Pontic army, and the troops of Lucullus beyond it, by what is now the little town of Bandirma. A single bridge connected their island, which was given by Zeus to Persephone 'by way of dowry',[27] so that a black heifer was usually sacrificed at her festival. During the siege there was none to offer and they were making a substitute of paste when a miracle happened, and a black heifer swam towards them from herds grazing in the Bandirma meadows. With the Queen of Death on their side the people of Cyzicus resisted, the Roman army defeated Mithradates, and the storms scattered his ships. As Lucullus pursued him through Pontus, the thirty thousand Galatian porters who carried corn were no longer required, in the plenty of a hitherto unviolated land (73 B.C.).

Amisus was invested, and Themiscera, home of the Amazons, also, and the winter passed. Mithradates, with declining fortunes punctuated by desertions, was astride the Lycus valley: his western adventures were over and the prudent among his followers had left him, and his cities were besieged. He was training a small force of forty thousand cavalry that, even so, was larger than the army of Lucullus. His mountain fortresses held their hidden wealth (for he never lacked money), and the nobles in their strongholds remained firm. The feudal pattern of the coming centuries was taking shape. The valleys of Pontus were Iranian in their sparse servile villages round heights of castles or scattered on temple lands, and in the names of their nobility and the worship of their armoured pre-Greek God. From Scythia and Sarmatia across the sea the splendid cavalry could be increased indefinitely as long as the money lasted. Its long duel with the infantry of the West began here, to continue along Tigris or Euphrates, first defeated and finally victorious, through the years and the nations to come.

Mithradates, now over sixty, would have been comforted to know this as he fought his losing war.

His immense strength, his endurance and his horsemanship – he would drive sixteen horses abreast among the Greeks at Pergamon – are well attested. Doubt has been thrown on the tales of his youth when he was said to have lived in the forests for seven years, afraid of being poisoned by his mother. It seems to me, however, that he could not have endured the same life, as he did in his old age, nor held the fidelity of his shy subjects in their solitudes, if the pattern had not been made familiar long before.

*   *   *

I travelled about his country in 1958 and often wondered how much of it belonged to the past. Greek profiles like those on their coins are still seen at Amisus, though the name is now Samsun, a growing commercial city, and the line of the ancient mole is almost submerged by a harbour in the making, and NATO radar installations flash on an acropolis sloping gently under corn.

Amasya, the old inland capital, is far away in a sanctuary of the rocks. Above its crowded gorge of trees and houses, nameless royal tombs in niches of their mountain sit shining in the sun: and here in time of crisis the king gathered his followers and sacrificed to the older gods. It is still a proud and conservative little city and, a few weeks after my visit there, caused a small diplomatic ripple by expelling two tourists for being improperly dressed.

I was constantly confronted by this resolute quality in Pontus. A subdued, almost completely veiled woman, for instance, suddenly reproached a busful of soldiers for singing (presumably) improper songs. They were instantly silenced: and in the neighbourhood of Nicopolis, which Pompey built when victorious near a little town now called Su-Shehri on a hill above the Lycus, the village people were not afraid to rescue me in an estrangement with the police.

Mr Wingfield, restoring Byzantine frescoes in Trebizond, had given me a note to the modern village which is now called Purk, but is only to be found on the maps through the usual desperate variety of Turkish names. I sat enquiring for it at a long day's end in Su-Shehri's café with a little crowd of elders, and had just arranged for horses next morning when a police commissar came by with a few jaunty English words and no greeting, and remarked that there was a law which prevented people from going to villages, and if I had been a man he would have arrested me. 'Then I thank God I am not a man', said I, and we reached a deadlock, made worse by the elders who all laughed.

A young student landowner called Ruhi now appeared, explaining in perfect English that he would himself take me, and, turning to the policeman, added that nothing but Roman ruins would be looked at: the commissar agreed, the horses were arranged for, and next morning failed to appear. It was then that I began to see the country's character, for Ruhi's face darkened when he heard the news: 'I will get horses', he said quietly, and arrived half an hour later with two good ponies and a guide. A stray mining engineer joined our party, and we rode for about ten miles across the necks of peninsulas that here launch into the broad and open Lycus valley (now the Kelkit), filled with corn.

The village had one hundred and ten houses winding almost invisible in the shade of walnut and willow, apples and quince: many Armenians had lived in it and it dwindled when they left it, and little except an Ionic capital, two column bases and a Greek inscription were there from a remoter past: but its people made me welcome, and while lunch was cooking set us to rest under an apricot tree on carpets, beside the oxen that were treading out the corn. In this peaceful atmosphere, two soldiers armed to the teeth rode up to take me to the commissar: our finding of the independent horses had annoyed him, and his permission of the night before was forgotten.

An arrival of this sort instantly produces a desert in almost any part of the Levant; but not at Purk; the village came in relays to assure me

I need fear nothing, and invited the soldiers to lunch. While they sat rather constrained I admired their weapons – pistol, rifle and bayonet – and then remarked that 'it seems a lot, for one woman', which plunged them once more into gloom; but the delighted village again burst out laughing and decided in a body to come with me to the town. Seven horses, two donkeys, and a little number of people on pillion or on foot gathered in and out among the soldiers, and I – better mounted – trotted ahead under my parasol with Ruhi, through a country full of flowers: blue thistle balls, caper, ageratum, yellow achillea, blackberries and roses, among fields of corn or maize, beetroot, lucerne and hemp. 'It looks more like a wedding than an arrest', said Ruhi, looking back: 'If there were an election, they would choose you for their deputy'. When we approached Su-Shehri I dropped behind to let the military save some scraps of its prestige and waited in my inn for Ruhi's competent handling of the commissar.

It was, I must say, an exception to find police so disagreeable for they and the army were usually as helpful, definite and kind as everyone else. The very next day, during a lorry's interminable waiting, an over-zealous soldier took me to his commandant, who explained that they had 'to be very careful so near the frontier as the villagers attack everyone they think a communist'. He had just rescued a Turkish geologist: the toughness persists. In the little town of Niksar, in the night, looking out from the window of one of the world's worst hotels, watching a poor man settling to sleep on the pavement opposite, moving his head from side to side like a creature of the woods till he could find a place to fit it with least discomfort into a hole in the wall – I turned reconciled to my so much, but not so *very* much, less squalid bed. Mixed as the inhabitants may be, the toughness of the valleys of Pontus has not changed.

The Long Resistance in The Lycus Valley 72–63 B.C.

Mithradates fought Lucullus round Niksar, which was Cabira. It was at Cabira that his palace and water mill were built, with zoological gardens and hunting grounds and mines near by; and here his most precious treasures were kept, according to Strabo, 'enclosed by remarkable walls, except the part where they have been pulled down by the Romans'.[28] A less ancient fortress still stands on a hill overlooked by the taller height where Lucullus camped and commanded the northern passage to the sea.[29] The Cabira hill is jagged with ruins. Their stones have been used over and over again, with cemeteries inserted from time to time among them as if in a mosaic of death, and the Islamic traces have ousted Mithradates; but the plain remains, five miles wide and flat as water, where his cavalry fought. Alexander alone could win battles with the unstirruped riders of the ancient world, but the Pontic horsemen had nearly beaten Sulla at Orchomenus and were superior to the Roman; and though Lucullus out-generalled them, it was not without anxiety and loss.

Mithradates in the beginning had followed the royal habit of Persia and never led his own troops until he was nearly fifty. He was now, in 71 B.C., sixty-one years old; his Greek generals had deserted him, and he learnt the art of war independently, training his infantry to abandon the massed formation of his youth and to meet the legions in line. The details of these campaigns are not necessary to my frontier story and need not be followed, though their Homeric world is comforting in the bourgeois smugness of Rome: for the mountain people, the peasants, and the nobles who traced themselves back like their king to Iran, fought till – through an accidental panic and confusion – the camp and fortress with its treasures were taken in a night. Lucullus four days later marched on from valley to valley to the richest of the fortresses at Talaura (Daurla?).[30] He spent a month removing treasure, but the old king had escaped. The Euphrates near by has steep forbidding tributaries by any of which Armenia could be reached, and thither the Roman destiny followed the Pontic king.

In 70 B.C. Lucullus wintered in Cabira (Niksar), and then marched eastward, and the next chapter will take his battle across Euphrates, where the main current of this history now flows. But as for Mithradates, he spent nearly two years in exile, until his Armenian son-in-law Tigranes was also defeated, and they then fought the Romans together on the Armenian plain.

After this, in the late autumn of 68 B.C., he was back again with eight thousand men among the river-loops of the Lycus; and the people of Pontus welcomed him, though the cities of the coast were lost.

Lucullus was in the south, and the Romans were surprised. The Thracian mercenaries deserted to Mithradates their old commander, and the Republican army was beaten and blockaded in Cabira before a second contingent could come up. An uneventful winter (68–67 B.C.) went by in fortified positions, but Mithradates forced a battle before the arrival of Lucullus in the spring. Seven thousand men, twenty-four tribunes, and one hundred and fifty Roman centurions were lost; and Lucullus when he came could do little, for his own army was disintegrating. The armies watched each other, and the summer passed, while the Pontic king in Talaura recovered his kingdom, refusing to fight since his troops were poor and few. It was a last flicker of fortune, for Pompey, Lucullus' rival, with fresh and devoted men to supersede the disaffected soldiers, was on his way.

Outnumbered and outmatched by this fresh onset, Mithradates once again fell back on the Lycus valley, and held the Romans at the hill of Dasteira, identified – wrongly, I think – with my village of Purk-Nicopolis. Here the mistakes of the over-eager cavalry were repeated and they were lured and destroyed in an ambuscade.[31]

Pompey, free of his enemy's horse, could now draw supplies from Cappadocia, and his Cilician reserves had come up; he was able to surround Mithradates and cut off his water on a mountain height.[32] After a forty-five day blockade, the Pontic king yet managed to deceive the Roman sentinels and to extricate his army, marching to where the Bulgur Su rises in marshy patches and winds round a small green eminence in the lap of the larger hills. It is as it were at the gate of the Lycus valley, where the Armenian border ran over a vast downland some 2,060 metres high above sea level, now called Chaldakli Dagh, where Vespasian a century later established his frontier and the Turks beat the Russians in the First World War. The Pontic sea and the deep Euphrates valley are out of sight below, one on either side of its bare and empty shoulders.

Pompey attacked at night from the opposite heights: ' . . . at that very time Mithradates, it is said, saw a vision in his dream foreshowing what should come to pass. For he seemed to be under sail in the Euxine Sea with a prosperous gale, and just in view of Bosporus, discoursing pleasantly with the ship's company, as one overjoyed for his past danger and present security, when on a sudden he found himself deserted of all, and floating upon a broken plank of the ship at the mercy of the sea. While he was thus labouring under these passions and phantasms, his friends came and awakened him with the news of Pompey's approach, who was now indeed so near at hand that the fight must be for the camp itself, and the commanders accordingly drew up the forces in battle array.

'Pompey perceiving how ready they were and well prepared for defence began to doubt within himself whether he should put it to the hazard of a fight in the dark, judging it more prudent only to encompass them at present, lest they should fly, and to give them battle with the advantage of numbers the next day. But his oldest officers were of another opinion, and by entreaties and encouragements obtained permission that they might charge them immediately. Neither was the night so very dark, but that, though the moon was going down, it yet gave light enough to discern a body. And indeed this was one special disadvantage to the king's army. For the Romans coming upon them with the moon on their backs [from the west therefore], the moon, being very low, and just upon setting, cast the shadows a long way before their bodies, reaching almost to the enemy, whose eyes were thus so much deceived that not exactly discerning the distance, but imagining them to be near at hand, they threw their darts at the shadows without the least execution.[33] The Romans therefore, perceiving this, ran in upon them with a great shout; but the barbarians, all in a panic, unable to endure the charge, turned and fled, and were put to great slaughter, above ten thousand being slain; the camp also was taken. As for Mithradates himself, he at the beginning of the onset, with a body of eight hundred horse, charged through the Roman army, and made his escape. But before long all the rest dispersed, some one way and some another, and he was left with only three persons, among whom was his concubine, Hypsicratia, a girl always of a manly and daring spirit, and the king called her on that account Hypsicrates. She being attired and mounted like a Persian horseman, accompanied the king in all his flight, never weary even in the longest journey, nor ever failing to attend the king in person, and look after his horse too, until they came to Inora,[34] a castle of the king's, well stored with gold and treasure. From thence Mithradates took his richest apparel, and gave it among those that had resorted to him in his flight; and also to every one of his friends he gave a deadly poison, that they might not fall into the power of the enemy against their wills. From thence he designed to have gone to Tigranes in Armenia but being prohibited by Tigranes, who put out a proclamation with a reward of one hundred talents to any one that should apprehend him, he passed by the headwaters of the river Euphrates and fled through the country of Colchis.'[35]

So, in Plutarch's story, the Pontic king departed, and the wild people of Colchis received him. After a winter at Dioscurias, the 'furthermost run for ships',[36] he slipped by the Caucasus in a makeshift way and recovered the Crimea, where the chieftains welcomed him, and a son who had submitted to Rome committed suicide.

Even in the most hopeless misfortune and exile he still kept the name of 'king',[37] and planned to reach Italy by the Danube with a new fleet and an army equipped in Roman fashion; but his overstrained subjects revolted. The poison that he tried to take had no effect upon him from the homoeopathic treatments continued since his youth; and at sixty-eight, his own wrist too unsteady with age to strike, he died by the faithful hand of a bodyguard. He held, says Cicero, 'a place before all the kings with whom the Roman people have made war[38]'. His women were all dead with his help or by his order; and his son Pharnaces was confirmed by Pompey in the Crimean dominion, to be defeated fifteen years later under Caesar's *veni*, *vidi*, *vici* at Zela near Comana. The Pontic lands were divided among minor kings. Their mountain fortresses were destroyed. They ran in a strong line along the great east–west road of the north, and Strabo, some fifty years later, came upon them with their wells filled up with stones. But the cities were resuscitated, or new ones were founded, by Pompey, who – like Mithradates' mother, the Seleucid Laodike, and unlike Mithradates himself – was a builder. He left eleven of them in Pontus alone, but they never became, like the Alexandrine and Seleucid foundations, outposts for the civilisation of the West, with the exception of Purk-Nicopolis where the invalid soldiers settled, and where Mark Antony nearly half a century later was to send for the Armenian king.[39]

Verdict on Mithradates and Rome

In spite of the ins and outs – mostly outs – of a family life singularly drastic even for his time, and many unscrupulous murders, the human verdict is favourable to Mithradates. Unlike most oriental sovereigns he was loved in misfortune; not by his own mountain people only, but by Scythians and Thracians, the Colchians whose landscape baffled the Pompeian army, the pirates to whom he confided his person, the mercenaries whom he paid in advance, the Cappadocians who held to him in spite of their 'liberation', together with the Greek towns where he had spent his childhood – all their various loyalties remained with him through all the strains of his long career. 'He is known', says Pliny, 'to have spoken twenty-two languages, and no man of his subject peoples was ever addressed by him through an interpreter during all the fifty-six years of his reign.[40] The vanquished rarely enjoy a panegyric and we are left to guess at qualities which nursed this devotion, though here and there, apart from the superb courage, a hint of generosity, of respect for faithfulness in friend or enemy, and gaiety too and a love of music and 'beautiful things' comes through. *He was a man, take him for all in all*, and fought with the greatest generals of his time,[41] and even at the end 'his soldiers remained steadfast and silent, for there was nothing mean or contemptible about him, even in his misfortunes'.[42] His life went down like a stormy sunset, and Rome settled to exploit her wider boundaries with no enemy in sight.

In the panorama of twenty succeeding centuries, a misgiving as to the completeness of her victory creeps in. With Antiochus, with Carthage, and now with Mithradates, her basic policy was ever the same – *to remove from the immediate Roman periphery any power that seemed to be getting too strong*. 'By an ironic paradox', Professor Maurice Holleaux writes, 'the two enterprises which brought the Romans so much glory and laid the foundations of their world-supremacy [the destruction of Carthage and the defeat of Antiochus] had their origin in a groundless fear. Had they been more keen-sighted and less easily alarmed, they would not have come to dominate the Hellenic world. More probably they would have concentrated their efforts in the neighbouring barbarian countries west of Italy – and that with more reason and more advantage to themselves.'[43]

Mr B. L. Hallward in the same volume goes on to say that 'the danger from Carthage [before her destruction] was not that she was too strong, but that she had become too weak, and that her weakness might make Massinissa too strong' on her meridian border.

These two movements constitute the whole discord and defeat of world dominion – the plunging of a boundary into weakness and the

BLACK SEA COAST, SOUTH

THE WALLS OF ANCIENT SINOPE

subsequent necessity of strengthening it against what promises to become strong on its outer edge. Rome pursued such a policy in each of the three cases quoted and was to continue to do so in her dealings with Parthia in the future. She was successful with Carthage, for no strong enough opponent rose in the wastes of Africa; and she seemed to succeed with Mithradates, for no serious threat came across the northern steppes until the Huns appeared. The consequences of Antiochus and Parthia we will presently come to.

Before doing so, we may glance back over the wars of Mithradates and see whether they were indeed necessary, for, as far as our evidence carries, he himself had no idea of fighting the Romans until he was attacked. 'All this', he said to Sulla, after the assault of Nicomedes of Bithynia, 'they did for money. . . . When war had broken out through the acts of your generals all that I did in self-defence was the result of necessity rather than of intention'.[44] The facts bear out this plea. After his defeat by Sulla, the next attack was a private enterprise of Murena's, and 'unless a small country has no right to fight for its liberties against a big one',[45] Mithradates, with four hundred of his villages raided and his capital threatened, was compelled to fight.

Until these things happened, and particularly until Bithynia and the Bosphorus fell to Rome, Mithradates was interested only in the lands adjacent to his northern kingdom and in the development of his Pontic trade, for which the western markets *were all in Roman hands*. With so decisive a trump card in its possession, the Republic could have followed the example of the Greeks with their Black Sea traders, who had interchanged a profitable diplomacy for generations. Where supply and demand are advantageous on both sides of a frontier, war is unnecessary: it is a principle that impresses itself upon one as one traces the slow Roman defeat along her south-east border. The destruction of the Pontic kingdom, which could have been a bulwark, was the second important step after the wearing away of the Seleucids, in the melancholy history of this defeat.

IV

Across the Euphrates

The invasion of Armenia – a consequence of the Mithradatic war – is followed in its oriental aspect, leaving on one side the more generally emphasised personal rivalry between Lucullus and Pompey, for which it set the stage. The conquest of Tigranocerta brings the Romans within striking distance of the main commercial highway of the East.

> *Medumque flumen gentibus additum*
> *victis minores volvere vertices,*
> *intraque praescriptum Gelones*
> *exiguis equitare campis.*[1]
>
> (Horace: *Odes*, 11.9)

The Euphrates

Between Kemakh and Divrik the Euphrates moves in its higher reaches through tributary defiles and chrome-streaked gorges, whose thousand spires plunge it in cathedral shade. Swift as a javelin and mottled green like marble, it carries its own light within it, under walls that exhibit an unimaginable, unresponsive dignity of stone. They dive, porphyry and gold and intricate as armour, with scarcely a lip of earth; the train burrows in tunnels and there is no room for a road; until they open

again to a wider stretch near Melitene (Malatya) before reaching the
liver-coloured gorges that break through Taurus and lead to Samosata in
the south. The river then settles, careless as man of what it has devoured,
and winds through open desert towards marshy estuaries impossible to
fancy in these its upper labyrinths of rock.

In one of its milder breaks, the first Roman to visit it officially was
Sulla, in 92 B.C. He established his country's superiority by seating
himself on its bank in a middle position between the king of Cappadocia
and the Parthian envoy – a carelessness in protocol for which the Parthian
was executed on his return.[2]

Some twenty-two years later, Lucullus, marching from Cabira, came
to the Melitene crossing and sacrificed a bull to Jupiter as he led the
Roman destiny into the unknown. Appius Claudius Pulcher, his brother-
in-law, had prepared it, sent 'on a barren messenger's job'[3] to Tigranes
the king of Armenia, to ask for the surrender of Mithradates.

Tigranes had kept his father-in-law in a distant unhealthy exile for
over a year and was presumably ready to treat; but Lucullus, kind and
civilised, was unskilful with subordinates, or possibly in this case not
averse to war: Appius, even if not as bad as Cicero painted him, was
evidently unsuited to a delicate oriental negotiation if one wished it to
succeed – 'it is astonishing how he holds proud kings to hate',[4] and when
he made an arrogant demand, Tigranes refused – being also annoyed by
the Roman ambassador's intrigues with his Kurdish subjects, as many
rulers on the Euphrates through one dynasty or another have continued
to be annoyed ever since.

Lucullus therefore marched from Pontus with two or three legions
and some five hundred horse or so,[5] in autumn when the mists lie shallow
in the sun and poplars shimmer behind the jade-green willows.

From Sivas he crossed the Kizil Irmak, the Red River, and climbed
to open highlands where grass and stubble offer no obstacle except,
in its season, a shortage of food. The soil is thin on a rocky uplifted
floor, the poplars glitter in the lap of small declivities, the flocks shine
stationary in the distance like islands: it must, one thinks, have been the
sight of Cappadocian sheep catching the sunlight that gave the idea of
a halo to the first Asiatic painters of the saints. Across the watershed,
eastward-flowing streams gather in short grass where the best horses in
Anatolia are browsing,[6] and brooks tumble between mudbanks soft as

earthworms towards Euphrates. Their currents shine like snakes in the Malatya gardens in the dawn.

'The whole of this region,' of Melitene or Commagene, says Strabo, 'is planted with fruit trees, the only country in all Cappadocia of which this is true, so that it produces not only the olive, but also the Monarite vine, which rivals the Greek wines. It is situated opposite to Sophene; and the Euphrates river flows between . . . On the far [east] side of the river is a noteworthy fortress, Tomisa by name, [by the modern Isogli crossing]. . . . presented by Lucullus as a prize to the ruler of Cappadocia who fought at his side in the Mithradatic war.'[7]

The river, as one draws near it here, takes control, dominating a landscape where slopes have been torn, and every track scooped out, and the very shape of the ground is modelled by headstrong floods. Reddish cliffs dip like claws of an animal drinking where the train now takes the ancient crossing; and from here Lucullus marched over the plain of Elazig, climbed to the Göljük lake, and followed the small dragon stream of Tigris born from its southern rim. The Romans usually avoided defiles, and seem to have kept to the western heights until the range of Taurus, breaking in eroded waves above the Dyarbekr plain, rose once again to the subsidiary range of Tur Abdin, the ancient Masius. The name Tur is yet Taurus; and the height of Mardin and the lowland of Nisibis are tossed along its southern slopes.

Tigranocerta

These ranges of Taurus were the frontier between ancient Armenia and Parthian Mesopotamia[8]; and Tigranocerta, Tigranes' new capital, was on the edge of one or another of them – on the southern range at Kizil Tepe or Tell Ermenek, along the 'royal road' of the Achaemenians and close above the later route of the legions, according to Strabo and Tacitus; or on the northern range and edge of Armenia, along the south of the main Taurus foothills, according to Plutarch, Ptolemy and Pliny. The geographical difficulty has led various travellers to explore the region, and the evidence, as given by Rice Holmes, Guse, Eckhart, Lehmann Haupt, and most recently Dilleman, is too lengthy to be gone into in detail here.[9] Calder and Bean, in their excellent map of Roman Asia Minor, are non-committal and put Tigranocerta on both

sites with a query; the *Cambridge Ancient History* inclines to the east,
Dilleman is definite for the west. I spent a week in the district, most
kindly lodged and taken about by the Keir and Cawdor Arrow Drilling
Company who were drilling oil for Shell – and very tentatively, with
the volumes of my predecessors in my hand and the landscapes before
me, decided to stick to the north-eastern slopes above the Tigris, with
an open mind towards any other conclusion whenever the experts may
reach it and in the hope that one or other of these sites may soon be
examined.

I made, however, two small observations of my own: the first, that
Nisibis, if only thirty-seven miles away in an easy land with no obstacles
between, strongly garrisoned, and held by the king's brother, would
surely have given some sign of life during the investment of its sister city
by an army which evidently seemed to the Armenians most manageably
small? There was, indeed, no point in having two strong cities so close
together. And, secondly, that it was much easier for Tacitus or his copyists to mistake a number of miles in a country unknown to them than for
all the other writers to invent a fact as definite as the crossing of an important river. One may also note that Lucullus, pointing out the Taurus[10]
as he came from the north-west, was probably looking at the main range
and not at the smaller and subservient southern curtain of Masius.

For better or worse therefore, I see him marching in open formation
eastward along the curve of Taurus, 'using no manner of violence to
the people who came to him and willingly received his army'.[11] 'And
when the soldiers were desirous to plunder a castle that seemed to be
well stored within, "That is the castle," said he, "that we must storm,"
showing them Taurus at a distance: "the rest is reserved for those who
conquer there"'.[12] He hastened his march, and crossed the Tigris where
it is low at the summer's end, probably some twenty miles above the
bridgeless hollow where ancient Amida and modern Dyarbekr were to
stand; and 'came into Armenia', picking his way over limestone débris
so closely scattered that there is hardly room for a horse's foot between
them, or for the thin stubble stalks of the corn.

The hospitable plains have given harvests since wheat was first discovered. Mounds of lost habitations strew their dusty horizons, and
Xenophon saw them already forgotten as he marched in the opposite
direction four centuries before. Behind Lucullus, in the distance just

visible, was the western lacework of the Euphrates hills. Plutarch's 'castles' are still there – villages with corner towers, and storks' nests upon them, a well in the level ground before them and flattened cakes of dung for winter fuel plastered against some wall in the sun. They use the wooden plough as Strabo describes it,[13] and their women still wear the many-coloured turbans and clothing of the Kurds.

Tigranes was territorially the most powerful monarch of the East. He had built Tigranocerta with the plunder of his conquests, which included Sophene down the east bank of Euphrates, and all that was left to the Seleucids in Syria and Cilicia in the west. His new capital is mentioned later by the Persian king Shapur as the first Armenian city coming from the south[14]: if it is the present Silvan, it had been built by Assyrians long before on an octagonal platform in the Babylonian way. Passing from civilisation to civilisation – a Greek inscription, a Persian rock-relief, a martyr-church of the Byzantines 'on the site of Tigranocerta' according to Faustus of Byzantium, an Islamic general who said 'I wish God would give us this town without a swordstroke', and had hardly spoken when the eastern gate opened of itself,[15] – it has come down as small in its walls as a shrunken old man inside his garments, with a stream flowing round two sides beneath the Assyrian platform and a stagnant ditch as Tacitus observed it on the north.[16]

The king's palace was in a suburb, with hunting grounds and lakes, and he had surrounded the town with walls and built his stabling at their base; and made the principal inhabitants of the country live there,[17] so that 'it was a rich and beautiful city, every common man and every man of rank . . . studied to adorn it',[18] and large numbers of citizens were collected from countries overrun or conquered in the west.

The Battle

The Roman attack came as a surprise, for 'no one told the king that Lucullus was advancing'[19] and he had the man hanged who first brought the report. He was not one whom we hear of as being loved. But he was obeyed: two thousand of his cavalry recklessly sent out were cut to pieces, and his Greek mercenaries settled down in the citadel to be besieged. He himself retreated northward to collect an army and march south again from the plains of Mush, dropping across the wall of Taurus

ABBASSID BRIDGE (A.D. 1147) ACROSS THE BATMAN SU
COUNTRY OF THE UPPER EUPHRATES (NEAR DIVRIK)

GÖLJÜK LAKE, LOOKING SOUTH TOWARDS THE SOURCE OF THE RIVER TIGRIS

LANDSCAPE OF THE UPPER TIGRIS

LOW WATER IN THE TIGRIS GORGE

among wooded precipices of Kulp and the headwaters of the Batman river which opens, before its junction with the Tigris, into a narrow oblong plain.

Here, in full but distant view of the city on its hill, the battle of Tigranocerta, which Mommsen describes as one of Rome's greatest, was fought in 69 B.C. The disproportion of forces was enormous – more than twenty to one according to Livy, or more probably seventy or eighty thousand Armenians to Lucullus' sixteen thousand foot.[20] Of these he left six thousand to continue the siege on the hill behind him, while he marched with the remaining ten thousand, a thousand slingers and archers, and three thousand horse, down between high reddish banks through the poplar thickets of the little Farkin valley. Where it opens into the Batman river it became visible to Tigranes, camped some three miles away on a low hill.

'Too many for ambassadors, and too few for soldiers,' the king remarked: and thought them retreating as they doubled towards a broad and sandy ford. But Mithradates' envoy said: 'Oh king . . . the Romans do not wear their best clothes on a march, nor use bright shields, and naked headpieces, as you see them, with the leathern coverings taken off: this is a preparation for war.'[21] Lucullus wheeled while he was speaking; the first eagle appeared; and the cohorts prepared to wade across.

The battle was fought on the 6th of October. The river at that time meanders in shallows among white stones, where donkeys shamble across laden with sand, and the piers of an old bridge are close to the crossing. Tigranes, surprised and unprepared, began to wheel his army on the crest of his hill to face west, while Lucullus disorganised the heavy-armoured Iranian horsemen at the bottom by a flank attack against which they were helpless 'on account of the weight and stiffness of their armour, with which they are, as it were, built up'.[22] Their shins and thighs, before the invention of the stirrup, used to be left naked to give a better grip on a horse, and the Roman infantry were instructed to hack at this vulnerable surface while Lucullus, in his fringed cloak with his sword out of its scabbard, took two cohorts round the back of the mêlée and caught the Armenian infantry in the disarray of wheeling at the top of the steep short hill.

The Roman infantryman's shield covered a man from neck to knee but was lightly made of leather on a frame, and he had no spear to carry, but a sword in his right hand and two javelins heavy with iron in his left. These he threw before closing with an enemy, and he then had a free hand behind his shield with which to help himself in close fighting or when dealing with obstacles on rough ground. On this occasion Lucullus told his men to dispense with the javelins so that – having dealt with the armoured horsemen – they scrambled unimpeded up the grass to join him and his two cohorts in a victorious assault at the top.

*   *   *

The Tigranocerta garrison meanwhile had held out well against the small besieging army, harassing them with arrows and burning their engines with naphtha. But their commander, seeing the Roman victory from his walls, thought it prudent to disarm the Greek mercenaries, who then 'wound their clothing round their left arms to serve as shields, ran upon their assailants [i.e. the Armenians] courageously, and immediately shared the arms of all those they killed . . . then seized some of the spaces between the towers, and called to the Romans outside'.[23] Lucullus' victory was complete. He found '8,000 talents of coined money as well as the usual valuables, while each man got 800 drachmae from the general spoils'.[24] He sent the Greeks home, 'allowing them money for their journey; and the barbarians also, as many as had been forced away from their homes . . . and by such aids, at that time, even without the help of arms, succeeded in reducing the barbarians'[25] – for the whole neighbourhood south and east (except Nisibis) submitted.

Lucullus first introduced gladiators to Asia Minor, but he was, like Julius Caesar, humane in a society where compassion was counted by Cicero and his contemporaries as one among the soul's 'disorders'.[26] As far as he could he repaired the damage of his wars. He lamented the sight of pillaged Amisus with tears, and gave clothes and money to the survivors; and Cyzicus remembered him with games for generations. He incurred the enmity of the equestrian order by giving back Syria and part of Cilicia to the Seleucids and reducing Sulla's monstrous indemnity in Asia:[27] the shattered province recovered under his hand and was able to clear itself in four years only. 'By the whole of Asia he was beloved . . . desirous as he was far more of praise for acts of justice and clemency, than for feats in war.'[28]

Yet even by these reputable means, he was able to collect his almost legendary wealth, to become – as Pompey called him – 'Xerxes in a toga',[29] and to leave among other things fishponds worth five million drachmae and a palace that eventually was to house the last western emperor of Rome:[30] 'Both Lucullus and Pompey made the war pay, and we may estimate that a total capital of at least 350 million drachmae was carried out from the East.'[31]

Like Mithradates he had a perfect knowledge of the Greek language: he only 'interposed a few barbarisms ... as a clear proof that what he wrote was the work of a Roman',[32] and, brought up with Greek philosophers, he opened his library to them and loved to be among them, though his values were never quite theirs. Plutarch describes those whom he feasted, 'coming to Rome day after day, ashamed and declining the invitations, where so great an expense was incurred for them – when with a smile he told them that "some of this ... is for your sakes, but more for that of Lucullus"'.[33] That too was a 'barbarism'.

For, among much riff-raff of the Republic, he yet showed, in a more favourable light, some of the qualities that fundamentally divided the Italians and the Greeks. 'There is no comparison', Plutarch writes, 'between the south wall of the Acropolis built by Cimon, and the chambers and galleries with their sea-views, built at Naples by Lucullus',[34] and the difference between the love for visual pomp and the abstract passionate cherishing of a nation persists, I think, in Latin and Greek to this day. I have often noticed, in a Mediterranean summer when citizens walk up and down in their good clothes in the evening coolness, how the Greeks in their interest in the world around them forget themselves completely, while an Italian will never miss a glance directed at himself. The remarks of Lucullus, his Roman ostentation, his pride in being able to pay for his fleet out of his local fund, his virtues indeed, all underline this Latin concern with other peoples' opinion. He had to suffer under the defections of his soldiers, the persecutions of Pompey, and the indifference of Rome; and it is painful even now to consider what humiliation a generous and sensitive nature must have undergone. But Plutarch is surely wrong in representing him as 'less desirous of praise for acts of war'? Later, when he was deprived of his provinces and disappointed, digesting injustice and anger for months on end, this may have been so. But at Tigranocerta he was superbly victorious, forty years old or little over, and ready – and surely eager – to venture 'with too great and ill-advised speed'.[35] He must have known that he was doing great things, 'pushing the frontiers of the Roman dominion from the setting of the sun to the river Euphrates'[36]; placing – far more than Pompey of whom Cicero said it – 'the boundary of the empire of the Roman people at the limits of the world'.[37]

Whether he meant to invade Parthia or not is uncertain, but one may remember that in Spain he had been ready enough to engineer a war for the payment of his debts. Plutarch declares that he sent envoys who found the Parthians 'double-minded, dealing privately with Tigranes' – a circumstance which surely could not surprise him or anyone else in the Middle East, but which, 'as soon as Lucullus understood, he resolved . . . to try the power of Parthia . . . thinking it would be a glorious result, thus in one current of war, like an athlete in the games, to throw down three kings one after the other. . . . ' He sent, therefore, into Pontus for his other army, which had had enough of the war and refused to come.[38] Lucullus then, according to Plutarch, gave up the thought of invading Parthia, and in the height of summer, 68 B.C., turned into Armenia, following the Batman-Kulp river to its headwaters, and thence crossing over the pass that gives them birth, due north from Tigranocerta, towards the eastern Euphrates across the plain of Mush.

Invasion of Armenia

Now indeed he went out 'into an unknown extent of country every way enclosed with deep rivers and mountains, never free from snow' (I have seen patches in August on Jilo) – 'which made the soldiers, already far from orderly, follow him with great unwillingness and opposition'.[39]

It seems strange that, after getting to know the fringes of the country for the better part of a year, he should have made so little provision for hardship. He had marched through Galatia with thirty thousand porters carrying corn, but here, when he reached the highlands, 'he was filled with apprehension at the greenness of the fields' and the lateness of the harvest. One must infer that in the earlier campaigns he had been well informed by his Cappadocian allies and had met docile and reluctant subjects of Tigranes, 'the effeminate men of Sophene', in the south. He now ventured into a purely Iranian land enclosed in mountain walls, and was unprepared for the difference not only in the people, but in the leadership also, for Mithradates – drawn by his son-in-law out of exile – was once again organising the resistance to Rome.

Even today the road that breaks by Hazro through a naked 'gate' behind Silvan finds a sudden remoteness. It is the most recondite of the four passes to the north – Ergana, Lije, Kulp and Bitlis.[40] Spacious but enclosed, small hills billow in cross-currents between two walls that hem them in and isolate them from the downlands that roll to Ararat and from the Assyrian plains. The land is scattered with poor but peaceful villages, and the women move in autumn to vineyards bright as new patches on old gowns, whose grapes are boiled in cauldrons till they thicken, and are spread, like glue, on cotton cloths to dry. The road, just feasible for a jeep, follows the track of a much older stone-edged Turkish road, through holmoaks and pistachio, by wooded precipices where the Kulp and Lije rivers meet under what was probably, in later wars, the fort of Atachas.[41] From Kulp itself, high up on the wall of the bowl, a mule track cuts north in two days to the Arsanias river, the modern Murat Su or east arm of Euphrates. Here, on good cavalry ground, the old king Mithradates took the war into his more competent hands. He comforted and clothed the fugitive Tigranes, for the difference in generosity of these two monarchs was very great; and 'having enrolled almost the whole population of Armenia, selected some seventy thousand of the bravest and half that number of horse'.[42] He trained them hastily in Roman methods, refusing every inducement to fight in the plain and cutting off the country's supplies, – until Tigranes, by losing another battle, allowed Lucullus, in spite of immense difficulties, to force his way north and east.

Artaxata, the Armenian capital, was designed, it is rather improbably said, by Hannibal on the folds of Ararat[43] and must have been almost in sight when the patience of Lucullus' troops finally gave way. They forced him to return, by a route equally abrupt but warmer (possibly through the present country of the Hakkiari), to reduce Nisibis and winter in the 'fruitful and sunny' south. From this time onward the wars of Lucullus were practically over. He marched back to Pontus to relieve the harassed armies there, and watched the old king recover his kingdom while his own men stood merely on the defensive, until Pompey's arrival put an end to the hopes of Mithradates and to those of Lucullus as well.[44]

*   *   *

The verdict of history has been against Lucullus as a leader of men, though probably few of the historians have fully realised how hard a country to fight in Armenia must be. The harvests were not ripe in July and the cold had already settled in September, with 'hoar frost and ice which made the waters scarcely drinkable for the horses by their exceeding coldness, and scarcely passable because the ice broke and cut their sinews.'[45] A generation later, Mark Antony failed in the same sort of country, although, with less generalship than Lucullus, he still kept the loyalty of his men. Even in the south, before the end of September, I have been nearly blown off the ridge of Taurus by an icy wind strong enough to shift my mules and muleteers.

It seems to me that the failure was not carelessness but an under-standable want of information — the fact that Lucullus expected the people in Armenia to be like those of Sophene and the southern slopes, co-operative and amenable and ready to supply his troops. If he had realised that in moving across Taurus he was leaving a country recently and unwillingly conquered, to march into the King's own hereditary highlands, he would surely have done as Pompey did who marched in the north with one thousand skins of water,[46] he would have taken supplies as he himself had done in Galatia, from the fertile plains where the harvest had just been gathered, and would probably have reached the 'Carthage of Armenia' in spite of his soldiers' reluctance.

The important fact is, however, that the mutinous soldiers were right. They were ready to defend the frontiers of Pontus, or to march to rescue their fellows in the north: but they objected (from whatever mercenary motives) to a quite unnecessary war. Lucullus himself gives a clue as to how unnecessary it was. When told that Mithradates and Tigranes were preparing their forces, 'he wondered much why the Armenian . . . did not assist Mithradates in his flourishing condition . . . instead of beginning the war when its hopes had grown cold, and throwing himself down headlong with them who were irrevocably fallen already'[47]; the answer of course being that Tigranes unless attacked would never have fought the Romans at all — and did, very soon after, abjectly surrender.

It was much the same pattern as the Pontic invasions, though the background and the motives were different: not led for booty, it was still a Roman army out for adventure, far from the will or even knowledge of its senate at home. In this case, as the profit (to the soldier) was small, the general's manner evidently unfortunate, and the adventure extremely severe, the soldiers objected. Pompey replaced Lucullus (67 B.C.); with his wider grasp of the situation, his small vain mouth and easy ways, he carried his troops along, and at the instigation of Tigranes' son crossed Euphrates and received the Armenian king's surrender without a battle. But he too was foiled by the climate and the landscape when he reached the cliffs of Caucasus that Mithradates had somehow negotiated with the help of his wild friends. Pompey abandoned the pursuit and deviated to the Caspian borderland, where drought, dysentery, and the multitude of adders in the lowlands turned him back from a 'seemingly superfluous campaign explained by a desire to develop a trans-Caspian trade route to the farthest East . . . or to gain the glory of a triumph over peoples whose very names were new to the Romans'.[48] T. Frank estimates that the Mithradatic wars cost the kingdom of Pontus about a hundred and twenty thousand inhabitants. Sulla, in need of gold took some 9,000 lb from the temples,[49] and the country's cash reserves, together with those of Cappadocia, Armenia and Cilicia, mostly found their way to Rome.[50]

It is impossible now to grasp the relative strength of the strands that drew these Republicans to the Euphrates battle ground. Fear, their first leading motive in Asia, had brought them through gradual involvement and the greed of individuals into control of a commercial machine whose delicate preservation in the hellenistic chaos they could not understand. As the later Mongols destroyed in a generation the irrigation that fed Babylonia, so the earlier Romans destroyed (temporarily) the threads that had fed the hellenistic kingdoms in spite of all their wars; and the beginnings of a Levantine education, visible in Pompey and in others, were continually cut short by ignorance or bloodshed at home.

These things held Plutarch with the mixed emotion that inspires most of us in spite of reason: for in one and the same paragraph he sighs over the failure of Lucullus, but for which, with 'his fortitude, vigilance, wisdom, justice, the Roman Empire had not had Euphrates for its boundary, but the utmost ends of Asia and the Hyrcanian [Caspian] sea'; and then goes on to say how 'by other's agency he did Rome greater harm than he did her advantage by his own. For the trophies in Armenia, near the Parthian frontier, and Tigranocerta, and Nisibis, and the great wealth brought from thence to Rome, with the captive crown of Tigranes carried in triumph, all helped to puff up Crassus, as if the barbarians had been nothing else but spoil and booty; and Crassus, falling among the Parthian archers, soon demonstrated that Lucullus' triumphs were not beholden to the inadvertency and effeminacy of his enemies, but to his own courage and conduct.'[51]

Having been led into the Armenian tangle which is to clog the feet of Rome for centuries, we move on to the Parthians in the south.

V

The Seleucid Kings and the Empire of Trade

T he amount of damage done to Asia Minor by the Roman Republic is hard to assess, since most of the Seleucid documentation is lost. Having destroyed Antiochus III and Mithradates, the policy of the *weak periphery* is followed, through the destruction of the Seleucid dynasty, to the breaking of the bridge of Asia under its hellenistic kings (92–64 B.C., from Sulla's arrival on the Euphrates to Pompey's ousting of the last Seleucid). This chapter deals with the great highway of commerce whose very existence is now to be endangered by the culminating folly of Crassus at the Republic's end.

> 'Thou didst think to drink up the kingdom of Arsaces in thy great cups.' (Parthian epitaph on the defeated Antiochus Sidetes; from Athenaeus: X.439e.)

Kingdoms Along the Euphrates

'I have done my best,' Cicero wrote on his way to Cilicia in 50 B.C., 'to get the king of Cappadocia to pay Brutus. . . . He has no means to pay. He has no treasury and no regular tribute: he levies taxes on the method of Appius. They are scarcely sufficient for the interest on Pompey's money. . . . Messengers come back with the reply that he has no assets. I can believe it, for I have never seen a kingdom more plundered or a king more needy.'[1]

Just south of Cappadocia, the little kingdoms of Commagene and Sophene that held the Euphrates were in no better case. All were poor lands, their richest produce gall-nuts[2] and medicinal plants,[3] cattle, or slaves in whom they trafficked[4]: 'The Cappadocian king is rich in slaves but lacks coin,' says Horace.[5] The high rocky soil grazed by wild asses, the bitter climate, the small fertile patches, gave no more than a chance of simple and frugal prosperity in times of peace. Cappadocia had astonished the Roman publicans by choosing, when the choice was given her, to revert to her kings. 'When the royal family died out, the Romans, in accordance with their compact of friendship with the tribes, conceded to them the right to live under their own laws: but those who came on the embassy not only begged off from the freedom (for they said they were unable to bear it), but requested that a king be appointed for them. The Romans, amazed that any people should be so tired of liberty, permitted them to choose',[6] and in 93 B.C. they elected Ariobarzanes and continued their hard and ancient ways round the temple of the Cataonian Apollo, or the Venasian Zeus in Morimene, or in their mountain strongholds – fine names, Azamora and Dastarcum – or in their only two cities – Tyana on the legions' road to Melitene, or Mazaca which is now Kayseri that leans against the volcano of Argaeus, from whose summit Strabo thought one could see the gulf of Issus as well as the Pontic shore. It was a poor site for a city, 'without water and unfortified by nature . . . in districts utterly barren', or 'marshy, and flames rise therefrom at night',[7] but the mountain was clad with timber and stone for building, and flocks could find a summer pasture in its folds; roads crossed it from the Black Sea in the north to Cilicia in the south, and west to east from the Aegean coast to Melitene; so that its importance continued to grow into the Roman age.

The possession of a country in the ancient world meant no more than the holding of its roads and cultivated districts. Most of Asia Minor and what lay east of it had remained unsubdued since Alexander's first advance, and the Seleucids left the north to its dynasts. Pontus soon began to be hellenised. Its first four kings, socially superior by their ancestry, were able to intermarry with Macedonian princesses, who eventually began to break up the Iranian seclusion of Cappadocia also, together with its domestic peace. These kings too were hellenised: Ariarathus and Attalus, from Cappadocia and Pergamon in the second century B.C., were class-mates in Athens and together dedicated a statue to their teacher. Yet they continued to foster the Iranian tradition which persisted along the upper Euphrates borderland. They wore the tiara and the Persian dress, the loose trousers and sleeved tunics that one sees today among the Chaldaeans of Iraq; and in Pontus Mithradates at any rate always carried a sword, and wore – barbarous in Greek eyes – a dagger in his belt.[8] His country was rich chiefly through the Pontic trade; but south of him, in the more austere highlands, the kings struggled with their debts – until, south of them again, the most opulent of the trade routes opened through Nisibis.

This drained the Babylonian storehouse and fed the Seleucid empire both in its greatness and decline. More than a hundred years after Magnesia, Cicero mentions an Antiochus whose wine-ladle 'hollowed out of a single precious stone with handle of gold'[9] inspired the cupidity of Verres. The Syrian kings through all their miseries continued to be rich while traffic reached them from the east; and continued to spread their riches through their own Syrian harbours and across the mainland gateways of Anatolia into the Asiatic provinces of Rome.

These recovered whenever the drain of war or extortion lifted, with a speed only to be explained by two factors: the basic Anatolian village policy on which hellenistic organisation was built up, and the golden stream of trade.[10]

Economic Result of Roman Civil War in Asia

One has seen, after the Second World War, how quickly rural countries like Italy or Belgium recover, though agriculture alone is not enough for actual wealth. Rhodes was diminished after Cassius' siege in 43 B.C. because the mainland terminal cities had seized her trade[11]; but thirty-seven years before, Lucullus with four years of good government had enabled the province of Asia to pay off the indemnity of Sulla; and Heraclea recuperated, after a two years' siege and a sack.[12] Pompey managed Asia well between 67 and 62 B.C. His municipal charters proved lasting; he increased the Roman income[13]; rewarded the allied

kings by distributing the poorly hellenised regions among them; and he
let them and the new provinces of Syria and Bithynia collect their own
taxes.[14] His immense prestige was proved by Asiatic loyalty towards
him throughout the Civil Wars.[15]

Before the renewed ruin of these wars, there had been a respite of
fifteen years in Asia. But from 48 B.C. onward, the Roman armies fought
for Roman motives on the Asiatic soil and the Mithradatic horrors were
repeated on a weakened population. The loss was not in money only but
in actual destruction – cities, Samos and Halicarnassus, 'dismantled and
almost deserted'[16], prisoners sold as slaves for 12 million sesterces[17]
in Cicero's small Cilician war alone.[18] Unexpected objects flooded the
Western world. Pompey's victories 'made fashion veer to pearls and
green stones'. The earlier ones 'had done the same for chased silver,
garments of cloth of gold, and dining couches inlaid with bronze',[19]
and Mummius, from the smoking wreck of Corinth, had 'caused the
dispersal of bronzes from a number of the towns of Achaia' and given
their name to the Corinthian lamps.[20]

The sums already extracted in earlier wars were so immense that in
67 B.C., after the annexation of Macedonia, direct taxation in Italy had
been abolished.

By the time of the Civil Wars most of the booty no longer reached
the treasury but was intercepted by victorious generals.[21] Pompey's
son was offered 70 million denarii as an indemnity for his father's
property[22]; about twenty of his lieutenants received nearly 25 million
denarii between them; and his personal secretary pulled out 4,000
talents.[23] Requisition of unpaid grain; bribes from the provincials for
their law-suits and complaints; billeting of troops and sales of captives,
etc. all went to swell the profits. Vast private fortunes filled the pockets
of benefactors and oppressors alike. Mithradates had raked 2,000 talents
by a single fine in Chios; the senate, 4,000 from Crete; Sulla, 20,000
from the province of Asia. The ever-increasing bribing of their armies
put pressure on the generals: Lucullus gave over a million denarii to his
soldiers and handed only 2,700,000 to the treasury.[24] In the Civil War,
Brutus writes from Illyria that 'the need for money, which is just as great
in the armies of the other generals as in mine, makes me regret so much
the more the loss of Asia'.[25]

The dealings in Anatolia strike one with sadness even now: the cities, uninterested in either side, were smitten by both.

In Tarsus one faction had crowned Cassius, the other had done the same for Dolabella: 'After Cassius had overcome Dolabella he levied a contribution . . . of 1,500 talents. Being unable to find the money, and being pressed for payment with violence by the soldiers, the people sold all their public property and coined all the sacred articles used in religious processions. As this was not sufficient, the magistrates sold free persons into bondage, first girls and boys, afterwards women and miserable old men, who brought a very small price, and finally young men. Finally Cassius . . . took pity and released them from the remainder of the contribution.'[26]

The speech of the Rhodians may be recorded. Cassius in 42 B.C. was preparing a fleet against the great republic, in the bay of Myndus behind its screen of islands. Here Rhodes sent to remind him of the treaty of friendship between them; and when this failed, sent Archelaus who had been his teacher. The old man pleaded, taking his hand familiarly: 'Oh friend of the Greeks, do not destroy a Greek city. Oh friend of freedom, do not destroy Rhodes. Do not forget . . . what the Rhodians accomplished . . . our services to you . . . when we fought with you against Antiochus the Great. . . . So much for our race, our dignity hitherto unenslaved, our alliance and our goodwill towards you. As for you, Cassius, you owe a peculiar reverence to this city in which you . . . attended my school . . . who hoped that I should some time plume myself . . . with different expectations, but now plead on behalf of my country, lest it be forced into war'.[27]

The old man shed tears, but Cassius drew away his hand and watched from a hill the battle in which the Rhodians were defeated; he then surrounded the city with land and naval forces, and after another of their desperate sallies and a short siege, entered and planted a spear on the tribunal 'to show that he had taken it by the spear'. He seized all the money in the temples and public treasury, and ordered the private citizens to bring what they had left. He finally supplemented these gains by a ten years' tribute in a lump sum from the other cities of Asia.[28] In the last act, when Antony was living on the country with at least 87,000 thousand foot soldiers and some 125,000 to 140,000 men in his fleet, he in his turn asked for nine years' taxes in advance. 'The Civil Wars', says Tenney Frank, 'left most of Asia bankrupt for a generation.'[29] Such was the swiftly mounting climax of extortion from the days when the Attalids invited the Romans[30], and crucified a grammarian for making an unfashionable comparison of their royal purple with the bloody weals on the back of a slave.[31]

The Miserable Greek

The victories over Tigranes reinforced the legend of eastern degeneracy that began before Herodotus and lasted to Kipling. They inspired Caesar's *Veni Vidi Vici* in Bithynia, undeterred by the warning of Carrhae, and were, one may say, a misfortune for the whole later history of Rome.[32] Even before the Romans came, Flamininus, making a heap of the Asiatic peoples, had called them all Syrians, 'far better fitted to be slaves', and Apollonius of Tyana, over a hundred years later, complains that the Greeks are denied (by the Egyptians as a matter of fact) 'any and every sort of good quality', are declared 'ruffians ... addicted to every sort of anarchy, lovers of legend and miracle mongers ... making their poverty not a title of dignity, but a mere cause for stealing'.[33] The gates of Rhodes, Appian suggests, were opened by 'the more intelligent' of the Rhodians.[34] Henceforth the *Graeculus* of Cato, the corrupt unreliable Levantine, is met more and more frequently, and no doubt the stigma became more and more true. Corruption followed subservience: there is in Cicero a whole unconscious gallery of sketches that illustrate not only the process but its causes: consular candidates indicted for bribery; the king of Egypt held up to auction[35]; the governor of Syria draining from the treasure house of 'that rich land now completely pacified an enormous mass of gold',[36] and waging war upon its quiet peoples. He describes the inhabitants of Lampsacus on the coast of Marmara, 'whose nature, habits, and training made them the gentlest of human beings: by their status the allies, by their condition the slaves, by their position the humble suppliants, of the Roman nation', so that the worst outrage alone could bring them 'to the point of being more influenced by loathing ... than by fear'.[37] Such poison works, and we have seen it, sadly enough, in our own age. 'I do not expect much from a Greek', Cicero writes to Atticus,[38] and later, embittered, says, 'a Greek witness does not think of the worth of his oath but of words that may injure. . . . My speech would never come to an end if I cared to describe completely the untrustworthiness of this whole people . . . managed by irresponsible seated assemblies . . . [39] trained by a long course of servitude to show an excess of sycophancy . . . [40]; you complain that I strongly recommended . . . an undoubted matricide from Phrygia; concerning this case and all others like it, if you should wonder at my courting popularity so strongly among Greeks, pray observe what follows. Perceiving that their complaints have more influence than is right, owing to their natural habit of exaggerating, I soothed . . . all such as I heard complaining about you. . . . Hermippus I muzzled not only by talking to him, but by admitting him to my intimacy . . . the most trivial creatures I compassed with my affability, even Nympho of Colophon. I did all this, not that such men, or even their whole nation, delight me; I am sick of their levity, their obsequiousness, their devotion, not to principle, but to the profits of the hour.'[41] The sound of this echoes in modern ears from other nations.

When the Parthians threatened the Asiatic provinces 'upon which the revenues of the Roman people depend',[42] Cicero found 'our allies either so feeble that they cannot give us much assistance, or so estranged owing to the harshness and injustice of Roman rule that it looks as though we ought neither to expect anything of them nor entrust anything to their keeping.'[43]

This breaking of the human mainspring, this intimate corruption, is what the historian cannot forgive: 'I myself', Professor Tarn writes,[44] 'venture to entertain considerable doubts whether the true Greek, the racial aristocracy of the Aegean, really degenerated. . . . The Roman Republic tended to break the Greek spirit, and probably ended by convincing many people besides the kings of Syria and Egypt that efforts doomed beforehand to be fruitless were not worth while.'

There is little to stem the darkness – a few efforts by Sulla, Pompey lending money to the king of Cappadocia,[45] Caesar with his unifying vision,[46] gleams of a constructive dawn; and a few civil servants were remembered with desperate affection for what their short term of office had allowed. Men continue to be born the same in every generation, but the system of the republic was a corrupting one, ignorantly operated at a distance and inspired by greed and fear; 'colonial, arrogant,

THE AUTHOR'S CARAVAN NEAR THE EUPHRATES

THE EUPHRATES NEAR ZEUGMA

PARTHIANS AT PERSEPOLIS

HARRAN (CARRHAE) FROM THE MEDIAEVAL FORT

corrupt, cruel and inefficient' according to Professor Roztovtzeff[47]: and in nothing worse than in the treatment of its Seleucid neighbours in their kingdom of the east.

The Seleucid Kings and Their End

The Hellenic complexion of this kingdom was based on military colonies which Alexander and his successors established in the third century B.C. They were drawn from traditional recruiting grounds in Macedonia rather than in Greece[48] and from both of these the treaty of Magnesia cut them off. The kingdom became gradually more oriental while it continued to be rich. Its first ruler, Seleucus Nicator, began with the advantage of knowing the Persian nobles whose cavalry he commanded under Alexander; and he had married and continued to live with, a Persian wife.[49] Like a wild animal as opposed to a tame, a hellenistic king had to be intelligent and strong to survive, and there were resolute men among the later kings. Theirs was the only bond that held a heterogeneous people together from Bactria to the Mediterranean, by a loyalty not centred on nationalism or race, but on the royal house. Primogeniture was not essential, but the heir must belong to the dynasty – the nuance became a cause of misunderstanding with Rome, and their rule differed profoundly from anything known in the West. Only one outsider ever gained power in the flux of the Seleucid wars.[50] Once recognised and invested with the diadem – the white linen headband – the purple cloak, and the ring engraved with an anchor that was the emblem of the dynasty, the king became the Living Law. He ruled the 'free' cities[51] with courteous forms which they were well advised to follow: his absolutism was tempered by good manners and it was largely the absence of the latter which hurt when the Romans came. Under Antiochus IV, a century-and-a-half before Actium,[52] the Godhead of royalty was developed, possibly – like the later Roman divinity – to unify a rule that spread so far.

Like God, the king was expected to attend to any task however small, even to the changing of a barbarian's name into a Greek one. Cicero quotes Antiochus the Great as expressing gratitude to the Romans for relieving him of half his burdens.[53] Seleucus, the Founder, is reported to have declared that no one would pick a diadem off the ground if they realised how much letter-writing it entailed. Nor had they any regular help in these tasks. Their 'friends' were a purely personal choice. They would cluster in purple hats and cloaks in the royal tent at dawn on a campaign, and be available for any work that might be needed; they would be gathered for a council, to advise; they formed a 'court' from which an Antiochus would sometimes try to slip away in private; but there was no regular civil service such as that on which Rome and Byzantium later could rely. With the not-free, or with a conquered town, the Seleucid king could do as he pleased: his acts might be thought cruel, they were not illegal; a pronouncement of Delphi praises Seleucus I for maintaining Smyrna in the possession of her lands; the liberty of the cities, which was considerable, was founded and had to be confirmed by the king.[54]

This centralised power was such that the cities 'were very rarely involved in external warfare, and the accumulation of capital and the introduction of improved methods in trade and industry brought the hellenistic states very near to the . . . industrial capitalism of Europe in the nineteenth and twentieth centuries'.[55]

Under Antiochus III the kingdom had once again touched the Himalayas, and his successors hoped, leaving Rome undisturbed in her West, to face away from her and build themselves up in their oriental inheritance. The Seleucid policy had been conciliatory from the first as it followed the milestones of Alexander along its eastern border. Throughout nearly two centuries, it succeeded remarkably with the kings of India and the despots of Bactria, and – more interruptedly – with the kingdoms of the north. The preservation of the roads was the incentive. Seleucus I gave up his Indian claims so as to avoid a 'continuous war',[56] and traces of his and his successors' Greek intercourse survive in the pattern of the Indian theatre to this day.[57] Antiochus III fought for communications and re-established them with an alliance in Bactria. It was only in the late third century B.C., when the semi-nomadic westward-moving Parthians reached the Caspian shore[58] and threatened the lucerne-bearing[59] uplands of Media – it was only when these pasture-lands of their heavy cavalry horses were endangered, that the kings of Babylonia were bound to fight and two of the best of them, after Antiochus the Great, were killed.

*   *   *

The Parthians belong to the dim intercourse of Scythian and Iranian, and for over a century their pressure continued. One of their kings,

Mithradates I, governed from Susa and conquered Babylon before 141 B.C. when a cuneiform document shows him entering Seleuceia in triumph. He was evicted, but the Seleucid king was captured soon after, and was kept, kindly treated with a royal Parthian daughter for a wife. The seventh Antiochus was his brother and the last strong Seleucid king. He gathered an army and fought. The Greek cities of Babylonia stood by him until he was killed, and a document of June, 130 B.C., in his name, is the last cuneiform dating we have of a Macedonian king. The Parthians, with a certain chivalry that distinguished them, sent his body home to Syria, where a great mourning was made, as though men knew that 'the effective history of the dynasty was ended'.[60]

The Seleucid tragedy then tailed away into obscurity, amid family disruptions and the merciless trammels of Rome. Only the latter concern us. 'No service or subservience could secure the genuine friendship of that immoral state; and few of the excesses or injustices of any ruler of Macedonian blood can compare with the practice of the Republic in its later days.'[61] When, in 164 B.C., the heir to the throne, at that time a hostage, had 'asked that he should be installed in the kingdom, the senate would not allow it. They thought that it would be more for their advantage that Syria should be governed by an immature boy than by a full-grown man.'[62]

Pushed to the west of Euphrates, the Seleucids were ousted by the Armenian Tigranes from what was left them, and in 64 B.C. Pompey turned Syria into a province 'by right of war', and trampled out the last Seleucid claim.[63]

Four-citied Antioch, Tetrapolis,[64] became a Roman pivot in the East. Its harbour lies, spiked with reeds and cut into waterways, silent now and pleasant in the sun, and here the first Antiochus built a tomb – long since lost – for his father. The broken threads of history get knotted with new colours and few keep their identity under the shuttles of Time: the work of Antiochus IV on the temple to Zeus in Athens was finished and named by Hadrian, in whose day, on the hill beyond the Acropolis, the monument now called Philopappus held a statue of Alexander's young cavalry general, Seleucus, the Founder, the Victorious – an echo from Commagene on the Euphrates to a dispossessed descendant[65] of the past.

The Hellenistic Bridge of Asia

We cannot begin to compute the European debt to the Roman occupation of Greece and particularly of Greece in Asia. Not only philosophy and religion, commerce and banking and a good portion of law came by those roads, but every colonnade or dentilled roof reminds us of an Ionian architect or a Lycian builder.

'I declare the Greek statues seem to be in business as landscape gardeners, and to be advertising their ivy', Cicero writes, and remarks to Atticus that no class-room is complete without a Hermes: 'If you can come across any articles of *vertu* for my gymnasium, please don't let them slip . . . and keep your promise to consider how you can secure the library for me. All my hopes of enjoying myself, when I retire, rest on your kindness.'[66] The art and the beauty of living were captured by the Roman tycoons for their homes and thence for ours, and even Verres, looting his gods, did something for the West.

This book, however, has little to do with the Western dawn and turns towards Euphrates; and here the most significant result of the Roman advent was the snapping of the bridge that, since Alexander, had been linking Asia to the commerce of the Mediterranean under the hellenistic kings.

From the Great Wall of China the land melts away intersected by blue ranges, whose repetitions move thin as paper across pale horizons till they reach the similar expanses of Iran. It is all one world: there are mountains and deserts, but no unbridgeable geographic lines between the great Asiatic civilisations – the Iranian and Indian and the Chinese[67] – and from the days of the Babylonians and through the Persian age the caravan trade prospered – drawing wealth from India certainly and from China probably, in whose art the traces of their intercourse remain.

The Bactrian two-humped camel can still be seen now and then under the sloping walls and the round archways of Peking, padding silently into the shaggy winters of Mongolia, and no mere river of water can be compared to this perennial stream of the caravans, that has carried a half of human history from stage to stage, from wasteland to wasteland and climate to climate, on the puny strength of men. These knowing neither the beginning nor the end, but only the days' or weeks' stretch of their journey, buying their gaunt provisions in wayside bazaars founded for this purpose perhaps by Alexander, in their dim and cheerful hearts know the earth they tread on for their home. There is no security safer than that of accepted danger. When from some metalled road on the highlands of Asia I see their gathered bales and small fires, and watch them squatting in friendly circle for the fleeting sojourn that leaves no traces on the surface of the earth — even now in my old age a longing takes me to wander in the hard and naked beauty of their world.

The stream of trade flowed uninterrupted through Babylonian, Assyrian, Lydian and Persian ages, until in the fifth century B.C. the Ionian revolt and the great battles of the Greeks set up a western barrier of the sea. Alexander's dream came to be, in effect, the elimination of this barrier with the return, or indeed the enlargement, of a united world. The great achievement of the hellenistic age that followed him was the partial fulfilment of this dream.

'The idea emerges of an . . . inhabited world as a whole, the common possession of civilised men; and for its use there grows up the form of Greek known as the *Koine*, the common speech which might take a man from Marseilles to India, from the Caspian to the Cataracts. . . . Commerce is internationalised. . . . Thought is free as it was not to be again till modern times.'[68] The Arabs in their turn went some way in establishing such uniformity of language; and there can be a hope that English may look like the *Koine* of our age.

The Seleucids held the depôts of this trade in Babylonia, and were therefore particularly instrumental in the hellenizing of Asia. If Rome 'made a city of what was once a world' we may say that Greece made a world of what was once a city. The Greeks' language and their legal forms took hold of the business life of Mesopotamia and were never relinquished even when the Parthians came; and the native language retained so many Greek terms that 'communication was less difficult and the way of thinking less oriental than might be supposed'.[69] *'The scanty attention which the Seleucids paid to the loss of the eastern parts of their empire is due to the fact that the Arsacides, their [Parthian] successors . . . were equally concerned to maintain the profitable safety of the trade routes, which was to the interests of both.'*[70] Rostovtzeff mentions the enormous importance of commercial considerations in shaping the foreign policy of the hellenistic kings.[71] Rapid strides in pure and applied sciences helped agriculture and industry; a new plough was used; novelties like cotton, lemons, melons, sesame, olives, dates, figs, ducks and the Asiatic ox, eventually reached Italy from the East.[72] Exploration was encouraged as never before; the mass production of goods for an indefinite market developed, and with it a kind of common civil law valid all over the Levant. With all this, there was direct fostering of the Founder's cities, a care to keep the precious tradition: it worked through the *gymnasia* – which played the part of public schools in England; through the women – who followed the extremely emancipated lead of Macedonian princesses and became poetesses, magistrates, and even philosophers; through plays and games, for which a Greek theatre and gymnasium existed in Babylon; and most of all through education – so widespread that excellent Greek was written right into the second century A.D. under the Parthians, as it was in many parts of the hellenistic world[73]: a textbook of the early third century B.C. in Egypt is almost exactly like one used centuries later in Christian times,[74] and in Syria the hellenistic literary foundation was so strong in Roman times as to rival any province of the Empire.[75] Seleuceia on the Tigris had nearly the same facilities for philosophical and scientific scholarship as Antioch, the metropolis of the hellenistic world.[76]

These Greek cities kept their pride. Even in the first century A.D. there were race-overseers to keep the Greek blood pure in Dura on the Euphrates, where the aristocracy in hellenistic, Parthian and Roman times bore almost exclusively Greek or Macedonian names.[77] The Babylonians too were cared for, and the well-to-do members of the past upper class came to be important in their own cities, employed as administrators and soldiers,[78] as agents for the rulers, or as organisers of the caravan trade which was largely in their hands. Their carpets and embroidery were famous; their purple and their asphalt were exported,[79] and their calendar adopted[80]; their temples were re-built, and their cuneiform literature and astronomy revived, their last extant cuneiform document being dated 7 B.C.; their coloured tiles continued, and came eventually through the Arabs to Europe[81]; and the Babylonian weight, the *manah*, was used by both Greeks and Indians.[82] Their relations with the Greeks seem to have been equal and cordial, though hellenisation – encouraged by the rulers as the supply of true Greeks diminished – was a key to prosperity, and therefore coveted. 'I should be turned into a Hellene . . . and be able to mix with the Hellenes'[83] is the hope of Apollonius' Babylonian disciple, and 'it is a fact that, in spite of separation, the islands of Greek culture in the East never lost their Greek character. . . . They showed in this respect an amazing tenacity and persistence. . . . The hellenistic monarchies, while they survived, continued to absorb and hellenise their oriental elements without suffering themselves to be disintegrated. . . . Even the outposts . . . in the Parthian kingdom, and in Bactria and India, though they lost the support of the government, kept intact some prominent features of their hellenism – their language and their ancestral institutions – though they succumbed in their religious and domestic life.[84] The Greek script was adopted by the founders of the Kushan empire, the nomads in Bactria, who retained it till the eighth century A.D.[85] More than this: the oriental kings, who followed the hellenistic rulers in some parts of Asia Minor and Syria, never in their early history discarded the hellenistic traditions or forcibly sought to destroy the nuclei of Greek life within their states.

These traditions made no political unity; local and various customs were preserved – even such as regarded women's rights which were different from those of the Greeks.[86] The cities selected their calendars or, like Cappadocia, kept the Achaemenian month names if they wished; they stamped their local gods on their small coins; and every new colony – of which the first kings had founded a great number – was able to develop in its own way in a common climate which the Seleucid kings carefully preserved. Their cohesion was fostered in social ways, by the *proxenia* or honorary citizenships that distributed the freedom of one city among other friendly individuals or states; by the system of inviting judges from neighbouring communities, and by many inter-actions of this kind.[87] It was above all the world of the great trade route, which kept its personal interests and human relations moving in a steady stream across the latitudes of Asia.

The Seleucids 'turned the hamlets into cities',[88] but failed with the Iranian countryman, whose life was based on the village[89] as it is today. These the hellenistic monarchies never developed into a national state. Aloof from Greek or Babylonian alike, the serfs were bought and sold with their land – and in spite of improvements when Greek cities or kings took them over, they, like their fellows in Cappadocia, continued to prefer the ancient way. The problem they present has ever pained the oriental reformer and is likely to cause modern trouble too: it has never yet, except partially in Turkey, been solved. Queen Laodike buys land near Cyzicus 'and any hamlets there may be in the land, and the folk . . . with their household and all their property . . . so also any of the folk of this village who have moved away to other places',[90] and though the royal lands were much reduced by the establishment of colonies or cities, and the system of serfdom had practically passed away in the old city territories of western Asia Minor, it continued in the eastern provinces, especially in Pontus and Cappadocia, unimpaired into Roman times.[91] Man does not live by bread alone: what he does live by is often unexpected: the Parthian victory when it came could well be considered as the countryman's revolt; and the hellenistic kings remained what they had been at first – military rulers dependent in the last resort on foreign or colonial arms.

The townsmen, however, remembered the dynasty that had first colonised and founded them, and counted the 'years of the Greeks' under their new Parthian masters, and welcomed attempts at rescue from the West. There were many Greek cities strung from the Aegean coasts through Syria, Babylonia and Media to Bactria and Sogdiana – 'Greek cities in the heart of barbarian countries . . . the Macedonian tongue among the Indians and the Persians, among which are Laodiceia, Apamea, and the city near Rhagae (near Teheran), and Rhagae itself which was founded by Seleucus Nicator', and Ecbatana (now Hamadan) which had been the royal residence of the Median Empire, where the colonnaded palace covered twenty-five acres of ground. 'The Parthians continue to use it even now, and their kings spend at least their summers there . . . but their winter residence is at Seleuceia, on the Tigris near Babylon.' So Strabo,[92] at the turn of the Christian era, when the population of Babylonia must have totalled some five to eight million inhabitants.[93]

The cities strung themselves along the eastern trade route and their main routes and rivers were well protected by military or police in normal times. No less than nine towns were founded on the shores of the Persian Gulf, including what is now Bushire.[94] At Seleuceia, founded by Seleucus Nicator, the Tigris was navigable from the south, and Babylon and the Euphrates were being superseded; all roads here converged, and the city stretched – with a population of six hundred thousand[95] – between walls shaped like 'an eagle spreading its wings'.

The Trade Route

The Seleucids inherited their road system from the Alexandrine past, and this in its turn had inherited it from the Persians,[96] who had produced three centuries of peace before ever the Macedonians came. When they did so, Alexander sent the value of gold down 50 per cent by his victories,[97] and added another cornerstone to the edifice of trade: his currency encouraged Greek uniformity, and was 'so famous and so popular in the hellenistic world that, after Magnesia, many of the cities ... agreed to begin their own autonomous coinage by the issue of uniform Alexandrian and Lysimacheian money'.[98] The early Seleucids established mints along the trade routes[99] – Susa and Persepolis for the southern way to India; Hamadan, Herat and Bactra for the north; and a particular money for the Indian trade; and these rich streams all converged on Seleuceia – a town not even in Pliny's day '*in barbarum corrupta*', and the main eastern centre for the transit caravans.

Here one journey ended and another began, from Seleuceia on the Tigris to Seleucia of Antioch, through Nisibis and the roads that creep along the southern margin of Taurus. Here streams come down and fodder could be found in evening camps; until the Edessa downlands dropped to the Euphrates at Zeugma or at Samosata, which is so small and lost now that when I asked for a permit to go there it was refused in Ankara 'because we cannot discover where it is'.

The garrisons and places of passage were built where the gorges end and the river opens below Zeugma to the desert. Here Antiochus III,[100] in his prosperous days, married Laodice of Pontus, his cousin, with great pomp, 'whose honours are increased by her husband because of her affection and devotion to him in their life together'[101]; and here probably Sulla first of the Romans sat with the Parthian envoy on the bank. He must have been a witness to the wealth of Asia pouring through.

Plutarch, writing of a time just before the Roman arrival in Asia, remarks that Ptolemy's or Seleucus' stewards' slaves were richer than all the Spartan kings taken together.[102] The income of Alexander's empire was computed at 30,000 talents, and the Asiatic portion alone of his successors' empire at 11,000 talents[103]. Its value increased rather than diminished until, a decade or two after Magnesia, a gradual decline set

in. A year of the Roman war in 190 B.C. has been calculated to have cost
Antiochus 8,000 talents; even then, and to their very last, 'the prosperity
of the kernel of the Seleucid monarchy and the income from the caravan
trade guaranteed a steady revenue'.[104] When the philosopher Apollonius
and his disciple reached the customs' post in the second century A.D.,
'the tax gatherer . . . led them into the registry and asked what they were
taking out of the country. . . . "Temperance, justice, virtue, continence,
valour and discipline," said Apollonius,' and the man, 'already scenting
his own perquisites, said: "You must then write down in the register,
these female slaves." Apollonius answered: "Impossible, for they are not
female slaves . . . but ladies of quality!"'[105]

The Weak Periphery: Seleuceia

In Cicero's day, the Romans had already established customs for the Asiatic ports,[106] and they kept the post at Zeugma. East of it, the Parthians,
as one region after another fell into their hands, took over the maintenance of the roads.[107] The defeat of Antiochus III gave them their innings,
and the last Seleucid king to make a successful stand against them was
Antiochus IV Epiphanes, his second son. He died during the expedition –
an event which Rostovtzeff describes as the turning-point of calamity in
the history of the Greek, Semitic and Iranian East. 'Eastern hellenism
might have experienced a renascence had he survived.'[108] The conclusion
is best quoted in his words:

'The fact that Antiochus IV would have been successful but for two
accidents . . . caused the Romans uneasiness and they decided to play for
safety in future and to keep the East in a state of anarchy . . . and put
obstacles in the path of the few talented and patriotic Seleucids, such as
Demetrius III (captured by the Parthians) and Antiochus VII, who took
seriously their positions as champions of Greek civilisation against the
Iranian tide. . . . It was certainly owing to the Roman efforts that none
of the successors of Antiochus IV was able to . . . stop the advance of the
Parthians and Armenians.'[109]

Here as elsewhere, the elusive pursuit of *the weak periphery* prevailed:
the Romans were haunted by fears that Syria and Egypt, the Seleucid
and Ptolemaic houses, might unite – fears that were to reach their tragic
end with Cleopatra: and they used the means which came easily enough

in the hellenistic chaos to weaken a dynasty which could have been their bulwark in the East. Had Rome profited by the Seleucids (as these had done by the Bactrians), to keep her farther enemies at bay, she might have saved herself a number of Parthian wars. As it was, her theory that only the sea or an unarmed nation must exist on her borders, again defeated her, and in 64 B.C. when Pompey consummated its end, 'the Romans in Syria simply inherited the great problems of the Seleucid Empire, and had to solve them as best they could'[110] when the Parthians took over.

'Far from continuing the careful yet progressive policies of the Attalid kings the Roman Republic had exploited in peace and pillaged in war the human and material resources of the eastern provinces until all their available resources were exhausted. . . . It was only after the régime of Augustus brought recovery . . . that the economic and social movements initiated by the hellenistic kings could reach their fullest development.'[111] But 'the [eastern] frontier of Europe was withdrawn to the Euphrates'.[112]

VI

The Parthians and the Trade Route

The survey of the trade route across Mesopotamia continues while
the Parthian campaigns of Crassus and Mark Antony are the opening bars to seven centuries of discord. The importance of Crassus lies in
the influence of his tragedy on public feeling in Rome; that of Antony in
the gradual freezing of Asia against him. Set up by a Roman conqueror,
any ultimate chance of success was precluded from Cleopatra's oriental
dream; and she seems, in fact, to have been averse to the whole Armenian expedition. The added disaster of his failure lost Antony the only
army capable of giving him his victory against Augustus and the West.

> 'The Gods . . . who punish those who violate treaties, did not fail to support
> either the craft or the valour of our enemies.' (Florus, I.xlvi.4–6.)

Mesopotamia Under the Parthians

The Parthians have been seen through the eyes of their enemies – desert
warriors fighting desert wars. The few notices that come from the
interior of Babylonia give a more easy-going picture, and their portrait-
statues, dug up at Hatra, show a series of not excessively intelligent, but
obviously honourable men, wearing embroidered coats with the sheep's
fur inside as they are still worn today, and on their long bearded faces,
with half-barbaric simplicity, that expression of innocence that often

goes with the soldiers' life. One could meet their long thin cavalry legs without surprise emerging from the Guards' Club in Piccadilly.

They conquered the Seleucid inheritance, and left it more or less intact, and no anti-Greek feeling accompanied their victory.[1] The hellenistic climate remained much as it had been, not more than slightly tinged; the Greek cities kept their moderate autonomy, their lands, their worship, their Greek coinage with a change of portrait and of name, their courts and their gymnasia. The Parthian governor took the place of the Seleucid; the kings appointed Macedonian judges; the properties of the citizens were respected. Life went on much as it had done before, and the demand for Eastern luxuries continued to increase in the West throughout the last Seleucid struggles, and to be provided for through every sort of hazard.

New trade routes opened new oceans,[2] and about 120 B.C. Eudoxus of Cyzicus explored the sea-route to India and prepared a way for the discovery and use of the monsoon.[3] The control of the irrigation system was continued[4]; the Seleucid cult for experiments in agriculture brought skilled cattle-breeding to Babylonia; and the mechanical inventions of the time – water mills and presses, fertilisation and manuring, the *sakiye* of modern Egypt and the Archimedean screw – were used.[5]

The 'silk road' (a later and Byzantine name) was fostered with embassies; cucumbers, onions, jasmine, saffron, vines and lucerne were taken to,[6] and peaches, apricots and sugar-cane brought back from China: a Greek diptychos from Dura with folded wooden leaves is possibly the ancestor of the first true book[7]; and the use of paper in China (instead of silk) perhaps originated with Chang-K'ien's embassy and his first sight of people writing 'in rows running sideways' on the parchments of Mesopotamia.[8]

The economic brilliance of the age of Augustus was being forged out of sight in the second century B.C., and, when the Parthians stabilised their control of Babylonia, the economic centre of the world became the Tigris for over four hundred years.[9]

Yet the cities, Greek or Babylonian, remained unreconciled in spite of all. They carried on their activities and paid their tributes, while the Parthians themselves remained feudal and decentralised Iranians, fighters on horseback and shepherds of flocks, members of a world that begins where, with a strange emotion, one can watch streams drain severally to

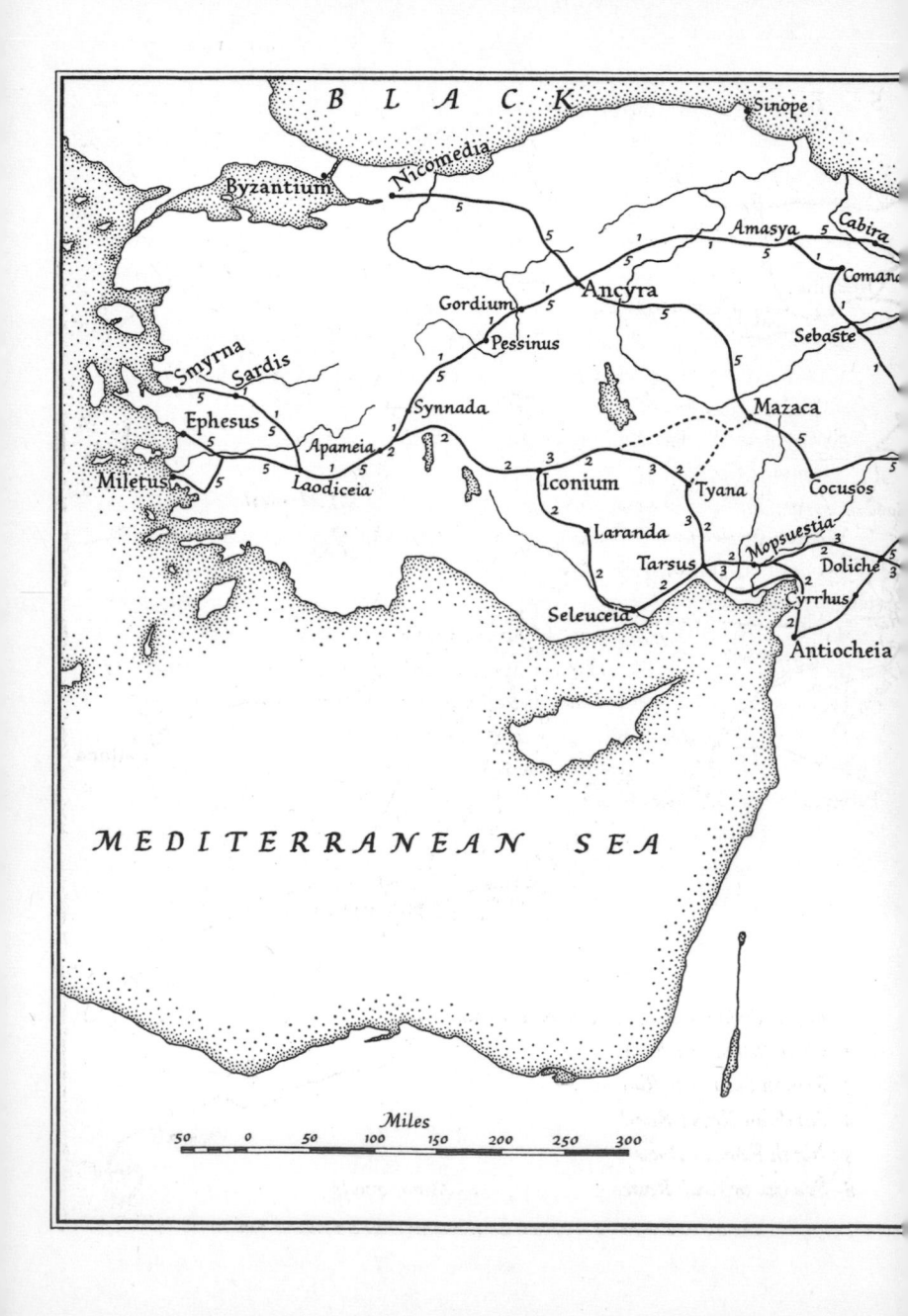

BLACK

Sinope

Byzantium   Nicomedia   5

5   5   1   Amasya   5   Cabira
5   1   1   5   1   Coman
Gordium   1   Ancyra   1   Sebaste   1
5   5   1
Pessinus   5   5   Mazaca
Smyrna   Sardis   1   Synnada   5   5
5   5   1   1   1   Cocusos
Ephesus   Apameia   2   2   3   2   2   5
5   5   Laodiceia   2   3   Iconium   3   Tyana
Miletus   5   Laranda   3   2   Mopsuestia   2   3
2   Tarsus   2   3   Doliche   3
Seleuceia   2   Cyrrhus
2
Antiocheia

MEDITERRANEAN   SEA

Miles
50   0   50   100   150   200   250   300

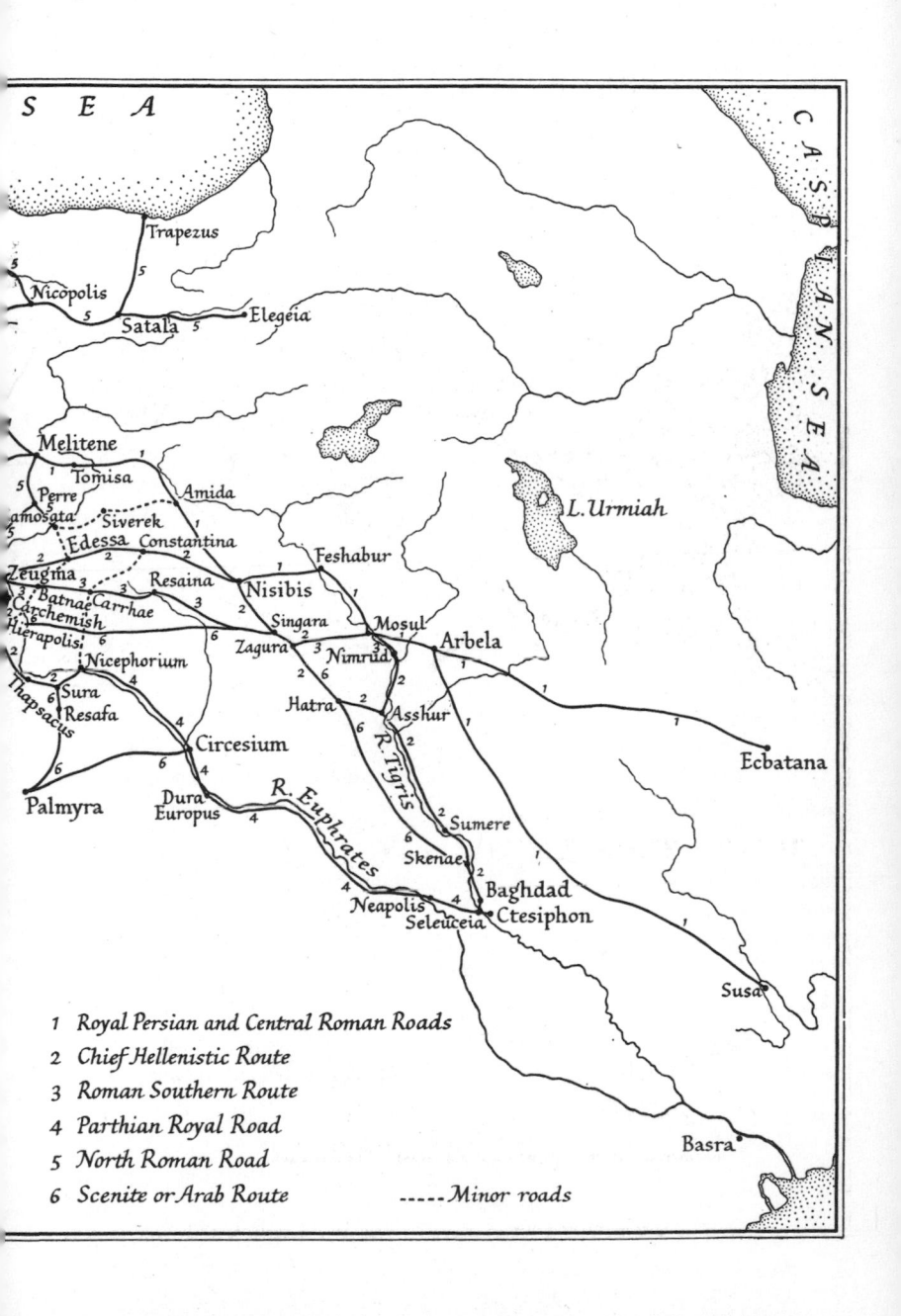

S E A

Trapezus

Nicopolis
Satala   Elegeia

CASPIAN SEA

Melitene
Tomisa   Amida
Perre
amosata   Siverek
Edessa   Constantina
Zeugma   Resaina
Batnae   Carrhae   Nisibis   Feshabur
Carchemish   Singara
Hierapolis   Zagura   Mosul   Arbela
Nicephorium   Nimrud
Sura   Hatra   Asshur
Resafa   R. Tigris
Thapsacus   Circesium   Ecbatana
Dura   R. Euphrates
Palmyra   Europus
Sumere
Skenae   Baghdad
Neapolis   Ctesiphon
Seleuceia

L. Urmiah

Susa

Basra

1 Royal Persian and Central Roman Roads
2 Chief Hellenistic Route
3 Roman Southern Route
4 Parthian Royal Road
5 North Roman Road
6 Scenite or Arab Route   ----- Minor roads

the Persian Gulf on one side and the Mediterranean on the other across
a scarcely perceptible divide.

The Syrian Desert Routes

Two thousand and more years of camel or donkey tracks crisscrossed
among the sands and stones of this watershed in its half-desert reaches.

The Parthians continued to maintain the Seleucid roads and to keep the
desert tracks provided with caravanserais and wells, mounted police, and
camel-riding Gods for caravans. The horseshoe was invented, though
it is not known whether in East or West, and the posts offered such
rapid travel that a journey of three hundred and fifty miles in two days is
recorded.[10] Oriental regions were now as well known as those encircling
the Mediterranean and are described by the geographers in the same
spirit, with the same interest and accuracy from material derived from the
official records of the hellenistic monarchies, a demonstration accessible
to everyone of a well-established fact – the unity and homogeneity of
the hellenistic world from the point of view of civilisation and mode of
life.[11] An Alexander coin found by Mallowan with some earthenware in
the northern steppes of Asia shows the unbroken chain.[12]

From Asia Minor, the 'royal road' of the Achaemenians came down
to Euphrates by Melitene,[13] led through Nisibis to the Feshabur crossing
of the Tigris above Mosul, and then left the (Arbela) Erbil riverlands to
climb to Ecbatana or Susa.

South of it, and far more level, the crossing of Euphrates at Zeugma,
a little way above the fine modern Birejik bridge, was that most used
in the hellenistic age. Its (pontoon?) bridge was famous, and crossed to
Apamea – also founded by Seleucus Nicator – on the opposite bank of
the river.[14]

Two routes with a number of cross-tracks ran east and roughly
parallel from Zeugma – the one through Edessa (Urfa) and Viran-shehir,
travelling 'to the fortified town of Caphrena, which formerly measured
$8\frac{3}{4}$ miles . . . and was called the court of the Satraps, being a centre for
the collection of tribute, but has now [first century A.D.] been reduced
to a fortress,'[15] thence to join the Achaemenian road before Nisibis;
the other more southerly and out in the open steppe, through Carrhae
(Harran) mentioned as a market town by Pliny,[16] and Resaina and the

lost marshy headwaters of the Aborras, (Khabur), and thence north of the isolated outpost of Jebel Abd-el-Aziz and south again through the saddle of Singara where a milestone of Trajan's remains. It crossed the Tigris by the mound of Nimrud in the open plain. This route partly coincided with that of the ancient Assyrians, who crossed the Tigris at Asshur where their mound still stands, and made north to Singara and Nisibis[17] through what later were to be the lands of Hatra.

There were several Euphrates crossings by which these main routes could be reached. Samosata – a later headquarters of the legions – Carchemish (Jerablus), Hierapolis (Membij) used by Julian, and Thapsacus used by Alexander.

Downlands of corn lead easily from Samosata to Edessa, but otherwise the river north of Zeugma and south of the Melitene-Tomisa crossing makes its own defences in its own gorges. I have been towed up it for an hour or two to the castle of Rum Kalesi in the southern defile, in a boat like a box, with an old fisherman punting and three chairs set for me and my companions, so that we must have looked from outside like those half-figures of late Greco-Roman tombs. Two men clasped a rope knotted over short sticks for holding, and swung us clear of boulders in the windless reaches; low in summer, they opened one into the other under precipices in their world of stone.

All that they contained – their hamlets and narrow watered gardens and pistachio trees thinned as if stylised against the binding of the cliffs – all seemed to be immured in sunlit silence below the level of the living world; and the green ripples of the water slid down as quietly as a snake asleep. Centuries of history – the first Assyrian builders; Antiochus' wedding; Sulla with the Parthians; Crassus in the storm and then the routine of the legions – all hung in the still air. From Berasil upstream (could it be Barsilion?), three men floated on a bundle of hay that settled in the water beneath them; and round a corner, beyond cliff openings of ancient steps and tombs, the castle appeared with marks of its many chisels still fresh upon it, as if it alone had a voice in the world of silence. The earliest builders had smoothed the valley sides to lift its unapproachable walls without a break, cut an Assyrian defile to separate it from the rocky snout of the cliff where it belonged, and carved an interior circular ramp to the water with fragments of stone steps that still appear.[18]

The hellenistic traces are there too in snatches of stone finely jointed and (I think) in a square tower on which later Byzantine or early Arab inmates have carved memorial peacocks and eagles in their day. An Islamic gateway and heavy machicoulis of the crusading age hang over a side-valley, the Marsyas of Pliny and modern Merzem, where the traces of three bridges are reported.[19] This spectacular ruin must be described somewhere in detail,[20] but I have not been able to lay my hands on anything modern beyond V. Chapot, who does not give the distance from Birejik – which is thirty-seven kilometres to Halfete by a good road, and then one and a half hours either walking or by water. F. Walpole describes the Samosata ferry as not used in 1850, 'Rum Kalaat, further south, being the route frequented . . . and Bir, the eastern bank of which is called Zeugma, or the bridge, to this day'.[21] There is a whole line of these castles along the Euphrates openings, dating from the Assyrian defences of the land.

Caravans followed easier routes built by the Romans[22] later with hard surfaces on the desert edge to the south. The Parthians too, when they came from their highlands, were equipped, as it happened, for what Rome was never naturally equipped for, the desert traffic and the desert camel war. Their conquest coincided with a time of anarchy in Syria during the decline of the Seleucids and the brief flash of Tigranes, when the western end of the trade route was unsafe. Their own 'royal road'[23] therefore crossed the Euphrates in the security of the south, and followed the river from Neapolis near Fallujah by Dura to Nicephorium (Raqqa), twelve miles from the older Thapsacus of Alexander. It then left the river and reached the Nisibis road by way of the Balikh tributary, and made for Zeugma by Carrhae[24]: that is to say that it came into the northerly main routes from the south. A short cut from Dura to Palmyra took off from this route and seems to have come into use about 100 B.C.,[25] and Poidebard,[26] who photographed all this desert from the air, considers the ruins between Euphrates and Palmyra to belong to Parthian settlements along this 'royal road'. As it was expensive and became insecure, the ' Scenitae' – the Arab camelmen who actually led the caravans – organised a new route of their own which made more or less a third west-east parallel, running south of the two main tracks and ending a little north of Seleuceia on the Tigris.

The Nomad Route

This route of the nomads went from Hierapolis (which was also one of their places of pre-Hellenic pilgrimage) by Edessa, through the desert to Skenae which was 'a noteworthy city situated on a canal towards the borders of Babylonia. The journey from the crossing of the Euphrates requires twenty-five days. And on that road are camel-drivers who keep halting-places, which sometimes are well equipped with reservoirs, generally cisterns, though sometimes the camel-drivers use waters brought in from other places. The Scenitae are peaceful, and moderate towards travellers in the exaction of tribute, and on this account merchants avoid the land along the river and risk a journey through the desert, leaving the river on the right for approximately a three days' journey. For the chieftains who live along the river on both sides [i.e. along the Parthian 'royal road'] occupy country which, though not rich in resources, is less resourceless than that of others, and are each invested with their own domains and exact a tribute of no moderate amount. For it is hard among so many peoples, and that too among peoples that are self-willed, for a common standard of tribute to be set that is advantageous to the merchant.'[27]

So Strabo near the end of the first century B.C. and, soon after, Pliny notices the goat-hair tents and desert quality of the road,[28] along which there were of course branching tracks to right and left to Batnae, Edessa, Resaina, Nisibis, or the Euphrates.

The account as it comes down to us is one of the normal Arabian struggle, sometimes successful and sometimes not, of merchants in the towns to keep the travel safe. Their antipathy to the nomad has ingrained itself through many thousand years, with a display of arrogance rarely diminished in the presence of people so easy in the grip of their desert hardships. When crossing one summer from Baghdad to Damascus with a few city Iraqis, our car was stopped by two herdsmen of the Aneizah who asked for water: theirs was finished and they had been out four days with their camels, and had two more days to go; yet they listened with a cool disdain while the city men refused, drank from my flask leaving me a little, and gave me – as if the rest of the car were non-existent – the news of the invisible desert grazing and of the moving tribe. To each his own virtue. The other travellers reproached me when we started. ' You might be left without water yourself.' 'Had you been thirsty', I tried, quite uselessly, to explain, 'they would have given you water at one of their tents, though it had been their last drop in the world.' If the times had been unstable, they might have robbed them first.

The Roman frontier was at the Euphrates when Crassus reached it with his army. When he had crossed it, of the three routes described above, he was rash enough to take the one that led through the desert of the tribes.

Crassus

In 55 B.C. when he was sixty, Crassus was made consul and rewarded with the dream of his life – the chance to rival Pompey in a war of his own. This desire had gnawed at him since the days when they were both young under Sulla, and Pompey stole the limelight every time. The rivalry went on; it left Crassus with a reputation smirched by his business methods,[29] his profits under Sulla, and by the undesirable people he collected to be useful – but also very rich. A rich man, he said, must be able to support a legion on his income – and he owned 'numberless silver mines' and 50 million denarii worth of land.[30] He was brave but not dashing, kind but not incapable of improving his troops' morale by decimation, or of massacring Sulla's captives for him after the taking of Rome.[31] According to Cicero he 'was half deaf; still he suffered a worse annoyance, in hearing himself spoken ill of, even if, as I thought at the time, unjustly'.[32] The strictness of history has treated him harshly, for he had according to Plutarch many qualities and one fault only – and who among us all can say as much? His entertainments were great, but plain, and 'pleasant through taste and kindness'; and he 'never met any citizen however humble and low, but he returned him his salute by name'. He was the first, according to Pliny, to design chaplets of gold or silver leaves to give as prizes.[33] Eloquent, good-looking, it vexed him to see Pompey and Caesar preferred 'yet he mingled no hostility or malice with his jealousy . . . but trimmed between them, making advantages of both, and changed sides continuously, neither a trusty friend nor an implacable enemy . . . as he found it to his advantage'. His one friend, a poor Aristotelian philosopher who used to accompany him on his travels 'received a cloak for the journey, which was demanded from him again when he came home' – peculiarly hard on someone whose philosophy held no brief for poverty. Plutarch devastatingly concludes that 'sordidness and avarice tarnished all the lustre of his actions', and Cicero supposed that if one were able to offer a Crassus the power to be named heir, when he was not really heir, he would 'dance in the Forum'.[34] After 133 B.C., when Rome accepted the province of Asia, a new spirit in foreign policy began to mark the commercial class, of which one may consider Crassus a member.[35]

In Italy, when I was young, a number of our neighbours lived on their lands, and if one asked what they did, the same answer was always given *'fanno i low interessi* – they are attending to the advancement of their affairs'. One could have said it of him and it is perhaps creditable to the human race as well as to Plutarch that Crassus has been unloved through the ages in spite of his bourgeois qualities and because of his utilitarian code. He was indeed a bourgeois out of water or an earthen pitcher between the iron of the other two triumvirs; and yet there was a streak of romance, as well as profit, which, when his fate took shape, 'so transported him that he let fall vain and childish words unworthy of his age and contrary to his usual character ... that he would not limit his fortune with Parthia and Syria, but looking on the actions of Lucullus against Tigranes and the exploits of Pompey against Mithradates as but child's play, he proposed in his hopes to pass as far as Bactria and India, and the utmost Ocean'. One may notice the perennial allurement of Alexander's dreams. 'Not that he was called upon by the decree which appointed him to his office to undertake any expedition against the Parthians but it was well known that he was eager for it, and Caesar wrote to him ... commending his resolution, and inciting him to the war.'

He left Rome on the ides of November in 55 B.C., Cicero writing from Tusculum that 'he made a less dignified start in his uniform than L. Paulus of old, who rivalled him in age and in his two consulships. What a poor thing he is!'[36] Many people at that time still thought it impious to make war without a provocation, and the tribune Ateius cursed him and his army as they left the gate of Rome.

The Battle of Carrhae

Cicero, two years earlier, had enlarged on the peace of the Levant, on the *pacatissimae et opulentissimae gazae*[37] of Syria, their ancient untouched wealth: 'For wars abroad with kings, people and tribes have long ago so completely ceased, that we get on brilliantly with such as we treat as pacified dependants.'[38] Just before Crassus' arrival this tranquillity – punctured, one may remark, by innumerable small robber potentates and bands – had been shaken under Crassus' legate, Gabinius, who planned to profit by a civil war in Parthia and then tried for quicker dividends by reinstating the Egyptian king. Crassus took over his own troops, and started with seven legions (28,000 men) and one thousand Gallic horsemen sent to him under his son Publius by Caesar. His quaestor was Cassius, the friend of Brutus and, later, one of Caesar's murderers, brilliant and steady both during the coming defeat and later, when he commanded what remained of the Roman army and pushed the enemy from the Antioch walls.

The troops, reformed by Marius and, since the Social War, not limited to the propertied classes,[39] were now professional soldiers ready for long term service and no longer clamoured to be disbanded after each campaign. The Caesarian regime had nearly doubled their pay,[40] grain and slaves had been distributed by Julius[41]; bonuses of money and of land had been added, and they had been forged into the instrument that was to control the history of Rome. They spent a winter weighing out the gold of Syrian temples, and followed gloomily foreboding but apparently uncomplaining when Crassus led them with adverse omens across Euphrates in a storm in May. It is already hot at that time and the harvests are gathered; there seems to have been no reason to delay so long. It is on the other hand unfair to criticize Crassus for not attacking in winter, since the clayey deserts of Iraq are practically impassable after rain, and all Arab warfare stops; (outside Baghdad, before the days of metalled roads, dinner parties would be cancelled for dust-storms or rain). The Parthians, like everyone else, made no war at this season, the only time of year when a dampness in the air might slacken the tension of their bows.[42] They had been taken by surprise in autumn when Crassus left garrisons in the little semi-Greek settlements across the river; these they spent the winter in harassing, and in spring sent an embassy to ask whether this war was seriously meant or was a caprice of Crassus' own. Being told to take it seriously, the Parthian king marched against Armenia, while his kinsman Surena waited south of Carrhae for the Roman army, in a land of imperceptible gradations[43] that stretch out to 'regions entirely deserted', where the last Assyrian mounds vanish in scarves of dust. Timber for roofs or even lintels has stopped here and the villagers' small barnacle-domes of mud settle in the soil that made them, and the last tillage also fades into the desert drought. In the west, some thirty miles away, the tongue of hills that runs from Edessa and hides the wide cradle of Euphrates sinks too and disappears with its strange whiteness into the whiteness of the sky.

Carrhae (Harran) is on a long platform with a mediaeval wall gnawed to the bone by the desert winds and man's destruction. The gates are gaps over a pale grassy ditch for sheep to browse in, and fragments of mosque and basilica share the great ruin-field under the castle with modern beehive huts whose last foothold is threatened even now by the drying up of water, their tiny path of life. A faint holiness lingers in a shrine below the southern wall, where, when I came to the place, a group of people had carried an open stretcher and were burying their dead.

The city was in the Edessa territory, but independent,[44] and old long before the Romans; and its terrace platform is characteristic of the Assyrian towns. Abraham visited its Moon-god temple about 1800 B.C.,[45] and there the Assyrian survivors fled twelve centuries later when Nineveh was destroyed. The Babylonian Nabonidus then had a dream, and revived the ancient cult; and it flourished long out-moded, like a dinosaur, through the classic ages into the Muslim day, when Arab travellers write of the inhabitants as Sabaeans. The Moon-god's temple is somewhere buried in the castle walls, and looked out, as one still does from later stone embrasures, over imperceptibly sloping expanses towards the desert's Gioconda smile. Beyond sight there, the troops of Crassus marched in from the west.

Professor Tarn suggests that the expedition would have faced the same problem whichever way it took.[46] To differ from him is perhaps rushing in where angels fear to tread, but I cannot help thinking that a river on one side – if they had followed the 'royal road' of Persia along Euphrates – was as protective as a wall at one's back, apart from its facility for transport and the inestimable boon of water in a climate that runs to 128°

in the shade in summer. The allied king of Armenia suggested a northerly route – not mentioned by the pre-Byzantine writers, though since, and now, much used – that led through Edessa by Severek to the Tigris[47] and, though exposed in winter to the terrible weathers of the highlands, would have turned the desert position, out of reach of a cavalry attack. The usual caravan route from Edessa to Nisibis, followed by Antiochus III[48] and Alexander below the wave of Taurus, also had water available and a hard detritus of limestone all the way: in the event, the Parthian cavalry pursuit ceased as soon as its hills were reached. The desert routes and their climates have not changed much,[49] and by all these tracks a far shorter stretch of open cavalry country would have to be crossed – in the south, to the friendly neighbourhood of Greek Seleuceia, and in the north to the riverlands of Tigris, in the steps of Xenophon and many others, through lands that had harvests already gathered and, for most of the way, a tolerable climate into June.

Artavasdes, the king of Armenia, strongly urged the hill route and, being coolly received, 'went his way' with his cavalry, to fight his own war in Armenia and soon come to terms with the Parthian king. Cassius urged the Euphrates but was overruled. Abgar and Alchaudonius, the kings of the little kingdoms round Edessa, actually brought their horsemen, but deserted before the battle. Abgar was accused of treachery, on what seem to be insufficient grounds: it was he who advised the nomad's road which was taken – 'not a bough, not a stream, not a hillock, not a green herb, but in fact a sea of sand, which encompassed the army with its waves'[50] – good enough for camels but not for infantry. The desert Arab has no inferiority complex and despises the shortcomings of others, unaware of his own: Abgar's jeer; 'Do you think you march through Campania?' has a genuine ring, though the geography was probably not so precise. The Armenian king sent a last message urging a return to the mountains – which Crassus disregarded. His army, any Arab could see, was vowed to destruction. A day's advance to the Balikh river was in fact, though the historians describe it as 'far into Mesopotamia',[51] a mere first step through semi-cultivated land into the long emptiness that lay before them: no road to a gas chamber ever had a more certain end than theirs. When this becomes obvious, the Arabs think it is time to go: they like one to be 'lucky' – and luck is the gift of Allah: they will give a new house for a year free of rent to try out its luck. It was not particularly treacherous for the Arab king to leave a friend who was obviously doomed, or take a hand in plundering what was evidently going to be plundered.

It seems unfair on the other hand to criticise the *softness* of the legions.[52] They were hurried in heavy armour along disintegrating tracks where every man except the front one breathed dust as thick as soup: they were given no time to rest by the mangy little Balikh river when they reached it, but told to eat as they stood, and hurried on, 'not leisurely and with halts to take breath' but at the pace of the cavalry, in the heat of noon in May, with the silly idea that the Parthian horsemen could be overtaken. The desert rather than the enemy defeated them, yet 'they followed and no one said a word'.[53] Nor did they disobey their leader until his absolute incompetence was plain. There is a genuine voice behind Plutarch and even at the far end of the rhetoric of Dio – a worm's eye view of the battle with inaccurate assessments, but a clear memory of pain. The 'dead hollow noise of the drums' they beat on brass with hammers lined with leather,[54] 'like the bellowing of beasts'; the barbarians circling round the squares of the cohorts to raise as much dust as they could – it is only a first-hand memory that remembers in a battle the choking of the Mesopotamian dust.[55] Yet the Parthians captured no Roman alive at that time; for seeing them standing upright in their armour and perceiving that no one either threw away his weapons or fled, they supposed they still had some strength.[56] With their cavalry defeated and the head of Publius, Crassus' son, thrown back among them, the legions held out till dark though 'their battle cry made but a faint unsteady noise, while the shout of the enemy was clear and bold'. When night came they left their wounded on the ground and made for the walls of Carrhae.

Polybius over a century before had noticed that it was to cavalry that Carthage owed its victories and Rome its defeats.[57] The battle of Carrhae was won by Parthia with little over eleven thousand horsemen, about a third of the Roman strength, and its victory was the young Surena's achievement. Taller and finer than any of his men, 'the delicacy of his looks and effeminacy of his dress did not promise so much manhood as he really was master of'. The Arabs of the desert even now wear their long hair in plaits and encircle their eyes with black antimony against the glare of the sun, which gives them a dashing girlish look; but Surena went further, with painted face and hair parted in the Median fashion; nor was he an ordinary person, but in wealth, family and reputation the second man in the kingdom. He had a retinue of at least ten thousand horsemen,[58] and the family of the Surenas were still mentioned by Tabari in Arab times.[59]

Cavalry

The Parthians when they first came from their steppes seem already to have had two types of cavalry: the armoured, with great spears that at Carrhae 'ran through two men at a time, making large and mortal wounds'; and the common people who, when mounted, were light-armed horse archers.

The heavy-armed on their huge Nisaean horses were fore-runners of the mediaeval knights, coated with mail to the knee, with helmets and mailed greaves, and horses armoured too. Antiochus III had met them in Persia and used them at Magnesia; and Lucullus had defeated them at Tigranocerta. The Armenians copied Parthia after Tigranes had raided Media for horses; the heavy armament reached China, and Wu-Ti sent two armies to Ferghana to obtain a few of the coveted Nisaean chargers; and in the hands of the Sarmatians and Sassanians the mailed (cataphract) cavalry became the weapon of Asia. One thousand were present at Carrhae.

At this time it looked, however, as if the light horsemen were to dominate the scene. With their lower bow cut short to be held from the saddle, they took the place of mercenaries or footmen in the desert wars, where javelin and short spear had been abolished and the whole nobility, Parthian and Iranian, armed their retainers with the bow. 'By Crassus' time the re-arming of Asia was complete, and a Parthian army consisted of just two formations, the mailed knights and their retainers the horse-archers.' It was Surena's genius that provided one reserve camel loaded with arrows for every ten men, so turning them into probably the first 'trained professional force depending solely on long-range weapons and with enough ammunition for a protracted fight'.[60] This and the desert together gave him his victory.

*   *   *

Crassus, wrapped in his cloak, hid himself in the night with his thoughts, and Cassius and Octavius his lieutenant 'came to comfort him, but he being altogether past helping, they themselves called the centurions and tribunes, and agreeing that the best way was to fly, ordered the army out, without sound of trumpet and at first with silence. But before long, when the disabled men found they were left behind, confusion and disorder, with an outcry of lamentation, seized the camp, and a trembling and dread presently fell upon them, as if the enemy were at their heels. By which means . . . sometimes taking up the wounded that followed, sometimes laying them down, they wasted the time – except for three hundred horse, whom Egnatius brought safe to Carrhae about midnight; where calling, in the Roman tongue, to the watch . . . he bade them tell the governor that Crassus had fought a very great battle with the Parthians . . . and not so much as telling his name, rode away at full speed to Zeugma.' The governor, suspecting some mischance, ordered out his garrison, and met Crassus and his army, and brought them into town.

The Parthians were not particularly involved in this war. They were a sporting nation, and having caught four of the scattered cohorts on a hillock next morning, let twenty survivors go because of their courage, opening their ranks to right and left to let them pass.[61] Lucan, writing about a century later, makes a consul say that they are invincible 'in the pleasant land of Media, on the level plains of Mesopotamia and beyond; . . . But you cannot make them scale steep ranges, or fight in steep ravines, or swim across swollen rivers, or sweat all day under a stifling sun on a dusty battlefield. They keep no battering rams nor any other form of siege engine . . . and when they attack, any arrow-proof shelter will keep them out as easily as a city-wall.'[62] The consul or his author evidently knew little about Media, but he was right about the Parthian incapacity for sieges, as their Syrian campaign was soon to show. The Romans might probably have held out in Carrhae and retreated in good order when delay and the advancing summer had brought boredom, the chief oriental enemy, on their besiegers. There must have been *some* provision in the fortress, since Cassius had in the first place urged a stay in these garrison towns, Eknai and Batnae and Anthemusias, the small centres for trading. Eknai to the south was known to be friendly, and Edessa was no doubt ready to turn with a turn of the tide, and there were Macedonians in Carrhae who had helped Pom-pey's officer before, when he 'had wandered from the way' and encountered the winter and its hunger.[63] Steadiness and compactness might have won, and it does not do to remember Xenophon similarly placed.

Egnatius got away with his horse, and Cassius with five hundred more followed; with no apparent difficulty they reached and crossed the bridge at Zeugma. No wonder the desert Arab loves his horse! But the infantry too reached the edge of safety. Crassus' legate Octavius brought five thousand men to the walls of Sinnaca which must have been east of Edessa in one of those stony bays. From its security he looked back, and saw his general, deceitfully entangled among fens and stupid about country, making for a small untenable ridge two miles away – and left his walls to help him. Here they all gathered to defend themselves, and Surena, seeing them about to escape out of the cavalry world, offered a safe conduct which the Roman troops forced their doomed general to accept. Before he was killed in a final and probably accidental scuffle, he summed up, unconsciously, the story of the battle between cavalry and infantry, Europe and Asia. ' "How is this?" said Surena, as they met: "A Roman commander on foot, whilst I and my train are mounted?" But Crassus replied that there was no error on either side, for they both met according to the custom of their country.'[64]

After Carrhae

Had Crassus, as a prisoner, reached the Parthian court, it is possible, though not likely, that an agreement about the Euphrates frontier might have been come to. There was no great wish in the East to overleap this boundary; the aggression came from the West, produced by a single-minded pursuit of riches that appears both directly and indirectly in the literature of the time.

> *si quis sinus abditus ultra,*
> *si qua foret tellus, quae fulvum mitteret aurum,*
> *hostis erat, fatisque in tristia bella paratis*
> *quaerebantur opes.*[65]

In the beginning, both Lucullus and Pompey had offered to restore to Parthia such portions of Mesopotamia as Tigranes had snatched: but a change had come over Pompey with his conquests, and he distributed territory regardless of the treaty, and set up Abgar – whom we have met in Edessa – to shut or open the gate of Euphrates at his will. 'Parthia never forgot Pompey's double dealing; it was the breach of faith of which Surena afterwards reminded Crassus.'[66]

Livy had already said long before that troops volunteered because they knew of the wealth acquired in the east,[67] and Pompey distributed 384 million sesterces among his soldiers and left another 480 million for the Roman treasury.[68] Wearing, 'if anyone can believe that', the cloak of Alexander that had been found among the treasures of Mithradates,[69] he was followed in his triumph by a trophy representing the inhabited world.[70] He annexed Syria partly to complete his hold of the Mediterranean shore against the pirates, but chiefly from the prevailing Roman fear that someone on the frontier might get strong; and he seems to have toyed with the idea of Mesopotamian conquest in his time and put it aside.

The Parthian invasion that followed the shock of Carrhae was easily dealt with, and gave Cicero his single experience of military leadership[71] while Cassius held the walls of Antioch. Cicero describes disaffection here and there among subjects and allies. When the Civil Wars developed, the Pompeians themselves were ready to call the Parthians in, and it is doubtful if the second and far more serious Parthian invasion of 40 B.C. would even have been attempted, if the young Labienus had not deserted to the enemy and been there to spur them on. 'When news of the defeat [at Philippi] reached him, and it appeared to be the intention of the victors to spare none who had resisted them, Labienus remained among the barbarians, choosing to live with them rather than to perish at home. . . . He promised to assume command in the war, and assured Orodes [the Parthian king] that if allowed to follow this course he would detach many of the provinces, inasmuch as they were already estranged from the Romans through the constant ill-treatment they had experienced.'[72] The tragedy of Carrhae stiffened the whole history of the frontier, and increased the north-south rigidity as against the east–west incline of trade. It offered, for one thing, revenge as a more respectable war façade than greed. Generals 'should have hurried towards Bactra' was the cry, 'leaving the Dacians and Germans to their own devices until Susa and Seleuceia had been destroyed'.[73] Even Seneca, after the lost eagles had actually been returned, wrote of 'Parthia, from whom Rome has not yet got vengeance'.[74]

THE GATE AND LANDSCAPE OF CARRHAE

GATE OF TAHT-I-SULAIMAN (ANCIENT PHRAASPA?)

SEPTIMUS SEVERUS

TIGRANES

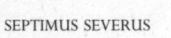

THEODORA

A KING FROM HATRA SECOND CENTURY A.D.

THE KASHGAI NOMADS NEAR PERSEPOLIS

The Parthians echo through the literature of their day, and the Asiatic lands in general are mentioned in one sense or another in half the odes of Horace. Julius Caesar continued to think of a Parthian campaign up to the time of his death. He had nearly doubled the legionaries' pay and he needed money. He prepared his way – nursing the Roman provinces as bases[75] to keep them quiet and prosperous behind him; subduing Pontus and conferring favours on its coastal cities; and scattering military colonies there and in Syria. He did away with such of the hated tax collectors as were left,[76] and dealt with the cities directly; and he took the burden of military service from the Jews.

A rumour that had gained currency in Rome – the prediction that success against the Parthians depended on a Roman king – became the equivalent of a Parthian victory; for though Caesar declined the crown, and 'was wholly engaged in hastening his departure', anti-monarchists were spurred to kill him notwithstanding, and in 44 B.C. Mark Antony, without his genius, inherited his plans.

Mark Antony's Adventure

In 36 B.C., seventeen years after Carrhae, Antony's eastern expedition, less discreditable in leadership but equally futile in conception, left things as they were except for the hastening of two private destinies, already doomed. The dreams of Antony and Cleopatra were political dreams in spite of all the poets, and died against the Roman swords as Hannibal's and Mithradates' dreams had died:[77] in all these cases Rome succeeded: it was only against the Parthian-Iranians that she failed.

Antony's Iranian venture was as purely aggressive as any – yet it scarcely counted as a Roman failure: in Italy it was a part of the oriental fear which finished at Actium; and Antony, when he had denuded Asia Minor and marched (in spring 36 B.C.) with his splendid troops from Zeugma to Malatya, was already cast off from the hearts of his people. He marched along Euphrates by Satala[78] and Erzerum and east of Urmiyah across the Persian border – sixty thousand legionaries and ten thousand horse from Gaul and Spain – and there was no public thanksgiving when the rumour of an Armenian defeat reached Rome.

His attack is attributed by Florus[79] to the wish to have Araxes and Euphrates inscribed beneath his statues and, like many others, he thought of himself as Alexander: he had covered Brutus' body at Philippi with his cloak. Yet the more immediate influence was no doubt that of Caesar's plans, though he made mistakes impossible to either Alexander or Caesar. He trusted the weather-cock king of Armenia against whom even Cicero – no professional soldier – had been on his guard[80]; and the Armenian cavalry deserted on the salt-encrusted flats of Urmiyah, in the gradually solidifying resistance of Asia. Three hundred Roman waggons with the battering rams for sieges, and two legions were lost. Their eagles went to join those of Carrhae, while Antony climbed twelve thousand feet above sea-level, south of Tabriz towards the Parthian summer capital of Phraaspa,[81] among the rugged pastures of Sahand Kuh.

The Germans, who are now excavating there,[82] have thrown doubt on Taht-i-Sulaiman, as the actual site of Phraaspa. Unaware of this, I took much trouble to reach it, a place of pilgrimage more ancient than the history we are dealing with, where the landscape rises like an altar to a flat-topped hill and the cone of a dead volcano, and the calcareous streamlets seep down on raised beds of their own making, through ancient walls still twenty-five feet or so in height. Their gates north and south enclose what is visibly left – a few pink sandstone bits of pillar or door-jamb faintly carved. The Sassanian fire-temple was destroyed by Heraclius in the seventh century, and what else is standing is Muslim of a later age; and the whole circular panorama is like the raised rim in the middle of a Chinese saucer, overlooked by a higher skyline which in May was barred with snow. At some time, probably early, a dam below the walls sealed and fed the short delicious turf of these highlands, in which, as early as Polybius, 'the royal stud-farms were entrusted to the Medes owing to the excellence of the pastures', and supplied 'nearly the whole of Asia'[83] with horses. The damp expanse when I was there was filled with grape hyacinths dark as a midnight sky, and at Mianduab near by I was pleased to be told that the Government horses are still kept. In the Parthian day this whole district must have been, it seemed, less a city than a fortress, a holy Iranian *yailagh*, the summer resort of cavalry whose defence and nourishment would not be concentrated but scattered over a vast zone of mountains and mountain hamlets lifted above the Maragha and Tabriz plain where the Iranian aristocracy lived through dynasty after dynasty in fortified country houses surrounded by villages. These were gradually walled in by their feudal lords so that – as in Bactria and Sogdiana – the land came to be described as richly studded with towns.[84]

Our track here as we rose was fit only for jeeps in good weather, and the air grew cold and brilliant as the nomad emptiness intruded upon it. Black turbans and padded waist-coats of the Kurds appeared, and a Mongol look in the horsemen, sitting wide and squat with saddlebags on squat ponies, with rifles aslant. The villages grew farther apart, clustered on beds of torrents round the mountain massif as if on the spokes of a wheel: between plantations of wheat and ghostlike willow white as aluminium, a clean wind blew across the untended heights.

We met nothing else on wheels; and saw the circular walls of Phraaspa, as I thought it, in failing light. Close by is a hamlet called Nusratabad which belongs to Arslan Afshar Aga who had kindly helped me, and here in one guest-room all together, two drivers and a friend and the headman, we slept. These Kurdish homes are not humanly comfortable like the peasants' houses in Turkey, and when I went out hoping to find a more private refuge with the women, I met nothing but darkness and an open court of mud and stones where an oil lamp showed the wife in a corner cooking – a sad plain woman speaking Kurdish only, bowed under the shame of having produced six daughters to one son. Behind her on a tall loom was her unfinished carpet: some dim unconscious joy had found its way through her rough fingers in the squalor, and glowed on its reds and blues, rich as cathedral glass in the poor flicker of the wick.

*   *   *

Antony meant to take Phraaspa in his stride to Ecbatana; but without his siege train, massacred below, he failed before its walls. With timber for cutting and building in the hills around, Alexander would probably have succeeded. But the country here has a seven months' winter under snow and the food ran out as the autumn closed around them. The Parthian too 'was full of apprehension that if the Romans were to persist in carrying on the siege . . . he should be deserted by his soldiers who would suffer anything rather than wintering in the open'.[85] He promised safety to the invaders in their retreat.

Antony's character was always at its best in calamity and showed very well in this time of trial. 'There was no man of his time like him . . . for carrying soldiers with him by force of words. . . . But when the baggage was collected, and they were to set out, for shame and sadness he could not find it in his heart to speak himself but employed Domitius Aenobarbus. And some of the soldiers resented it . . . but the greater number saw the true cause and pitied it', for there was love between them. 'When five thousand were carried back to the camp wounded, he went from tent to tent to visit and comfort them, and was not able to see his men without tears and a passion of grief . . . for, in short, never in all these times can history make mention of a general at the head of a more splendid army, whether you consider strength and youth, or patience and sufferance in labours and fatigues.' It was the greatest that ever a Roman general had assembled,[86] and might perhaps have turned the fates at Actium – a consideration which makes the Parthian defeat of Antony more important than that of Crassus in its historical perspective.

Verdict on Mark Antony

Though Plutarch disapproves of Mark Antony, his immorality, luxury, drunkenness – distasteful to a moderate Greek but no doubt looked upon with equanimity by his troops – the likeableness which underlay his success breaks through the story all the time: 'For there was much simplicity in his character; he was slow to see his faults, but when he did see them, was extremely repentant, and ready to ask pardon of those he had injured; prodigal in his acts of reparation, and severe in his punishments, his generosity much more extravagant than his severity; his raillery sharp and insulting, but the edge of it taken off by his readiness to submit to any kind of repartee.' 'You allow him to say anything he likes', Cicero complains: there seems to have been a lack of that *gravitas* about him,[87] and when he rode in a chariot drawn by lions with the actress Cytheris beside him it was 'a thing that outdid even the portentous occurrences of that disastrous period'.[88] He had once fought an old friend, 'bravely while alive, but on his death sought out his body and buried it with royal honours[89];' and because of this good fellowship and generosity of nature his men followed him through the twenty-seven days of the retreat with only a break of a few hours under the strain.

His optimism helped him, for when advised to mistrust the Parthians and keep to the mountains above the cavalry stretches of the plain, he trusted and followed the advice. When the expected attack came, he marched in a square battle with his squadrons kept close, riding high above the Mianeh Valley and making for the highlands of Armenia; and when, at the descent of a hill, the Parthians let fly their arrows as the troop moved slowly down, 'the full-armed infantry facing round, received the light troops within; and those in the first rank knelt on one knee, holding their shields before them, the next rank holding theirs over the first, and so again others over these . . . the whole affording sure defence against arrows, which glanced upon them without doing any harm. . . . After this rate it was every day, and the trouble they gave made the marches short; in addition to which famine began to be felt in the camp, for they could get but little corn, and that which they got they were forced to fight for; and, besides this, they were in want of implements to grind it and make bread. For they had left almost all behind, the baggage horses being dead or otherwise employed in carrying the sick and wounded. Provision was so scarce in the army that . . . barley loaves sold for their weight in silver. And when they tried vegetables and roots, they found such as are commonly eaten very scarce, so that they were constrained to venture upon any they could get, and, among others, chanced upon an herb that was mortal.'[90]

Not much of this army survived the twenty-seven days and the following march through Armenia, nor could its quality ever be repeated. Yet the soldiers continued to love Antony, and even after Actium, five years later, 'would not give up their desires and expectations, still fancying he would appear from some part or other, and showed such a generous fidelity to his service that, when they were thoroughly assured that he was fled in earnest, they kept themselves in a body seven days, making no account of the messages that Caesar sent to them'.[91]

But along the banks of Euphrates and on the desert fringes as elsewhere the Roman Republic, after Actium, was dead. The Principate came leading on to Empire; and the blood of the Parthian wars had an interval of leisure to dry in the Augustan sun.

VII

The Rome of Augustus

The Augustan effort to rule the eastern Roman world from a
Roman setting failed: the wealth and civilisation of the Orient
proved too strong; their influences were too subtly persuasive; and
a *mixed* Mediterranean voice was to be the voice of Rome. The long
duel that soon opens between Empire and senate will demonstrate,
ever more feebly, the attempt at government from Rome: but the
reign of Augustus, with the splendour of its literature that so soon
collapses, is already the last battle of Italian Rome. It is worth a digression. If Magnesia and the oriental influences it brought had never
happened, the Italian Italy of Augustus might have survived and developed, and the history of the world would be different for better or worse
today.

'The Scythian plant...is brought from the marshes of Maraeotis...
Britannica from islands in the ocean lying beyond the mainland, Aethiopis...
scorched by the constellation of heaven, and other plants passing through
the whole world for the welfare of mankind, all owing to the boundless
grandeur – *immensa Romanae pacis maiestate* – of the Roman peace.... May
this gift of the Gods last, I pray, for ever! So truly do they seem to have given
to the human race the Romans, as it were a second sun.' (Pliny: *Natural
History*, XXVII.1.3.)

The Elder Pliny

The rhapsody of the elder Pliny gives an exact picture, however botanical, of the feelings of his time.

The age, bestriding the dawn of the Christian era, was weary and rich like ours. As soon as it was given scope, when Augustus turned to forbearance, industry and intercourse did the rest: country after country appeared to be reborn, and Pliny's *Natural History*, voluminous and uneven, gives a safer picture than do the satirists, whose truths are sharper but less general for a society that in its nervous fatigue and voluntary descent to the second-rate had many points of contact with our own. Juvenal, Martial and Petronius are keen but not universal. They seize the point – when big words are used for little things – that makes an age, theirs or ours, vulnerable to satire. In Pliny the ingredients are involved with others in a more natural proportion, and what is noticeable on his Roman canvas is not only the swift increase of riches, but a genuinely international atmosphere of comfort – also typical of today – spreading in the 'second sun'. The Roman transition in its literary aspect is worth a digression from our scene on the Euphrates, since it sprang from causes which were to affect every quarter of the new Imperial world.

Pliny, like Horace, was a countryman, born in Verona nine years after Augustus' death. He had the severe life of the provinces still in his remembrance, but came into the new age with a mind undistracted by strains of the Civil Wars. What he looked back to, with interest and disapproval across the luxuries and their inventors, were the times when there were no bakers in Rome and the citizens baked for themselves[1]; when linen awnings were first brought for the forum by Julius,[2] and mosaic floors in Sulla's reign[3] superseded the painted Greek[4]; when the first marble was used by Lepidus on the finest house in Rome before Lucullus, and the art of carving it was scarcely known. Caesar's chief engineer in Gaul introduced it[5] as a veneer on his walls, and Julius Caesar had already used it, for the transition to luxury was rapid even before Augustus.[6] Travertine began to replace tufa, the Roman cement was invented,[7] and the censors still thought 6,000 sesterces[8] too high a rent for houses[9] when Cicero's idea of a gentlemanly income had reached 600,000 sesterces a year.[10]

'Clipped arbours were invented within the last eighty years by a member of the equestrian order . . . a friend of his late Majesty Augustus'[11]; cypresses from Crete were trimmed for gardens to represent hunting scenes or fleets of ships[12]; and citrus wood was brought from Mauretania for 'the table-mania which ladies use as a retort to the men against the charge of extravagance in pearls'.[13] Cicero with his slender resources paid 500,000 sesterces for a table.[14]

Few flowers for chaplets were known beyond roses and violets,[15] but pearls came in after the death of Cleopatra, and Horace in his *Satires* mentions one worth a million sesterces.[16] They entered into the definite range of Pliny's disapproval with Drusus' wife, 'who adorned her favourite lamprey with ear-rings'.[17]

'I have seen Lollia Paulina . . . a single little lady reclining at Caligula's side . . . covered with emeralds and pearls . . . all over her head, hair, ears, neck and fingers, the sum total amounting to 40 million sesterces . . . acquired in fact with the spoil of the provinces. This is the final outcome of plunder, it was for this that Marcus Lollius disgraced himself by taking gifts from kings in the whole of the East, and was cut out of his list of friends by the son of Augustus,[18] and drank poison – that his granddaughter should be on show in the lamplight covered with 40 million sesterces.'[19]

The women came off badly, as they do with most of the first century's authors. Seneca's 'silk garments provide no protection for the body, or indeed modesty, so that when a woman wears them she can scarcely . . . swear that she is not naked'.[20] When it comes to gold, of which Pliny remarks (he is often very inaccurate) that the first Roman coin was struck in 217 B.C., it is the men's turn to be criticised. 'The Roman nation did not even use a stamped silver coinage before the conquest of King Pyrrhus',[21] (in 275 B.C.), and in the Republican period not even members of the senate had gold rings, not even Roman generals in their triumphs.[22] But nowadays, says Pliny, 'even men are beginning to wear on their fingers a representation of Harpocrates and figures of Egyptian deities'[23]; the horns of animals to be immolated are gilt, and ceilings are covered with gold even in private houses, when the use of gilding passed to vaulted roofs and walls.[24]

Luxury extended to plants, most of whose names, though not all, are unknown: the *agnus castus*' purple panicles – so-called because the

Athenian matrons 'preserving their chastity at the Thesmophoria, strew their beds with its leaves'[25] – are still brushed by every passing car in the lanes of Asia Minor, and the plant that grows in Bactria must surely be hashish – 'causing phantoms and laughter if taken in myrrh and wine'.[26] Nard from Arabia cost 100 denarii to the pound,[27] and the double-dyed Tyrian purple wool over 1,000 denarii.[28] A myrrhine bowl from the Persian Gulf, such as Petronius destroyed on his deathbed to deprive Nero of his pleasure, was sold to Nero himself for one million sesterces. Slaves ran to 700,000 for a linguist and the same for a grammarian,[29] whose profession could command anything from 100 to 400,000 sesterces a year[30]: a commissary strangely enough was bought and liberated by Nero for 13 million sesterces.[31]

An actor's meal of singing birds is mentioned at 6,000 sesterces apiece,[32] and 'even the Parthians bestowed their fashions on our cooks'.[33] Pliny says that his countrymen knew the goose by the excellence of its liver, and officers in command of auxiliary troops would frequently get into trouble for having sent whole cohorts away from outpost and sentry duties to make *pâté* on the German frontier with these captured fowls.[34] The goose, he adds in one of his engaging deviations, is remarkable for coming all the way on foot from Gaul to Rome while the partridges of Paphlagonia have two hearts.[35] The censors' resistance to these gastronomic excesses seems inadequate: they forbade the serving of dormice at dinner.[36]

The arts grew expensive together with everything else, and their prices compare with those of modern buying, though it was bad taste to show too much knowledge about them.[37] 'I do not think you would hesitate to concede', Velleius Paterculus wrote in the year A.D. 30, 'that it would have been more useful to the state for the taste in Corinthian art to have remained uncultivated to the present day, than that it should be appreciated as it is now'.[38] Lucullus ordered a one-million-sesterces statue and Tiberius, a much-tried man, found comfort with a picture valued at six million sesterces[39] which he tried in vain to keep in his own rooms. 'No wonder the art of painting is degenerate', Petronius complains, 'when all . . . think a block of gold more beautiful than any work of . . . those madmen Greeklings'[40]; and Pliny reports painting as 'now entirely ousted by marbles, and indeed finally also by gold-embossed marble slats carved in wriggling lines to represent objects and animals. . . . [41] People leave behind them portraits that represent their money, not themselves, and display all around their bedrooms . . . likenesses of Epicurus. . . . In the halls of our ancestors it was otherwise . . . wax models of faces were set out each on a separate sideboard, to furnish likenesses to be carried . . . at a funeral in the clan, and always when someone died the entire company of his house that had ever existed was present. . . . Outside the houses and round the doorways there were other presentations of these mighty spirits, with spoils taken from the enemy fastened to them, which even one who bought the house was not permitted to unfasten . . . as a mighty incentive, when every day the very walls reproached an unwarlike owner.'[42]

The Admiral was not one for abstract art, and while giving their due to Caesar and Augustus, who placed paintings in the forum, and even to Agrippa, a 'rustic man and unrefined' who suggested they should be national property and not banished to country houses,[43] his genuine approval goes to the painted horse of Apelles that made other horses neigh recognition, or to the Emperor Claudius who cut out a face of Alexander 'and put in Augustus instead'.[44] He enjoyed the wall paintings of 'country houses and landscape gardens, porticoes, groves, fishponds, canals and hills . . . and people fishing and fowling or even gathering the vintage', the charming fancies that we have still found at Pompeii[45]; and he admired the novelty of perspective[46]; and admitted that, after the Greeks under Nero, the skill of the bronze workers had declined.[47] The antiquarian interest of the time left him cold, and while old graves in Corinth had been dug over by Caesar's colonists to find vases and bronzes for the Roman dealers, Pliny probably agreed with Horace in preferring 'gladiators with their straining legs drawn in red chalk or charcoal' to the things admired by the 'fine and expert critics of the antique'.[48]

There are a good many Plinys in all ages, with their *Times* every morning, and their reliable virtues and unfashionable prejudices. 'Perfumes, for instance,' says the old Blimp, 'the most superfluous of all forms of luxury. . . . The Emperor Caligula had the bath tubs scented, and so also later did one of the slaves of Nero – so that this must not be considered a privilege of princes! Yet what is most surprising is that this indulgence has found its way even into the camp: at all events the eagles and the standards, dusty as they are and bristling with sharp points, are anointed on holidays – and I only wish we were able to say who first introduced this custom! No doubt . . . our eagles were bribed by this reward to conquer the world! We look to their patronage forsooth to sanction our vices, so as to have this legitimation for using hair-oil under a helmet! I could not readily say when the use of unguents first made its way to Rome. It is certain that in 189 B.C. the censors . . . issued a proclamation forbidding any sale of "foreign essences" . . . and the brother of Lucius Plancus who was twice consul and censor, when proscribed by the Triumvirs was given away in his hiding place at Salerno by the scent . . . he had been using – a disgrace that acquitted the entire proscription of guilt, for who would not consider that people of that sort deserve to die?'[49]

Commercial dishonesty too he disliked – 'wines adulterated as soon as they are put into vats',[50] a practice that persists to this day. But he appreciated the eighty notable kinds of liquor that can properly be understood as coming under the term 'wine',[51] and was proud that two-thirds of the best of them were Italian. This too was a recent change from days when the city used milk for its libations, before the Grecian wars. 'When Lucius Lucullus was a boy he never saw a fulldress banquet in his father's house at which Greek wine was given more than once, but when he himself came back from Asia he distributed more than a hundred thousand jars in largesse . . . '[52] and the same swift progress was made by Italian oil, which began to be exported under Pompey,[53] and by glass manufactured with the Volturno sand.[54]

These were healthy things which the Admiral approved of, while he felt that 'receiving Asia as a gift dealt a serious blow to our morals, and the bequest of it that came to us on the death of king Attalus [in Pergamon] was more disadvantageous than the victory of Scipio [at Magnesia]. For . . . in the interval of fifty-seven years our community had learnt not merely to admire but to covet foreign opulence. That nothing might be lacking, luxury came into being simultaneously with the downfall of Carthage, a fatal coincidence that gave us at one and the same time a taste for the vices and an opportunity for indulging in them'.[55]

Scattered about in his collection are sums that one after another the generals brought to Rome – from the younger Africanus' 4,370 pounds of silver[56] to the 300 million sesterces booty of the Macedonian wars. It was then that the Roman nation left off paying the citizens' property tax in 167 B.C.[57] Other authors show the scale ascending; 3,000 talents of loot from Antiochus, apart from the indemnity[58]; 600 million sesterces were brought by Caesar, and Pompey endowed Rome with nearly twice the total amount of revenue that she had ever received from her conquests before.[59] A century later Crassus alone owned 200 million sesterces – 'the richest Roman citizen after Sulla ... and we have subsequently known many liberated slaves who have been wealthier'.[60] C. Marcius Censorinus, dying in A.D. 8 after great losses in the Civil Wars, left 4,116 slaves, 3,600 pairs of oxen, 257,000 heads of other cattle and 60 million sesterces.[61]

Pliny emerges out of the novelty and welter with admirable coherence, unaffected by his extraordinarily indiscriminate judgements. He liked the world; it is called pure, he says, *mundus*, 'because of its pure finish and grace'[62]; and he collected all he could that was tangible inside it. In its spiritual springs he took no interest and, though he praises their industry,[63] never misses a chance of criticising the 'wanton imagination' of 'those parents of all the vices the Greeks'.[64] He quotes their listing of the stars by Hipparchus as a 'bold thing, reprehensible even for God',[65] and complains of their frivolity in offering a golden radish, merely because they liked radishes, in the temple of Apollo. Even Sophocles, in spite of his 'noble Athenian lineage, his public achievement and his leadership of an army' (Pliny was evidently not a reader of drama), comes in for reproaches, because he mentions birds that weep amber tears for Meleager: 'Can one imagine a mind so childish ... regarding a substance that every day of our lives is imported and floods the market and so confutes the liar?'[66]

This would be all very well if Pliny himself were not constantly ready to adopt the wildest certainties. He repudiates the phoenix – a golden pheasant apparently – that was displayed in Rome during the censorship of the Emperor Claudius[67]: but there is hardly anything else that he will not accept. I can never resist his bye-ways, and if anyone finds them boring they must skip the next pages: the plane-tree, for instance, that 'neutralises the poison of the bat'[68]; or the Pisidian iris root, 'those who are going to dig it up pour hydromel round it three months previously, as it were a libation to please the earth. ... It is especially enjoined that those who gather it should be chaste'[69]; or the laurel, that is never struck by lightning[70]; or the desert-gazelle that sneezes as the dog-star rises[71]; or quails, the only creatures besides man liable to epilepsy[72]; or Venus wandering two degrees from the Zodiac and causing 'some animals to be born even in the desert places of the world'.[73] I find almost any animal story enjoyable, but constantly wonder at the certainty with which the old Admiral mentions their most unsponsored ways: he could surely, near Naples, where scorpions abound, have verified whether they were 'always fatal to girls and almost absolutely so to women, but to men only in the mornings'[74]; and there must have been plenty of people moving about from the eastern trade route to tell him whether camels really enjoy their water more if they 'trample it with their forefeet before they drink'.[75] So glibly does he tell it, that he might actually have seen the deer swimming from Cilicia to Cyprus 'with their heads resting on the haunches of the ones in front of them',[76] and talks almost as a witness of Nero and Britannicus' starlings trained to talk Latin and Greek.[77] The stories of the bees, that go to bed and rise with the Pleiades, are more familiar – taken from Greeks who spent their years among them, and apparently saw them overtaken by nightfall, 'reclining on their backs to protect their wings from the dew',[78] and when evening approaches 'the buzzing inside the hive grows less and less, till one bee flies around as though giving the order to take repose with the same loud buzz with which she woke them, in the manner of a military camp'.[79] Their cells, he rightly says, are hexagonal 'each side being made by one of the bee's six feet'.[80]

It is difficult enough to be sure of anything anywhere, but how can one tell for instance that insects are more deadly if they have eaten their own kind before attacking?[81] Or that serpents in Syria never touch Syrians when asleep?[82]

He is hard as usual on women and makes them either unlucky, like the poor creature who was delivered of two male and two female quadruplets 'which *unquestionably* portended the food shortage that followed'[83]; or else frivolous because, unlike the ostrich who is the only bird with lashes on both eyelids, the Roman ladies dyed their lashes every day.[84] The human race itself is scarcely better treated: 'One feels pity and even shame in realising how trivial is the origin of the proudest of the animals, when the smell of lamps being put out [we used to use those Tuscan lamps when I was a child and they were very smelly] usually causes abortion.'[85]

A gay little tale which I hope was true is that of a knight of Volterra, who owned a racing four-in-hand and 'used to catch swallows and take them with him to Rome and despatch them with the news of a win to his friends, as they returned to the same nests; they had the winning colour painted on them'[86]; and there is an unexpectedly domestic detail which says that 'vessels into which food is put foretell dreadful storms by leaving a smudge on the sideboard'.[87] It sounds like a butler's invention, and some of these legends have come down to our time. When, as a child in north Italy, I suffered from ear-ache, a peasant woman was sent for to squirt a little milk from her breast into my ear.[88] Pliny however reports, without batting an eyelid, how 'the governor of Gaul wrote to the late lamented Augustus that a large number of dead Nereids were to be seen on the shore'.[89]

In spite of discoveries, our world is still wrapped in essential darkness. It was then even more thickly shrouded, and – as Pliny truly asks – 'who ever believed in the Ethiopians before actually seeing them?'[90] Much of our knowledge of his time depends on his eccentric mass of information; and there are moments when enthusiasm carries him beyond the bare facts to their essence – and this happens nearly always when he speaks of the country and country things, the stars or the turning of the seasons or even simple, basic occupations – the weaving of baskets in winter and cutting of vine props, 'squared at the rate of thirty and rounded at the rate of sixty a day', or the Dolphin rising at dawn, and the star in the breast of the Lion, when 'the ground should be turned up with a double mattock – seventy hands are enough for an acre' – and the darkness before daybreak should be used for sharpening tools.[91]

He saw the horrors of Caligula and Nero and came sanely out of them, ignoring those creatures that 'when they cross our path forbid us to act or to be of service to life. . . . But in this matter also Nature's grandeur is the same: how many more good men has she engendered as her harvest! How much more fertile is she in products that give aid and nourishment! We too will then continue to enrich life with the value we set on these things and the delight they give us, leaving those brambles of the human race to the consuming fire that is theirs, and all the more resolutely because we achieve greater gratification from industry than we do from renown. The subject of our discourse is indeed the countryside and rustic practices, but it is on these that life depends and that the highest honour was bestowed in early days.'[92]

He talks of the stars not as a poet of the city, but as one who thanked and used them in their visitations – trying to introduce them 'to the ignorance of the rustic',[93] or watching the 'cold star Saturn',[94] or seeing honey come out of the air at the rising of the Dog-star just before the dawn.[95] Anyone who has slept out in Arabia or with the Alpine shepherds, must recognise his feeling. 'I have seen a radiance of star-like appearance clinging to the javelins of soldiers on sentry duty at night in front of the rampart: and on a voyage stars alight on the yards and other parts of the ship, with a sound resembling a voice, hopping from perch to perch in the manner of birds. . . . They also shine round men's heads at evening time.'[96]

Mystery, recognised or unrecognised, was still around him – though his world is already spherical, revolving or static according to the conflicting theories of his day; and he speaks of lands on the far side of this sphere, unattainable because of the encircling Ocean.[97] He is enthralled with the life of earth, 'even that odour of the soil . . . which often occurs when the ground is not being turned up, just towards sunset, at the end of rainbows . . . or when the soil has been drenched with rain after a long period of drought'.[98] His best words are for the 'earth that belongs to men as the sky belongs to God; she receives us at birth, and gives us nurture after birth, and when once brought forth she upholds us always, and at the last when we have been disinherited by the rest of Nature she embraces us in her bosom and at that very time gives us her maternal shelter; sanctified by no greater service than that whereby she makes us also sacred, bearing our monuments and epitaphs and prolonging our name and extending our memory against the shortness of time'.[99]

These sterling tastes and qualities go with a Poona complacency for his own country and a most unsailorly mis-liking for the sea. Rome, he considers, produced 'more men of distinction in every branch whatever than the whole of the rest of the world'[100] and 'the one race of outstanding eminence in virtue' among the races of mankind.[101] As for the sea, he blames Daedalus who 'made man perish where no burial awaits him',[102] and no execration is adequate: everything to do with navigation he objects to, from boats that ship marble 'so that Nature is flattened and we remove the barriers created to serve as the boundaries of nations',[103] to the growing of hemp, which seems harmless enough (as hashish was not yet discovered) – except that its fibre was woven for sails: 'And how audacious is life and full of wickedness for a plant to be grown for the purpose of catching the winds and the storms, and for us not to be satisfied with being borne on the waves alone.'[104]

We must leave Pliny, regretfully, as he goes up almost literally in the smoke of Vesuvius.[105] Having listened to his words we need not linger over others, for his was a general voice, spoken with deeper or lighter accents by Virgil and Horace. Foreigners like Strabo echoed it, or Dionysius of Halicarnassus, who from his perfect climate writes to say that of all countries fertile and self-sufficing, Italy basking in her wealth is the best.[106] 'But neither Media's groves . . . not beauteous Ganges, nor Hermes, thick with gold, may vie with Italy's glories – not Bactria, nor India, nor all Panchaea, rich in incense-bearing sand.'[107]

Architecture, Travel and Philosophy

'We have come to fortune's summit; we paint, we play and sing, we wrestle with more skill than the well-oiled Greeks.'[108]

Rome beautified herself with her plunder – with colonnades such as the ageing Augustus loved to sit under on the Palatine,[109] and libraries 'among cold baths and hot baths'.[110] and the first theatre built by Pompey in stone, where early in the first century cushions came into use under Caligula and senators took to wearing Thessalian hats against the sun.[111] Most of the building in the central and north Italian towns is Augustan[112] – either Pompeian-hellenistic in fashion after the Punic wars[113]; or round structures derived from Neolithic ages, or broad-façaded temples lifted high on the Roman podium, devoted to the trinity of the Etruscan Gods. In the south, Naples 'tried in a manner to imitate the customs of the Greeks',[114] and Pompeian homes had long ago spread into large and beautiful buildings, with columns and porticoes, peristyles, fountains, wall-paintings and gardens, and an industrial life where shops first show connected with the houses.[115]

There is no break in continuity; in the Augustan period, though fashion was derived from Alexandria rather than Asia Minor, the pleasantness and perfection were the same; and though the Roman invention of cement was as revolutionary as ours, when Caesar and Augustus came to build their forums they found the main structure of their architecture prepared.

*   *   *

Travel increased in this easy atmosphere, helped by the cheapness of a tideless sea.[116]

Pompey's settlement of the pirates in 67–6 B.C. had opened intercourse with Asia Minor, and both the Italian and the Asiatic trade revived.[117] The hellenistic guidebooks were imitated,[118] adopted and increased for tourists; *cicerones* multiplied, invented in the early second century B.C. for the art centres of Greece; and a golden milestone in the forum gave the distances of the chief cities of the Principate from Rome.[119] Rest houses improved; and litters for hire, or the light two-wheeled *cisium* or four-wheeled *reda*, would cover an average of fifty miles a day on roads which Augustus steadily urged his unwilling senators to pave.[120] Julius Caesar is reported to have done a hundred miles a day for days in succession and despatch bearers could cover one hundred and sixty in the twenty-four hours.[121] It pleases me to think that I have still met someone who, born in Baghdad and sent over eleven hundred miles along the Tigris by Dyarbekr to Istanbul for his studies, spent forty-three days in a carriage twice every year. Another old friend, Guy l'Estrange, used to travel seventy to eighty miles a day in Persia, where the Achaemenian arrangements still survived in his youth; and even in the days just after this war, in Italy before the posts recovered, a letter would drop down as it might have reached Cicero in the early morning, brought by some casual military cyclist in the dawn. In the heyday of the first century, it took ten days to travel from Rome to Southern Gaul; Caesar's letters to Cicero took twenty-six or twenty-eight days from Britain; the same or a little more was needed for Cilicia,[122] unless, if the winds were bad, six to twelve weeks might be taken[123]; eighteen days from Rome, or nine from Puteoli the main western port, to Alexandria; and seven from Cadiz to Ostia. There was a choice of routes to Alexandria, by sea, or overland by the Egnatian road to Thessaly and the Black Sea and thence across the Taurus, or coasting by Byzantium.[124] The time had been when crowded galleys could carry water only for a day or two and crews had to beach them where they wished to sleep: but now, while the descendants of the huge hellenistic warships became ever lighter and smaller and swifter, passengers and goods travelled in larger bottoms, and followed a regular schedule from port to port.[125] There was a direct service of cornships from Alexandria between May and September,[126] and most of the population of Cadiz, according to Strabo, was constantly at sea.[127] Levantine shipping companies were advertised on the white and black mosaic floors of Ostia; and Horace, most suburban of poets, yet thought of a forgotten promontory south of Smyrna,[128] where even lately the only approach was by sea; where the north-sheltered waves still lap at a low acropohs, and wooded hills hide the plains of Ionia – 'a townlet more desert than Gabii and Fidenae, there would I wish to live forgetting and forgotten ... and watch the distant fuming Neptune from afar'.[129]

*   *   *

Not only 'tourism' and commerce, but students, athletes and doctors, artists, pilgrims, religious impostors and philosophers all travelled, and the principles of Zeno and Epicurus migrating in this company, were soon adapted to the capacities of Rome.

The splendid bourgeoisie succeeded, as it has done before and after, in tempering philosophic precept to the rich. Stoic ethics were adapted to the requirements of the Roman upper classes from the late Republic onwards[130]: and it must be added that this alone produced a fit philosophy for ordinary life; for 'nothing can prevent some seats in the theatre from being better than others', said Chrysippus.[131]

A very little philosophy was thought sufficient, and Agricola would have gone further 'than was befitting to a Roman and a senator' had not the wisdom of his mother restrained him.[132] Cicero's 'one should know what philosophy teaches us but live like a gentleman,' puts the matter in a nutshell. There was little enough left in common with Zeno, or with Cleanthes,[133] his follower, who came from Assos that looks to Mitylene, where no one had ever worried about what a Roman might think.

The discrepancy increased as time went on. 'Zeno's philosophy was transformed into a moral stiffener for a spiritually bankrupt Roman aristocracy.... Its steady decay as a philosophy was matched by its increased spread, at a lower level, as a guide to conduct ... it is difficult to avoid the feeling that it meant little more than elaborate justification for the immediate political or psychological *fait accompli*.'[134] Cicero makes fun of it: 'The philosopher surmises nothing. . . . A philosopher is never angry. . . . "To lie", he says, "is the action of a criminal; to change one's opinion is disgraceful . . . to pity is a crime" . . . if you had gone to better teachers, Cato [he concludes], you would have been a little more given to kindness.'

In its measure, the Stoic creed served as a cement for Roman unity. St Paul used its conceptions and phrases,[135] and it has been popular in England because its main teaching was self-restraint, though the uninvolved harmony with the heart of the universe which was its target is rarely attained by such approaches. The woman who 'had loved much' reached her peace by being everything that a Roman stoic would dislike.[136]

Epicureanism – escapism as it would now be called, (as if the wish to attain could not be independent of the wish to run away!) – Epicureanism with its charities, its personal individualism and practical ethics,[137] appealed to the provincial and the lesser people, as it does, in fact, appeal to the Italians today. Hope for the future, gratitude for the past, patience for the present, are its virtues: and it is 'not impossible that it facilitated the spread of Christianity'.[138] Whether its standards survived their transplantation is another matter; but it comforted men in the loneliness of their growing cities and was immensely popular towards the end of the Republic, especially among the Greek Italians of the south.

The Social Order

Decisive no doubt in the long run, philosophy was a minor preoccupation in the first Christian century, and many other stimuli – drain of civil wars, emancipation of Italy (the very word Italy as a living entity dates only from about 90 B.C.),[139] acquisition of empire, deluge of slaves, industrial concentration and the rise of the business men – equestrians and freedmen – all these things were altering the outlook of the Romans.

For one thing they became very mixed. Some ninety per cent in the Assembly seem to have been of foreign extraction. There were well over two hundred thousand slaves in Rome before the end of the Republic and, though free labour paid better especially in an unhealthy district,[140] the emptiness left by war in country places was gradually turned over to grazing and thereby to slave labour: 'There was no other means of bringing these lands under cultivation again.'[141] Domestic servants, secretaries and the like were at this time wholly of the slave class[142] and, more wide-awake than their masters, were also needed in most professional concerns. The great numbers sent home from the East during the wars were now coming to an end,[143] and a shortage began to be felt under the *pax Romana*, so that kidnapping, as it still exists in Arabia, grew frequent.[144] Yet right through the second and first centuries B.C. the stream of slaves never ceased to flow; they managed the properties acquired by the old and the new aristocracy, pupils and heirs of the hellenistic landowners, most of whom had made their fortunes in the East; and as the slaves were increasingly manumitted as they bought or were given their freedom, a growing foreign strain seeped into Rome.[145]

The end of the Civil Wars and the battle of Actium meant the victory of the non-political classes.[146] In the first decade of Augustus' constitutional rule, he employed not a single noble among the legates commanding his provincial armies, and only three men of consular standing.[147] The aristocracy had been decimated as never before at Philippi, and was hampered by the theory that almost every way of making money except by robbery was vulgar. The road was therefore open to a new order 'patently, though not frankly, plutocratic . . . a formidable collection of hard-faced men in the purified senate – enriched by war and revolution'.[148]

It was urbanisation[149] not only in Italy but over the Roman world,[150] the day of administration and bureaucracy in the undemocratic hands of salaried knights and freedmen. These and the equestrian order together exploited the Roman economy, and no Imperial edict could keep them separate for long. Birth counted for a little, but the main passport was money,[151] and a rich man's daughter could soon become a priestess of Vesta.[152] Claudius was humane in many ways in his slave-legislation, but severe on this point – a freedman would be sold back if he usurped equestrian status, or even showed a lack of respect to his former master; a free women's child, if the father were servile, was a slave.[153] The rulers tried, like Mrs Partington, to sweep back the sea. For the 'paradox of Rome is that of a nation whose ruling passion was money, but whose ruling classes nevertheless ignored and despised the means by which their

AUGUSTUS

NERO

money was made'.[154] The country gentleman in his modest comfort did not realise that Italy now lived by her business men's efforts and imports. His panacea was 'a gentle nostalgia for the peasant virtues of his ancestors', when the armies that had vanquished the world were peasant armies, when vices were peasant vices enlarged and the touchstone of virtue the *mos maiorum*. The satirists who criticise him were no wiser than he: 'they shared the Rousseau vision of an idealised antiquity'[155] and blamed him for leaving it, and there can be no more painful criticism for the early Empire than the fact that its more respectable members looked back with nostalgia to the blood stained Republic before it.

Augustus

Most enigmatic of all great Roman rulers, the aged and tired Augustus steered this world. His greatness is undoubted, for he belonged to that small company that has made history permanently different. His secret is, I think, a sympathy amounting to identity with the character of his own people, a Latin complexion which, right into modern times, has been rarely comprehended in the north. Like Heathcliff to Catherine in *Wuthering Heights*, Italy to Augustus was 'more me than I am myself' and in nothing more so than in the perennial Latin devotion to a 'façade'. 'On all sides prevailed a conspiracy of decent reticence about the gap between fact and theory'[156]; the names of Antony and the other Romans were never mentioned, for instance, either at the time of Actium or after, to imply that it could be proper to celebrate their defeat.

The façade, the principle that it is the show and not the actual existence of a thing that matters, not only built up the Principate itself but appeared in the smallest details of daily life. That indifference to public opinion which the great Julius had so lavishly practised was, according to Cicero, the expression of 'a total want of principle'[157] and of that *gravitas* which prevented 'singing in the street or any other gross misconduct!'[158] Tacitus assumed a general to be haughty because he wore breeches and parti-coloured cloak,[159] and Juvenal later on enumerates fast driving among the major sins. In Augustus' own family, where a constant *malaise* is perceptible, the young grandsons were 'inclined to insolence[160]; for example, Lucius on one occasion entered the theatre unattended'. Hypocrisy about women had the Latin complexion which has talked about chastity without necessarily practising it for several thousand years: the 'modest virgin looks with hand before her face' at the feast of Priapus,[161] and though the prostitute (indelibly registered, her dress, hair, and civic disabilities conspicuous) could be met openly at theatre or banquet – Cicero was nervous, having met Antony's Cytheris at dinner – the profession was frowned upon, and one would think scarcely required, for there were a great many amateurs. This bourgeois insincerity, that relies not on intrinsic values but on the promiscuous approval of strangers, is yet a factor of stability and an anchor of order to which the easy-going Italian race has ever been desperately attached – the shield of *pietas* and *gravitas* and that boring Mother of Gracchi, right down to the speeches of Mussolini. Augustus was its supreme manipulator, and the façade ever since his day (and possibly before) was and is a reality in Italian life[162]: family, church and state depend upon it: discriminating French or Greek intellects shatter it to bits . . . and cease to govern: in cliché after cliché, or decency after decency, it has come down the ages, preserved with Roman pride and accepted by other good administrations with less frankness but equal relief: for it is an instrument of government, and to govern without an instrument is hard indeed.

'The existence of the gods is expedient; therefore let us believe they exist', says Ovid, with a frankness which landed him in exile. Galileo, centuries later, murmurs '*eppur si muove*' while bowing to the stationary world and its façade.

Augustus may or may not have been aware of the divergence, but he was sincere in that he meant and expected the façade to remain and the facts to conform behind it, and it *has* remained, preserved by the enthusiasts of his time and the piety of posterity, while the facts go their way as they usually do. The divergence (which has ruined so many other periods of greatness), has cast its enigmatic complexion on a man remarkable not for his effort to twist facts into a pattern – which many try to do – but for the intensity of passion, courage and sagacity which accompanied his perfectly normal Latin indifference to abstract truth. The measure of this passion is the cruelty – *adulescentulus carnifex*[163] – which stained an otherwise friendly nature whenever this particular harmony was infringed. Family affection was one of its notes – the family is almost the strongest tie in the Latin magic – and no ruthlessness was too great where the murderers of Julius Caesar were concerned. For six years after the assassination, the young Octavian let his beard grow as a sign of mourning[164]; forty years later he dedicated the temple of Mars the Avenger as he had vowed it on the eve of Philippi, and there is no notice that the blood of the proscriptions hung heavy on his mind. Later on, when 'the tutor and attendants of his grandson Gaius took advantage of their master's illness and death to commit acts of arrogance and greed in his province, he had them thrown into a river with heavy weights about their necks';[165] and bitterness towards Antony was made indelible by the offences offered to Octavia: Antony seems to have been genuinely surprised that his respectable marriage with Cleopatra did not make all well.

Yet it was never family emotion alone acting in that singularly strong nature. Augustus exiled his stepson Tiberius[166] when the façade was threatened, and no affection could help his daughter Julia in her disgrace. When the people urged him to recall her, 'he answered that fire should sooner mix with water. And the people threw firebrands into the Tiber'[167] till she was put back on the mainland. Augustus would not have her buried in his family mausoleum,[168] and when a friend of hers, a freedwoman called Phoebe, also implicated, hanged herself, his comment was, 'I would rather have been Phoebe's father.'[169]

It is clear that he loved Italy more than any human being – the traditional Italy of his mother and of Virgil, the solid home of peasant armies and homespun squires, and land-rooted gods. The rural life and the religion of Numa came back into practice. His 'loyalty to the traditions of Italy did more than give its character to the Augustan age. It endowed the Roman Empire with its significance in the history of Western Europe.'[170] These traditions were on the verge of submersion in an atmosphere in which Rome was still a learner. If Augustus had ever shared Caesar's easy freedom in that equal and larger world, he soon rejected it as either undesirable or unattainable – and in any case as too near in essence to what Antony had been building in the East. The Julian empire, a gigantic client state as Antony inherited Caesar's conception, he soon rejected, and citizenship, that Julius pictured universal in one imperial culture which would include the best that Rome and Greece and the East could furnish, he conceived as something to be attained by service and merit under the unquestioned predominance of Rome.[171] Italy too wished for no equal empire after her conquests, as her antagonism to the liberal policies of Claudius was soon to show. *Parcere subiectis et debellare superbos*[172] was the feeling of Horace and of Rome.

Augustus' Handling of Power

In 36 B.C., at twenty-seven, Augustus held the Western Empire – forty-three legions and six hundred ships of war: at thirty-one, after Actium, he was master of the Roman world. He had the wealth of Egypt in his possession, and did not underestimate its importance. He had begun his career almost bankrupt when the news of Caesar's murder hit him, and his immediate thought had then been the treasure prepared for the Parthian war (which in the event fell into his enemies' hands).[173] Later, when the Roman world was partitioned, the poorer half only had fallen to his share – which he ruled with lavish donatives, but taxing Italian incomes at twenty-five per cent[174] until the battle of Actium gave him Alexandria, and diplomacy with Cleopatra the treasure of the Ptolemies as well. Tenney Frank estimates the Egyptian revenue before the ruin of war at 75 million sesterces.[175]

'Cleopatra had collected all she could lay her hands on in the tomb which she was constructing in her royal grounds, and she threatened to burn it all up with her if she should fail of even the sHghtest of her demands. So he [Augustus] sent Thyrsus, a freedman of his, to say many kind things to her,'[176] and continued to pay his troops with promises, counting on the Egyptian gold. When that finally fell to him, every citizen received 400 sesterces in gold[177]; arrears of tax were remitted; the value of real property in Italy increased; and the rate of interest dropped from twelve to four per cent. A rhinoceros and a hippopotamus, never seen in Rome before, appeared at the shows; and the statue of Cleopatra was allowed, in gratitude one hopes, 'defeated and captured but glorified',[178] to remain in the temple where Caesar had placed her.

'To begin first with the least important consideration,' Maecenas is made to remark to Augustus in a very unlikely way,[179] 'it will be necessary for you to procure a large supply of money from all sides.' This necessity was now provided for: the treasure of Egypt paid for everything and continued to pay while that rich country was administered like a farm: sums are recorded that 'add up to over a thousand million

sesterces, much of which seems to have come from Egypt'.[180] They
made the Principate possible, for they enriched Augustus sufficiently
to let him undertake what the senate could no longer afford. 'The
senate never protested against these encroachments. The reason was the
same ... fear of assuming responsibility for the enormous expenditure
necessary for the state. ... The emperors emerged from the civil wars
as the richest men in the Empire.'[181] The nobility could not compete
with them. Even if lucky enough to have retained their ancestral estates
they were now deprived of the profits of political power, and debarred
from Egypt, whose large estates were owned and exploited by members
of the reigning dynasties or prominent partisans.[182]

In the delicate handling of his great power Augustus made no mistakes. He *was* the Italy that was being governed, *tam similis sibi nec ipsa*,[183]
and what is more he was a banker's grandson, a traditional member of
the Italian middle class under which Italy was feverishly growing, developing her riches, running her model farms on hellenistic patterns,[184]
centralising her banking and the transits of the west.[185] He had a gift for
publicity and was helped by his generous virtues – a capacity for affection
that enabled him, like Alexander, never to mistrust or need to mistrust
his friends. Agrippa and Maecenas altered his letters as they thought
best[186] in his absence; and with all his wealth he gave away enough
money, in donations, in public works, in help to senators and others, to
die relatively poor.[187] In the *Res Gestae* he declares himself the first ever
to pay the towns for the lands which he took for his soldiers – about
600 million sesterces in Italy and 260 million in the provinces.[188]

He was a master of advertisement and missed no chances – dissemi-
nating his own speeches or circulating Antony's will snatched from the
Vestal Virgins; or reading his rivals' calumnies to his troops among the
sand hills near Alamein[189]; and no other power in the state was rich
enough to shoulder or compete with the enormous expense of propaganda[190] into whose service literature, religion and art were pressed.
Art for the Romans was documentary, acknowledged as a system of propaganda – the beginning of that pictorial teaching which the early ages
of Christianity were to develop.[191] In the Augustan religion, even the
little gods of the cross-roads, the *Lares Compitales*, brought the poorest
citizens into the pride and dignity of Rome[192]; and in the long struggle

with Cleopatra Augustus managed, by sheer publicity, to crystallise the fear that divided West and East.

Not only his virtues but his habits belonged to the bourgeoisie. 'No less distasteful to the *nobiles*', says Syme,[193] 'were the domestic parsimony and petty superstitions which the Princeps imported from his municipal origin.' He walked, when he was Consul; he treated his senate with courtesy; and enjoyed the theatre, where he avoided Caesar's unpopular habit of answering letters as he sat. He was amused by things for which Nero was criticised later – distributing surprise presents at festivals,[194] enjoying the sight of aristocratic dancers and even of a 'Woman of High Birth' on the stage.[195] He disliked – and how much he must have suffered from them – the 'odour of farfetched words',[196] parodied Maecenas' scented style, and like a good Victorian had a tendency to think foreigners inferior. Having lived in Greek lands in his youth he never wore anything but Roman dress.[197] He praised his grandson for not visiting the temple in Jerusalem,[198] and himself never entered one in Egypt; and where Julius would have paid his respects to the tomb of Alexander, and the Macedonian himself went on foot to that of Cyrus, Augustus sent for the sarcophagus to decorate it with a gold wreath and flowers – a vulgar touch.[199]

These bourgeois symptoms narrowed the spacious atmosphere left by Julius Caesar, whose soldiers could reek of perfume so long as they fought, and whose omens 'will be favourable when I wish it'. 'It should not be regarded as a portent if a beast has no heart',[200] he had said. (Another Claudian ancestor, exasperated by the Sacred Chickens who refused to eat before a battle, threw them into the sea and said that they might drink.[201] This aristocratic levity tended alas! to disappear.)

Although the great Julius must have been the strongest influence of his adolescence, Augustus showed no tendency to follow him: there was no discipleship such as existed later in Tiberius towards himself. Everywhere, so far as we can judge, there was a narrowing, no doubt into the bounds of possibility, of what the Dictator had sketched out in broad and visionary lines. The dream of a world of equal cities melted: the hellenistic halo of sovereignty came later, by its own compulsion; the republican forms, which Julius was ready to scrap as useless, were saved by Augustus to build the great façade.[202] Julius scattered the Roman franchise: it grew from less than half a million citizens in 70 B.C. to over

4 million in forty-two years.[203] Augustus at his death asked that too many
more should not be created; Rome was to be the centre on which alone
a new empire could build.[204] Carving his pattern, he hit his age with
unhesitating values, and the Roman quality of a Cato seems a bludgeon
beside the rapier glance of Augustus that liked to bend all eyes before
it.[205] His power was the greater because he never ceased to be its servant,
and the length of his reign was given him in addition to make his lasting
fame: more than perhaps any other ruler of antiquity he is visible – for
good and also for ill – as the background of everything that happened –
in state or strategy, art, architecture, or literature, or private life. What
he built lasted three hundred years until it 'decayed at its Italian heart',[206]
and Rome ceased to be the universal city 'with no peer and no second',[207]
a symbol of human aspiration, and 'her eternity an article of faith for
every civilised man'.[208]

These are strong words and not quite true, for the Rome of Augustus
had disappeared almost with its founder; yet many would have echoed
them who knew him – Virgil and Horace and Livy and lesser names.
'There was nothing men might pray for to Heaven, and nothing Heaven
could grant to men – nothing desire could conceive, or fortune could
bestow which Augustus . . . did not realise for the people of Rome,
and the world. . . . And it seems to me', says Dio, who is not unduly
favourable, 'that he acquired these privileges not by way of flattery, but
because he was truly honoured; for in most ways he comported himself
towards the Romans as if they were free citizens.'[209]

That there were people who found it trying to be fenced in the
beneficent compulsion is clear from the small but frequent trickle of
conspiracies against him, and from the lack of ease in his family, whose
marriages he organised in a disastrous way. In his Greek and Latin reading
he 'sought for nothing so keenly as precepts and examples of salutary
application to the commonwealth or to individuals,' which he copied
word for word and sent to his captains and provincial governors[210] – a
method to exasperate in any age.

Tragedy of the Façade

As the policy of Augustus developed through the century that followed
him, the appalling fact emerged that Rome as a growing spiritual power

had ceased. 'If a passion for writing carries you away, bravely tell of the feats of Caesar, the unvanquished',[211] Horace had already been advised; and by the time, soon after A.D. 117, when Tacitus, the last of the great Augustan writers, was dead, Seneca, Lucan and Petronius had been forced to suicide and Ovid and Juvenal had suffered exile. What other civilisation, says Peter Green, 'can show such a political casualty rate among writers – till our own times?'[212] The phenomenon, with all that it carried with it, was too frequent to be merely accidental. It was the dark side of the façade.

Towards the end of the first century Juvenal 'saw the Empire as one long continuous process of degeneration. . . . He realised (although perhaps his audience did not), that it would be trivial to satirise only the men and women of his own time. They were end-products of a process which began with the lash of Julius Caesar and the wet sword of Augustus, which ran on through the lunatic Caligula, through Nero and the Civil Wars, to the fiendish emperor of yesterday and perhaps another monster tomorrow. This realisation was one of his chief contributions to satire'[213] which presents the façade with money and want at its root. There is shipwreck everywhere, says Petronius.[214]

In Rome, suicide and servility, a dislike for war among the elegiac poets, a taste – in literature as in the circus – for details of horror, descriptions of disease, decay and death,[215] fill most of the first century of Christ. 'The Roman people use their hands not for defending the constitution but for clapping,' Cicero had already cried long before; and Ovid's mild and futile complaints, punished for an unknown indiscretion and for the *Art of Love*, set the tune for a long litany of lies in the sad squalid volume of his exile.

'What am I saying, madman that I am! Even my very life I deserved to lose by offending the divine will of Caesar!'[216]

To Martial, the Emperor Domitian is the 'blest guardian and saviour of the state', until long-lasting terrors turn to flight and truth is brought back by Trajan and he can say what he thinks.[217]

Seneca writes tragedies forgetful of the Stoics, and lets his feelings through, in their disguise: 'let brother fear brother, father fear son and son father . . . let a murderous wife lift hand against her husband . . . let lust exult triumphant. In this sin-stained house let shameful defilement be a trivial thing; let fraternal sanctity and faith and every right be trampled underfoot.'[218] The family life of the Claudians – Claudius, Britannicus, Agrippa, and every one of Nero's witnessed crimes, is through Seneca a source from which the Elizabethan bombast is directly descended. A horror haunts him, of brutality that 'has reached the farthest limit . . . when cruelty has changed into pleasure and to kill a human being now becomes a joy'.[219] The sad man sits in the theatre with his stoic cloak wrapped round him, none too warm:

'The morning's show was merciful . . . then men were thrown to the lions and bears; but at midday to the audience. There was no escape for them . . . "Kill him, flog him, burn him alive. Why is he such a coward? Why won't he die willingly?" Unhappy that I am, how have I deserved to look at such a scene as this ?'

And when he writes that; 'Though none should teach them the ways of treachery and crime, the throne will teach them',[220] it is not Thyestes he is thinking of, but Nero.

Suicide under the Claudians is not only often imposed, but is also indulged in for its own sake with an eagerness that verges on ostentation. Poenius Postumus, praefect of the IInd legion in Britain, killed himself on hearing of the successes of the XIVth and XXth, having cheated his own legion of a similar renown,[221] and Velleius Paterculus tells how his own grandfather ran himself through with his sword because he was too old and infirm to travel with a friend.[222] One is reminded of Vatel the cook who committed suicide because the fish failed to arrive for Louis XIV's dinner. The excellence of the time was to die well.[223]

A part of the decay may have been encouraged by the oral quality of education which, like the visual today, endangers the written word and cheapens or obliterates its meaning; but a more embracing corruption is required wholly to explain a catastrophe as sudden and complete as the Augustan decline.

'Pindar', writes Peter Green, 'can start from premises of unchallenged validity and, without an effort, make the transition from the *mousikon* that is operative in the present performance to the power of harmony that governs the world. Horace had no such ground to stand upon, and he was fully conscious of it. His poetry, his "music", was not the joint product of an effort of his individuality and of something that was there before he was born, that existed independently of him and had its roots in a supra-normal sphere. . . . In Rome, poetry had no proper standing because the spirit had none. . . . Any poet whose work was unrelated to practical purposes because it was exclusively devoted to the concerns of the mind and heart, saw the fruits of his earnest endeavours classified as play-things.'[224]

This seems to me to reach the heart of the matter (as it also does in much westernising of the East today). The façade of Augustus like many others lacked the universal and elastic element which alone allows of growth: it soon shackled the human mind, and was obliged either to kill or die.

> Zeus the guide who made men turn
> Thought-ward, Zeus who did ordain
> Man by suffering shall learn.
> So the heart of him, again
> Aching with remembered pain,
> Bleeds and sleepeth not, until
> Wisdom comes against his will.[225]

That organ voice had ceased, and Terence too was long silent, who had found his welcome and understanding two hundred years before, in the Rome of the Scipios and their friends. His world was never again to reappear till the Renaissance re-invented the *Commedia dell'Arte*.

In it too there had been cruelty enough – slavery, abduction, torture, infanticide; but it was a liveable world, balanced on decency however precarious, and the courtesan talks like a human being, and the well-brought-up virgin does not have to look at Priapus through her fingers; the perennial husband fears his wife, the slaves run the machinery in Figaro style with no rights but a great deal of humanity, and fathers and sons in particular, in a relationship singularly free from *gravitas*, seem to have felt more genuine affection for each other than in any literary convention before or since.[226]

What happened to bring so sunny a literature to the gloom of Seneca or the bitterness of Petronius?

The doubt and nostalgia can be followed through the Claudian age, from Martial's picture of the farm at Baiae,[227] to Seneca's young friend hovering insecure:

'I do not like a couch made up for display, nor clothing . . . pressed by weights and a thousand mangles to make it glossy, but homely and cheap, that is neither preserved nor to be put on with anxious care; the food that I like is neither prepared nor watched by a household of slaves . . . but is easy to get and abundant; . . . the servant that I like is a young home-born slave without training or skill; the silver is my country-bred father's heavy plate bearing no stamp of the maker's name, and the table is not notable for the variety of its markings or known to the town from the many fashionable owners through whose hands it has passed, but one that stands for use. . . . Then, after all these things have had my full approval, my mind is dazzled by the magnificence of some training-school for pages, by the sight of slaves bedecked with gold . . . and a whole regiment of glittering attendants; by the sight of a house where . . . riches are scattered about in every corner . . . and the whole town pays court and escorts an inheritance on the road to ruin. And what shall I say of the waters, transparent to the bottom, that flow round the guests even as they banquet, what of the feasts that are worthy of their setting? Coming from a long abandonment to thrift, luxury has poured around me. . . . My sight falters a little, for I can lift up my heart towards it more easily than my eyes. And so I come back, not worse, but sadder, and I do not walk among my paltry possessions with head erect as before. . . . None of these things change me, yet none of them fails to disturb me.'[228]

These little voices mingle with Pliny's full-blooded applause or with such happy men as Velleius, whom the Augustan façade chances to fit – who find nothing comparable in any race, age, or rank, to a career such as that of Metellus: 'For, not to mention his surpassing triumphs, the great honours which he held, his supreme position in the state, the length of his life, and the bitter struggles on behalf of the state which he waged with his enemies without damage to his reputation, he reared four sons, saw them all reach man's estate, left them all surviving him and held in the highest honour. These four sons bore the bier of their dead father to its place in front of the rostra; one was an ex-consul and ex-censor, the second ex-consul, the third was actually consul, and the fourth was then a candidate for the consulship . . . which he duly held. This is assuredly not to die, but rather to pass happily out of life.'[229]

Such and so mixed was Rome about A.D. 40 with its old and its new fashions, when the things that these decent army officers wished for, and that other frugal and moderate Italians wished for, had not yet turned into monsters above Augustus' grave. The Rome they represented was departing for ever; the city itself to be washed over, during the next seven centuries, by foreign tides first of the East and finally of the West. One wonders what would have happened to the history of the world if Rome had remained intact at heart? Not until Gregory the Great held the Papacy in the Dark Ages was a clear Italian voice to be heard again: and we have digressed because of the importance of this moment, which Augustus strove so passionately and so vainly to maintain.

He was spared the sight of the change, nor could he see and be comforted by what lay across the centuries – remote and eventual results of his labours. His long life closed in peaceful weariness with its object accomplished, and his cheerfulness is said to have increased as he drew near his end.

VIII

Nero's Armenian Wars

The commercial policy of the Roman East appears along the trade routes of Arabia and of the north. The client system fails in Armenia and is followed, through a dismal attempt at annexation, by a successful but temporary period of friendliness under Nero. To keep trade and intercourse open, with a bridgehead possibility of invasion into Mesopotamia ready but unused, was the frontier policy required, and obtained, through Corbulo's diplomacy. It had no time to take root in the streams of waste and blood that accompanied and followed Nero's death, and a strategy based on the non-aggressive nature of Parthia was too subtle for Rome before Hadrian. Her only other choice was either the holding of the Euphrates, for which she had too few troops, or of Armenia, which was a perpetual threat to the right flank of Parthia. The attempts to carry out this latter policy were the main cause of all her troubles with Parthia throughout the next few hundred years.

> Stet Capitolium
> fulgens triumphatisque possit
> Roma ferox dare iura Medis.
> (Horace: *Odes*, III.3.)[1]

Policy of Peace

At the death of Augustus, the process begun by Pompey was complete, the Mediterranean was a lake and Rome ruled its shores. But its far eastern ingress from Asia was in the hands of Parthia, who could close, open, or charge for the trade as she pleased, and this simple proposition embraces Rome's 'Middle Eastern' policy, peaceful or warlike, for the first few hundred years of the Christian era. It does not dominate the general picture, for it leaves the West – Africa, Gaul, Germany to the Rhine, and Britain later – out of account – the best of the Roman labours and those on which Augustus' heart had been set. Here most of the Italian export flowed,[2] and most of his colonies were planted, and here history rewarded him; and as early as the elder Pliny's day Spain could be considered the most fruitful of the Roman possessions. The western debt can never be counted. But it is out of my picture, and I mention it only so as to set the events now gathering round the Armenian East in their just perspective.

Augustus retrieved Crassus' standards[3] by diplomacy and developed his peaceful policy by necessity – the necessity of an insufficiency of legions. This continued to haunt the immensely long Roman frontier, and the loss of Varus' three[4] in the German forests which so desolated Augustus could never be enduringly made up. After having settled the military legacy of Actium, he left himself with twenty-eight[5] – about 140,000 men altogether – -just sufficient in a world sick of wars; and he established the army, that had become professional ever since the reforms of Marius,[6] on an independently financial basis of its own.[7] Its cost, at the time of the Civil Wars, is estimated at about a million denarii a year per legion,[8] and (apart from the independent levies of the kings[9]), it was composed of Roman citizen infantry and of auxiliaries – chiefly cavalry, archers and slingers – foreign or allied. The infantry (legionaries) had to be not only landowners, which led peasants to sell their small holdings so as to remain free of conscription,[10] but also citizens. Augustus twice overlooked this rule after disasters in Pannonia and Germany,[11] and a way to obtain local troops was found for eastern armies in particular by granting citizenship separately to individuals.[12] After Hadrian, the political difference between legionaries and auxilia gradually disappeared, though the basic problem remained as it must ever remain – of how to make other people fight without letting them snatch at the prize. This utopian objective was never securely reached.

Apart from the dearth of legions, Augustus was driven by circumstance and his own temper towards a policy opposite to that of Antony, and above all towards a period of peace. Peace 'was, so to say, an indispensable condition of the permanence of his power'.[13] His gentle method was successful: he relied on diplomacy with Parthia, fortified by the fact that the son of the Parthian king had fallen into his hands[14]; Rome celebrated the return of Crassus' standards with pride and joy; the trade route functioned amicably through three succeeding reigns; and Augustus' young grandson, Gaius Caesar, picnicked on the banks of the Euphrates: 'On an island in the Euphrates, with an equal retinue on each side, Gaius had a meeting with the king of the Parthians, a young man of distinguished appearance. This spectacle of the Roman army arrayed on the one side, the Parthian on the other, while these two eminent leaders not only of the empires they represented but also of mankind thus met in conference, it was my fortunate lot early in my career as a soldier', says Velleius, 'to see. . . . As for the meeting, first the Parthian dined with Gaius upon the Roman bank, and later Gaius supped with the king on the soil of the enemy.'[15]

It was a makeshift solution, and its pragmatic character soon appeared when Augustus sent an expedition to Arabia. This too was probably pragmatic – no deeply aiming policy, but a natural interest in the port dues of Egypt and the customs of the Arabian spice trade, interests which could easily encourage isolated ventures apart from the main objectives of an age. Historians are constantly trying to discipline deviations which a glance at the accidental character of politics makes plain. Without, therefore, imputing a 'commercial policy' to Augutus, one may suppose that he was interested in securing a trade terminus on which a twenty-five per cent duty was soon to be placed by his successor,[16] just as his further measures in the Black Sea also showed a commercial interest beyond mere defence, at the other free end of the Parthian caravan route, in the north. Before his day both Julius Caesar and Gaius Gracchus, without being very mercantile, had planned the colonising of harbour towns to produce an income[17]: this was not commerce so much as the good estate management ingrained in the Roman character, and Augustus – the bankers' grandson who so definitely did what he could for the depleted

THE LION OF COMMAGENE ON NIMRUD DAGH

LANDSCAPE OF CORBULO'S MARCH:

HOSHAB ON THE PERSIAN BORDER

THE MURAD SU (E. EUPHRATES) SOUTH OF MUSH

reserves of Asia – was naturally concerned in the rapidly increasing revenue of Egypt[18] which was his own estate. On the Red Sea frontier of the Nabataeans, at Leuke Kome, where Antony had met Cleopatra on his return from Armenia, a centurion is soon mentioned as a collector of dues on imported merchandise from the small Arabian vessels of the south.[19]

The Arabian Expedition

The Arabian expedition is only indirectly in our range, though alluring as the first western venture into the lands of Sheba. It was an effort to break a monopoly which the Arabs of the south jealously guarded, allowing no western ships along the eastern Red Sea coast. Even the origin of valuable spices like cardamom, or of the famous steel that drifted from Merv along the caravan route to Parthia, were kept secret through the first century A.D., and western merchants never themselves gathered the products of India, Arabia or Africa.[20] The Arabs lifted them at Aden and carried them north to Petra by camel caravan, and the Ptolemies knew little about this trade until an interest in elephants under Ptolemy II (285–247 B.C.) brought them to the opposite African coast and made them organise regular transport from Berenice to Coptos (Koft) on the Nile, and thence to the elephant park at Memphis.

This led to a Red Sea fleet against pirates; and in the course of two centuries elephants were neglected in favour of Indian goods and Arabian spices, which a growing Italian demand began to make ever more lucrative. There is an Indian dedication on a temple to Pan beside the Egyptian desert road at Redesiya[21]; and, about 120–117 B.C., an Indian sailor, found half drowned on a beach, guided exploration into the southern Ocean which no one before had entered 'except against his will'.[22]

There were Indian traders in Somaliland and Alexandria under Cleopatra; if her stars had helped her, her dream of a Red Sea empire could have been sober fact; and after her death, in the first century A.D., when other routes were impeded by the Parthian wars,[23] the discovery of the south-west monsoon enabled ships to reach India in the height of their prosperity.[24] The first voyages were made under the Romans, touching South Arabia and Socotra and presently sailing from

Aden direct, and the Emperor Vespasian was the first person to dedicate chaplets of cinnamon in the temples of the Capitol and of Peace. Livia consecrated a cinnamon root in a golden bowl to the memory of Augustus, 'out of which drops used to distil every year which hardened into grains'.[25]

Maritime traffic, once run by the royal Ptolemies, was now owned privately by Greeks[26] with Roman capital, and run almost entirely by Arabs in cargo boats of two or three hundred tons that 'carried seven sails'; while the Nabataeans, from their clearing house at Petra, held a strangle-hold over the camel caravans by land. It was through their territory, in the hope 'either to deal with wealthy friends or to master wealthy enemies',[27] that Aelius Gallus, Augustus' praefect in Egypt in 24 B.C., led his troops into the deserts of Sheba, though he would have done better to sail to one of the more southern roadsteads like Mocha, that even now export a trickle of coffee, as once they sent spices, to the West.

Mocha is one of the few places where I have had anxious moments during a journey in Arabia, shut up for a night with its Yemeni governor in a rough fortified tower on a gaunt shore. His family were away in the heat of summer and I rested in a bed with satin quilts in a stone-walled room, from whose small windows little could be seen but a few palm-leaf hovels and half a dozen slaves and guardsmen talking in the light of a lantern far below. As I lay there in the middle of the night, I heard the latch lifting and saw the governor returning and felt trapped, for there was no escape through the inner darkness of the tower: but I pretended to sleep, deciding to slip to the window if things got difficult and disgrace him by calling to his guards; and lay, breathing peacefully, as I hoped, with my eyes shut, while a feeble torch was turned upon me, and a heavy object presently deposited close to my cheek. Shambling around, and evidently debating whether to awaken me, the governor presently departed, while before I dared open my eyes a whirring sound beside me on the pillow produced a thin metallic melody – a musical box of all the unexpected! – an incongruous little descendant of luxuries that travelled for centuries along the Arabian harshness of this road.

Aelius Gallus failed, but extricated his army after many months of near disaster, through one of the most stubborn desert marches in history:

and the Indian trade with Rome developed independently, encouraged by a hold-up on the Chinese land-route at this time.[28] Lighthouses were built along the coast in Pondicherry,[29] and many embassies came to Augustus, and one to Claudius from Ceylon. A Tamil poet speaks of Greek (Yavana) ships bringing gold and taking away pepper,[30] and describes the stern looks of the Greek mercenaries who guarded the commander's tent.[31] The Roman customs on the Red Sea, at Berenice and Leuke Kome, were probably taken over from the Ptolemies; a temple to Augustus appeared in Mysore.[32] The Roman hour was adopted; Greek pots reached Pondicherry; Roman coins are found here and there; and the activity of the Alexandrian mint became so marked that it has been held to reflect the discovery of the monsoons, since it was probably due to a sudden expansion of the Indian trade.[33] In the age of Nero larger ships were needed for the transport of cinnamon[34]; Vespasian converted his great arcade into a spice market[35]; and in the middle of the first century an Italian community is quoted as established in Petra. Yet the Romans, ever shy of deserts and the more so after their expedition's failure, were forced to continue to pay the high prices of the Nabataean caravans with a balance heavily against them: the Indian and Arabian trade sold a million pounds a year or more, according to Pliny, at a hundred times its original cost.[36] The *parvenu* Nabataean tombs of Petra were built out of the Imperial deficit, though the southern route, whether by sea or land, was never a substitute for the main route of Asia.[37]

The Black Sea

Augustus had declared that the Empire's frontiers were not to be exceeded, and was probably unaware of how his own annexations[38] in the Black Sea and the north were to prepare the long Armenian tangle. For there was no threat to Rome, until the mere crossing of Euphrates menaced both the southern and the eastern lands of Parthia, and was bound to produce a war.

Antony, when the attack on Armenia was in his mind, had given a precedent of annexation[39]; but his *defensive* measures had soon shown themselves to consist in a ring of client kingdoms[40] – a policy which Augustus followed at first, but was gradually forced to abandon because it failed: the client kings one after the other were pushed out or died.

The Black Sea kingdom failed in the emptiness left by Mithradates, and the kingdom of Cappadocia only survived to fall into disgrace under Tiberius and become a province like the rest. Augustus gradually merged any principality that fell vacant into the province of Galatia, and Tiberius continued the process in eastern and south-eastern Asia Minor, until all save eastern Pontus and Cilicia Aspera had become provincial territory of Rome.[41]

The South Russian steppes had long been producers of corn for the ancient world, and as the Roman armies began to move towards the Black Sea shores, the corn of the Bosporan kingdom became ever more necessary to feed them.

The landowners there with their families and their armed retinues would leave the cities in springtime in heavy four-wheeled carts or on horseback, and settle in tents on their fields to supervise and tend their flocks and their harvests. In the autumn they returned to their houses in the city; the corn was shipped, and the Bosporan king received an annual subsidy from the governor on the opposite coast of Bithynia. The great Bosporan merchants supplied the ships.[42]

But there was now no longer a Pontic king on the frontier of the Parthian power strong enough to hold both shores and guide the trade towards Aegean harbours, for ever since his death a substitute for Mithradates had been sought for and not found. His shade must have been satisfied. The attachment to his dynasty survived through his granddaughter Dynamis,[43] who married one after the other four of the Bosporan rulers and ended at the age of seventy as the friend and ally of Rome. Little is known about her, except that she was the deciding factor in the people's acceptance of a king – and seems indeed to have kept the sovereign power in her hands. Her third husband, Polemon, the son of an orator of Laodiceia, had followed Mark Antony's fortunes and then made his peace with Augustus, and had been made king of Pontus; and Augustus sent him to marry Dynamis and unite the two kingdoms across the sea. He lasted for a year, then married another remarkable matriarch, Pythadoris,[44] a grand-daughter of Antony's; and Dynamis fled to find a fourth husband among the Sarmatians, while Polemon was captured and killed. The line of Mithradates was too strong, even for Augustus, and Dynamis was left, reinstated in her fierce and vulnerable land, with Pontus and Bosporus still divided.

Ovid, too old at the age of fifty to adapt himself to his exile, describes this northern world and its Grecian cities,[45] where 'the guard on the wall and a closed gate keep back the hostile Getae'.[46]

'Across the new bridge [of ice], above the gliding current, the carts of the barbarians are drawn by Sarmatian oxen. . . .[47] Greater hordes of Sarmatae and Getae go and come upon their horses along the roads. Among them there is not one who does not bear quiver and bow and darts yellow with viper's gall. Harsh voices, grim countenances, veritable pictures of Mars, neither hair nor beard trimmed by any hand . . . the knife which every barbarian wears fastened to his side. . . .[48] Without, nothing is secure: the hill itself is defended by meagre walls and by its skilful site. When least expected, like birds, the foe swarms upon us and when scarce well seen is already driving off the booty. Often within the walls when the gates are closed, we gather daily missiles in the midst of the streets. Rare then is he who ventures to till the fields, for the wretch must plough with one hand and hold arms in the other. The shepherd wears a helmet while he plays upon his pitch-cemented reeds. . . . Scarce with the fortress's aid are we defended; and even within it the barbarous mob mingled with the Greeks inspires fear. For with us dwell without distinction the barbarians, occupying more than half the dwellings . . . .'[49] Poor Ovid! dreaming of Rome: 'At times I have memories of you, my pleasant friends, at times thoughts of my daughter and my dear wife . . . and from my own house I am once again visiting the beautiful town, my mind surveying everything with eyes of its own. Now the fora, now the temples, now the theatres sheathed in marble, now every portico with its levelled ground comes before me, now the greensward of the Campus that looks towards the lovely garden, the pools, the canals, and the water of the Virgo. . . .[50] You will scarcely find in the whole world, I assure you, a land that enjoys so little as this the Augustan peace.'

Agrippa was responsible for the Black Sea as governor of Asia, and the honours decreed him attest the importance of the Bosporan kingdom. It continued to be held faithfully by Dynamis' Sarmatian widower, who left two sons and his second wife (also a Sarmatian) to keep it, in spite of another frustrated Roman effort to annex it to Pontus again under Polemon and Pythadoris' son.[51] The Sarmatian widow's stepson, Mithradates, tried to free himself from Rome and failed, but the nominal independence of the kingdom continued. By Nero's reign, the idea of a northern trade route beyond the reach of the Parthians had taken shape.

The strength of the great Mithradates had been based on four factors: on the wealth of the Pontic trade – his yearly tribute from south Russia was estimated at 200 talents and 270,000 bushels of grain[52]; on the mines; on the forests and rivers of the south-east Black Sea corner that gave him his timber for shipping; and on the inexhaustible supply of cavalry from the north, to obtain which 'an indefinite right of expansion north eastward'[53] was granted to Polemon by Augustus. But the unforgiving minute had gone by: none of the western kingdoms were strong enough in themselves or sufficiently buttressed by Rome to make an effective bulwark, and if they had shewn any sign of being so they would promptly have been suppressed.

'Except in a few instances he [Augustus] restored these kingdoms . . . to those from whom he had taken them. . . . He also united the kings with whom he was in alliance by mutual ties, and was very ready to propose or favour inter-marriages or friendships among them. He never failed to treat them all . . . as integral parts of the empire, regularly appointing a guardian for such as were too young to rule or whose minds were affected until they grew up or recovered: and he brought up the children of many of them . . . with his own.'[54] Yet Galatia was annexed in 25, and Paphlagonia in 6 B.C.; and in A.D. 18 Tiberius, seizing Cappadocia and Commagene, was carrying on the Augustan policy of absorption. 'Vassal status was by its very nature transitional',[55] and the little thrones must have felt permanently insecure.

Commagene

When Cappadocia was incorporated, it enriched Tiberius sufficiently to enable him to reduce an unpopular purchase tax in Rome by half.[56] Its mines of onyx, crystal and mica, its salt and cinnabar and silver and royal domains, were taken over as a third-class province and governed by a knight.

Commagene, its neighbour in the south, commanding the two Euphrates crossings of Zeugma and Samosata, was annexed for strategic as well as financial reasons.[57] It had been independent for about two hundred years under a long line of princes and kept its freedom after

Actium, and Caligula reinstated it in 37 A.D. under Antiochus IV, the legitimate heir and his friend.

The first of this branch of the Seleucids had welcomed Lucullus and Pompey when they came to Asia. He was buried on the highest of the little kingdom's mountains, remote enough but well known now as Nimrud Dagh, since its monuments are published,[58] a four hours' ride from the tiny hamlet of Eski Kiahta, under hellenistic Arsameia. A later castle and an inscription left by a son of Saladin's[59] stand half way down the rock of its ancient acropolis. We arrived here one night in a jeep, thankful after the Euphrates valley for cooler air and less dusty stars, and rode the four hours next day by small paths up steep hills until we reached a wide terrace on either side of a tumulus of stones, where Antiochus and his Gods sat with stone eagles and lions and their altar before them — vast portraits in the Iranian manner, with a faint Grecian flavour and Greek inscriptions on their backs. Their heads — all except that of the garlanded Fortune of Commagene — have fallen and lie scattered but entire, showing a singular and pure oriental beauty in the young and peaceful features of the king. Almost the whole of his country lies in sight below him — a lark's horizon that encircles the roundness of the world. The villages disappear, built out of the earth that bears them, and patches of forest show blurred among the pencil lines of rock: blue in the west are the wild hills of Melitene, and fair and majestic in the south-east the scimitar curve of Euphrates from his gorges, breaking in faint white cliffs to Samosata, where Lucian, 'still a barbarian in language', was born. There the Parthian lands come down and the Parthians took refuge when Pacorus their king's son was defeated, and there a later Antiochus bought off Antony's besieging general, and possibly Antony as well. The Roman record in Commagene was not too good, and a small buffer state kept in with both sides if it could. The wide cornlands with Kiahta stream meandering through them swept like an avenue to feed the garrisons of Samosata, and are still crossed by the bridge and the road rebuilt by Severus. Birejik and the Zeugma crossing are beyond, invaded by desert dust out of sight; and high in the north and north-east the rounded shoulders of Taurus hide Euphrates, the abrupt southern defence of Melitene.

From this point, says Pliny, the river formed the frontier of Commagene and carried a bridge even where it forced its passage through the Taurus; 'And there for the first time in this combat Mount Taurus carries the stream out of its course, and, though . . . cleft in twain, gains the victory by . . . forcing it to take a southerly direction. Thus this duel of nature becomes a drawn battle, the river reaching the goal of its choice but the mountain preventing it from reaching it by the course of its choice. After passing the cataracts the stream is again navigable; and forty miles [downstream] from this point is Samosata the capital of Commagene.'[60]

I rode here for an August week with two godsons, taking mules near the castle of Gerger above Samosata and following the river by hamlets perched in the cliffs where the steep slopes join. They were so poor that eggs were often unobtainable, though we found the flat bread that Pliny mentions as Parthian,[61] and twisted ropes of hay for our animals. The villagers let us sleep on their round threshing floors of battered earth, surrounded like small Druid circles with stones. No wide track can ever have clung to these shelves, and we found no ancient building except a ruin, as it seemed to me, of a hellenistic watch-tower at Deraso, where a ferry towards the Dyarbekr road probably existed then as it does today. The path's uncertain corners, polished by the feet of mules, were nearly always high above the river, dominating the snaky backbone of its current as it threaded the descending ridges. Its company enlivened us, and the landscape seemed dead when we drew away from it, and in the silence of noon or in the night it filled the solitude with the majestic voice of its wandering, and, as we climbed towards the north, brought us the growl of rapids in its gorges, muted to their summer lowness through the moonlit air. The mountains steep as walls on the eastern shore became familiar but unattainable, and become even more so when floods rise in spring to the height of houses, melted from the snow that has imprisoned these unmapped villages for five months of their year. There are said to be one hundred and fifty rapids in three hundred kilometres below Melitene, and no one so far as I know has risked them except Huntingdon and Norton,[62] and Von Moltke, who, as a young and attractive Prussian officer seconded to Turkey, shot them twice on a raft at the risk of his life.[63]

We left the river where its sharp bend to the west occurs, came to flat cultivation at Thilo, and were given a bath in extremely cold water and a roof to sleep on, and an excellent dinner in the house of a sheikh. A government official and a policeman ran the whole wide roadless area, and became very friendly – and so did the women of the house. They asked my name, to give to a grand-daughter just born: and when the official guests had gone, brought her up, pinned over with amulets and swathed in bands, and laid the warm little bundle in my lap, breathing with tiny jerks in the moonlight. It makes a bond with a place so far away. From Thilo in two days we crossed Soguk Dagh, the height of this Anatolian Taurus, treeless and naked and dangerous as it happened, for we met a storm that blew our muleteers thrice off the path; and were glad to descend to a little town called Pötürghé among running waters, with what looked like the foundations of a Roman camp beside it – and so by the Byzantine ruined fortress of Claudiopolis (Kerer in the Siraj valley) by jeep to Melitene.

Castles that go back to Assyrian[64] or Urartian history[65] hold the Euphrates' openings all along its fiercer stretches; and there must have been a track, but never an easy one, from one guardhouse to another along the river bank.[66] The main military road went from Samosata to Melitene through Perre, which is near modern Adyaman. But where the columned bridge of Kiahta led to – which Ibn Haukal called a world wonder with its Roman inscription and which is used to this day – is a mystery, for it seems too imposing to be merely a short cut to the Euphrates, as it appears in Calder's maps, unless it led perhaps by an important ferry to Severek on the Dyarbekr road. Its westerly objective must eventually have been Melitene.

Under Nero, who planned an offensive war, the whole policy of this river front was tightened.

East of Euphrates, the little district of Sophene.[67] and west of it Lesser Armenia were prepared by being entrusted to new and foreign kings. In A.D. 64–5 western Pontus was added to Galatia, annexed by Augustus in 25 B.C. as we have seen:[68] this brought the whole Pontic sea coast to beyond Trebizond under Roman control. Rome took over the suppression of the pirates – who continued to be notorious there – with a royal squadron which grew in a few years to a fleet of forty ships stationed at Trebizond; she was now up against her Parthian-Armenian problem from the Black Sea to the Euphrates, and from north of Erzinjan to Syria.

The Frontier Policy

Two peaceful solutions were possible: an alliance with a strong Pontic power, such as that of Mithradates which had been destroyed; or a simple holding of the line of the Euphrates, relying on the unaggressive nature of the Parthians, which had been the first, partially carried out policy of Augustus.[69] Both were consciously or unconsciously dependent on the basic frontier safeguard, that consumers and producers are equally important if there is to be any traffic at all across a border – a mercantile concept beyond the Roman horizon, but which had worked for centuries with the Black Sea trade and the Greeks.

The Parthians, without a regular standing army or commissariat or siege trains, were incapable of a long aggressive war, 'both because they encounter an entirely different condition of land and sky and because they do not lay in supplies of food or pay'.[70] Augustus had been aware of this, or he could not have relied on holding the whole Anatolian front from Syria only, where four inadequate legions were stationed: as soon as war was imminent, the impossibility of his arrangement had become apparent. The defence of the frontier was then assumed to have two alternatives only – either a strong military command in Cappadocia (behind the gap of Melitene), or the establishment of Armenia as a buffer against Parthia in the north. The latter was the policy chosen. A third alternative was never formulated, but was put into practice under Nero, as in 1914 by the French and German armies when each tried to break through on its own right flank: the Parthians and Romans could play this game, the Parthians through Armenia into Cappadocia, the Romans across the bridge to Babylonia: with fairly balanced forces such a deterrent, threatening invasion, is usually strong enough to operate: it was not only tried, but showed itself repeatedly successful under Nero.

*   *   *

Augustus had always been pleased to manage the family affairs of others. There is a touching entry in the *Res Gestae* describing the various kings who took refuge with him, such as Phraates 'seeking out friendship by means of his own children as pledges ... and a large number of other nations experienced the good faith of the Roman people ... '.[71]

Genuinely convinced that he could run the private lives of family and Empire, he met the disappointments incidental to this belief.

It was he who had chosen the policy of the Armenian buffer state and, feeling that Parthia could wait, tackled the wooing of a friendly neighbour with zest. Little he knew that the whole weight of history was unable to make Iranian and Mediterranean coalesce. In the intricacy of events, the basic Iranian quality of the Armenian civilisation soon appeared. It was spreading, not in Armenia only but in Pontus, Cappadocia and Commagene, on the west bank which had long been far more hellenised than the east; for two hundred years already it had been assumed that the ruler of Armenia was to be a Parthian and a brother of the Parthian king.

A pretender from east of Euphrates had been sheltered shortly after Actium, by Augustus, who at the same time had welcomed the envoys of the legitimate ruler and released the Parthian king's son, his prisoner. After a certain amount of diplomatic pressure he got the Crassus standards in exchange. With this prestige the patriot poets were satisfied, Tiberius was sent to crown a Roman nominee in Armenia, and the king of Parthia lent four princes, his sons, to live in Rome. Hostages from Parthia had soon become familiar sights, seated in the theatre or driven by Caligula in his chariot; and Pliny collecting miscellaneous snippets, noticed how the Parthian upper classes 'smell from too much wine' and add lemon pips to their drink as a cure.[72]

The frequency of the royal Armenian nominees makes one agree that there are too many duplicates in the human race. The first one soon died, his anti-Roman son was elected and evicted, and the next reign, supported by Roman troops and ended by the Parthians, was short. Their own candidate finally closed the deadlock by himself accepting Roman suzerainty; and the Parthian king, with an Italian mother known as the Goddess Musa, came to terms. It was on this occasion that the meeting had taken place on the island of Euphrates, as Velleius Paterculus describes it.

Murders, and an astonishing number of natural deaths continued to make Armenia difficult, and soon disturbed the precarious royal family lives of Parthia too. Vonones, one of the hostage princes, sent from Rome to be crowned, was spewed out of Mesopotamia, turned out of Armenia also, and allowed to live as a refugee on his own riches in Antioch. Only Zeno, the son of Polemon and of the excellent Pythodoris, who had brought him up to the country life of Pontus so that he endeared himself to his sporting subjects, broke the Armenian record by ruling for sixteen years. By the end of Augustus' reign the folly of the policy seemed clear in spite of this brief success, for at Zeno's death trouble started with another Parthian, and the youngest of the four hostages was sent from Rome to supplant him. There was war everywhere in Armenia; savage Iberians of the Caucasus fought Albanians, Sarmatians and Parthians on its soil. The governor of Syria now showed the possibilities of the 'threatened invasion' policy by spreading a rumour that he was about to cross into Mesopotamia, and the Parthians were withdrawn from the north.

In the middle of the century, under Claudius, Rome again threatened a Mesopotamian invasion, and again the Parthians were kept safely in the south: it was obvious that with the Zeugma bridgehead in hand there was indeed no need to occupy Armenia at all. Events there continued to give trouble: the brother of the Roman nominee was handed to his enemies by a venal garrison commander and his murderer crowned in the presence of the procurator of Cappadocia; and Vologaeses of Parthia, who happened to be a particularly energetic king with a Greek mother, seeing his chance, marched up from the south to place his own brother Tiridates on the polluted throne. After two more years of revolution, the news of Armenia's successful re-occupation by the Parthians reached Rome just after Nero's accession.

Seneca and Nero

Nero at seventeen was steered in friendly partnership by his praetorian prefect Burrus and by Seneca, and it can never be accurately known how far the responsibility for the break with Augustan policy in the east was divided between them. Its first definition was a letter from Corbulo to Tiridates in A.D. 55 when the two advisers were in power, but its application was postponed till after Burrus' death in 62 and Seneca's retirement, and must have been carried through by Nero alone, who was often conscientious in his attention to affairs.[73]

He too, like Augustus, is no easy figure to interpret – a not vicious, not even originally cruel, human child wrecked by circumstance and power. His mother Agrippina must answer for a good deal in him along with her other crimes: the facet that perhaps the haunted Seneca saw, 'shedding blood on land and sea'.[74] Seneca himself had a philosophy that, in practice if not in theory, amounted to prostration in the House of Rimmon,[75] and must have helped in perversion. 'Wicked we are,' he thought, to begin with, 'wicked we have been, and always shall be,'[76] and never hesitated in subduing the means to the end: 'If the state is too corrupt . . . if it is wholly dominated by evils, the wise man will not struggle to no purpose[77] . . . if some necessary business summons him he will . . . placate . . . and not deem it improper to pay something . . . remembering that even on some bridges one has to pay to cross.'[78] In Nero's young formative years he was building up 300 million sesterces[79] largely by usury, and happy enough with 'ampler material for displaying his powers, since in poverty there is room for only one kind of virtue – not to be bowed down and crushed by it – while in riches, moderation and liberality and diligence and orderliness and grandeur all have a wide field. The wise man will not despise himself if he has the stature of a dwarf, but nevertheless he will wish to be tall.'[80]

Seneca lived up to his detachment and could say to his critics that riches 'if they slip away, will take from me nothing but themselves'.[81] He was never heard to regret them when they went, and his generosity was as strong as his courage. He fulfilled 'all that the very constitution of the universe obliges us to suffer . . . the sacred obligation . . . to submit to the human lot'. It is true, but it was probably not so evident nor, in itself, inspiring to a young autocrat with an artistic temperament whose tutor – let us face it – was almost as much of an exhibitionist as himself and far more selfconsciously efficient in his death.

Seneca could write lies with the best, and showed it in the abjectness of flattery to Claudius, but he believed in Nero's state unstained by blood.[82] 'It is the rarest praise, hitherto denied to all other princes, that you have coveted for yourself – innocence of wrong . . . and today your subjects . . . confess that they are happy, and that nothing further can be added to their blessings, except that these may last.' It must have read strangely very soon.[83]

Nero was eighteen at that time and the happiness that Seneca contemplated was Seneca's own doing. 'If peace fills all the earth', he wrote: 'if no cities groan and no man stains with sin his altar fires; if crimes have ceased, admit this soul, I pray thee, to the stars.'[84] He is, one prays and hopes, admitted and there was nothing ignoble; yet he dealt in dark colours: his world was like a city just stormed, in which all regard for decency and right had been abandoned,[85] and the post that Nature assigned was the post of a hero.[86] Pity to him was a weakness of the mind overmuch perturbed by suffering, like requiring a wise man to moan at the funerals of strangers.[87] The kindly hope of service, the help that the highest in the land stands in need of[88] – these hopes ebb. Bitter misfortune becomes the price that a king's friends pay when, in his terrible description of anger, 'oft-repeated indulgence and surfeit passes at last into cruelty, and so these men laugh and rejoice, and wear a countenance utterly unlike that of anger, making a pastime of ferocity'.[89] All this he knew well.

In this net of sorrow and fate Seneca struggled, and had nothing but his stoic virtue to support him, 'which needs no gift from chance'[90] in a world where indeed a gift of grace was sadly needed. For himself he did well, and died satisfied, with a public dignity which poor Nero might have envied, trembling and unable to press the dagger home. Him no Seneca or stoic could help. For him the façade was too much, and like Caligula before, and Domitian and Commodus and Caracalla after, he stepped onto his throne too young. Yet his legend was to be remembered with affection, particularly in the East where family murders count less, and his grave was to be visited with flowers. A personal magic that can deal with the Orient seems not to have been lacking in him, and his brief interlude with Parthia gained more influence than all the military triumphs of the succeeding reigns.

Corbulo and the Policy of Annexation

Meanwhile, at the beginning of the reign, with Seneca advising, Armenia was to be treated firmly, not without a possibility of compromise at the end. Gnaeus Domitius Corbulo, the best Roman general, was sent there, with a reputation made in Germany seven years before. There the legions, 'lethargic in their toils and duties as they were ardent in pillage',[91] had been toughened by him with the utmost discipline, until Claudius so firmly forbade fresh aggression that he ordered the garrisons to be withdrawn to the west bank of the Rhine. 'Happy the Roman generals before my time',[92] said Corbulo, and after retreating to the digging of canals and a triumph, was kept kicking his heels in

Rome as a senator for the next seven years. The only notices of him are a tussle with road contractors unsupported by Claudius – who evidently suspected or disliked him – and an utterance in the senate when he compared a fellow senator to a plucked ostrich, and reduced him to tears.[93] His reputation remained, and Tacitus remarks that 'apart from the routine of sycophancy, there was genuine pleasure in the senate at Nero's appointment of Domitius Corbulo . . . this gigantic and grandiloquent soldier . . . to save Armenia: a measure which seemed to have opened a career to the virtues'.[94]

Orders were given to move recruits up to the eastern legions and the legions themselves were stationed closer to the border; two surviving independent kings prepared to cross into Parthia and pontoons were built for the Euphrates. The Parthians were having trouble with their original kinsmen in Hyrcania with whom Rome contemplated an alliance (a chance which was never repeated), and in the nick of time a rival to the Parthian king appeared in the person of his son: the king, with the threat of trouble at home, evacuated Armenia.[95] The danger of an invasion in the south had cleared the north again.

The war gained momentum slowly.

Corbulo had been given half the Syrian legions, and they came from their easy quarters unprepared. Syria had no rugged camps like the north. Thickly populated behind a curtain of desert, its soldiers and its inhabitants lived side by side[96] in camp and city, among gardens famous for their vegetables,[97] whence the legionaries looked on ramparts and fosse as novel and curious objects.[98] A very few years later they rallied to Vespasian when a rumour of removal reached them from his rival, for there was nothing that angered the province and the army so much as the idea of a transfer from Germany to Syria and from Syria to the climate and labours of Germany.[99] Stationed no farther east than Antioch or Cyrrhus, they saw the desert and the mountain world with equally unaccustomed eyes, and Corbulo, when they reached him, hastily applied for reinforcements. He obtained a legion with auxiliaries from Germany, whose hardships he shared, and proved the excellence of his severity by experience, 'the camp showing fewer cases of desertion than those in which pardons were the rule'.[100]

*   *   *

Kinnear, in the nineteenth century, regarded it as impossible to make war in any part of western Armenia during four or five months of the year[101]; and the Hon. Robert Curzon, carried sick in a winter litter to Trebizond, remarks that 'at this moment the greater part of the artillery of the Turkish army is, I believe, buried under the snow in one of the ravines between Baiburt and Erzerum, whence it has no chance of being rescued till next summer'.[102]

When the snow melted off dead travellers, the villagers went to bury them at the passes[103] (as they still do in the Hakkiari south of Van), and Kinnear in 1813 found five villages near the Mysian Olympus 'exempt from taxes because obliged to see that no traveller dies in the snow'.[104] 'Hunger and fatigue were, and ever will be,' the guardians of these marches.[105]

Today, whenever there is a crisis, it is towards the desolate eastern region that one sees the young Turkish lads devotedly entraining, in a climate where spring lasts for a fortnight only,[106] and beards are frozen, and camels covered with icicles,[107] and partridges are caught in winter before the sun rises to thaw their wings.[108] 'The weather', says Curzon, 'may as a general rule be considered as on the way from bad to worse.'[109]

In the tenth century a Turkish army and all its prisoners and booty were drowned in the broken ice of the eastern Euphrates,[110] and towards these sources, after two and a half years' training in the already rigid climate of Melitene, Corbulo led his subdued but, one hopes, inspirited soldiers to winter in camp, probably in the neighbourhood of the later Erzerum, at an altitude of six thousand feet above the sea. They were all excellent now, selected from his half of the Syrian garrison and added to by recruits from Galatia and Cappadocia, where the best Roman asiatic troops were to be found.[111]

In the spring of A.D. 58 they marched on Artaxata, trying to pin the Parthian Tiridates[112] to a battle which he wisely avoided. He vanished into inhospitable spaces from under the walls of the surrendering town.

Corbulo had no garrison to spare, so he burnt and left the town, and marched south, to attack Tigranocerta, meeting no one on his way except the Mardian Kurds on their seasonal move between pastures. He had left his communications behind him, and found, with relief, that the harvests were ripening as he came into (probably) the lands of Mush.

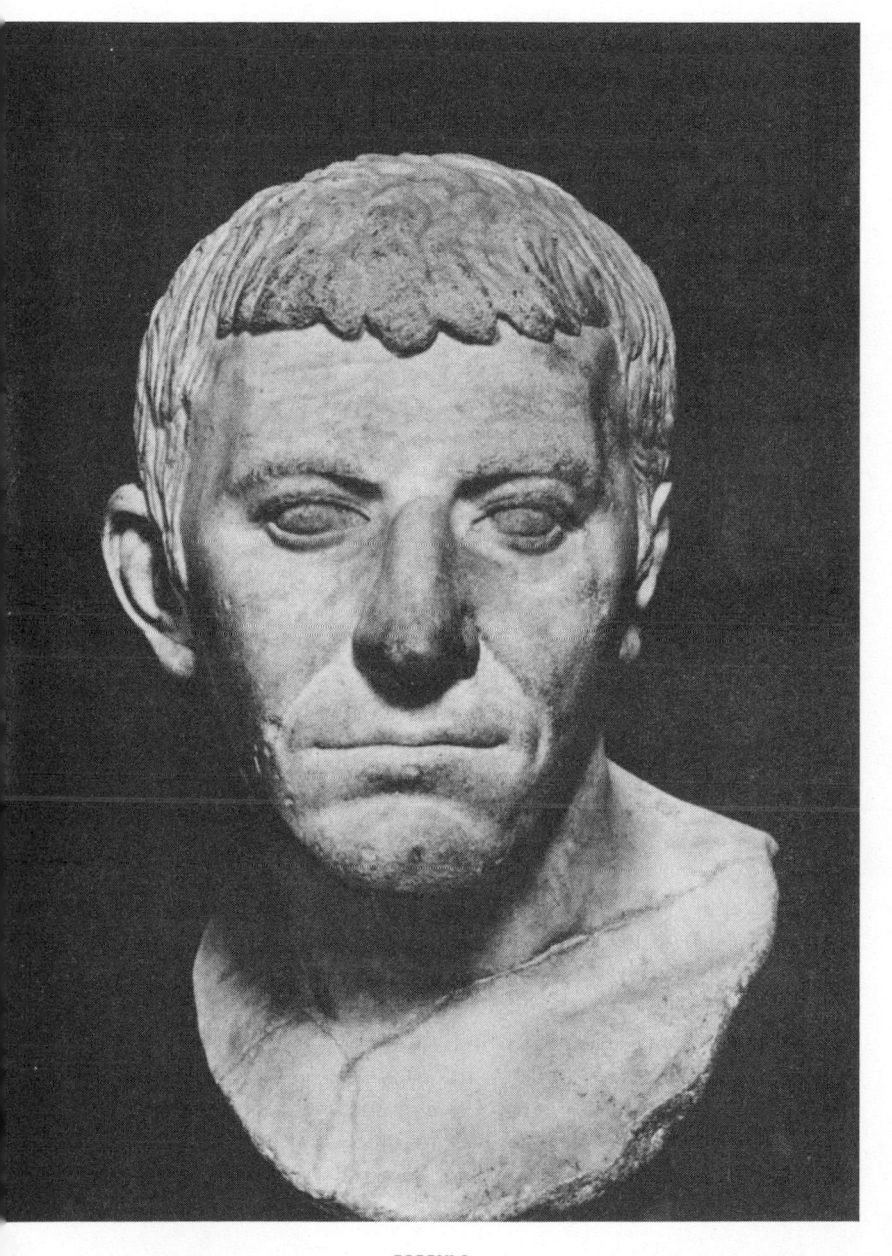

CORBULO

THE RIDGE OF TAURUS SOUTH OF MALATYA (MELITENE)

THE UPLANDS OF ANATOLIA

The Armenian frontier here wandered through a labyrinth of valleys, safe only behind some breastwork where a castle looked down on the caravans, and there is a good deal of vagueness both for the dates and the geography of this campaign: I follow Dilleman's 'itinéraire normal entre Artaxata et la grande Sophène par le défilé du Qoulp'[113] – Kulp, the charming country into whose remote and intricate recesses Tigranes had marched and Lucullus had pursued.

Somewhere on the route, envoys from Tigranocerta met the Roman army with a golden crown, and Corbulo entered the southern capital peacefully, but stormed the pleasant little town of Ilidja or Lije (Legerda)[114] which holds the most westerly and easiest pass between north and south: the remains of a wall barricading the valley can still be seen, below a secondary Tigris source which the Assyrians celebrated with inscriptions.[115]

Tiridates made another attempt and failed, and peace was in sight when a new Armenian king came out from Rome, 'reduced to docility by his long residence as a hostage.'[116] Docile or no, that is to say with or without the knowledge of Rome, he soon attacked the neighbouring subject-kings of Adiabene (Azerbaijan) across the Tigris, and started the war again.

*   *   *

The adjective *implacable* has been applied to the Parthians ever since the days of the Augustan poets, yet their moderation is witnessed by Roman historians and by all the evidence we have. 'The Parthian king', says Tacitus, 'apprised of Corbulo's feats . . . and anxious . . . to avenge the slur cast upon the Arsacian line by the expulsion of his brother Tiridates, was drawn . . . to different lines of thought by considerations of Roman power and by respect for a longstanding treaty. For he was by nature prone to temporise . . . and was still in doubt when [the new king] Tigranes ravaged the bordering country of Adiabene.'[117]

The Parthian nobles were humiliated at being harried not by a Roman general but by a hostage, and Vologaeses now bound the diadem on the brow of his brother Tiridates, transferred a body of cavalry to a noble named Monaeses, and sent him to besiege Tigranocerta with the Roman nominee inside it. He himself laid aside his quarrel with Hyrcania and called up his internal forces as a threat to the provinces of Rome.

Corbulo had become governor of Syria in the south, and asked for a separate commander. Syria was the graver danger if Vologaeses attacked. Covering Egypt, which represented a third of the Roman corn, it was so vital an outpost that it ranked highest among all the Imperial governorships,[118] and Vespasian was later able to gain the Empire largely by holding the Syrian and Egyptian supplies.[119]

Corbulo took precautions. He stationed his best troops on the Euphrates, and sent two legions to reinforce the puppet king – not the best, but with good officers in charge, 'whom he advised to be circumspect rather than rapid for he was more desirous to have war upon his hands rather than wage it'.[120]

Dubiously as Tacitus puts it, this circumspection seems natural enough, since there was every reason to wait for the arrival of a capable Roman general: it was impossible to run the widely spaced campaigns of Syria and Armenia from a single centre; and it is also possible that Corbulo could see more chances for a temporising diplomacy than were evident in Rome.

He had begun, presumably with his government's consent, by suggesting a policy to break the Armenian deadlock, which was in fact finally adopted; Tiridates was to be sponsored not only by the Parthians but by the Roman Emperor as well. But Tiridates, when still undefeated, rejected this reversion to the client-policy of Augustus, and the Roman government had decided on undisguised annexation, encouraged no doubt by Corbulo's successes. L. Caesennius Paetus, the legate chosen as his colleague, came out like a new broom to Cappadocia, and by pure inefficiency shocked the Roman policy back into grooves of moderation. While he was busy in the north, and a few Roman cohorts were still besieged in Tigranocerta, Corbulo sent a centurion to King Vologaeses in Nisibis to threaten invasion in the south.

'With Vologaeses,' Tacitus writes, 'it was an old and deep-seated principle to avoid the Roman arms'[121]; nor at the moment was the current of events too smooth for him. The siege of Tigranocerta had been fruitless; the Roman nominee was safe there with his garrison and supplies; and the Parthian cavalry was incapacitated for lack of fodder, for a swarm of locusts had made its appearance and destroyed every trace of grass or foliage. The Parthian king therefore promised to send an embassy to discuss a permanent peace in Rome on the terms already suggested by Corbulo, and agreed to an armistice meanwhile, withdrawing his troops from Armenia while the Romans in the south crossed back to the west bank of Euphrates. It is remarkable how these threats of invasion served time after time to keep the Euphrates line clear.

All this diplomacy however both Rome and her legate disregarded. Paetus crossed the Euphrates from Melitene and left a base half built at Rhandeia, on the northern bank of the Murat Su, the eastern Euphrates, the 'finest pasturage in the world' and 'Water of Desire'.[122] Pertek is the nearest modern site, and on the southern bank opposite is Shimshat, an old fortified city then called Arsamosata, 'near the Fair Plain' (of Kharput) between Euphrates and Tigris, once already besieged by the Great Antiochus one hundred and fifty years before.[123] Here Paetus left his family and the non-combatants on the wrong side of the river and exposed to the enemy, and followed the illustrious route of Lucullus through Sophene, failing to reach Tigranocerta. With the winter closing in upon him, he returned to his half-built camp, where his only good road to Melitene was cut off by the Murat Su. He thought the season over and sent men on furlough, and when he heard of the unexpected approach of Vologaeses, scattered his troops, 'divided his very vanguard into two isolated detachments; left them without supports; placed a river between his main army and the advance guard; practically sacrificed this to annihilation . . . and reluctantly sent off an orderly to Corbulo with the bare tidings of Vologaeses' approach'.[124]

Corbulo had already started with a large train of camels loaded with corn, when a second more desperate message hurried him through the hills to Melitene and thence to the Tomisa crossing. Here 'the first of the beaten army whom he met was the centurion Paccius, soon followed by a crowd of private soldiers', and after that by Paetus himself: Rhandeia had been surrendered with 'so much corn that they set fire to their granaries', when Corbulo was three days away. The Armenians had entered the camp even before its evacuation, 'lining the roads, identifying and dragging off slaves or sumpter animals which had been captured long before: even clothing was snatched and weapons detained, our terrified troops offering no resistance. . . . Vologaeses, after piling up the arms and corpses . . . to serve as evidence of our disaster, abstained from viewing the flight of the legions: he was laying up a character for moderation, now that his arrogance (*sic*) had been satisfied, *fama moderationis quaerebatur, postquam superbiam expleverat.*' Mounted on an elephant, he charged through the river not trusting the bridge which, by the terms of their surrender, the Romans had been forced to build.[125]

Armenia was evacuated, and Corbulo and Vologaeses came to terms while a reply from Nero was awaited. The policy of annexation was dead.

Peace with Parthia, A.D. 63

At the beginning of the following spring Vologaeses wrote to accept the proposals made by Corbulo eight years before: Tiridates, although Parthia had been victorious, was ready to do homage for his crown before the Roman standards. It was now a matter of prestige: and after a show of bargaining and force combined which an eastern court could appreciate, the final climax in Rome was planned, with a prelude on the very scene of the disaster at Rhandeia.

It is clear from various touches that Corbulo's moderation and adroitness were behind these discussions, and according to Dio[126] he displayed great bravery and great fairness and good faith towards all, both friends and enemies. 'Unconditional surrender' was wisely left out. 'Matters had not yet come to a pass where war to the bitter end was necessary,' he wrote as he once more took Lucullus' road towards Tigranocerta, and met the Parthian envoys: Rome had been favoured with many successes and Parthia with a few, so that both had received a lesson against arrogance. It was therefore to the advantage of Tiridates to receive an unravaged realm, and to the interest of Parthia to cultivate friendship with Rome. 'The name of Corbulo was regarded by the barbarians themselves without bitterness and with no rancour' – and they believed his advice to be trustworthy.[127]

They met at Rhandeia, where the river runs green among villages and castles as if in a trough of summer between the basalt rocks; and they clasped hands standing beside their horses. The Roman general praised the young man who was choosing the safe and salutary course: and he replied that he would go to Rome to carry to Caesar 'a new distinction – an Arsacid in the guise of a suppliant, though the fortunes of Parthia were unclouded'. After a few days' interval, standing before the statue of Nero on a curule chair with the legions and the cavalry ranked round it, Tiridates lifted the diadem from his head and placed it at the feet of the image, 'arousing among all present a deep emotion increased by the slaughter of the Roman armies still imprinted on their eyes'.

Vologaeses requested Corbulo by special courier to see that Tiridates should be exposed to no signs of vassalage, should not give up his sword, nor be debarred from embracing the provincial governors or be left to stand and wait at their doors, and in Rome should receive equal distinction with the consuls. There must be a great many humiliations behind these touching requests. 'Evidently, accustomed as he was to foreign pride, he lacked all knowledge of ourselves who prize the essentials of sovereignty and ignore its vanities',[128] was Tacitus' rather unsympathetic comment.

However this may be, it was a gentleman's agreement among the four principals, and the young king rode with his wife and sons, and Vologaeses' two sons, and Roman and Parthian cavalry, for nine months round the Mediterranean shores at a cost of 144,000 denarii a day, which was charged to the treasury: and the splendour of Rome, and Nero's welcome left so strong an impression that Artaxata – rebuilt by Italian workmen – was called for a brief instant Neroneia. When the news of Nero's death came soon after, the king of Parthia asked the senate that his name be remembered with honour. The implacable Parthian comes out of this story in a gentlemanly light.

Corbulo was too great to survive. Whether or not he took part in the plots that were gathering, his was a name round which they were bound to cluster. He appears in the Capitoline bust as a straightforward soldier, quite free of the brutality which repels in so many busts of the time and later, but with an expression of disenchantment, *désenchanté*, a word less casual than unhappiness and deeper than disillusion, a confession that the mainspring of life has gone. He is not known to us like Pompey or Lucullus, but one may infer that he had faced his private problems as well as those of his profession, for when Nero's order for suicide met him in Greece as he landed, he said only one word, '$\alpha\xi\iota o\varsigma$ – your due', the word used for heroes, and killed himself on the spot with his sword.[129]

And yet 'when I was a young man, twenty years after his death', writes Suetonius, 'a person of obscure origin appeared who gave out that he was Nero, and the name was still in such favour with the Parthians that they supported him vigorously and surrendered him with reluctance'.[130] And in the reign of Trajan, fifty years after, Dio Chrysostom wrote that most men longed for him and believed him to be alive.[131]

But the peace lasted fifty years, and the caravans moved without disquiet across the ferries or the pontoon bridges until what Henderson calls 'Trajan's splendid retaliation' broke it up.[132]

IX

The Trade Routes and Trajan's Wars

The Flavian tightening of the frontier and Trajan's campaigns now lead through Armenia and Mesopotamia to Babylonia. The Roman effort to obtain the Chinese and Indian trade sufficiently far north to evade Parthian customs, and the Parthian effort, soon to follow, to enclose the Black Sea in their net, are to bring war for many generations to come. Trajan's northern campaign had been foreshadowed under Nero, but, in the south, he opens a new chapter, or one that had lain dormant ever since the failure of Augustus' Arabian expedition. Instead of circumventing the Parthian trade of the south, he planned to annex the Mesopotamian route itself at its receiving end, a futile policy based on the fallacy that the wealth of a trade line can be mastered at any one particular point. However far they marched towards the east, the Romans would have found dues to pay for the luxuries they needed; it is only by paying for what is received and selling it again at a profit that a trade route can live, and peace with Parthia and a development of their western markets alone could solve the Roman problem on the Euphrates frontier. The reaction to Trajan's enterprise by the business people of the Parthian communities, and the peace and prosperity that followed Hadrian's reversal of his policy, clearly condemn the policy of annexation.

> Non qui profundum Danuvium bibunt
> edicta rumpent Julia, non Getae,
>   non Seres infidive Persae,
>   non Tanain prope flumen orti.[1]
>   (Horace: *Ode*, IV.15.)

'Trajan . . . making more stringent the ferry dues for camels and horses on the Euphrates and Tigris . . . (M. Cornelius Fronto: *Correspondence*, II, p. 215.)

The Great Road from China

I sometimes think of the saga of East and West as if it were music – an orchestrated symphony with solos, mostly sad, here and there, flashes and discords: and ever in the background heard in its quieter moments, moving in a rough repeated harmony, the padding footsteps of the caravans. That austere stream carries the wealth of Asia from city to city and leaves it in suburbs, and finds its own well-known and dingy quarters where the news of the road goes up and down; and in the Eastern bazaars one can still recognise the desert walk and faces in the streets of the weavers or saddlers, knitters of girths or workers in leather, those who knot bright tassels or sew the great sacks of the water-skins for the journey, or beat out the honey-coloured brass of the camel bells. It has often seemed to me that this breath that carries with it the constant reminder of hardship is what in spite of the corruption of poverty and riches has kept the oriental city and saved it, even at its worst, from the degradation of cities in Europe, whose luxury is paid for without the everyday tangible contact of men's lives.

The Great Wall of China was built towards the end of the third century B.C. to guard against the Hiung-Nu, a nomadic people thought to be early ancestors of the Huns.[2] In its shelter commerce gradually ventured westward through the Tarim basin in the reign of the Han emperor Wu-ti (140–87 B.C.). Silk had as yet no part in this traffic, and did not reach Rome till Antony introduced it[3]; Martial mentions that its wear was forbidden to men by an edict of Tiberius; and the famous name was not given to the road till the Byzantine age.[4]

The functioning of this highway in its length, through the centuries and the difficulties of nature and the vicissitudes of dynasties and races, with a general continuity seldom interrupted if we take into account the enormous forces arrayed against it – the permanence of this stream of Asia – is one among the triumphs of the human reason over chaos, though its virtual obstruction at the Roman end through eight centuries of unnecessary war is the melancholy subject of this book.

About 139–126 B.C. Chang K'ien, a Chinese ambassador, brought home news of trading nations and discovered the walled cities of Bactria; and caravans soon after his death numbered twelve yearly.[5] Traffic became established, between the Han capitals – Singan-Fu first and then Lo-yang (Ho-nan-fu) on the Yellow River – and Bactria where the Yueh-Chih, ruling from Peshawar, had inherited the power of the Greeks.

Parthia, about 115 B.C., made a treaty with China to facilitate and continue the traffic through Iran, and, immediately after, Wu-ti extended the Great Wall to the gates of the western limit, beyond the Gate of Jade.[6] Thence a road now untravelled led to Lou-lan,[7] with the swamp of the old Lop Nor on one side and a desert of sand dunes on the other, which the Chinese likened to white headless dragons, their tails and bodies convex to the wind.[8]

The roads branched under the rampart of Lou-lan, one through the middle, one joining it and longer on the north from Hami, and a third along the south of the Tarim basin, to Kashgar or Yarkand, according to the safety of the lands. All three were in use about 100 B.C.[9] The middle and shortest route by Lou-lan[10] became deserted because of the shifting of the waters; but the southern, known in many stretches, was mentioned later by Marco Polo in regions east of Khotan,[11] by streams of chalcedony and jasper.[12] Six crossings between south and north are referred to in the Chinese annals,[13] across what is now the central desert of Taklamakan.

In these outer lands the raid of a single enemy was enough to ruin an oasis for ever. 'Many travellers stick in the swamp. On the northern road, the Hiung-Nu fall upon one. On the southern there is neither food nor water, and on many uninhabited stretches there is hunger'[14]: there was in fact a ten days' trek without habitation worth mentioning, and

the settled places when reached were too poor to afford the traveller
sufficient provision for the way. The Chinese solved the problem through
colonies of soldier-peasants: an imperial komissar was established to
watch over crops and harvests and care for the visiting ambassadors; and
the northern route in the second half of the first century B.C. came to take
eight days less than the southern,[15] while the Hiung-Nu were kept down.

Traffic soon found its way from Yarkand or Kashgar to Tash-Kurgan,
or the 'stone tower', where agents from India, Oxiana and China met,[16]
and to 'Lan-schen, which is the capital of Bactria, a forty-nine days' journey from Lo-yang'. The immense solitudes of Thibet were unknown.[17]
Merv, walled by the Seleucids and famous for its iron, the limit of Roman
knowledge under Augustus, was also on another way from Samarkand.
These roads passed on together, skirting the Parthian homelands of
Hyrcania south of Damgan (Hecatompylos) to Hamadan. When, about
A.D. 115,[18] the first embassy was sent to Parthia, the king there ordered
twenty thousand cavalry to meet it on the eastern frontier. He sent an
embassy to follow the Chinese embassy and offered to the Chinese court
large birds' eggs (ostrich) and jugglers from Petra.[19] From Hamadan the
route led across Euphrates to the final factories where the silk was woven
in Berytus (Beirut) and Tyre, 16,590 *li* from Bactria. The interesting
point is that these *li*, not being Chinese at all, nor corresponding to
the Persian *farsakh*, but to the Greek *stadium*, show that the itinerary
must have been taken over from the Parthians as it stood – possibly
from a Parthian translation of an earlier Chinese.[20,21] Coloured stuffs
and carpets and seventeen sorts of weaving from Syria; glass, metals,
jewels and drugs[22]; horses from Hyrcania, purple and coral, papyrus
and styrax were carried. Lucerne and wine and pomegranates reached
China, and henna was transplanted to Canton from Parthia or India in
the early centuries of the Christian era, when the glass and copper of
Khotan were also made with materials from the West.[23] The whole
Indian trade shifted gradually north-west because of the overland route
through Bactria, until the Hiung-Nu in A.D. 23 fell upon it and made it
impossible again for fifty years. In A.D. 73 the Chinese began to resus-
citate it, and again advanced along both sides of the great chain of oases
of the Tarim basin to 'open the roads that lead to China and establish
peace'.[24] Merchants along the trade line, from Parthia and Bactria and
India, sent their requests and prayers to the Celestial Court; and it was

during this renascence of the trade around A.D. 100, that the Syrian-Roman merchants and the Chinese tried to link up their trade directly, and failed[25] because Parthia lay between.

At this time, the trade was in its heyday; 'peasant colonies were founded in the fertile lands; inns and posts for changing horses were established along the main routes; messengers and couriers travelled in every season of the year; and the Merchant Strangers knocked daily on our gates to have them opened'.[26] It was the period of the Roman peace with Parthia and the never-to-be repeated summit of the Asiatic trade in the ancient world. By 127 A.D. the Tarim relapsed into chaos, while traffic increased in the Persian Gulf or Aden as it waned in the north[27]: that there was any connection between the Chinese of the north (the 'long-lived' *Seres*[28] of Lucian) and those of the south (the *Sines*), was still undiscovered in Ptolemy's day.[29] In A.D. 166 after the destruction of Seleuceia, a little party of Syrians were to reach the Chinese capital with great difficulty – private traders probably, who gave themselves out as ambassadors from Marcus Aurelius.[30] Their visit marks the first direct intercourse with Rome in the Chinese annals, though an embassy from India had reached Antioch in the days of Augustus by the overland route – all except three killed or disabled by the long journey – with a message in Greek from their king.[31]

From Bactria westward the Parthians took on the trade. Their whole prosperity depended on it, so that the cities on its routes were cared for, and a camel corps was probably kept armed to guard the desert caravans.[32] These were brought through kindred peoples, the homelands of Parthia and Iran, to Seleuceia as we have seen. There were still Parthian princes on the Lower Indus in the time of Trajan, and related Sakas[33] in Seistan till 390 A.D.[34] Apollonius of Tyana, travelling from Babylon to India in the first century A.D., was helped across the Indus by a letter from the Parthian king; and found Taxila 'fortified after the manner of Greek cities', with bronze tablets on the exploits of Alexander and Porus along its temple walls.[35] All trade between the Persian Gulf and the Taurus, direct by sea from Indian Barygaza, or sea-borne from Hormuz through Seistan, or overland altogether, was obliged to pass through the Parthian sieve.

But the distant Romans had a good name in China. 'They traffic by sea with Parthia and India . . . honest in their transactions and . . . their kings always desired to send embassies to China, but the Parthians wished to carry on trade with them in Chinese silks, and it is for this reason that they were cut off from communication. This lasted till the ninth year of the Yen-hsi period (A.D. 166) when the king . . . An-tun (Marcus Aurelius) sent an embassy.'[36] The trade was continually thwarted, and regular only when Romans and Parthians were at peace[37]; and about A.D. 160 – when the straits of Malacca were crossed and direct commerce with China started – the peak of the sea trade was already over.[38] By then the strengthened Roman frontier held the South Arabian spice route at one end and the Pontic route round the Caspian at the other, the only two trading channels that could escape the Parthian dues.

The Northern Trade Route – Pontus to the Caspian

Pompey had built five out of his seven Pontic cities on the strategic northern route[39] already fortified by Mithradates.

Pontus was desirable on its own account. Polybius had praised its cattle and slaves, honey, wax and fish[40]; and Pliny the sweet-scented 'amomum that flowers twice a year'.[41] Wormwood came from there, hellebore and many perfumes, and wool from Themiscera and Gazeloni-tis, protected on its sheep with a wrapping of hides.[42] Its rivers flow among orchards of apples or quinces, and a silver lining of poplars and alders flutters when a wind blows along their banks. 'Pontus, the Pontic mists, and the habitation suitable for exile, the mountain crests . . . and the air which you have to measure, and the sun for which you long', St Gregory wrote from Cappadocia, but St Basil remembered his 'moun-tain range with its moon-shaped windings . . . and single entrance, of which we are the masters, and the breezes from the river and sweet exhalations from the earth'.[43]

Metal was its wealth, and the discovery of iron and steel was almost unanimously ascribed by the ancient world to the Chalybes of Pontus. Its working was established at many points from the bronze age onwards[44]; it brought the earliest Greek colonies to the Black Sea coast, and made Sinope its clearing-house and Trebizond its harbour; in the tributary valleys of the northern Euphrates one can see the open-cast mines busy like ant-hills to this day.

Beyond Pontus were three little kingdoms – Colchis, Iberia, and Albania – 'free people without kings living about the Araxes', Plutarch[45] describes them erroneously, for they had numerous kings. They held the southern Caucasus, from whose uplands at least seven summits rise to over fifteen thousand feet. The people in summer fasten to their feet 'broad shoes made of raw ox-hide, like drums, and furnished with spikes . . . and descend with their loads by sliding down upon skins'.[46] Of the three passes, even when Bryce travelled there some eighty years ago, only the Dariel had a road.[47] On the south-west of this range the Phasis, and on the east the Araxes and Cyrus, linked the Black and Caspian Seas by a four days' journey with a paved road between them, the Phasis 'made passable by one hundred and twenty bridges . . . with a rough and violent stream'.[48] At its estuary stood a statue of its god together with the legendary anchor of the Argo,[49] and a fort with walls and towers and four hundred men inside it: and in the mountains above, the Iberians lived 'like the Scythians and Sarmatians of whom they are both neighbours and kinsmen . . . and assemble many tens of thousands, from them and from their own people, when anything alarming occurs'.[50] Below the slopes on the eastern side, the Albanian nomads who had been free throughout their history, simple people who could not count up to a thousand,[51] lived quietly on the Caspian plain, which was 'better watered by its rivers and other waters than the Babylonian and Egyptian and consequently keeps a grassy appearance always, and is good for pasturage'.[52] Here the Albanian, or Derbend pass led northward by the shore. The only other passage is the Dariel in the middle of the range, a gigantic crevasse within four thousand feet vertical walls,[53] and both are confusingly apt to be called the Caspian or the Caucasian Gates.[54] Pompey, making for the more central pass, attacked the Iberians. He left a garrison and advanced to the Cyrus, until the conquered Iberians concluded a treaty.[55] He was securing the gateway to Sarmatia.

North of the Caspian

The legend of a trans-Caspian sea trade has been demolished by Professor Tarn,[56] and only a more northern route is left, that led from the steppes north of the Caspian to the plains of Mongolia, 'quite independent of the routes through Chinese Turkestan'.[57] It finally reached Pliny's *Seres*, who were not the peaceful Chinese traders of the Yellow River, but tall nomads of the steppes with 'flaxen hair and blue eyes who speak in harsh tones and use no language',[58] famous for their pure steel which the Parthians bought. Horace imagined them:

> *times*
> quid Seres et regnata Cyro
> Bactra parent Tanaisque discors,[59]
> (Horace: *Odes*; III.29.25–27)

They were the metal workers of the Altai whom the Parthian envoy referred to when he threatened to load Crassus with their chains.[60]

These were the people Strabo thought of when he reported goods brought from India by the Oxus[61]; and their traffic along it at the end of the first century A.D. was observed by the Chinese.[62]

Pliny describes their country ungeographically – 'the chilly lurking places of the north wind' and 'beyond (if we can believe it) a happy race of people called the Hyperboreans, who live to extreme old age. . . . Here are believed to be the hinges of the firmament and the extreme limits of the revolutions of the stars, with six months' daylight and a single day of the Sun in retirement . . . a genial region where all discord and all sorrow is unknown. . . . Nor is it possible to doubt about this race, since so many authorities state that they regularly sent the first fruits of their harvests to Delos . . . brought by virgins . . . until because of a violation of good faith they instituted the custom of depositing their offerings at the nearest frontiers of the neighbouring people, and these of passing them on . . . '[63] a fair enough echo of a trade route, apart from the virgins at its end.

Centuries later, Hayton, a king of Lesser Armenia, reports that beyond Cathay are to be found 'men like great hairy dogs, and women endowed with reason'.

It is now ascertained that from the days of Herodotus and before, the Black Sea appears to have communicated with the Altai steppes across the flat lands of Dzungaria.[64] These lands, slowly desiccating but geographically easy, where horse and horsemen were at home, are slowly opening out to the fascinated eyes of the West. Their salty grasslands are excellent for sheep in the two per cent area of their oases, and their climate, with ups and downs of a few centuries, has not greatly varied[65];

NOMADS NEAR LAKE VAN

a route across them was followed in the sixth century from the Crimea to China by the ambassador of the Byzantine Emperor Justin II[66]; and it must have been already known to a good many merchants from whom Ptolemy – about A.D. 150 – got his information, for he shows himself well at home in the geography of the Don and the Volga to about 55 degrees North.[67] The importance of Asia in his day may be gauged from the fact that only ten out of his twenty-six maps deal with Europe, as against twelve for Asia and four for Africa[68]; and he got much of his vast information from these slowly accumulated reports of unrecorded travellers. Along the great eastern trade routes the Parthian frontiers impeded Roman merchants,[69] but the northern information seems to have had the traditional itinerary of the steppes to rely on. 'The itineraries consulted extended much farther north than most commentators have supposed; no doubt they continued the ones traced across western Scythia, the great Turkish-Siberian steppe.'[70] North of the Caspian, the route crossed a pass to Dzungaria and made for Mongolia.[71] The discoveries of the Tarim basin, says Berthelot,[72] 'have concentrated attention on the high passes of the Karakorum, Pamirs, and Altai, but the far easier route of Dzungaria must have been the more usual one in the age of Ptolemy as in that of the Milesians and Mongols' before and after.

Two passes, Dzungaria and Ferghana, form corridors which connect the Asiatic and Euopean portions of the vast and gradually sand-invaded plain where the nomads, divided rather vaguely into Massagetae, Dahae, Sacae, Scythians, lived a uniform life and spoke a more or less homogeneous Iranian language under conditions that were much the same from the Don (Tanais) to the ice-preserved graves of the Altai that have shown them as they lived. 'Countless tribes of the Scythians extend over territories which have no ascertained limit; a small part of whom live on grain. But the rest wander over vast deserts, knowing neither plough time nor seed time; but living in cold and frost, and feeding like great beasts.'[73] So wrote Ammianus Marcellinus in the fourth century A.D. Their carpeted tents lined with patterned rushes as their Luristan descendants still weave them, their Chinese carts and mirrors, their gay and rich horse trappings and clothes[74] are there from the fifth century B.C. intact.

*   *   *

The Achaemenian gold stream to Bactria had been cut in the hellenistic age just as the amber route to the Baltic was cut and not restored till the reign of Nero[75]; but the Mongolian trade route remained when the gold supply ceased, and its existence has been established and the Scythian influence on Chinese art is noticed from the fourth to at any rate the first century B.C. Indefinite as it is, the evidence locates it as an El Dorado of that time, a tradition of gold possibly as non-existent as the North-West Passage was non-existent when the Elizabethan ships went out to find it. The rumour of things is greater than themselves, and the rumour existed; and so did the truth, however long past, of Strabo's legend of the gold. 'It came to Bactria, as it came to south Russia, from Siberia – the "griffin-gold" whose guardian griffin adorned the coinage of Panti-capaeum. This was the main Asiatic source of supply. . . . The antiquity of the Siberian washings is shown by the discovery . . . near Damgan, of a gold treasure . . . from about 1500 B.C.'[76]

Throughout the latter half of the first millennium B.C. the nomads of Siberia must have been in regular touch with the people living on the fringes of China.[77] Their baggy trousers and close-fitting tunics, an oriental variant of Scythian dress, were adopted by the Chinese for riding,[78] and 'Greek, Iranian and Chinese products and art motives all met in distant Mongolia'.[79] The south-western end of this northern trade which reached Ferghana, must have been closely connected if not identical with the gold route,[80] which certainly existed before the Greeks reached Bactria, and left its metal scattered beside Chinese mirrors in later tombs, as far south as the Black Sea coasts.[81]

While the nomads continued to drift from north and east, the Assyrians raided from south-west to supply their cavalry with the great Nisaean chargers, centuries before these reached China in 101 B.C.[82] The Mitannians, inhabiting what became loosely Kurdistan, were transmitters of horsemanship to the West, and the cult of the horse during the second millennium B.C. supplants that of the stag.[83] 'Almost immediately following the Scythian penetration into Asia, the technique of riding was suddenly mastered throughout the Middle East.'[84] Strabo tells how the upper Aorsi, who ruled over most of the Caspian coast and imported the Indian and Babylonian merchandise, could send out more than two hundred thousand horsemen in his day.[85]

The Parthians sprang from this mixed but remarkably uniform background, and were noticed by Chang-K'ien on his embassies in 128 B.C.[86] They settled and became a main barrier against their own nomad Scythian kinsmen of the East.[87] The sedentary western Iranians whose civilisation they saved never welcomed them,[88] and the popularity of both Seleucids and Romans in Media was a constant protest against the victory of the eastern nomads, who had defeated Darius, and killed one of Alexander's generals,[89] and held the steppes until other nomads, the kindred Sarmatians, moved with their new invention of the stirrup across the face of Asia (400–300 B.C.). These Tacitus describes as: 'No people so cowardly on foot, but when they attack on horseback hardly any line can resist them.'[90] They could cover a distance of eighty miles a day easily in waterless desert, and their horses, unsheltered in winter or summer, never tasted oats or barley.[91] (I have myself cantered in Arabia for five hours almost continuously on a pony fed exclusively on chopped straw.)

Armoured with scales of hide or iron, and their horses also, the Sarmatians registered another victory for cavalry in the history of war. When, after the middle of the first century A.D., Nero brought the Bosporan kingdom and all the Caucasian coast under the direct control of Rome, it was the Sarmatians he had to deal with before their migrations swerved westward to merge with those of the Germans in Moesia.

Roman Interest in the North

Roman interest in the north could be due to several causes: to the trade route; or to the growing military demands of Black Sea communications; or to the financial difficulties which the Parthian customs' barrier did nothing to alleviate; or to a mixture of all three motives, of which the first had already attracted the attention of the Seleucid kings long before. Patrocles in the third century B.C. had explored the Caspian for King Seleucus, who dreamed of linking it to the Black Sea by a canal[92]; and Demodames of Miletus, about the same time, had erected altars to the Didymaean Apollo on the banks of the Jaxartes. When Pompey built his strategic road up the Lycus valley and opened a gateway from Iberia to the Sarmatian steppes, he was following in the track of

Mithradates; and Vespasian added a link to the chain by placing a garrison at Harmoriza on the Caucasus to overlook the Dariel pass, whence the road was safe to Samarkand: for at this pass 'the road terminates . . . cut off by cliffs and . . . no way out appears except a small gate set there by nature . . . which has been called from of old the Caspian gates. From there on there are plains suitable for riding . . . used as pasture land for horses and level besides. Here almost all the nations of the Huns are settled' and can come with their horses fresh to the pass: but by any other way must suffer difficulties and fatigues. The pass was a key to the whole Caucasus.[93]

The second or military Roman motive became apparent as soon as armies moved into Armenia and the great roads from Ankara and Sebaste (Sivas) eastward came into use.[94] Corbulo made Trebizond his base and linked it to his camp under Ararat by a chain of blockhouses across the enormous passes.[95] It grew steadily more important. Its anchorage, reported by Arrian to be useful in summer only, was turned into a harbour, with a statue of Trajan which Arrian complains of, pointing to the sea.[96] Ever notorious for pirates, the Pontic Sea was held by Nero with forty warships, but as they mostly remained at Byzantium, 'the barbarians still roamed at will . . . in boats . . . fastened together without spikes or bronze or iron. When the sea is rough, the sailors build up the bulwarks with planks to match the height of the waves, until they close in the hull like the roof of a house. Thus protected these vessels roll about amid the waves. They have a prow at both ends and their arrangement of oars may be shifted, so that they can be safely propelled in either direction at will.'[97] I believe I have seen boats very like them today, drawn up on the small dark lunar beaches near Trebizond.

The third, financial, Roman motive is at the back of Mommsen's theory that all the Armenian wars derived from Pompey's discovery of the Caspian trade.[98] Though too simple an explanation, and though the English and German interpretations differ,[99] it will not do to keep finance entirely out of the picture. Nero's plan, when it started, had Seneca behind it, a man with 'large estates scattered about the world, who lent out money to provincials'.[100] 'Any land in the whole world will offer kingdoms', he makes Jocasta say.[101] The increasing expenses that fell upon the private treasury of the emperor, his extravagance, the need

to safeguard and perhaps to extend Roman commerce, supplied tempta-
tions which must have appealed in an age when wars were still profitable,
and the Roman exchequer needed to be constantly replenished.

'Solvency depended on the Princeps,' Buchan says of Augustus,[102]
but some economic flaw apart from mere personal extravagance must
help to explain the almost permanent poverty of the Empire. Egypt
alone was producing well over £5 million yearly, yet the general Roman
balance never again reached the sums which Augustus left at his death.
Even careful men like Marcus Aurelius, in the golden age of the Empire,
'held a public sale in the forum of the deified Trajan . . . and sold goblets
of gold and crystal . . . even flagons made for kings, his wife's silken
gold-embroidered robes, and indeed, even certain jewels which he had
found . . . in a particularly holy cabinet of Hadrian's'.[103] Commodus
intended to kill fourteen consulars 'since the revenues of the Roman
Empire were insufficient to meet his expenditures'.[104] Extravagance
was vast: games and donations, informers too to be paid[105], bribes to the
crowd, and bribes to the army for granting the throne; (Claudius was
the originator of this ominous practice,[106] and Galba when he tried to
economise on it, was murdered). Domitian increased the army pay by
a third; Trajan gave immense donations though his campaigns probably
paid; and there was vast expense in building. During the century of
peace from Augustus to Nero the revenues of the Empire had increased
amazingly; yet after Nero's wars Vespasian found a debt of 40,000
million sesterces at his accession, 'the largest sum of money mentioned
in antiquity'.[107] One would scarcely credit so great a personal capacity
for spending if the difference between one emperor and another did
not make it manifest. Caligula, who would sell his gladiators at the
circus, gave a present of a million pounds when he reinstated the king of
Commagene, and spent 2,700 million sesterces in one year.[108] Nero is
said to have squandered 2,200 million sesterces in gifts,[109] 2 million to
Tiridates alone. 'The reckless extravagance of his last years contributed
not a little to the partial ruin of Italy'[110]; the coinage was debased,[111] and
the Ostia canal given up for lack of funds;[112] and, in penury from A.D.
64 onwards, he simply put wealthy people out of the way. Vespasian,
economising to stem the enormous deficit, was taunted by the crowd
in Alexandria for not knowing 'how to play the Caesar'. It is possible,
I imagine, that the sudden retrenchments may explain the diminished

respect of the Parthian king, and his omission of the Imperial titles in a letter to Vespasian, under whom the glamour of Nero's generosity had vanished.

All this made a background to encourage any financial experiment and particularly one that had as many respectable Roman precedents behind it as a war.

Defence (against the southward-pressing Sarmatians or Alani as they now came to be called)[113] was at any rate not the only motive of the Roman interest, if indeed it was a motive at all. Until the following century off and on, the tribes of the northern Black Sea coasts were friendly to the Greek protected cities, that gave them supply centres and trustworthy agents 'because of their need for traffic with the Greeks.'[114] The 'Chief Interpreter' of the yellow-haired Alani[115] was an important official in the Bosporus. Though a strong 'iranisation' was proceeding, altering arms and dress and language, it was an uneasy but not a menacing relation – its impact more against Parthia than Rome. Vespasian refused to cooperate when the Parthian king asked for help[116]; and the southern Alani were soon to show themselves ready to join the other Black Sea peoples in homage to Trajan when he reached Armenia.

*   *   *

There is thus a whole background of interpretations for the undoubted Roman interest in the north: defensive against the Alani; precautionary for the Trebizond supply route[117] (which was aggressive in its very nature); or a mere evasion of the Parthian customs; or a subsidiary fringe to frontier affairs farther north, where Dacia and the main road of the Empire were soon to blaze into war.

Some influence in the complicated skein may also be allowed to the insubstantial lure of Alexander, whose legend, from Nero's day at latest,[118] was connected with Armenia and the Caucasian region. Nero's 'Phalanx' of six-foot Italian soldiers was called after the Macedonian, and the wraith of Alexander continues to flit in and out of the Roman history, with Pompey's cloak,[119] and Antony at Philippi, and Caligula's breastplate 'taken from the sarcophagus',[120] and soon, and more destroyingly expensive, the harsh reality of Trajan's dreams.

Whatever the inducement, Nero's plans against Sarmatia never matured; but the Colchians, the Bosporani, and all the coastal tribes were adopted by Rome, and the Romans under Vespasian built their fort opposite the Caucasian pass. Willingly or unwillingly the king of Pontus was persuaded to abdicate, and in A.D. 70 his country was incorporated, together with lesser Armenia, first in the new and growing province of Galatia-Cappadocia, and then from Trajan onwards in Cappadocia itself. A freedman of Pontus, impatient of the change, massacred a cohort and set fire to the fleet and escaped to one of the coastal kings, but his protector had to choose between 'the reward for treachery and the alternative of war', and handed him back to Rome.[121]

Most of the Black Sea export now went to the armies of the Danube or of Cappadocia, and the commerce of south Russia was in the Black Sea cities' hands.[122] 'The increasing volume of trade from the Caucasian regions determined the Flavian emperors to convert the kingdoms into provinces and to control all the approaches to the Euphrates with Roman garrisons.'[123]

The Flavian Frontier

By A.D. 72 the frontier line of the Euphrates could be drawn tightly and held in force.[124] Strong garrisons were settled at Satala and in the rectangular camp of Melitene, and both soon grew to cities in these sparsely populated hills.[125] Flavian milestones, and those of Nerva, as well as later ones, are found scattered about the northern roads, through Galatia, Cappadocia, Pontus, Pisidia, Paphlagonia, and over the heights between the sea and the Euphrates where Mithradates' last battles had been fought. The milestones of Nerva and Trajan particularly show a care for the lines leading to the frontier, especially the Pontic highway.[126]

Pannonia was now the military centre of the Empire, and the mastery of the Adriatic loses its importance; no legions pass along the Egnatian way; the Black Sea has become the quickest route for reinforcements to Euphrates. Nerva bridged the Kizil Irmak, the Red River, and carried a route through Amasya to join Domitian's backbone of defence from Samosata by Melitene and Satala to Trebizond; and fourteen repairs at regular intervals between A.D. 97 and 323 testify clearly to the military importance of the northern roads to Satala.[127] Vespasian and his sons made the frontier still more definite: 'undesirable gaps were steadily closing . . . the legions were given the maximum striking

power . . . while, in their rear, supply route areas for production were
carefully organised. . . . Under the Flavians, and Trajan after them, the
limes[128] system, elastic and adaptable . . . was a basis for methodical advances'; it was only later, in the third century, when the tide had turned,
that the frontier became a bulwark in retreat.[129]

The Social Widening of the Empire

The Empire was getting into gear.

Most of its inhabitants were happy and an era of municipal felicity
opened under the Flavians, with loyalties more centralised than those
felt for the scattered kings.

Vespasian, one of the most likeable emperors, 'the only one who
was changed for the better by his office,'[130] slipped his rugged humour
between the storms before and after, that rocked the ship of Augustus
on its course: the figure of Pax Augusta reappeared on his coins,[131] and
the temple of Janus was closed. 'The tone of society was set by the
ruling class and the composition of this had changed.'[132] The nobility
were dead and in any case Vespasian was not one of them; his father
had farmed the port dues of Asia and he himself had been a trader[133];
and the middle class provincial bourgeoisie, the Egyptians who wished
to trade in land,[134] the Spaniards to whom he granted their Latin rights
en masse,[135] the municipal aristocracy of the East for whom the ranks of
the Imperial nobility were opening,[136] now came into their own.[137]

'There were still to be rich men, though not many *nouveaux riches*,
but they would indulge less in display . . . and the larger fortunes of
the second century are reported chiefly from the provinces.'[138] War
and politics were abolished.[139] The Empire was made unhealthy for the
aristocracy, but the provincials outside Italy, and the trading people going
about their business were – unlike the Roman nobles – too decentralised
to be coerced. Claudius, though liberal in his time, had degraded a Lycian
citizen because he spoke no Latin[140]; from the Flavian age onwards there
were senators, and even consuls from Lycia.[141] There were still three
thousand statues in Rhodes, seen by Pliny,[142] and in Delos 'the number
of dedications by eastern princes, Pontus, Cappadocia, and even the
Parthian Arsaces . . . increases so rapidly that we feel ourselves hardly
in a Hellenic place of worship'.[143] Nor did the government interfere

except in cases of riot or disorder, such as the town clerk in Ephesus had feared with St Paul. The Empire was becoming a great and prosperous pool with trouble only at its edges.

Many things went under in the tightening of the frame. The free cities of Byzantium and Samos were given by Vespasian to the provinces of Bithynia and of Asia, and so was the city of Rhodes, one of few that still kept its walls in repair, not for use but from pride – the only city that had refused the abolition of its debts when offered by Augustus: it was the richest of the Greek states according to Dion,[144] and Vespasian desperately needed money, and freedom was apt to mean exemption from taxes[145]; and the better emperors did by annexation what the worse ones did through murder, nor can one say that a province or a city was more badly treated than a senator on the average of those times.

In the general reorganisation the little kingdom of Commagene too went under with Antiochus, the last of its Seleucid kings. Caesennius Paetus, recovered from his partnership and disgrace with Corbulo, marched upon it. An eagle on a column still looks out over the restless pastures on the far side of a tumulus where another figure, an ancestor, is talking to his god. When the river is low, a ferry with a crooked pole can punt across Euphrates to where Samosata clusters a few poor houses of mud and whitewash beside the mound that was its citadel and the slightly raised outline of its vanished walls. Antiochus had been the first to ride to Beirut to join Vespasian when he was elected emperor by the Syrian legions; his son had been wounded fighting for him, and when the old king, 'conscious of innocence or of impotence, would offer no resistance', the young man and his brother engaged the Roman forces, with some success. But the troops would not continue to fight without their king. The princes escaped to Parthia where Vologaeses received them with honour, 'till a centurion came with a mandate from Vespasian to fetch them and . . . the bounds of the province of Syria were defined'.[146]

Trajan in Armenia

The aims of the Flavians seem to have been pacific, but as they tightened the border, and extended it towards Palmyra and the Nabataeans in the south, it was natural for the friendship of Parthia to cool. The Euphrates frontier, Mr Lepper writes, had 'too many powerful and uncontrolled neighbours, and, along the upper Euphrates, though protected by a formidable series of gorges, did not adequately dominate the country beyond'.[147] People dislike to have their country dominated by a potential enemy, yet the maligned Parthian continued to be averse to war. Trajan was soon on his way (A.D. 113) 'with a programme of rational aggression without match or parallel as yet in the history of Rome',[148] and had got as far as Athens when an embassy from Osroes the king met him, asking for peace and proffering gifts.[149]

Trajan paid no attention, travelled to Antioch and through Samosata up the familiar gorges to Melitene, which was now declared a metropolis. From there he secured his flank at Arsamosata, and then continued to Satala, where the first of the troops he had sent for from the Danube possibly met him, on the slopes of a southerly tilted plain surrounded by little hills.

It is now called Sadagh, and remained for several centuries a purely Latin centre, and is a small village with a brick or two of the XVth legion and a dedication to Aurehan left there forgotten. I have driven there, 6,640 feet up the Zigana pass from Trebizond, thinking how no man-made fortress can compare with these depths and steepnesses of valleys, this breadth of slopes scattered with summer *yailaghs* and lower all-weather houses, pastures and woods and corn and sheets of the Pontic azalea, and empty peaks of grazing patched with snow. At the pass all changes suddenly and turns to arid ridges; the Hashret and Choruk rivers lie pale as jade below, the fierce enormous ranges lead to Kelkit in the south. Gothic pinnacles of rock, tense as anatomic muscle, are spewed among them. The velvet of the northern slopes is forgotten, till all subsides to new plains and passes that stretch towards Ararat in billows of cultivated ploughland, and the Byzantine and Seljuk walls of Baiburt – Mithradates' Sinoria ? – hold the emerging defiles in their sight.

Satala is sixty kilometres away to the south-east by an earthen track, across an almost treeless landscape that has smoothed away its detail, as if the grassy hills were waves with their strength inside them. The villages shine scattered and rare against empty slopes, the land is bright with geometric patterns of corn and grass, or the various shades of ploughing – rusty colours like ripened corn or bread; the clouds boil up from the Black Sea suddenly and meet the blue strength of the sky, and disperse; and the rounded hills look soft unless a cut shows their massive solidity of rock. The skin of earth, like civilisation, is thin; but its grass is full of flowers – scabious and dianthus, borage, and poppies in the ditches, achilleia and gypsophila, and white and pink convolvulus in clusters, and purple lupins on the edges of the corn. And shining on its slope in a silvery light is Satala, one hundred and fifty houses, with bits of Byzantine wall and an acropolis not high but clear beside it, and four arches of an aqueduct, and broken pillars, and here and there an inscribed stone built in the walls. Turning back towards it from a track not meant for cars, I saw it as romance personified, caught in a far shaft of sunlight among the sweet-scented grasses of its meadows, forgetful of the roads of the Empire that met here, Lycus and Euphrates, Kelkit, Eriza, Melitene, Bithynia or Trebizond. The high Soghan range, with only two dips, outlines its northern sky: and many a soldier watched its alien harvests.

*   *   *

The king of Parthia, for some unknown and probably domestic reason, had deposed one relative from the Armenian throne and put in a brother, without consulting Rome. Chaos no doubt ensued, but his ambassadors in Athens now requested Trajan to overlook and grace this *fait accompli* with the diadem – a matter for argument rather than war.[150]

The young king, Parthamasiris, wrote signing himself royally, and, getting no answer, wrote again, this time omitting the unsanctioned titles. But he hesitated to come to Satala with the other client rulers when Trajan held his court there, and waited to meet him at Elegeia (later Erzerum). There Trajan received him 'seated upon a tribunal in the camp'. The king, saluting him, laid the diadem at his feet, and the rest of this sad story is best told in Dio's words, for he ' . . . stood there in silence, expecting to receive it back. At this the soldiers shouted aloud and hailed Trajan *imperator*, as if because of some victory. (They termed it a crownless and bloodless victory, to see the king, a descendant of Arsaces, a son of Pacorus, and a nephew of Osroes, standing before Trajan without a diadem, like a captive.) The shout terrified the prince, who thought that it was intended as an insult and meant his destruction;

and he turned about as if to flee, but seeing that he was hemmed in on all sides, he begged that he might not be forced to speak before the crowd. Accordingly he was conducted into the tent, where he obtained none of the things he wished. So out he rushed in a rage, and thence out of the camp; but Trajan sent for him, and again ascending the tribunal, bade him say in the hearing of all everything that he desired. This was in order to prevent anybody, ignorant of what had been said in private conference, from making up a different report. On hearing this command Parthamasiris no longer kept silence, but spoke with great frankness, declaring among other things that he had not been defeated or captured, but had come there voluntarily, believing that he should not be wronged and should receive back the kingdom, as Tiridates had received it from Nero. Trajan made fitting replies to all his remarks, and in particular declared that he would surrender Armenia to no one; for it belonged to the Romans and was to have a Roman governor. He would, however, allow Parthamasiris to depart to any place he pleased. So he sent the prince away together with his Parthian companions and gave them an escort of cavalry to make sure that they should associate with no one and should begin no rebellion,'[151] and he was murdered on the way.

Tiridates, the friend of Nero, watching a wrestling match in the theatre, had once seen one of the contestants struck by his opponent as he fell. When the king saw this, he exclaimed: 'The fight is unfair. It is not fair that a man who has fallen should be struck.'[152] Fronto, years later, writing to Marcus Aurelius, remarks that Trajan's glory was dearer than the blood of his soldiers, 'for he often sent back disappointed the ambassadors of the Parthian king when they prayed for peace . . . and it is not easy to absolve him from the murder of a suppliant king'.[153] Trajan's letters give him a very different record from his action in Armenia; and the senate conferred the title of Optimus upon him, while Dante enshrined him in his Paradise.[154] Among the emperors he was conspicuous for his justice, his bravery, and for the simplicity of his habits, 'and even if he did delight in war, nevertheless he was satisfied when success had been achieved . . . and his countrymen exalted'.[155] He was not scholastic: Dio Chrysostom described Socrates to him as an old and poor Athenian of whom he might have heard[156]; and he would have made an excellent colonial governor, ancient or modern. It is impossible to doubt the accumulated evidence of the contentment and prosperity of his time,[157] and Tacitus reserved the history of Nerva's reign and Trajan's rule for his old age because of the rare good fortune of feeling what he wished and saying what he felt.[158] For many ages, unnumbered ages perhaps, private men have been able to measure themselves and grow by some divine standard, while public or patriotic morality is assumed to be different, so that there can be no real change of direction in the world; and Trajan was not the first conscientious man to give this demonstration. *E manubis* (from the spoils) is the inscription on his column.[159]

Trajan in Mesopotamia

The private tragedy of Parthamasiris was probably no more to Trajan than a detail in the larger picture which he brought from Dacia. The Parthians seem to have been in touch with the Dacians across their fluid steppes, and any interruption of the trade was followed uniformly and always by outbreaks on the lower Danube and the Rhine.[160] The Flavian plan had been to build the eastern frontier so as to *serve it in the nature of a wall.* Trajan destroyed this possibility by the annexation of Armenia. By pushing out a great promontory, that automatically put the Tigris in place of the Euphrates, he made the conquest of Mesopotamia essential if the Parthians were not to enjoy that 'salient' which had served them so well at Rhandeia. This was the second time in Armenian-Roman history that a plan of straight-forward annexation was tried, and it was a kindness of destiny that saved Rome a world of trouble by decreeing for the second time a prompt but not crippling failure. Henderson remarks that 'it was impossible to annex Armenia only. Both Trajan and Hadrian realised fully this truth, the former in acquiring, the latter in surrendering all three countries [Armenia, Mesopotamia and Babylonia] together'.[161] Trajan was now forced by his own policy to march south.

Apart from the strategic requirement, the military necessity to carry his conquests forward no doubt fitted his dreams[162]; when he reached Babylon he offered a sacrifice in the room where Alexander had died.

In the summer of A.D. 114, after sending some short raids among Kurds and Albanians, he moved south to Edessa, probably by the route that Corbulo had taken, and continued, meeting no resistance, to Nisibis to prepare for a Tigris crossing.[163] Adiabene at that time stretched out along both banks of the river, and the satrap in command retired to the eastern side.[164] The west, across Jebel Sinjar, was again in Roman hands as in the days of Lucullus, and the petty kings of Anthemusias and Edessa fled or submitted, the latter with a gift of two hundred and fifty horses and fifty thousand arrows: one can see him panoplied with the *ornamenta consularia* beside Trajan on the arch of Beneventum.[165] He was allowed to keep his kingdom through the good looks, it was said, of his son.[166]

A winter or possibly two were spent in preparation, and in the spring of 116, presumably before the rising of the Tigris, when laden donkeys can still wade across beneath the cliffs of the gorges, 'Trajan brought his boats on waggons, for they had been built in such a way that they could be taken apart'.[167] The Romans were expert at bridging, and would let one pontoon after another drop downstream and anchor with a basket of stones and a cable when it reached the side of the pontoon before it[168]; and these collapsible boats would be *kiliks*, rafts floated on goatskins filled with air and easily carried – as they are used today. 'He had great difficulty in bridging the stream opposite the [Kurdish] mountains, as the barbarians had taken their stand on the opposite bank,' but, attacked by boatloads of archers, 'and because of their consternation at seeing so many ships appear all at once in a land destitute of trees', they gave way, and the Romans gained the whole of Adiabene.

A separate force was left to finish the conquest of this district destined for annexation, and Trajan himself turned back[169] along the trade route through Sinjar to the 'river Aburas [Khabur] which empties into the Euphrates', and, with his transports drifting downstream beside him, followed the Parthian road.

Somewhere not far from Fallujah he pulled his rafts across the level gravels that separate the two rivers at their nearest point in the Mesopotamian plain. I have often driven here, and watched the mirage shimmering its phantom battlements; and in 1941 the taking of the ground by General Wavell's forces was the prelude to the capture of Baghdad. His was the first invasion from the West; Trajan however, following the right bank of the Tigris, had dropped down from the north and may have hoped, like Lucullus, to force a battle by attacking the Parthian capital.

KIZIL IRMAK RIVER
THE HINTERLAND OF TREBIZOND

He made for Ctesiphon, 'a large village . . . which the kings of the Parthians were wont to make their winter residence, thus sparing the Seleuceians, in order that the Seleuceians might not be oppressed by having the Scythian folk or soldiery quartered among them. Because of the Parthian power, therefore, Ctesiphon is a city rather than a village; its size is such that it lodges a great number of people, and it has been equipped with buildings by the Parthians themselves; and . . . been provided by them with wares for sale and with the arts that are pleasing to the Parthians; for the Parthian kings are accustomed to spend the winter there because of the salubrity of the air, but the summer at Ecbatana and in Hyrcania because of the prevalence of their ancient renown.'[170]

The details of the Ctesiphon siege are missing. The circular Parthian walls were taken, with Osroes' golden throne and his daughter inside them, and the senate voted Trajan 'as many triumphs as he wished'.[171] Reluctantly, at sixty-three or sixty-four, he relinquished the footprints of Alexander, and Osroes vanished unpursued out of the reach of Rome. A sort of stillness follows this conquest like that of Moscow before the fire. In the lull one can watch the old soldier opening the unknown world before him, following the two rivers in their desolate flat windings and untraced wanderings through the marshes of the south, and visiting the *entrepôt* of the Indian trade at Charax Spasinu, the 'palisaded town'[172] near modern Khurramshah.

The silting waters which have created the whole of Babylonia with scarcely a stone inside it continue to build it in shallow stretches, where nothing lives in blinding sunlight among the salt-encrusted fingers of the sea. Looking from the air at the head of the Persian Gulf, it is almost impossible to tell water from land, except where the two rivers, then separate, now cut their united path.

Pliny describes Charax 'in the uttermost recesses of the Persian Gulf, from which projects the country called Arabia Felix. It stands on an artificial elevation between the Tigris on the right and the Karun on the left, at the point where these two rivers unite, and the town measures two miles in breadth. The original town was founded by Alexander the Great with settlers . . . and with the invalided soldiers from his army who were left there. He had given orders that it was to be called Alexandria, and a borough which he had assigned specially to the Macedonians was to be named Pellaeum, after the place where he was born. The original town was destroyed by the rivers, but it was afterwards restored by Antiochus, the sixth king of Syria, who gave it his own name; and when it had been again damaged it was restored, and named after himself by . . . the king of the neighbouring Arabs, who is wrongly stated by Juba to have been a satrap of Antiochus; he constructed embankments for the protection of the town, and raised the level of the adjacent ground over a space of six miles in length and a little less in breadth. It was originally at a distance of one and a quarter miles from the coast, and had a harbour of its own, but when Juba published his work it was fifty miles inland; its present distance from the coast is stated by Arab envoys and our own traders who have come from the place to be one hundred and twenty miles. There is no part of the world where earth carried down by rivers has encroached on the sea further or more rapidly; and what is more surprising is that the deposits have not been driven back by the tide, as it approaches far beyond this point.'[173]

Here was a civilised town, where the kings shaved in Greek fashion. Trajan confirmed Attembalos king of Mesene as a client; and the whole of the Far East, the sea route from Malabar, the southern trade from Bactria that came through Seistan to the eroded coast and entered the sea route at Hormuz – *the wealth of Ormuz and of Ind*[174] – and of farther lands, Indo-China and Sumatra, and not luxuries only but useful wares like cotton,[175] fell into Trajan's hands.[176] Now, if not before, the financial aspect of his conquests must have presented itself to him in the strongest colours. He returned to Babylon and set about the tightening of tariffs,[177] until a world of whose management he knew nothing, a world 'politically divided but economically almost unhampered'[178] crashed like a hailstorm about him. He touched the middle class, the traders who managed the life-line of Asia, and he failed. Seleuceia turned for the first time against the westerners; the Jews, of whom Benjamin of Tudela later found one hundred congregations in the Zagros,[179] who were numerous in Nisibis[180] and even today guard the tomb of Ezekiel on the Tigris, and have been powerful in the land since their first exile in Babylon,[181] were against the Romans in general and their finance methods in particular; the Parthian army, still intact, appeared both in Armenia and across the Tigris in Adiabene; and the trade routes rose with their cities – Dura Europus possibly, Edessa under its king, 'and Palmyra's attitude may be guessed from the warm partiality she afterwards showed for . . . Hadrian'.[182]

The revolt was suppressed: the Parthians were beaten in the north after they had defeated and killed a Roman governor-general, probably in the pass of Bitlis: the records are obscure. Nisibis was retaken and King Abgar disappears in the sack of the 'impregnable' Edessa: and Seleuceia, recaptured by two legions, was burnt. 'This', in the strange language of the historians, 'restored order in the south, and Trajan was free to march off to the heart of the trouble.'[183] He left a client Parthian as king in Ctesiphon to keep a nominal and extremely ephemeral control of the trade route; Adiabene was lost; Armenia in chaos; and the desert route to Nisibis with its Parthian-built city of Hatra was out of control. But the fact that Trajan determined to capture it shows that he had no intention of giving up the riches he had seen. A milestone with his name remains on what was once his road across the pass from Singara.[184]

Hatra is possibly the unidentified Ho-to of the Chinese annals, a knot of wealth along a desert route that abandoned the Tigris near the mound of Asshur, and still does so; and many people who knew Iraq a generation ago must remember the spring beauty there, when herds of gazelle roamed at will and the Shammar drove to shoot them over the desert flowers, regardless of the absence of a road.

Cultivation, due to the tractor, in stripes like a beduin tent of varied browns, has almost reached the deserted city, and the wadi Tharthar, the only running water, is now bridged: but the walls, close on six miles in circumference, are still unobstructed on their horizon, chapleted with towers and roughly circular in the age-old tradition of the nomads,[185] with the courses of their building biscuit coloured and bitten like sea-cliffs by the wind. Inside, a deep round pool sinks and rises with the seasons and is visited by ducks in their migrations, and the rectangle ruin of temple and palace remain.

Any obstacle was important in the ages of hand-to-hand fighting, when a man had to use one valuable hand to hoist himself up or over; and though, to the town-bred eyes of Dio, the city looked 'neither large nor prosperous, and the surrounding country is mostly desert and has neither water (save a small amount and that poor in quality) nor timber or fodder', he saw that these very disadvantages afforded it protection, as also did the Sun-god to whom it was consecrated; 'for it was taken neither at this time by Trajan nor later by Severus, although they both overthrew parts of its wall. Trajan sent the cavalry forward against the wall, but failed in his attempt, and the attackers were hurled back into the camp. Indeed, the emperor himself barely missed being wounded as he was riding past, in spite of the fact that he had laid aside his imperial attire to avoid being recognised; but the enemy, seeing his majestic grey head and his august countenance, suspected his identity, shot at him, and killed a cavalryman in his escort. There were peals of thunder, rainbow tints showed, and lightnings, rain-storms, hail and thunderbolts descended upon the Romans as often as they made assaults. And whenever they ate, flies settled on their food and drink, causing discomfort everywhere.'[186]

These flies are familiar to any desert traveller, since they make for the moisture of lips or eyes in the dry air, with a constant nagging. The desert anyway was an experience the Romans never enjoyed.

Trajan departed, and all that remains of him is his milestone of A.D. 116 in the cleft of the hill behind Singara, where his new road came down. Later Romans (A.D. 162–226),[187] fortified this town, which, with a camp near by on the trade route,[188] and a few *castella* described by Sir Aurel Stein,[189] are all that is left of their buildings in Mesopotamia. The Ist and IIIrd Parthica were stationed there, the Moorish cavalry a little to the west, probably at Alayna; the Assyrian road ran a very little south of the Roman; and the medieval Arab station a trifle to the west. It is all cavalry land, heaving in low rises, bleached under shallow cultivation and thin scratchings: the teasing desert air beats the tent canvas against the tentpole like faraway thunder and dies at nightfall. As the morning returns dust envelops everything and eats the treeless backbone of Singara and the far blue circle of the Armenian hills, and the mounds rise out of it like barren breasts one behind another, and Time with its broken dynasties seems idle: the black asphalt road moves through it, flashing its dusty distance on the windscreen of a car.

There are few villages and treeless – the shadows only of houses show – the new on the open level, the old ones sloping to their mounds: and they go back to the first millennium or the second, Assyrian, Roman or Arab; the thin straw of their harvests blows about them. Sandgrouse fly with busily working wings over the seed-filled stubble: the crested larks run with tripping steps, their colours that of the wrinkled stone, which is nothing but hardened sand. All the colours are pale, as if washed or diluted, and the road and the railway and the telegraph travel together – symbols of union in the vast *separateness* of the desert. The camels alone unite it with a ritual detached but not brutal, walking from age to age, their eyes downcast under the loose eyelid, their colour that of the sand only darker, as if it were part of the long distance that creates and then buries its sons. From the rise of the Roman camp where a pale streamlet trickles one can look out and see no horizon – only perpetual wind and dust. The mounds swim in it, slowly drowning, and the sun or the moon float above them unimpeded, as if the heavens were not their path but their domain.

The strong tension of the earth, felt like muscle in the day beneath its harvests, is hidden in the vagueness of moonlight as it is by vegetation in gentler lands. The dusty steppe relaxes as if it breathed; and the solitude and silence continue the aeons of silence behind them. When the winter first comes and brings wild skies from Armenia, the rain is dissolved in the heat of the air before it can touch the ground: only when cooled by days of shadow can the rain come down.

I was last on this stretch of the trade route when the frontier was again closed between Mesopotamia and the West, and the road, planned and begun during World War II when traffic could go through freely, had faded into hummocks short of the frontier – desolate and drifting under stones and sand like the historic roads before them. Buses had ceased to run and the hamlets were back in their age-old life of isolation, 'though the Shammar tribes, if you know them, can get you across'. It was probably always so. As I drove along, I picked up a tribesman trudging home along the shadeless way with a withered hand. I stopped for him. 'I have no money', he cried, 'I am of the poor, the Bedouin, the people of the tents' (just as Strabo described him); their world has too few details to change.

The seleucid Macedonian colonies, frequent on either bank of the Euphrates and east of the Tigris also, died away in this middle area, where civilisations come and go and sink away in their own dust. Only two hellenistic towns or possibly three are certainly known, and even there most of the Greeks had departed. Trajan found a few Romans (i.e. Greeks?) in Ctesiphon; in Nisibis, when Lucullus took it, the Greek engineer Callimachus had been alone.[190]

The Roman world began at the Western 'port' of Zeugma: *Areae fines Romanorum: fines exercitus Syriaticae et Commertii Barbarorum* – the frontier area of Rome and the Syrian army, and of the Barbarian trade. This barrier Hadrian, following Trajan in Empire, promptly restored. The Euphrates again became the frontier, though the organisation of the Flavians was maintained along its banks.

Trajan, whose coins had *Oriens* stamped upon them,[191] who had steered himself across the Danube and swum the Euphrates at sixty and had loved soldiering for its own sake, was dead, dropped by the Fates on his way home beneath a Cilician headland, by Antiocheia ad Cragum where, on an unbridged river, the foundations of his square mausoleum still show: but he himself is buried at the base of his column in Rome, 'and the Parthian games, as they were called, continued for a number of years until they too were abolished.'[192] His policy did harm not only for generations but for centuries, but to Rome, 'Goddess of earth and of the nations', he appeared as his column shows him, and as indeed he was, 'a soldier strong, young and warlike' of whom she could say to the 'rulers of the Parthians and chiefs of the Seres, Thracians, Sarmatians, Getians, Britons, "I can show you a Caesar: come."'[193]

Like Alexander whom he longed to follow, he left his ring to Hadrian but named no successor. Very soon the Chinese and Indian trade, the apple of discord, was thrown for sixty-four years into more southerly routes by the activities of the Huns in the Tarim basin; and the interest of the next generation centred in the south.

X

The Antonine Climax

A mong the Antonines, Hadrian alone envisages a policy of peace. The others miss their opportunity along the trade-routes of the East. Marcus Aurelius returns to the sterile grasping of a receding frontier, and the permanence of Parthian enmity is accepted as many another *cliché* before and after. The world's missed opportunities become noticeable only after their disappearance, when the inevitable bill has to be paid: the result of the Antonine return to violence hardly begins to develop in this chapter: it will be found later, in the third-century devastations and the rise and fall of Palmyra.

An unexpected consequence of the doctrine of the weak periphery appears in the re-organised Flavian and Antonine armies: entrusted with the task of defence which no remaining ally was powerful enough to undertake, they themselves became sufficiently strong to dominate their employers. This disintegrating effect of a *domestic* periphery made stout enough to cope with external dangers and becoming dangerous to its own centre, will become apparent in the next century's revolutions.

'Some of them are even said to pick up something of philosophy so far as a race that is always in arms is capable of such knowledge. '(Quintus Curtius: VII.8.10.

The Provincial Renascence

The Aegean sea shows no horizon before the summer dawn. The morning breeze has not yet come to step between the islands; and in that enchanted hour day lies as if with closed eyes, iridescent as pearl and still involved in night. When the sun springs up with his spiked rays sea and sky separate, the horizon takes on its cutting edge of sapphire, and the colour of the day is born. And sometimes, under the fulness of light as it progresses, a wide and gentle wave with no apparent wind to urge it heaves across the hollow spaces. The shocks that conceived it are forgotten as it whispers by without an obstacle in sight, and carries on its back a universe of wavelets and fluid shadows; and moves to shores that must break it. In the heyday and beauty of its power, during three brief generations, the 'eternity of the Roman Empire' moved thus across the world.

Many changes had altered the Augustan dream. Most important among them, the victory of the provinces, with three Imperial Spanish rulers at their head:[1] between Domitian and Commodus (A.D. 96–180) no emperor resided habitually in Rome.

The aristocracy no longer came solely from Italy, and money, gathering along the main routes of the armies, had spread with the provincial renascence: it appeared in unexpected places, building the sarcophagi of Assos or the tombs of Lycia and Palmyra. 'Not only the municipal spirit was at its height during the first half of the second century, but the wealth concentrated in the hands of the city bourgeoisie both in East and West steadily increased.'[2]

There were not so many ways of spending as there are now, and civic and private generosity carried on its long hellenistic tradition. Drainage and water; modern bathrooms, noted by Seneca, with mirrors, marbles, silver taps, transparent windows[3]; professional cooks; divorces, introduced, according to tradition,[4] in early days shortly before the wars of Hannibal; the lighted and colonnaded streets which Antioch invented; the paved streets of Smyrna – good things and bad had been adopted from the East. A little country town like Aphrodisias celebrated at least six festivals named after their founders[5]; and the excesses of Rome publicised by Juvenal and Martial were rivalled by those of Alexandria and Antioch, where Apollonius found the people shut out from their baths 'because of the enormities committed'.[6]

Rome, 'a city made up of cities,' had discovered that double citizenship was possible, and spread her urban world until, in the fifth century, no one was to be alien except *the barbarian and the slave*.[7] The second century was drawing towards its general enfranchisement (in A.D. 212), yet even at this late date, when the gift of citizenship was losing its value, it was still being sought with eagerness and distributed with care.[8] The Empire preferred indirect rule as a system, recognised things as it found them in its annexations, and rarely changed them,[9] and it struggled for three centuries to keep the semi-independence of the city-councils in being.[10] It was drifting towards failure, but under the Antonines[11] the cities were still at their zenith. Both Trajan and Hadrian rivalled the Seleucids as founders, and the great bridges of the Empire, the aqueducts in Dalmatia, Asia, Arabia and Egypt, the harbour works at Ephesus, record Trajan's name: it lies carved in marble under the pines of Phaselis: and one can clearly see in a city like Ephesus, now being excavated, what the Antonine age looked like in 'the common treasury of Asia',[12] lavishly rich and full of beauty, full too 'of pipers, and effeminate rascals, and full of noise'.[13]

The rich provincials whose fathers had become knights and who themselves, as senators, could now reach the highest pinnacle of office,[14] devoted their wealth and leisure to their towns[15]: 'Everything', in Smyrna, 'is a blaze of gymnasia, markets, theatres, precincts, harbours, where natural and man-made beauties vie with each other, and there is nothing that does not serve both for ornament and use; baths so many that you would not know where to bathe, public walks of every kind . . . fountains and running waters for each house . . .'[16] Ephesus, Pergamon and Smyrna had populations of over two hundred thousand,[17] and smaller places – villages sometimes – gathered into townships 'free and autonomous from the beginning by the grace of Augustus'[18] (the sentence reminds one of the 'freedom of the cities' argument that brought Rome into Asia) – these little pleasant places like Stratoniceia, or Lagina, now nestling in the carved fragments of their ruins, all joined the urban procession with longer or shorter strides.

The peaceful reign of Augustus had brought recovery and help even to the smaller and the inland cities.[19] Debts had been remitted; one hundred talents of the tribute of Cos were cancelled in exchange for their Venus Anadyomene; the annual tribute of Asia had once been paid out of the Emperor's own patrimonial funds. 'The men of Nicopolis are wont to shout: "Yea, by the fortune of Caesar, we are free men."'[20] The gratitude of the towns was shown by the numbers that had once adopted the Julian and Claudian names,[21] and now took those of Trajan or of Hadrian; the care for the cities had continued till it reached its apex in the Antonine age,[22] and began to decline under the civil wars of Septimius Severus.[23] The maintenance of the roads too, military as it was and dependent on the tightening of the frontiers, helped the prosperity of the cities of Asia.[24]

They spent too much. Their finances were ever in chaos. Pergamon, even in the early days, although in desperate straits, erected five statues to one benefactor, two of gold and one of marble, one of each kind on horseback.[25] Trajan, or the Flavians before him,[26] appointed Imperial curators to the municipalities to advise them – who became general in the second century, were made regular officials in the third, and eventually became oppressive. In Trajan's correspondence with Pliny in Bithynia the insidious temptation of the administrator appears, with all the difficulties and disappointments of this toil: 'These paltry Greeks, I know, have a foible for gymnasia; hence, perhaps, the cities of Nicaea have been somewhat too ambitious in planning one: but they must be contented with such a one as will be sufficient for their occasions.'[27] Curators and procurators multiplied under Hadrian, and Imperial efforts to curb the spending of money seem to have had the usual negative effect. Cities were to spend on maintaining rather than building: the Emperor was to be consulted about new gates – yet the lavish tide went on through the second century undeterred,[28] while Imperial solicitude prepared that increase of bureaucracy in which the later Empire was strangled.

There was extravagance at home too: what one emperor saved another spent, and Lucius Verus' banquet,[29] if one believes the *Scriptores Historiae Augustas*, cost 6 million sesterces. 'The comely lads who did the serving were given as presents, one to each guest and . . . live animals tame or wild . . . and carriages together with mules and muleteers for driving home.' In Rome itself there was free food for 150–200,000 people and games for all.[30] Marcus 'groaned and bewailed the Empire's fate'.[31]

While the peace lasted, the state finances stood the racket. Hadrian's innovations tightened the Imperial bureaucracy to a pitch of high, if dangerous, efficiency[32] and made it possible to rise in the civil services without a term in the army – as had been formerly compulsory. Antoninus Pius left 2,700 million sesterces at his death.[33] Merchandise, inside the Roman area, declined in quality but spread more widely, and 'underdeveloped' countries gradually began to come into independent production of their own.[34] 'The almost complete security of travel . . . the absence of high [internal] customs duties, and above all the splendid system of Roman [paved] roads, produced an efflorescence of provincial commerce, chiefly along the sea or overland routes, never seen before,'[35] and we hear of a Phrygian merchant who travelled seventy-two times between Rome and Asia Minor.

The Roman achievement was urban: 'In the cities, if anywhere, were realised the ideals of social health and local autonomy which Rome showed to be compatible with her insistence on world-wide peace, and which were the motives of her policy even towards the rudest of the races she controlled.'[36] World-wide excludes, we must remember, the slave and the barbarian, an exclusion which spelt disaster in the end: it is surely an incorrect term in this context. But the cities rejoiced meanwhile. They were little interfered with, even by their curators; their jurisdiction over wide territories gave local politics plenty of scope; and they produced many of the best intellects of the Empire. Spain alone, apart from establishing three emperors and probably inventing the Norman arch,[37] had Seneca and Lucan, Quintilian and Martial to her credit: Fronto, the beloved teacher of Marcus Aurelius, came from Constantine in Tunisia: there were booksellers at Lyons, to Pliny's surprise[38]; and the eastern lands in which we are interested basked in the sunshine of Hadrian's hellenistic revival, which released philosophers, doctors and grammarians from paying their taxes and caused a renascence of theatres and gymnasia and all things Greek. The past which to Augustus had been Italic was, to Hadrian, the past of the whole Mediterranean world, all equally to be cherished. It shifted Italy, which was anyway declining, from the centre of the stage, and probably partly explains Hadrian's unpopularity in Rome.

Culture Under the Antonines

Vespasian, establishing public education, had catered for that touching oriental hunger for learning which existed then as it does today.[39] In the revival that followed the Flavians, the Hellenic world, Rostovtzeff says, recovered a sense of direction.[40] The cities of the Greek East had not forgotten their traditions, 'for the memory of those early writers still lingers [in Syria] and is not wholly lost, as it is in Rome'[41]; and even along the Black Sea's northern coast, hard pressed by the barbarians, although they no longer spoke Greek distinctly, 'almost all at least know the Iliad by heart'.[42]

The Greek literature still sparkles in eclipse. The cynical provincial Lucian can look at life cheerfully, and 'we of the household of Plato', says Apuleius 'care for nothing that is not festal and joyous and solemn and high and celestial'[43]; and Dio Chrysostom, diffuse as he is, 'took for his hearthstone the wide world which after all is man's common hearth and nourisher'[44]; and wandering through the Empire with a friendly eye for landscapes free of suburban amenities, lived equally with rich or poor, herdsmen and hunters,[45] enjoying the variety of a world unknown to the metropolitans in Rome. He feels what few writers describe – the poverty beneath the splendour, the cattle grazing in deserted market places,[46] and even the 'duty not to bear the mistreatment of outcast and enslaved creatures with indifference'[47] in the old struggle of rich and poor.

Plutarch glances even more easily through the chinks of the façade, finding presumption 'barbaric and cheap', and keeping his pride in its place, 'characteristic of a Greek and a man of refinement'.[48] Apart from his value in history, he is full of wise thoughts and sayings. 'Agamemnon', he writes in his *Moralia*, 'is suspected of having, for a bribe, released from service in the army the rich man who made him a present of the mare Aetha. He did quite right in preferring a good mare to a man of that type.'[49]

It is the atmosphere of a world already old: and one would like to have been a guest at one of Plutarch's little dinners.

There are regions far from the noise of wars, where life has slowed down to an outmoded pattern in 'cities long ago inhabited where we come on broken stumps and fragments of columns and find traces of walls . . . some destroyed by the hand of man, others by that of time'.[50] Pella is mentioned as a small poor village once great under the Macedonians[51]; and other long-neglected and decayed temples Apollonius restored.[52] The market place of Thebes is described as unrestored after the city's destruction, with only a small part inhabited, except for a statue of Hermes which the inhabitants set up again because it commemorated a victory awarded them by the rest of Greece for flute-playing long ago.[53] In a comfortable and generous world where, as in England today, the Parish Magazine was taking the place of *The Times*, there was a certain boredom:

> Menippus (Lucian makes him say): 'If you found the sameness tedious in life you will find it tedious here (among the dead) where everything is always the same.'
>
> Chiron: 'And what should I have done, O Menippus ?'
>
> Menippus: 'They say that the wise make the best of the present, and endure all things with patience.'[54]

'For see, if we enumerate the greatest blessings which polities enjoy – peace, liberty, material prosperity, populousness, harmony – as far as *peace* is concerned, the communities have nothing to desire from their politicians; every Greek, every barbarian war has departed from us and vanished; as regards liberty, they have as much as the rulers accord and perhaps as much as is good for them . . . fit to enjoy thorough quiet and concord, if men of sense will make the best of it, since fortune has left us no higher prize to win.'[55]

Dio speaks with the same nostalgic tranquillity to the people of Tarsus, absurd in their quarrels, since 'it is an ass's shadow, as they say, over which they squabble; for the right to lead and wield authority belongs to others'.[56]

The same peaceful stagnation meets us in Italy, in old and sleepy towns like Anagnia, which Marcus Aurelius visited on the way to their house in the country, about a mile off the main road – a tiny ancient township containing many antiquities and buildings – not a corner without its chapel or shrine or temple[57]: it reads like Assisi. And what one would now call a movement of decadence, a sacrificing of substance to form throughout the literature of the second century, was spread by teachers of rhetoric and paid for by the treasury of Vespasian. It cultivated 'the patina of antiquity,'[58] Hadrian's 'spurious pretence of ancient eloquence'[59] criticised by Fronto; and showed some modern features:

'It seems to me,' said Apollonius, 'that you are a past master of encomium.'

'Yes,' said the author, 'and that is why I have composed an encomium of gout, and of blindness and deafness.'

'And why not of dropsy too?' said Apollonius, 'for surely you won't rule out influenza from the sphere of your cleverness, since you are minded to praise such things?'[60]

The north and east of Asia Minor produced writers like Dio, Aristides, Arrian, Lucian; the west produced Epictetus: through all of these one can follow the blended pessimism and repose of the century, and an ethic quality intruding into the delight and curiosity that once enjoyed the world for its own sake alone. That has gone.

> *Also allow not sleep to draw nigh to your languorous eyelids,*
> *Ere you have reckoned up each several deed of the daytime:*
> *Where went I wrong? Did what? And what to be done was left undone?*[61]

'Behold now,' Epictetus the slave writes, 'Caesar seems to provide us with profound peace . . . there are no wars any longer, nor battles, no brigandage on a large scale, nor piracy, but at any hour we may travel by land, or sail from the rising of the sun to its setting. Can he, then, at all provide us with peace from fever too, and from shipwreck too, and from fire, or earthquake, or lightning ? Come, can he give us peace from love? He cannot.'[62]

Epictetus wrote with a warmth still Greek and a gaiety foreign to the Roman stoics. The Creator, he remarks, 'needs those who join in the holiday and the dance, that they may applaud rather, and glorify, and sing hymns of praise about the festival. But the peevish and the cowardly He will not be distressed to see left out of the festival; for when they were present they did not act as if they were on a holiday, nor did they fill the proper role,[63] . . . for your reason is the element of superiority which

ROMAN ROADS:

ALEPPO TO ANTIOCH

DÖSHEME NEAR ANTALYA

you possess; adorn and beautify that, but leave your hair to Him who fashioned it as He willed.'[64]

The language of Virgil yielded more and more ground to the hellenisers among the Antonines,[65] and Marcus Aurelius, bringing to its highest point the anxious preoccupation of his age with conduct, turns from the warfare of life and the forgetfulness of fame to philosophy that keeps 'the divine genius within pure and unwronged, lord of all pleasures and pains . . . waiting for death with a good grace as being but a setting free of the elements of which everything living is made'.[66] 'Let the good that is in thee be lord of a living creature,' he writes in his brave sadness, 'that is manly, and of full age, and concerned with statecraft, and a Roman, and a ruler[67] . . . that thou mayest speak the truth freely . . . and have an eye to law and the due worth of things: . . . then shalt thou be a man worthy of the universe that begat thee, and no longer alien in thy fatherland.'[68]

He leaves a sad little list of the things he has learnt from various people: 'To become aware of the fact that I needed amendment and training for my character; and not to be led aside into an argumentative sophistry; nor compose treatises on speculative subjects, or deliver little homilies, or pose ostentatiously as the moral aesthete or unselfish man; and to eschew rhetoric, poetry, and fine language; and not to go about the house in my robes, nor commit any such breach of good taste. . . .'[69]

Delight, that first of obligations, is missing, and in spite of loving a man so lovable, a parody of Keats – *A thing of duty is a joy for ever*, comes irresistibly to mind: 'The universe stretches forth into the infinitude of Time . . . and discerns that our children will see nothing fresh, just as our fathers too never saw anything more than we. . . .'[70]

It was a world that took no pleasure even in ships, the rolling adventure of which a normal man delights in. Apollonius, strolling down to the port of Rome 'about the time of the lighting of the lamps when these ships sail'[71] saw them as Lucian describes them[72] – one hundred and twenty cubits long and twenty-nine deep from deck to hold, and gently curved to the high carved stern and figure-head of Isis at the prow; but the sailors were little thought of – a wretched ill-starred rabble 'that dash their ships onto the rocks if their gains do not balance their debts'.[73]

And there were no end of other trades to be avoided: cosmetics and interior decoration, quoted by Dion[74]; acting, miming and dancing; harp and flute-playing; hawkers and town-criers bunched rather strangel with attorneys and advocates; and the keepers of brothels. Cicero (over a century before) had included tax gatherers and usurers, and those trades like fishmongers, butchers, cooks and poulterers, that 'cater to sensual pleasures'.[75] Apollonius gives the conventional view: if you acquired your wealth by inheritance or commerce 'such as befits free men and not by petty traffic',[76] all was well. Yet in Asia Minor, unlike Rome, the professional men and even actors were held in honour[77]; and Julius Caesar[78] who had been familiar with the Levant, gave their citizenship to teachers and doctors as well.

For the Romans themselves, who now scarcely read Latin for pleasure,[79] the *Pervigilium Veneris* is the swansong of their singing. In the silence of their literature after Augustus, and in the shadow of their architecture which continued to develop in splendour,[80] they devoted themselves to the study of rhetoric, and to poetry with which the years of their boyhood were filled[81] and which they continued, with very little profit, to write. They found their scope in the law courts, and strove with fair success for honest sentences, and continued, though with less conviction than formerly, to compare their *gravitas* with the levity of the Greeks.

The Imperial Divinity

The person of the emperor had grown from decade to decade, till it had come to be the one living symbol that held the Empire's loyalty together.

The kingly idea developed during the century that divided Augustus from Hadrian, and this not only through the efforts of philosophers to make it virtuous, but by a notion of its inherent divinity taken, with other notions, from hellenistic countries where the experiments in kingship had been made. It was natural that, succeeding to Alexander, the first kings of Babylon and Egypt should have been deified by their sons. Ptolemy II (285–247 B.C.) probably took the final step; his sister and consort Arsinoe was officially deified before her death as the goddess Philadelphus, and with her Ptolemy himself became a god while living.[82] The cult sprang up spontaneously in Pergamon.[83] The Seleucids were kings through victory and hereditary right and not essentially gods: they were deified externally as it were, in compliment for their deeds – for the Hellenes felt the possibility of the divine that 'still in this paltry body of death, doth none the less have his purpose set upon fellowship with

Zeus,'[84] and it was their error, according to St Jerome, to think every man above them a god. Antiochus IV, however, appearing deified on his coins among them,[85] exploited his divinity politically in his struggle against the farther East and Rome.

Altars to the Goddess Rome were first put up in 195 and 170 B.C. in Ionia at Smyrna and Alabanda, in gratitude for the war against Antiochus III; and worship of such governors as could be considered benefactors followed in ever-increasing numbers. Cicero tried to prevent his own, but hoped to get 'as near deification as possible'[86] in the shrine for his beloved daughter Tullia; Julius Caesar claimed origins both royal and divine in his aunt's memorial service.[87] His own status remained doubtful; but Antony and Cleopatra used deification as a political instrument in the Eastern way, and no feature continues to discriminate between the Levantine or Italian sympathies of the following emperors more clearly than their attitude towards this oriental manifestation.

Augustus (as well as Tiberius) accepted homage with reluctance: 'Silver statues of me, on horseback and in chariots were erected in the city to the number of about eighty; these I myself removed, and from the money thus obtained I placed in the temple of Apollo offerings in my own name and in the name of those who had paid me the honour of a statue.'[88] The eastern provinces however insisted on worship, and when Augustus died, the senate took the symbol of an eagle from Syria or Babylon, released it like Lucian's vulture[89] from the funeral pyre, and decreed the emperor's reception among the Gods.

> *Quos inter Augustus recumbens*
> *purpureo libet ore nectar.*[90]

After his death, the deification of Claudius was parodied by Seneca or some author unknown.

Nero hesitated, though his golden colossus showed him like a god. 'I find', Tacitus writes, 'that Anicius Cerialis, consul designate, gave it as his opinion that a temple should be built to Nero the divine . . . out of public funds. His motive, it is true, merely implied that the prince had transcended mortal eminence and earned the worship of mankind: but it was vetoed by that prince, because . . . it might be wrested into an omen of . . . his decease: for the honour of divinity is not paid to the emperor until he has ceased to live and move among men.'[91]

Caligula, however, enjoyed, and indeed insisted on his own deification, and Domitian 'as god-monarch of the Roman realm needed no senate to partner him, but only ministers and servants: hence the opposition of the senatorial order and its pitiless suppression'.[92]

Hellenism and the Emperors

The cold war of emperor and senate, which lasted and biased history for centuries, is beyond my geographic limits; yet the *leitmotif* that runs through it, the opposition between East and West, must be cursorily remembered: for it was never far beneath the surface. It was a cliché of the time and liable to become articulate whenever other circumstances tended towards it, and it existed from the day when Julius Caesar's imaginary intention to transfer the capital to the East had been the shadow of something which, however non-existent, had yet helped to precipitate his death.

Augustus, in his necessity to oppose Antony and by natural inclination, reacted against the hellenistic influences that already surrounded him. In the years before Actium he established by sheer propaganda the fear of the Orient which persisted until Constantine in A.D. 330 took his capital to Byzantium and the Orient won.[93]

> *Yet, warlike Roman, know thy doom,*
> *Nor, drunken with a conqueror's joy,*
> *Or blind with duteous zeal, presume*
> *To build again ancestral Troy.*[94]

The words of Horace express a fear that had reality behind it, and the eastern Mediterranean continued to entice one emperor after another, making hellenists of Titus and Domitian, reviving the Alexander dream, and influencing even those like Vespasian, Nerva and Trajan, whose roots were firm in the West. All built the dual edifice 'in which the ideas of Roman magistracy and hellenistic monarchy were subtly blended'.[95] And in spite of themselves they came to look for guidance to the Persian Empire and the hellenistic monarchies which had followed it.[96] The absolutism of the East was steadily pursued through the much-praised first five years of Nero's reign; the 'welfare state' with corn funds, and liturgies, and free festival tickets, were hellenistic inventions going back to the third century B.C.; the idea of law – Ulpian's *princeps legibus solutus est* – the prince is free of the laws – was a Seleucid conception,[97] with a voluntary adherence to law as its corollary; and even the keeping of tame philosophers and the complimentary naming of months like July and August, came originally from the hellenistic kings.[98] The inescapable forms and guards of court life that caused visitors to be searched under Claudius and that, under the Antonines and later, revived the Seleucid and Iranian custom of calling the king's friends to council – all drew away from the Roman tradition and continued to build the western resentment against the East.[99] The triumph of Augustus at Actium was not final and the prejudice so deeply inspired by the great Egyptian queen remained. Every intrusion of Greek superiority accentuated it in Rome. Even the vicissitudes of the Greek dress which Roman exiles had to wear when the toga, the citizen's symbol,[100] was taken from them – for the wearing of which Cicero had apologised[101] and Tiberius had been unpopular; which went out of fashion in Rome in the reaction after Nero, and was disapproved of in Domitian – even such indexes against a foreign fashion were straws in a persistent wind.

'The contact with the alien civilisation of Greece originally roused the Romans to become conscious of their own individual character as a people. While they took over and assimilated all that the Hellenes could give, they shaped their ... concept of what was Roman in deliberate opposition to what was Greek. Out of the war of Actium, artfully converted into a spontaneous and patriotic movement, arose a salutary myth which enhanced ... Roman nationalism to a formidable and even grotesque intensity.'[102]

Under Hadrian (A.D. 117–138) Hellenism and divinity were combined, and as he completed the temple to Zeus in Athens, he became himself Olympius, identified with the God.[103] The new name was deliriously welcomed by the Greeks: countless monuments celebrated it, and altars to the new Olympian as Saviour, Benefactor, Founder, were erected by private people in their houses; the East, which responds to personal influence and to personal influence only, was unified by this worship as by no other bond.

Hadrian himself worked hard at his legend. 'A learned ruler and a strenuous, loving not only to govern the world, but to go up and down in it, devoted to music and flute-playing, and withal a right good eater',[104] he was the first emperor after Augustus to cross the Aegean on a peaceful errand, and twelve years of his reign were spent in travel. His monies were minted in at least ten of the cities in the province of Asia,[105] and delicate marbles with his name carved upon them are scattered now in all the lonely places which once were the cities of his world.[106]

His genius smoothed the path of his successor, whose virtues were very different from his own. 'When I praised Hadrian', Fronto writes, 'I ran for my master, but today I run for myself.'[107] Marcus Aurelius, Pius Antoninus' adopted son, described his unsleeping attention and wise stewardship; his disinterestedness free from superstition, and soberness and steadfastness in all things.[108] For the last time in Imperial history the emperor was wholly at one with Rome and its centralisation,[109] however remote to his subjects in the East.

Under the burden of empire and disintegrating frontiers, Marcus Aurelius (A.D. 161–180) dreamed that his shoulders were made of ivory, strong to bear.[110] The generosity of his character appears in his tribute to Pius, and even more so in the letters to Fronto his teacher, written in the happy tumult of youth and brought to increasing sadness during the twenty years that end in the *Meditations*. The Gods, he says, put up with worthless men who are what they are and so many, 'but thou, though destined to die so soon, criest off, and that though thou art one of the worthless ones thyself. It is absurd not to eschew one's own wickedness, which is possible, but to eschew that of others, which is not possible.'[111]

'. . . thine associates, even the most refined, it is difficult to put up with, let alone the fact that a man has enough to do to endure himself.'[112]

'To pass through each day as if it were the last, without agitation, without torpor, without pretence.'[113]

Such were the three Antonines, so different, who carried the wave of Empire to where Commodus (A.D. 180–192) saw to its breaking; and if Marcus Aurelius is blamed for resuscitating the hereditary principle on behalf of so disastrous a son, it is only fair to remember that the preceding adoptions had all been carried through by childless men: with Augustus and Vespasian before him and Severus after, the dynastic feeling might probably have been awakened if there had been anyone to awaken it.

Development of the Army

The Roman army also had very gradually lost its Italian substance.[114]

The wars that had followed Nero's death gave plenty of scope for reform. 'Dishonour you have exhausted', was the taunt of Vespasian's general to the Praetorian Guard. 'A quarter of each company', Tacitus writes, 'would be away on furlough or loafing about the camp, provided the soldiers paid the centurion his price.'[115] Yet the troops had fought bravely enough for the unworthy Vitellius, and Vespasian himself, marching from Syria to seize the Empire, kept two facts about it clearly in his mind: that it could occur anywhere 'for the secret was now disclosed, that an emperor could be made elsewhere than at Rome'[116]; and that it was in the army's gift.

Both these vital truths went back a long way – to Pompey and the Lex Gabinia that had first allowed him to rule through lieutenants, and to Marius' professional reforms. Personal loyalty to an individual leader was one of the most frequent causes of bloodshed in Republican Rome, and Caesar, treating his soldiers as his friends, was the magnificent example. He borrowed their money when he crossed the Rubicon,[117] and raised their pay to 225 denarii a year, with bonuses and a third of the booty added for officers and men.[118] His colonising, however, aimed beyond the military, and was intended to create a miniature Rome in the East[119]: and it was Augustus who used this precedent to place veterans at military strategic points. He organised not only a separate army fund, but also the length of service and gave a bonus of 3,000 denarii after twenty years. The term was eventually fixed under Hadrian at twenty-five years, and at the end of that time the soldier, whatever his condition, received his donation and with it a diploma of Roman citizenship if he had not got one already.[120] He was then legally able to marry and beget citizens, while those children born to him before could become so by joining the army – an expedient that naturally suited the Imperial government, which had never been able to replace the central reserve of the legions and was always short of recruits.[121] 'Ten asses a day' says Tacitus, 'was the assessment of body and soul: with that they had to buy clothes, weapons and tents, bribe the bullying centurion, and purchase a respite from duty.'[122]

When Vespasian came to power in A.D. 73 his policy,[123] very gradually carried out, was – consciously or no – to eliminate the Italian proletariat from his army. His lavish granting of the Roman franchise, his efforts for education, and particularly for the training ground of his soldiers – the *collegia juvenum* – all pointed in this direction. Urbanisation, the encouragement of the provincial cities, particularly in the West, was pushed 'to the very limit of what was practically possible',[124] and the Flavian army becoming gradually less dependent on either citizenship or geography came to be recruited mainly from the most civilised and the best-educated classes of the urbanised parts of the Empire.[125] His son, Domitian, raised their pay to ioo denarii a month,[126] and the difference within the ranks between legionaries and auxiliaries grew ever less noticeable, until – after the second century – hardly any Italian troops remained except officers and praetorians. Severus replaced even these by Danubians, and the youth of Italy, according to Dio Cassius,[127] 'turned to robbery and to the gladiatorial profession in place of military service'.

The citizen army had now become the Imperial army along the Imperial frontiers.[128] Under the Antonines, after the Flavian reorganisation, Hadrian decreed that each province should see to the supplying of its own troops, and the legions were no longer moved in a body from place to place, but distributed in detachments here and there as they were required, while their headquarters remained fixed in their own province.[129] Their task was to defend the 'underbelly', the extremely vulnerable disarmed population of the Empire, from whose remoter districts they were now chiefly composed.

The Seleucids had used interpreters for their mixed nations,[130] but the Roman official language remained exclusively Latin even on the banks of the Euphrates. Many veterans must have taken a pride in their long service and brought, like the Nabataeans described by Rostovtzeff,[131] strange innovations to their villages, where they settled as small free landowners and gradually built up a new aristocracy with its own provincial roots. They tended to live near their camps, and even before it became customary to give them Roman citizenship on discharge, the auxiliaries who had been hearing Latin spoken throughout their service, and whose higher officers were Roman in outlook, took at least a surface of Roman culture away with them. The province of Africa for instance owed its romanised development in the third century chiefly to the uninterrupted settlement there of the III Augusta legion.[132]

The Parthian War of Lucius Verus

With these soldiers as we have described them Rome continued not only to imitate but to demolish the eastern half of the world. Wars in the Germanic north from now on dominate her history, and a turbulent fringe was beginning to seethe along her borders; and in the East, 'wherever she broke the power of a hellenistic state she destroyed at the same time a bulwark of defence against the frontier peoples'.[133] The policy of the *weak periphery* continued to drag its tragic nemesis behind it.

The implications of the northern wars are beyond my horizon, and so is the growing background of revolution except as it affects the eastern frontier. The Euphrates is my concern, and it flowed in peace through Hadrian's reign,[134] visited by the emperor in person when argument with Parthia arose. Trajan's nominee had been ejected from Babylon, and Hadrian settled him temporarily in Edessa, restored the Parthian king's daughter out of the booty of Ctesiphon and promised the golden throne. His successor, Pius Antoninus (A.D. 138–161) refused to send it, but was able to 'induce the king of the Parthians to forego a campaign against the Armenians merely by writing a letter' – a prestige more due to Hadrian than to himself, for the next Parthian war is said to have been planned under Pius.[135] It broke out in the reign of Marcus Aurelius, when the Parthian Vologaeses hemmed in a legion stationed at Elegeia, and shot down the whole force, leaders and all.[136]

What incidents led up to this action is not known, but a Roman legion at Elegeia was, as we have seen, a dagger pointed at the heart of Parthia and – like Mussolini's Abyssinian 'provocation' which started a hundred miles inside a victim's borders[137] – it prompts one to ask what the legions were doing there? The city of Elegeia, near the modern Erzerum, 'was held by a garrison of Romans' who had made it the foremost city of Armenia.[138]

Vologaeses settled his own candidate on the Armenian throne, refused a peace offer, defeated another Roman army, and advanced 'powerful and formidable against the cities of Syria', whose troops, according to Fronto, were more often found 'in the nearest café garden than in the ranks: their horses shaggy from neglect . . . saddled and with cushions [which do improve the comfort of oriental saddles]. Few of the soldiers could vault upon their steeds. . . . Not many could make their spears hurtle, most tossed them like toy lances. . . . [139] Mutinous, disobedient, seldom with their units . . . tipsy from one noon to the next . . . half naked', [140] they were furthermore 'accustomed to hot baths'. [141]

Avidius Cassius, an efficient Syrian, trained this unhopeful material and fought with it, while Lucius Verus, the emperor's colleague and adopted brother, travelled gently to Antioch, and the war under his generals returned to the familiar landscape of the trade route. In the north, a Roman Syrian senator – soon to be in trouble – was made king of Armenia; and in the south, Avidius Cassius, following in Trajan's footsteps, conducted a brilliant campaign down the Euphrates, rolling up the Parthian stations in his stride. The Parthians hurried back so as not to be cut off west of the river, and were beaten at Dura and again at Sura on the river-bank. Seleuceia opened its gates to Cassius, and Ctesiphon stood a siege, and both were equally destroyed. [142] The king of Parthia retreated behind his mountain screen as usual; the Roman army of the north crossed the Tigris; Alexander's route once more spread its fatal distances in front of the legions; and once more proved elusive: 'An image had been brought from Ctesiphon to Rome and placed in the temple of the Palatine Apollo, where it was formally dedicated to that God. . . . But it is said that after this statue was carried off, and the city was burnt, the soldiers, searching the temple, found a narrow hole, and when this was opened in the hope of finding something of value in it, from some deep gulf which the secret science of the Chaldaeans had closed up, issued a pestilence . . . which polluted the whole world from the borders of Persia to the Rhine and Gaul with contagion and death.' [143] The plague – endemic in Baghdad in spring and autumn even in my day – increased until it broke the invasion: year after year it carried desolation through the peoples of the Empire, and diminished their numbers, often piling up two thousand dead in Rome in a day, [144] altering the balance of classes like the Black Death later in Europe, and helping to bring the *humiliores* to the top. It was looked upon by many as a vengeance of the Gods for Seleuceia, [145] – the bastion of Hellenism, a

town at that time of three or four thousand inhabitants,[146] and founded
by the friend of Alexander. It never recovered; Greek culture was almost
extinguished east of the Euphrates; 'and it was probably now that the
kings of Charax put Aramaic inscriptions on their coins'.[147]

*   *   *

Lucius Verus, the nominal commander, did very little to further a war
which Marcus Aurelius had planned,[148] and Cassius and his colleagues
fought, and the finances of the Empire could not stand.[149] He spent four
winters at Laodiceia, four summers at Daphne, and the rest of the time
at Antioch, and left the Lotus Land reluctantly to celebrate his triumph
in Rome.

His 'well-proportioned person and genial expression' are remembered: the yellow hair onto which gold dust was sifted; the halting
speech and reckless gambling; the crystal goblet named after a favourite
horse,[150] and the anecdote that when a satrap in Armenia thrust his
sword in his face, he did not put him to death, but merely sent him to
the lesser equivalent of Britain.[151]

He did nothing to raise the Imperial prestige in Syria. 'I am ready,' he
writes to his teacher Fronto after his vicarious victories, 'to fall in with any
suggestion as long as my exploits are set in a bright light by you. . . . Do
not be in a hurry to come to my share . . . I think it essential to make
quite clear the great superiority of the Parthians before my arrival, that
the magnitude of my achievements may be manifest. . . . Whatsoever
their character they are no greater, of course, than they actually are,
but they can be made to seem as great as you would have them
seem.'[152]

A slant towards independence becomes noticeable in the eastern
provinces as time goes by. But the next event, the revolt of Avidius
Cassius in A.D. 175 seems to have been less a rising against the Emperor
Marcus – who was rumoured to be dead – than an insurance against
candidates from the other armies, by now almost completely separated
one from the other by Hadrian's reforms.

It was the age of the Syrians. Claudius Pompeianus from Antioch had risen to be a son-in-law of Marcus: and Cassius too came
from the Orontes foothills where Seleucus had once established his
Macedonian soldiers. After beating rebels in Egypt,[153] and bearing the

brunt of Mesopotamia, after disciplining his relaxed and demoralised army and governing Syria for eight years and almost the whole East for nearly six, Cassius felt strong enough to attempt the throne. Severe and capable, he was the first Levantine to revive the old oriental threat of East to West feared by the Augustans.

It drew Marcus from the German rebellions. He made a hasty Sarmatian peace and marched south, refusing the help of barbarian allies who might learn of trouble between Romans.[154] He was met by the news that a centurion had killed the rebel and averted a civil war: and he now made a progress through his eastern lands, which he treated with clemency and 'conducted many negotiations, and ratified peace with all the kings and satraps of Persia when they came to meet him. He was exceedingly beloved by all the eastern provinces, and on many, indeed, left the imprint of philosophy'[155] which must have been badly needed by all concerned; and as he brought his army back to Italy gave orders that the troops should assume the toga, the garb of peace.[156]

Armenia and Edessa were left garrisoned and Parthia remained desolate but intact. The policy of conciliation was resuscitated, without the cordiality with which Hadrian had grasped the last chance of peace: once relinquished, it never more returned. The Parthians cannot humanly have forgiven the second and soon to be repeated capture and burning of their capital, and the Romans had realised the possibilities and riches of the south. Wilhelm Weber writes that 'Rome's interest demanded the offensive, and Marcus pursued it with far-ranging strategic vision.'[157] If so, it was not far-ranging enough, for although – like most Romans and many other people later – he thought of the world as virtually ending at the Tigris, he was in fact cutting the ancient Asiatic openness in two. This operation, first fully effected fifty years earlier by Trajan, led to inescapable disaster sooner or later whenever the conquest of Mesopotamia was attained.

XI

The Lower Euphrates and the End of Parthia

The high-water mark of the Roman offensive is overlapped by a Persian advance in Babylonia and the end of Parthia. The Roman policy of the *weak periphery* has done its work; the Parthian goes down fighting, like Seleucids and Mithradates before him; and a more dangerous enemy fills the vacuum. From now on, with few and fallacious intervals, the Roman frontier in the south-east is defensive. A last chance of peace and traffic is to be given through Palmyra, whose dangerous prosperity will bring the Roman destruction upon her. The chapter ends in chaos and defeat.

> 'All that the Romans hold, occupy and possess is the spoil of outrage; their temples are all of loot drawn from the ruin of cities, the plunder of gods and the slaughter of priests'. (Minucius Felix: XXV.5.)

Palmyra

The French archaeological mission in south Persia has now reached the eleventh city level of Achaemenian Susa – or perhaps the twelfth, for I last saw it four years ago when its streets and houses showed clear as a contour map at the bottom of a shaft, with seven more cities still expected to appear.

Here King Darius, in the sixth century B.C., described his palace – the cedars brought by Assyrians to Babylon and thence by Carians and Ionians; the timber from north-west India and Kerman; gold from Sardis and Bactria; lapis lazuli and cornelians from Sogdiana; turquoises from Chorazmia; silver and copper from Egypt; and ivory from Kush and Sind. Ionian masons had built their limestone walls and carved the pillars, and the goldsmiths were Medes and Egyptians: a polyglot Empire was no Roman innovation and the Persian also had given to these people roads and bridges and three centuries of peace.[1]

The Romans began to be interested in the Babylonian south in the time of Augustus, when Germanicus visited and perhaps settled a representative in Palmyra, and sent a Palmyrene messenger to Mesene, at the estuary of Euphrates. He opened relations with the petty half-desert kings,[2] not only in east and west where there were a score at least between Singara and Hatra and Edessa and Anthemusias, but also in cities like Susa (Seleuceia Eulaeus at that time), and Mesene, Charax, Nippur and Tello – strong-points mostly inhabited by Macedonian settlers who were 'masters of their own cities and owners of their allotments of land'[3] under Parthia.

The first mention we have of Palmyra had been written long before, early in the second millennium B.C., on tablets of the Assyrian-Cappadocian traders[4]: but the Assyrians, using asses only, could not tackle the desert transport, and it was not till the tenth or ninth century B.C., when the two-humped Bactrian camel was well-known and the single-humped Arab was beginning to be introduced,[5] that Aramaic Arabs began to move about these empty spaces. They gave their language, and it lasted and spread through Persian, hellenistic Greek, and Roman ages, first as a literary language in Cappadocia, and then, when Greek ousted it, as the written commercial tongue of the Levant.[6]

There must always have been a halt by the clear water in the desert, and in 280 B.C. a Seleucid general had built a fort for a colony of Macedonian soldiers in Palmyra. It was probably one in a chain connecting Syria and Seleuceia – and so it remained, growing bigger and richer, and conveniently placed from Damascus to reach the Euphrates road eighty

miles away, that led by the river bank through Dura to Seleuceia or
Babylon.

Dura too has an Assyrian root,[7] and became Parthian late in the
second or early in the first century B.C., and remained so until it was
captured by Trajan. An important centre for textiles, with a school of
architecture and the names of several architects recorded,[8] it grew from
a mere fort to a main river strong-point, and was probably the most
northerly of the Parthian fortresses during this time. All the small Syrian
and Euphrates principalities were developing with the rise of Palmyra,
which was taking over the Nabataean caravan route at Damascus, was
organising the farther trans-Arabian caravans and was once more to open
the lower Euphrates to a traffic closed since the fall of the Seleucid kings.
Palmyra herself was not definitely heard of as a staging centre until
Mark Antony tried and failed to capture her with his cavalry and was
repulsed by her archers. In A.D. 32 she was already rich enough to lay
the foundations of her temple[9]; in 9 B.C. she had carved the first of the
discovered inscriptions of her tombs.[10]

The desert landscape embraces her with wide pale ridges – a concave
oasis from which the unseen convexity of the world is excluded – one
feels but does not see it in the unfettered air: and the colonnaded street
which was her thoroughfare and numbered over seven hundred columns
still holds its diminished beauty in the evening and morning light. In the
great days of Palmyra there were villages, gardens and vineyards and
cisterns around her, waterless now and invisible except from the air as a
faint writing under sand; the columns that Cornelius Loos saw thick as a
forest in 1711 have vanished more than half; yet the magic remains – an
Arabian Nights' quality in her gradual relaxation. More than in any place
I know, the voice of ruin speaks, clothed with a luminous austerity of
silence; from the black tents out of sight, propped in the desert among
obliterated fields, the camels come to drink at sunset; the women fill
their goatskins with the limpid water that saw the place rise and fall; and
nothing seems to speak in the nakedness of earth and the clothing light
except Time and the courage of mankind.

Palmyra never lost her tribal complexion even under Rome,[11] and
remained in fact independent owing to her monopoly of a climate where
no one else could venture. She held the vague eastern frontiers with
profit to all concerned, and policed the desert by methods of her own[12];

THE EUPHRATES DESERT

SPRING IN THE SYRIAN DESERT: CAMELS BROWSING

and the presence of a Claudian tribe in her territory in the time of Nero,[13] and of a Roman milestone on the way to the Euphrates (placed by Trajan's father, who was legate there) proves a merely nominal Roman suzerainty in the frontier line against Parthia.[14] In the time of the Antonines she was the only remaining power that could be either a link or a bulwark between Parthia and Rome. She had a Roman garrison after the wars of Verus, but still reached the Indus on her own affairs; and produced high officials for Charax in the south[15]; and kept, to protect her caravans, her own militia of mounted bowmen. These were soon to be used in Africa and Europe, when the Moors – so famous among the auxiliaries in the wars of Trajan – began to be eclipsed in the third century by the archers of Osrhoene. Partly Christian, and the best forces of the East under Aurelian,[16] they were to show their bravery in the Persian wars after they had tried to nominate an emperor of their own (in A.D. 235 when the last of the Severi was dead). The whole climax of Palmyra 'is but one reflexion the more of the might of these oriental archers'.[17]

Nominally Roman, and reckoned so by Corbulo for taxes,[18] Palmyra was fundamentally Arab and more Iranian than Greek. She remained neutral along the Parthian border, and was allowed to keep a garrison in Vologasia,[19] the Parthian emporium of the south. Objects from Sarmatia or Mongolia, found in her ruins, point to the silk road trade[20]; but throughout the second century, when she chiefly flourished, the Nabataeans, and the Kushans of the Indus, swung her commerce away from the Parthians and Greeks of Seleuceia towards the south. Metal goods, minerals, slaves, corals and textiles, wine and glass, styrax and sweet clover were exported, and tigers and other wild beasts reached the West from India through Palmyra.[21] Her local taxes were imposed on slaves, oil, clothes, hides and furs; on leather workshops, harlotry, and the use of water in the oasis; but her foreign customs, to defraud which was punishable with death, were controlled by Rome though managed by her own officials, and twenty-five denarii were imposed for each camel-load of myrrh 'in alabaster vessels', and thirteen for each in goatskins.[22] A sort of jute exported only from India has been found in Palmyra[23]; and the great caravans to and from Charax at the mouth of the Euphrates grew ever heavier with the sea-borne Indian trade. Their presidents and associations shuffled Persian, Babylonian and Hittite fashions in courts and colonnades,[24] and their tombs stand square in the sand, shorn of their pillars. Merchants rather than rulers, the inscriptions they left were mostly dedicated to the caravans and their leaders, and few to emperors or governors.[25] A garrison was put in by Marcus Aurelius, and the city was given its Italian rights – *colonia iuris Italici* – by the Emperor Severus, who may have visited it[26]: yet the oligarchy of commerce continued independent, and long after Palmyra's day other cities, Aleppo or Damascus, were to take up its heritage. Two hundred years after its fall the Indian, Arab and Persian ships were still sailing up the Euphrates as far as Muslim Hira.[27]

The Parthian South

Most of the Palmyrene inscriptions are related to the south, and show the desert route 'where Greeks dedicate girl children to serve in native temples'[28] in regions scarcely known, and carts (described by Chinese travellers) could move in summer only, up to their axles in dust.[29] Attembalos, king of the port of Charax, had been friendly to Trajan and remained so through the Mesopotamian rebellion, content with his harbour monopoly and unwilling no doubt to lose the Roman trade: but his lands remained vague to the Greek or Roman mind. The traveller Pausanias in the second century A.D. met no one who had ever seen Babylon or Susa,[30] and the Euphrates estuary was almost unknown, 'the greater part lost in a marsh and ends in earth: and some have a bolder tale, and declare that it runs under the earth to turn up in Egypt and mingle with the Nile'.[31]

The Syrian desert was held open for cavalry, with water kept underground till midsummer in cisterns, and the trace of some small guardhouse of the third century can be found in the desert landscape near every isolated spring.[32] Poidebard examined the ruins from the air, and describes low walls fanning out from gateways to get the nomad flocks quickly into shelter against the attacking horsemen[33]; and the auxiliaries could come from their camps at a gallop to help when the tribes were raided. Glubb Pasha, in the early days of the British Mandate in Iraq, describes such desert wars.[34]

The Parthian road reached this insecure land from earth-built fort to fort through reedy dusty stretches – west of the Ziggurat of Ur long deserted, by Forat, and Uruk, Vologasia and Babylon, by Sippar, and Neapolis whose crossing led to Ctesiphon, to the middle stretches that kept to the bank of Euphrates and were written down (from north to south) by Isidore of Charax in his *Parthian Stations.* Starting from the regions round Carrhae on the Balikh river he came down to Nicephorium (near Muslim Raqqa), and by the canal of Semiramis where 'the Euphrates is dammed with rocks . . . to overflow the fields; but wrecks the boats in summer' – to where the Khabur tributary comes in and the legions crossed over to Roman territory east of the river: then through Dura and the city of Giddan (Jabariyah) and the island in Euphrates 'where was the treasure of Phraates, who cut the throats of his concubines when Tiridates . . . invaded the land'. Anatho (Anah) is still flourishing with water-wheels and gardens, and Aipolis is now Hit – a dusky little town of black stone and bituminous springs. 'Beyond is Besechana in which is a temple of Atergatis, and then Neapolis where those leaving the Euphrates pass through Narmalchan (the Nahr-al-Malik canal) to Seleuceia on the Tigris'[35] as we have seen. Here Mesopotamia and Babylonia met.

The Roman South

Dura was the most southerly bastion of Rome on the Euphrates, until the Persian conquest in the early third century killed its commerce, and Diocletian fixed the border north of it at Circesium, and the Dura crossing was abandoned.[36] It was a hellenistic city built by the Seleucids like an American town in the square blocks of their day,[37] and garrisoned under Rome by the XXth *Cohors Palmyrenorum.*[38] As a military outpost,[39] its road led from one *funduq*,[40] to another, held by Palmyrene archers to shelter the mounted escorts of the caravans.[41] In the no-man's land south of it, the Parthian with his loose wide sleeves[42] and trailing gown that impeded fighting but helped against the sun; or a platoon of cavalry riveted, men and horses, in armour; or the bedu with a single rein and a flick of the hand on his thin horse to steer it, would alone find the way from castle to castle[43] beside their barren river, by heaps now indistinguishable beside Euphrates – ruined walls reinforced by Justinian, or built like the round mass of Najm by later Muslims for Aleppo caravans. The frontiers of Syria, Palmyra and Parthia melted into each other in the waste; and there is a picture of the Byzantine age, of a Christian monk and his disciples walking along there, singing psalms till hunger overtook them and some tribune with Roman soldiers invited them into their *castella* and gave them food.[44] Even in the days of Justinian this frontier line was vague.[45]

Its underground waters were tapped for wells, usually built some way below their springs in hollow places; and as one travelled up from the south, the bearded wheat no doubt softened the low undulations as it does in the Jazirah today. The population was greater than now; Czernik, in the nineteenth century, already found no more than one inhabitant for every ruined site.[46]

Diocletian ran his frontier north of Dura, at Circesium, which became the most southern Roman post, with possibly a pontoon bridge,[47] where the Khabur tributary fell in. In A.D. 363 the emperor Julian, when invading Parthia, was still to find a garrison here of six thousand men in a fortress between the two rivers, and to leave four thousand more. It became the customary crossing in the later Muslim age.[48]

North-west of it, the Palmyra track[49] came in and crossed the river at Nicephorium and Sura; and the river route continued as far as Zeugma, with the shrine of the Syrian Goddess at Hierapolis on its left hand. Nothing remains on the spot but a slender muslim minaret in a field of ruins, less living than Lucian's description of the courts, and the bearded Apollo[50] and the high phallic cones on which men would climb to spend a week in fear of falling – a singularly unchristian model for St Simeon Stylites to follow later on.

The Palmyra track was a backbone of empire, and Diocletian reinforced it. It crossed the river and moved into an earthquaky[51] area of cultivation and settled villages – the small kingships and Greek-speaking cities among which Crassus had got entangled – Anthemusias, Batnae, Zenodotium, Ichnae, Callinicum, Carrhae – *civitates multas et varias* 'in all of which were excellent men extremely sharp in business'[52] and where throughout the third century there was constant raiding. Apollonius, as early as the first century A.D., says that one of his governors sent a mission to the king in Babylon about two villages near Zeugma, complaining that the Romans had taken them, though long ago belonging to Antiochus and Seleucus. "'O Apollonius," said the king, "these villages were given to my forefathers by the kings whom I mentioned, that they might sustain the wild animals, which are taken by us in our country and sent to theirs across the Euphrates, and they, as if they had forgotten this fact, have espoused a policy that is new and unjust. What then do you think are the intentions of the embassy?" Apollonius replied, "Their intention, O king, is moderate and fair, seeing that they only desire to obtain, with your consent, places which, as they are, in their territory, they can equally well retain without it.'" And he added his opinion, that it was a mistake to quarrel with the Romans over villages so paltry that probably bigger ones were owned by private individuals; and added that it was a mistake to go to war even over larger issues.[53]

*   *   *

Latin inscriptions increase as one reaches the frontier zone of Euphrates but few are found beyond it to the east. None of the legions were permanently posted on the river banks below Vespasian's XVIth Flavia Firma at Samosata, though detachments must always have guarded a customs' post like Zeugma. The difficulties are great in the desert; and though the Euphrates armies were good customers for Syria and Asia Minor, no Greeks were allowed to traffic[54]; the more southern lands were left to Palmyra undisturbed. Italian traders had mostly disappeared from Asia during the first century A.D., beaten by the Orientals and particularly by the Syrians, who held the sea trade until the coming of the Saracen pirates, and were as ubiquitous as Genoa and Venice later on.[55] And these also were to avoid the hardships of the Euphrates in their day.[56]

Except on the Khabur, and the Jagjag river below Tigranocerta, and for a short interval along the route to Hatra[57] there were no Roman fortresses south of the Nisibis road, for the garrisons could not subsist beyond the zones of cultivation.[58] The legion nearest to the Euphrates below Samosata was the Xth Fretensis, winter-quartered in Cyrrhus (Kilis) since the reign of Tiberius,[59] and far enough from the frontier to show how little a Parthian attack was feared at that time. Easy roads reached it from Samosata and Zeugma through the vine-clad hills of Doliche (Duluk) where tombs are still scattered with pagan or Christian symbols honeycombed into the village hill, and Zeus Dolichenus, the god of the Chalybes, was a famous god of the Armies.[60] From Doliche to Cyrrhus and then to Antioch was easy marching, in and out of bays as if the open lands of Euphrates were a sea; until the hills of Antioch appeared, thin like greyhounds on their skyline, with Orontes below them, navigable to the city at that time.[61] At its estuary ran the coast-road that was to be repaired by Severus the great road-mender,[62] and Caracalla and Aurelian; the port of Seleucia, the base of the fleet and only port cared for by Rome, was near at hand – ruined already in the third century when the Persians came.[63]

All this river landscape, of which only the edges were fortified, was to be from the third century onward a battlefield of armies both coming and going.[64] Its free traffic, 'of merchants from Parthia selling and buying in all the Roman land',[65] soon came to be enclosed in 'gates'; and exports of military value – metals, corn, wine, oil and salt[66] – were forbidden. Its Roman coins, minted in the little cities and found at Sinjar, end with the end of prosperity and of the Severan dynasty, in A.D. 235.[67]

The dice for attack here were loaded against the Roman descending by Tigris or Euphrates into a hostile country easily traversed at any point by an enemy from the Persian hills; whereas an oriental invader moving upstream had an expanse of desert on his right to protect him, and only a frontal enemy to fear.[68] Just as the seizing of Armenia had entailed the conquest of Mesopotamia and Babylonia, that in its turn demanded the conquest of the Persian range beyond it to make it safe. And this is why, in spite of apparent success, the warfare carried on by Trajan, and after him by Verus, Severus, Caracalla, to Valerian and beyond, was doomed to failure even before it began. It was only the pacific character of the Parthian Empire that had allowed this strategic inequality to pass unnoticed for so long.

The Roman Army

In the second century, through the heyday of the Antonines, the varied army that held the eastern frontier was still disciplined and splendid. Behind a double line of scouts, the mounted Nabataean archers, the wing (*ala*) of the Isaurians (from Anatolia), the Rhaetian cavalry, the Ituraeans (south-west of Damascus), the mounted archers from Cyrene, the Celtic cavalry in double file, are described by Arrian for his province of Cappadocia. Infantry four deep follow with flags displayed – Italians and Cyrenians, mounted Bosporans and Numidians, and all there is of archers and horsemen before them and on either flank. The cavalry of the legions at the centre escorted catapults, legates, prefects, tribunes and centurions with their eagles; the javelin-throwers and the marching infantry and allies from Lesser Armenia, the heavy infantry from Trebizond, the spearmen of Colchis, the baggage and a guard of Getae from the steppes of Asia, brought up the rear.[69]

The camps were still those described by Josephus – the outward circumference resembling a wall, 'where between the towers stand the engines for throwing arrows and darts, and for slinging stones, and where they lay all other engines that can annoy the enemy, all ready for their several operations. They also erect four gates, one at every side of the circumference, and those large enough for the entrance of the beasts and wide enough for making excursions, if occasion should require. They divide the camp within into streets, very conveniently, and place the tents of the commanders in the middle, but in the very midst of all is the general's own tent, in the nature of a temple, insomuch that it appears to be a city built on the sudden, with its market-place, and place for handicraft trades, and with seats for the officers superior and inferior, where, if any differences arise, their causes are heard and determined. . . . '

' . . . in the morning the soldiery go everyone to their centurions and these centurions to their tribunes, to salute them; with whom all the superior officers go to the general of the whole army, who then gives them of course the watch-word and other orders, to be by them carried to all that are under their command. . . . '

'Now when they are to go out of their camp, the trumpet gives a sound, at which time nobody lies still, but at the first intimation they take down their tents, and all is made ready for their going out; then do the trumpets sound again, to order them to get ready for the march; then do they lay their baggage suddenly upon their mules and other beasts of burthen, and stand, as at the place of starting, ready to march: when also they set fire to their camp, and this they do because it will be easy for them to erect another camp and that it may not ever be of use to their enemies. Then do the trumpets give a sound the third time, that they are to go out, in order to excite those that on any account are a little tardy, so that no one may be out of his rank when the army marches. Then does the crier stand at the general's right hand and asks them thrice in their own tongue whether they be ready now to go out to war or not. To which they reply as often, with a loud and cheerful voice, saying, we are ready. And this they do almost before the question is asked them: they do this as filled with a kind of martial fury, and at the same time that they so cry out, they lift up their right hands also.'

' ... The readiness of obeying their commanders is so great that it is very ornamental in peace; but when they come to a battle the whole army is but one body, so well coupled together are their ranks, so sudden are their turnings about, so sharp their hearing as to what orders are given them, so quick their sight of the ensigns, and so nimble are their hands when they set to work; whereby it comes to pass that what they do is done quickly, and what they suffer they bear with the greatest patience.'[70]

These serviceable troops no longer flashed in scarlet and gold like the Seleucid armies. A tunic and heavy nailed boots and occasionally the loose barbarian trousers clothed the legionary, with sometimes an added military cloak and scarf; a leather corselet, and perhaps a coat of mail under, were worn by the ranks, and a metal cuirass by the centurions; and their arm was sword and dagger,[71] and in the second century or possibly earlier, a lance for hurling instead of the heavier *pilum*, while the auxiliary had a spear for thrusting and a long sword.[72] 'Of sixty-one soldiers serving in the Egyptian legions, in the first century, fifty-three are known to have been natives of Asia Minor, Syria and Egypt.' The division of the Empire is reflected in the armies of the Greek-speaking East and Latin-speaking West.[73]

The Limes Under Hadrian

The *limes* along which these troops were serving is too complex a subject to be considered here in detail: one may say however that its gradual growth was various – developing from a line of watch towers with scarce a path to bind them, to the elaborate sentry-walk raised high above the surrounding country and flanked by ditches and towers which Trajan – and Hadrian after him – built to protect the more threatened outlying regions of the Empire as though they were the precincts of a castle.

The *limes* never reached this perfection in the south-east on the desert border, partly because of the nature of the land with its difficulties of transport and subsistence; partly because of the river barrier which, with a desert steppe to reinforce it, discouraged invasion; but above all because of the unaggressive nature of the Parthian enemy. We are coming close upon the disappearance of Parthia under the impact of the Sassanians from Iran, and the inadequacy of the desert frontier was soon to be made plain.

Meanwhile, under Hadrian, the whole complexion of the *limes* had altered from the offensive to the defensive, with the general second-century alteration of the army. What had been a spear-head under Trajan was henceforth to be a shield, and by the end of Hadrian's reign the frontier's defensive reformation was well under way. Aware that bridges can be used for crossing in both directions, he had destroyed Trajan's greatest construction on the Danube and, although he left eight legions strung along the boundary from Satala to Bostra, had limited the Empire's total forces to the twenty-eight legions of Augustus and reorganised them defensively – the auxiliaries close to the frontier, the rest garrisoned in the rear.[74] During the second century if not before, the legion came to be used rather like the Greek phalanx, in a solid body kept for the later stages of a battle, while the auxilia, now extremely efficient, opened the attack.

The resistance in defence was first offered by the auxilia in a series of forts, each occupied by one of their cohorts, till the legions had time to march up from larger reserve camps connected by road with the front-line fortresses. In attack, on the other hand, it was equally necessary for the Romans to safeguard their line of retreat with the most seasoned troops, and leave the first impact to the auxilia, whose activity was particularly noticeable in the desert areas.

The Southern Route

Trajan's catastrophic Parthian policy shifted the interest of the Euphrates from Armenia to Mesopotamia: but, even before his reign, the Romans had discovered how the dues and harbours of the south could relieve their chronic embarrassment, when imports like spikenard had risen to three times the value they had in the days of Mary Magdalene[75]: a new Arabian chapter, or perhaps the continuation of the older chapter of Augustus,[76] was emphasised by Trajan in A.D. 106 when he annexed the

Nabataeans round Petra. The termini of all the southern trade routes –
Jerash, Petra, Gabala, Rabbat-Ammon and Damascus – were in their
hands.[77] They had their own docks, and warehouses to distribute the
Arabian spices even near Naples at Puteoli.[78] Their absorption gave little
trouble and they prospered under Rome. Their archers were used as
garrison troops to save the legions[79] and protect the trans-Arabian trade,
and the new capital of the new province was established in A.D. 106 at
Bostra (Bosra). The troops of Saladin later were to turn its amphitheatre
of black lava into a fortress, that housed a nervous French garrison in
the twenties of this century. When first I travelled in their district they
were politely convinced that I was a spy.

Under the Romans this south-western trade route was still the main
source of wealth for Egypt[80] as it had been through the ages, and city life
prospered along it, though Petra declined with the rise of Palmyra. Two
other great desert cities – Vologasia and Hatra – owed their existence
to it[81]; and others – Jerash, Amman, Edessa, Babylon – grew and
flourished, and so did Parthian Ctesiphon[82] in spite of its destructions.
The trade with Europe through Palmyra continued: the Egyptian linen
paid for Arabian spices and helped to limit the Indian circulation of
Roman money[83]; Trajan repaired his 'river', the Cairo to Suez canal;
and before A.D. 216 the Red Sea was to be patrolled and Coptos was to
be garrisoned by Palmyrenian archers officered by Rome.[84]

Hadrian exploited the situation, maintained a friendship with the
south Arabian kings, and was called the second founder of Palmyra. He
favoured the southern trade route in all its length, and kept friendly
intercourse alive between Syrian Rome and the Euphrates. Imperial
bureaucracy had not yet closed down on Palmyra; when peaceful relations with the Parthians were re-established, Hadrian was careful to
arrange for the free passage of the Roman (Palmyrenian) caravans, and
pushed his troops as far as the Euphrates,[85] possibly running a flotilla
there[86] when threatened from the East. He adopted the Parthian cavalry
equipment for his desert wars and a merchant of Palmyra was allowed
to dedicate a temple to him in Vologasia,[87] for his popularity was great
with the Parthians. They 'regarded him as a friend because he took away
the king whom Trajan had set over them'.[88]

There were other inducements. The Sarmatian-Alani, pressing continually against the northern frontier, gave a common defensive interest

to both empires in the north. There was no need for Rome to hold
Mesopotamia while Petra and Palmyra were under her control – just
as there was no need to hold Armenia while the Black Sea was open
and the Caucasus at peace. Whether Hadrian's policy was meant to be
permanent, or merely to tide over a crisis is not certain, but – reversing
that of Trajan – it was a policy of peace: his frontier system showed itself
useless only when his tactics were reversed by the emperors who followed him. The Roman defence then broke down and the thin frontier
crumbled, and only the strongest walled cities were able to survive.

Septimius Severus, A.D. 192–211

The four great Antonines went their ways into eternity, and whatever
one may think of philosophers, Marcus Aurelius' son Commodus was
a living example that their sons should not be kings. He was murdered
in spite of his love for the beautiful[89] and his guilelessness, the solitary
tributes made him; and Septimius Severus, in A.D. 193, deified him when
finally succeeding to his throne. He hoped to hitch the credit of his own
African dynasty to that of the venerated predecessors, and 'inveighed
against the senate for dishonouring that Emperor (Commodus) unjustly',
since most of the senators 'were worse in their lives than he'.

Severus, a cultured man and African at heart, was alien to Rome but
not unaware of the value of tradition – particularly of his own. He fought
the senate, and built up the African Hannibal's grave near Nicomedia
(Ismit), guiding himself like a surf-rider through chaos in the ominously
gathering divisions of his time. The loyalties of Syria and Asia were
increasingly local, and in the struggle with his Syrian rival, Pescennius
Niger, the oriental army was defeated by his Danube troops on the field
of Issus, through a ruse which Alexander had foreseen there and guarded
against five hundred years before.[90] Yet the Syrian army fought well;
and Byzantium stood a siege of more than two years (A.D. 193–96) and
frightful punishment when it was over; and the eastern feeling against the
northerners gathered strength with the Danubian triumph. The rulers
beyond Tigris and Euphrates had sent congratulations and promised
assistance to Pescennius Niger, and he, like the rebels before him and
the usurping emperor Macrinus after, fled towards the Parthians and was
caught and beheaded between Antioch and the Bridge. 'The Imperial

frontiers were ceasing to be mental boundaries'; the Parthian was no longer the foreigner; and so many of the defeated troops took their skill across Euphrates that Severus was forced to grant a general amnesty.[91]

In A.D. 194 he led his army across the river at Zeugma. Edessa had regained her independence, and the subjects of King Vologaeses, who could never resign themselves to the loss of Mesopotamia and their trade route, had been trying to shake off the Roman garrisons. Severus sent his commanders to the lands of the present Shammar tribes in north Iraq to raid the Skenite Arabs, and the Parthian king followed the familiar pattern of the wars and withdrew behind the Persian hills. Partly sailing and partly marching along the river, Severus found Seleuceia and Babylon deserted, and gave his troops the captured and then abandoned Ctesiphon to sack[92]: 'He used to declare,' says Dio, 'that he had added a vast territory to the Empire and had made it a bulwark of Syria. On the contrary, it is shown by the fact . . . that his conquest has been a source of constant wars and great expense to us.'[93] But the days of Parthia as a buffer state protecting Rome were nearly over, and a first serious Persian rising against the Parthians followed this defeat. Rome had destroyed another of her bulwarks in the East.

The Climate and Hatra

Sir Aylmar Haldane, commanding British troops in Iraq during a rising in 1920, remarks that the climate may be considered healthy apart from dysentery, malaria, typhoid, cholera and plague; and in 1943, during the Second World War, one in seven of our men went down with heat stroke while encamped (in a singularly shadeless place) under canvas. Severus' army 'encountered a dust storm that caused them great distress, so that they could no longer march or even talk . . . and when water did appear, on account of its strangeness', for it does not look appetising in the desert, 'it meant no more to them than if it had not been found at all, until Severus called for a cup, and . . . drained it in full view of all'.[94] The fierceness of the climate pervaded all the Roman invasions, and continued to do so when the Persians had replaced the Parthians and massacred their prisoners for want of water, and the warfare of the following centuries had destroyed the few mud habitations along the trade route.[95] Severus did not linger in the south. He 'did not even occupy Ctesiphon, but, just as if the sole purpose of his campaign had been to plunder this place, he was off again'.[96] On his way north he laid siege for a second time to Hatra, where water was so plentiful within the city walls that every street had a fountain,[97] but is hidden underground in the surrounding steppe. The suddenness of water peculiar to a limestone country saved Hatra from the Romans as the city wells with desert around them were to save Nisibis from the Persians throughout the coming century; and Severus failed as Trajan had failed before him.

At Hatra, Dio writes, the Arabian cavalry 'kept assailing everywhere in swift and violent attacks. . . . They inflicted the greatest damage on their assailants when these approached the wall; and much more still after they had broken down a small portion of it; for they hurled down after them, among other things, the bituminous naphtha [of which there still are pools near Mosul] that consumed the engines and all the soldiers on whom it fell. Severus observed this from a lofty tribunal. When a portion of the outer circuit had fallen in one place, and all the soldiers were eager to force their way into the remainder, Severus checked them by ordering the signal for retreat to be clearly sounded. For the place enjoyed great fame, containing as it did a vast number of offerings to the Sungod as well as vast sums of money; and he expected the Arabians to come to terms voluntarily . . . and allowed one day to pass; then, when no one came to him . . . he commanded the soldiers to assault the wall once more, though it had been built up during the night. But the Europeans, who alone of his army had the ability to do anything, were so angry that not one of them would any longer obey him, and the others, Syrians, who were compelled to make the assault in their place, were miserably destroyed.'[98]

The rifts between the Eastern and Western armies are plainly visible and the coming age was to bring them out fully: Severus already had several mutinies to contend with; but his campaign was successful in spite of Hatra,[99] and he left Mesopotamia diagonally established from Euphrates to Tigris across the trade route, a Roman province with Nisibis as capital and Singara as an outpost, where Trajan's road still swings across the pass. Into it Edessa, the 'daughter of the Parthians', was inserted as a client kingdom to be ruled by the Abgars with their Armenian-Nabataean-Parthian names.

Caracalla, A.D. 211–217

Caracalla in A.D. 211 followed his father as the Augustus of the East, and heard with ill-judged pleasure of the family quarrels that were now wrecking the Parthian dynasty. The war of conquest continued, and the heat of the climate is again mentioned, and the Parthian king hid again behind the Persian hills.[100]

Caracalla pursued the ghost of Alexander, whose 'achievements were ever on his lips'.[101] He instituted a phalanx of Macedonians, and wrote to the senate that the conqueror was once again alive in his own person.[102] Picking up the fragments of the great conqueror's dream, he thought to unite the two empires by marriage and asked for the daughter of the Parthian as his wife; and when the proposal was rejected, offended the Parthians by opening the captured tombs and scattering the bones of their kings. In the spring of A.D. 217, riding through the countryside of Carrhae by the mound now called Sultantepe where the Assyrian library of the Moon-goddess had been kept, he stopped to relieve himself and was stabbed by his equerry, at the instance of Macrinus, the praefect of the Praetorians.[103]

The great Alexander's shadow hangs over the eastern borderlands while the power of Rome is declining; 'it is said that those who wear the likeness of him carved in gold or silver are aided in all that they do'.[104] And when Macrinus and Elagabalus after him had also been murdered, and the last grand-nephew of Septimius, Alexander Severus, had been placed on the throne by the army, he too had a phalanx, and a guard of Silver Shields, and 'used to say that there should be a great difference between a Roman and a Macedonian Alexander'[105] – and so of course there was. 'And when he had with him friends of the military class he would serve them a goblet "in honour of Alexander the Great".'[106]

This ill-fated young man closed the dynasty of the Severi, and while thirteen out of seventeen emperors after Septimius had been or were to be murdered by their own soldiers, the destinies of Rome on the Euphrates are controlled by other hands: the three centuries of the Parthian wars come to their end and the rising sun of Persia lifts above the eastern horizon.

THE BRIDGE OF SEPTIMIUS SEVERUS NEAR KIAHTA

THE EMPEROR VALERIAN KNEELING BEFORE SHAPUR

The End of Parthia

In Iran, in the province of Fars, where the tomb of Cyrus is still visited, in the traditional centre of their race and out of the line of trade or interference, the people of Persia had guarded their memories and watched their sacred fire through the Parthian ages, under the cliff-sculptured tombs of their kings.[107] Their new capital of Istakhr was near Persepolis; and at Darabjerd, not far from there, a young man called Ardashir became their first ruler in A.D. 208 through the death of his elder brother – which surprisingly enough seems to have been natural. He rebelled against the Parthians and in A.D. 224 (or possibly 227) defeated the last Parthian King Artabanus; and gave the name of his grandfather Sassan to the new dynasty – known as the Sassanian.

The Kashgai tribe still pass through his country in their spring and autumn migrations. Moving in the distance along the straight roads, their black clusters appear like bars of music, flowing to summer pastures from the lands beyond Shiraz. Their white felt caps still vaguely resemble mitres and all day they pass by, with long thin faces and fine eyes like the sculptured tombs above them, where the cliff suddenly ends and the windowless fire-temple stands at the opening of the plain.[108] The trek lasts a month or more, they say. The camels heave along it with a black foam of goats around them like little crested waves. The foals trot free beside the ridden mares; the donkeys follow; the tent-poles lie horizontal along the saddle bags, and, from the cooking cauldron tied on top, a hen, or baby, or black lambkin's head emerges. In the hotel garden beside Persepolis, dust eddies all day over the pool and its pots of geraniums and beds of pansies, and over the trees – maple, pine and quince in blossom – and the lawn; until a thread of coolness shows evening coming, and gardeners go about with watering cans, barefoot on the grass. The diesel starts; lamps, yellow and red, reflect the water; and the clankety bells move in darkness, as it were from century to century, until their camp is pitched and their fires are lighted beside some rushy stream.

*   *   *

The young Ardashir routed the army of Artabanus in three successive battles, and killed him in the last one, and hung his head in the temple of Anahita near Persepolis. He then continued to defeat a coalition of Kushans and Romans and Chosroes the Arsacid king of Armenia – until the Romans and the Kushan king retired after two years of warfare, and the king of Armenia fought on for ten years alone.[109]

But the Parthians vanished, unobtrusive and inarticulate as they came, and their eclipse repeated that of the Seleucids before them; a stronger enemy gathered on the frontier of Rome. Ardashir had a long reign in which to consolidate his state-church and his rule out of the careless Parthian lands; and Rome was to be threatened and invaded for nearly half a millennium before the Arabs in the seventh century destroyed Syria and the Sassan power together in one mighty revolution.

In an eastern tradition, the Parthian country had been divided among ninety princes by the dying Alexander, to forestall any chance of their revenge.[110] Too nomadic to be acceptable to settled peoples, they had never been wholly adopted either by their Iranian kinsmen – whom they saved from further invasions from the steppes – or by the Greek and Babylonian cities whose trading welfare was their chief concern: and as they were indifferent to written words, and such as there were were mostly obliterated by the Sassanians, they left scarcely a memory behind them except in the nameless epic poetry of Asia, where they survive.[111]

They are slowly and laboriously being discovered as their mounds are excavated and the achievement of their unsung tradition comes to light. Their round camp-cities, taken from the Assyrians,[112] were imitated by Diocletian in Split and by the Arabs in Samarra.[113] The fashion of their palaces – a central nave with smaller naves beside it – still seen at Hatra and Asshur and carried on in Sassanian Ctesiphon[114] – was derived from tents open to or closed against the winds: and vaults built with gypsum mortar that sets quickly,[115] invented to supply the lack of timber,[116] substitute the flat roofs of Babylonia. The Islamic-Iranian house, with its fountained court and four vaulted *iwans* or open halls, such as one may see in Isfahan, or Damascus, or Cairo, all descend from this nomadic conception.[117] Pillars are no support here, but are mere hellenistic additions to an Asiatic substance, like the Parthian civilisation itself: under an essentially tolerant régime, Babylonian and Parthian styles were mixed in the houses of Susa, Dura, or Palmyra: and the Parthians' religion was as synthetic as their art.[118]

They survived in many visible things: in the armour of their warfare which the Sassanians carried on towards mediaeval Europe; in the crenellated parapet taken from the Neo-Babylonians and handed on to Persia[119]; in the stylised, frontal quality of their painting and sculpture, that looks forward to Byzantium[120]; in the royal gifts of garments which came down from Seleucid through Parthian and Sassanian to our day.[121] The architectural use of stucco made its first appearance in Persia,[122] though the type of the painting on their walls was taken from the West[123]; and in Palmyra, where the fusion is most complete, one can see the Parthian dress carved on tombs,[124] with loose embroidered tunic, and the jewelled shoes that the Syrian emperor Elagabalus was so much criticised for wearing, and trousers folded like the skin of a hippopotamus, as the Chaldaeans still wear them today.

The Sassanians, whose aim was to reinstate the Achaemenian kingdom of their ancestors, succeeded in almost eliminating the foreign interlude from their minds, and the Indian Parsees tell how Ardashir restored the sacred books mythically burnt by Alexander, omitting the Parthians altogether.[125] Yet Parthia, more Iranian than the Achaemenians, remains an indispensable link with them, even in details of hereditary ritual, conventions of feudalism and royalty[126] introduced into Armenia, for instance, which have descended to the West. The ancient Seleucid devotion to the royal house (as apart from its individuals) comes down intact[127]: the great families, their four heads of household, village, tribe and province, their temples, administration,[128] religion and general civilisation were all transferred into the more fanatic age of the Sassanians, whose chief innovation seems to have been a religious intolerance unfamiliar to either of the preceding dynasties.[129] Inevitably, whenever we seek connecting links between Sassanian and Achaemenian art, we find them in the art of the Parthians. The sudden renascence of the Sassanians is a myth. The liaison between them and the Achaemenians was provided by the Parthians.[130]

What is more important, they saved the western world from the menace of their own nomad kinsmen,[131] and held the frontiers of the Oxus while the last of the Greco-Bactrian kingdom was swept away.

Their army was chiefly 'an array of horsemen' – heavy armed cavalry using the horse-shoe that at that time had been invented, or light bowmen recruited from the lesser nobility of small landowners – 'private armies of the satraps and of the vassal kings', and king's guards largely foreign; sometimes foot soldiers, such as the army of twenty thousand concentrated at Ctesiphon against the Alani in A.D. 134.[132] They were never good at sieges, since they were uninterested in conquest and content to retire into their wildernesses when attacked[133]; yet engines of war were introduced by Roman deserters or captives,[134] and the Macedonian colonists, who had inherited a good training in the arts of war, garrisoned their own cities. All this, taken over with scarcely an alteration by the Sassanians, had been kept in constant training through western and eastern campaigns. The empire of other Iranian nomads[135] had been a perpetual threat on their eastern border; and the Kushans, straddling the Hindu-Kush and profiting by Roman wars, had captured Herat, Seistan, and all western India, so that the three main stretches of the silk road were in their hands[136]; yet, by constant diplomacy, the trade remained open – an example to the West. The trade route and the threat from the Kushans was the first problem to be tackled by Ardashir.

The Sassanians on the Euphrates

The Kushans had entered history in the first half of the first century A.D. with their king, Kujula Kadphises, who crossed the Hindu Kush, occupied the Kabul district and extended the boundaries of his kingdom to the left bank of the Indus, seizing these countries from the last princes of Parthian origin.[137] This expansion of the young Kushan kingdom occurred while the vigorous policy of Nero and his advisers was making itself felt, and Corbulo, marching south from Artaxata, was offering an escort to the envoys from Hyrcania.[138] The Kushans were, like the Parthians, middle-men in commerce, and Rome tried to enter into direct relations with them. But they seem to have been little attracted by the prospect of an attack on Parthia, who consistently tried to reduce the tension in the East to a rninimum while her decadence coincided with the rise of the Kushan empire. This remained a constant menace and threatened to weaken Iran still further by closing the trade route. The first Sassanians were fully alive to the danger, and the conquest of the Kushan empire was one of their earliest enterprises.

*   *   *

These eastern tangles explain the intermittence of the early Sassanian offensives in the west.

Ardashir defied Rome by minting gold – a prerogative which the easy-going Parthians had never claimed. His coins were no longer Greek but Aramaic,[139] though his horse still bears a Greek inscription[140] on the rock-carved sculpture that portrays him trampling the dead body of the Parthian king. Six years after the death of the Parthian, in A.D. 231, he met the last of the Severi who – struggling against mutinies and usurpers – was unaware of the radical change that had altered the Roman fortunes – whose embassies were rejected, whose invasion was defeated, both in Armenia (where his ally, the Parthian Chosroes, was still active), and again, after some hard fighting, near Dura. Victorious according to the *Life*, but in the silence of Herodian, the last of the Severi returned to Antioch with the European soldiers suffering severely from the climate, and though the frontier remained intact, the Roman offensive, as an offensive, had failed. Alexander Severus, Parthicus and Persicus, went to fight the Germans in the north; 'the tribunes were orderly, the centurions modest, and the soldiers courteous,'[141] in his command: but they murdered him and his mother notwithstanding, in A.D. 235.

Maximinus, the next emperor, was the son of a Thracian peasant and fought successfully along the German rivers until his own IInd Parthica legion killed him before the unexpectedly resisting walls of Aquileia. Two African emperors, Gordiani father and son, followed; then two senatorial emperors in Rome; and then the third and most popular Gordianus, 'who by his well-ordered ways restored and enhanced the ancient peacefulness of life'[142] opened the temple of Janus for the last time in its history, and barely in his teens departed in A.D. 242 to command against the Persians in what was becoming a habitual invasion.

Ardashir had captured Nisibis and Carrhae, and in A.D. 241 Shapur his son was threatening Antioch itself; but the young Gordianus was well guided and recovered the whole province along the trade route from Zeugma to Singara. Hatra – friendly now to Rome and with a Moorish cohort[143] in its garrison – fell to Shapur: the story was told that Nadira, the governor's daughter, saw the young Persian king from the walls and opened the gates to him, and the victors tied her by her long hair to a horse's tail: '*Hatra through Nadira is deserted and Mirb'a too in the lands of Tharthar*', the Arab poet sings.[144]

'*He lost his lordship and left his lands deserted*'. The trade route was uprooted and its riches deviated, and Hatra in her long solitude remained forgotten though the track was still used: when another defeated Roman army marched by, one hundred and twenty years later under Jovian, the place had long been derelict and there were leopards, or possibly cheetahs, around it in my time.

The young Gordian's hopeful triumph ended in A.D. 244 when he died in battle or was murdered by his soldiers on the bank of Euphrates[145] – 'nobly born, excellently reared' like many another, and 'pitiably slain'.[146] Philip the Arabian, his successor, ransomed the prisoners and arranged a peace which tacitly abandoned Armenia and those other smaller kingdoms that still clung to the Parthian cause; and the Arabian emperor then celebrated the city's millennium in Rome with a crowd of animals collected for the dead Gordianus' Persian triumph.

Philip too was killed (A.D. 249), and Decius followed him and died in Gothic battles (A.D. 251): the Roman emperors throw themselves with disintegrating powers into the Persian invasions as if they were waves. Shapur twice besieged and finally captured Nisibis[147] within ten years of Philip's peace, and the loss of Armenia involved, as ever, Mesopotamia, for whose protection 'the Persian king, in any future war with Rome, had secured his right flank, which had hitherto always been threatened'.[148] The ill-judged mountain bulwark of the Empire's eastern defences had collapsed.

Shapur succeeded Ardashir in A.D. 241 and now made a yearly raid into the Roman provinces, in the oriental fashion that waited for horses' fodder and weather dry enough for bowstrings in the spring. He added the lands beyond Iran to his title of King of Kings, and possibly reached Homs in Syria before a Roman usurper there stopped him. In A.D. 253 Valerian, a Roman general with an army, became Emperor – 'a wise senator, a modest senator, a respected senator'[149] – senatorial encomiums of little use. His son Gallienus was left with British troops to fight the Germans, while the father hastened to the East.

The Goths, who were to harass the Roman world for the next three centuries, now made their appearance in the Mediterranean. Their first sea-raid reached Ephesus in A.D. 253. During the next three years, Trebizond was sacked and a second naval expedition launched which gave them Chalcedon and opened up Bithynia. Brigandage increased.[150] Antioch was captured by the Persians in A.D. 256.[151] Valerian was afraid to trust any of his generals with an army, and, himself marching north, got no further than Samosata, while Shapur's son Hormizd had been undermining the walls of Dura (probably in A.D. 254).[152] Edessa alone stood firm with her high moated rock-cut citadel. In 257 Valerian minted a victory over the no-longer-existing Parthians: just as Lord Raglan in the Crimea always called his Russian enemies 'the French', so the title *Parthicus* long survived that enemy's disappearance. *Restitutor Orientis* too was minted: but the distress of Syria and Asia Minor had now reached a stage beyond the remedy of words, and deserters began to join the Persian king.

Dates are confused, historians disagree, and one invasion overlaps the other; behind the rampart of Edessa the Roman army was plague-stricken and badly led. In the face of another invasion, Valerian offered money which Shapur refused; and either in fight or during a treacherous meeting, he was taken prisoner somewhere around midsummer in A.D. 260.

Ruin was all around. The troops in Samosata withdrew to Asia Minor and a deserter opened the gates of Antioch by surprise: (he was burnt to death by Shapur in the end).[153] Tarsus had been captured, the Taurus crossed, and Mazaca (Kayseri) destroyed after a fine resistance, also by a traitor in its walls; and the sea shores were ravaged by the Goths. But the eastern provinces now pulled themselves together, and produced two Imperial candidates and a general who saved the Cilician coast. The empty scene was set for Palmyra.

*   *   *

Valerian disappeared and no news of him came back.

It is possible that a palace was given him in Shapur's city of Gundeshapur[154]: or the enemy, or more probably the climate, may have killed him.

Early in April, with the glass already at 107° in the shade, I once travelled through Khuzistan and came to Dizful on the lower Karun river whose cliffs and buildings shone brilliant and ravaged in the evening light. The water curved slack as a bowstring within the bow of the houses, and the bridge that spans the half-empty stream bed still showed some traces of its Roman work.

The seventy thousand prisoners of Shapur lived out their lives here, in a rectangular city built in the desert in the shape of their camps. They married Arab wives and were forgotten, as the prisoners of Carrhae before them. They built the great bridge of Shuster that remains with broken arches stretched across the Karun water, under thin peaceful headlands of corn. Mills trickle their handfuls of grain between stones and spout waterfalls down the river cliffs, and the children of Shuster play in the foam with no visible Roman blood to show. The country is poor, saturated with hot dust and held in an arid belt of the Bakhtiari foothills. Bee-eaters balance themselves like Persian gilded miniatures on stems of barley, that bend beneath their weight. Abadan is in the south, under palms that look, from the air, like dotted asterisks covering all except the rectangles of courts, avenues and bungalows, chimneys and plants of oil, and high aerial sky-scrapers of lights and girders, where molecules are rarified at various levels, and liquid bitumen and gasolene pour from a single tower. A daemonic admiration holds one, as in the second book of *Paradise Lost*.

Charax, the ancient port, is here near Khurramshah, and Susa is not far, between the waterways of Kerkha and Karun that made it rich. Older than all, since the earth hides the cities of Susa, the ziggurat of Jeva Zombil[155] is resurrected, Professor Ghirshman's labour of love, on a low ridge, with four of its seven storeys still intact: the barrel-vaulted steps with open landings make a pattern of shadow in the incandescent, desiccated land. Through a slit in mountains out of sight, an American dam holds the Dizful river, which feeds the emptiness that Trajan peopled with his dreams. Here the Roman prisoners wore their hearts out, and practised as captives their engineering skill.

XII

The Revolt of the Poor

The third-century revolution, the most interesting for its parallels and contrasts with our day, passes with the clamour of a disappearing world. When the light of history begins to shine again, it is as it were over a flooded waste; the landmarks of the Roman past are strewn like wreckage, and Byzantium is there. The Augustan visions are submerged and altered in the third century together with the middle class that had produced them, and the deluge – like the social revolution of our own age – is the true and dominating chord of its time. When Byzantium comes, it is the contrast and the development of the revolution, just as the revolution was the contrast and development of the bourgeois state that preceded it; these three milestones along the general road of our civilisation entered into all life and overshadowed the frontiers and their affairs, so that an account of them in outline seems necessary. By the end of this chapter the Roman hold in the south-east is loosened; it only tightens again with the transfer of its centre to the East.

'If then you understand how to govern, why are the cities incessantly declining?' (Philostratus: *Epistle of Apollonius.* XXX.)
'Men said they no longer had a kingdom on the earth.' (Shah-Nama on Parthia.)

The Too-Narrow Platform of Wealth

A modern phenomenon was occurring in the Roman Empire while its ancient world ripened towards catastrophe. The class struggle of the city state, the problem that had foundered Greece and constantly threatened the delicate absolutism of Alexander's hellenistic successors, the tension between the haves and have-nots – the *honestiores* and *humiliores*, honest and humble – the Latin names give the Roman bias – came to its head during this time. 'The aspirations of the lower classes were expressed by the army and countenanced by the emperors, and . . . the bourgeoisie and upper classes of society were destroyed.'[1]

The city civilisation was based on too narrow a foundation to survive. 'The few', says Epictetus, 'give all their time to one thing and one thing only – the study of the fair before they leave it.'[2] In a world of ease never again paralleled until the eighteenth century or later, they had produced most of the ideas by which we live today. Their splendour continued through the middle of the Antonine age while wealthy and civilised lands added new markets to the expanding Empire. The same causes had enriched the hellenistic world. But when conditions became static, the decay began. Without an increase of prosperity at home, the poor were unable to absorb an increasing production: and when the markets abroad themselves learned to produce, 'the only clientèle left was the population of the Empire'.[3] With Hadrian the expansion ceased, and by the time of Marcus Aurelius the Italian landlords were losing their best markets.[4] Rostovtzeff attributes much, perhaps most, of the decay both of Greece and Rome to the decline in production due to an increasing ability in outlying countries to make things for themselves.[5]

The danger was not met by any sound economic encouragement of the consumer. Benefits were confined to the 'better people' through whom it was Rome's consistent habit to govern. 'There is no need of guards to hold any citadel for you: the great and the influential in each city garrison it themselves.'[6] Even education was only paid for by the treasury so as to strengthen the class from which army and bureaucracy were drawn. The cities were numerous and rich: in Dacia alone more than one hundred and twenty towns were organised by the conquering race in the one hundred and seventy years of its occupation, and five hundred were said to be flourishing in the province of Asia[7] – far more than there are today. In the Christian age, even the east of Asia Minor hardly fell behind the rest of the Empire in the number of its cities and bishoprics; but their splendour had been created by, and existed for, a minority[8] not strong enough to support the world-state alone, yet unwilling to open its ranks.

Decay of Philanthropy

The bourgeoisie continued for a long time to be remarkable for wealth and generosity within its own limits and reached its climax in the reign of M. Aurelius. Careful emperors and their *curators* tried to save it from itself, for it spent money like water, on philanthropy as well as ostentation. Its prosperity continued through the Antonine age, while Trajan beyond the frontiers was already destroying the Empire's vital forces.[9] In his reign, in Italy as in Egypt, depopulation was spreading over the countryside. Remedies – buying and settling of lands by patriotic people like Pliny, the wholesale freeing of slaves, government loans to landowners, the institution of *alimenta* for the feeding of children – all the usual palliatives[10] applied through this and the following age, gradually failed.

The beneficent plutocrat of the past disappeared under lessening profits. Under an ever-increasing burden of coercion, the system of *liturgies*, by which public liabilities had been accepted by the wealthy in every state, was now tightened to suit the economic stress. Civic honours ceased to be voluntary; they became enforced and inescapable; gifts of corn, of oil for the gymnasia (a very big item in every city's expenses), of transport for the restless armies – were gifts no longer but ever-growing government assessments; the man handling public money was required to pledge his own property and, if necessary, to meet any deficit out of his own pocket, and this transfer of collective to individual liability caused many of the taxable people from the third century onwards to abandon their homes in despair. 'And how, respected Sir,' St Basil asks on behalf of an old man whom an Imperial decree had exempted from public burdens, 'did you drag him in again . . . when you commanded his grandson not yet in his fourth year to take his place in the municipal senate, what else are you doing than to drag the old man into public affairs afresh in the person of his grandson ?'[11]

In the fifth century, Synesius writes that 'leisure I shall enjoy when I succeed in freeing myself from entanglement in the political life of the Romans; and that will be when I am released from these accursed curial functions'.[12]

The Centralising of Government

The Emperor Severus developed the *liturgies* into a permanent institution, legalised, regularised and enforced by the state.[13] He made the responsibility of municipal magistrates personal, and added to the miseries of the upper classes a ruthless confiscation of his enemies' properties after the civil wars. 'We shall probably never be able to measure the extent of the economic upheaval that this change entailed.'[14]

The Imperial estates increased under him and his successors and he left more treasure than any other emperor to his heirs,[15] but the lands that had enabled the wealthy to carry the burden of civic expenses and services were now diverted to support the Imperial purse.[16] 'After the defeat of Niger, he was merciless in his raising of funds; thus, for example, he exacted four times the amount that any individuals or peoples had given to Niger, whether they had done so voluntarily or under compulsion.'[17] 'I venture the opinion', T. Frank writes, 'that if we had a reliable history of the third century, we should arrive at the conclusion that Septimius Severus dealt the fatal blow to the Empire by his confiscations . . . centralising the ownership of vast estates under Imperial control.'[18]

This false dawn of the modern policy of nationalisation is perhaps too heavy a responsibility to lay on one man's shoulders, and a long line of precedents – from the confiscations of Sulla[19] and the early civil wars' proscriptions,[20] through Domitian and the long senatorial liquidation[21] – led to a climax which was none the less catastrophic for being slowly prepared.

All freedom in the choice of a profession now came to an end, for corporations were obliged to hold their members to the same occupations for life.[22] Exemptions from the *liturgies* given to influential groups like shipowners, or farmers of the Imperial domains, only added to the burdens of the rest[23]; and some of the richest men being thus exempted, the owners of lands and shops and the middle class in general, remained the sole victims. For the maintenance of the soldiers, the chief payers were the large landowners who always had great quantities of food stuffs in store, for which no money was paid. Compulsory gifts to the government from cities and individuals added a capital levy 'very like robbery'.

The Widening Gulf Between Rich and Poor

If this fleecing of the rich had been compensated by any betterment for the poor, the Empire's economy might have righted itself at a prosperously mediocre level and a welfare state emerged. This however did not happen, and the pressure of the state on the people was never so heavily felt as under the Roman Empire. 'In the oriental monarchies the supremacy of the state was based on religion, and taken for granted. . . . In the hellenistic monarchies it . . . bore mainly on the lower classes, which were used to it from time immemorial and regarded it as a matter of necessity'; but under Rome, the larger the number of cities created, the deeper became the gulf between rich and poor,[24] and every increase in the numbers of the privileged meant heavier work for the others. This social canker lay hidden beneath the brilliant but economically careless apogee of the Empire in its century of greatness, and as the burden of state support pressed almost entirely on the working classes, and as they were the chief consumers of the industrial goods produced by the cities, their diminished purchasing power was directly felt by commerce and industry and produced stagnation.[25] The population of the Empire is estimated to have fallen by approximately one third.[26]

One may observe in passing how the sea, and the more primitive requirements of the great trade routes, provided, in their measure, a safety valve of persistent employment which, because of its hardships, the city bourgeoisie was unable to absorb. The sea remained chiefly in the hands of the East and was never a Roman delight: there was an attitude similar to that of the modern Turks towards it: 'Juvenal treats almost as a criminal the merchant who braves the wintry Aegean.'[27] The land routes required thousands of camelmen and artisans to keep them going,[28] and though there was everlasting tension between them, they united town and country in a mutual dependence which no other economic factor, in a society based on slavery, succeeded in doing before the advent of Christianity. It is a possibly distressing but noticeable fact that, whenever a stretch of peace allowed it, the barbaric world, however cruelly divided, was prosperous enough outside the Roman pale.

The caravan route helped also to mitigate the perennial grievance against government requisitioning of transport at a time when the movements of armies spelt calamity to any route they passed along. 'Your Caesarians come in, deserting the travelled roads, take us away from our work, press our plough oxen into service, and exact what we do not owe them'[29]: the Emperor Philip's peasants speak to him of lands already deserted in A.D. 244.[30]

The *humiliores* came to be divided by almost a caste system from their betters. Their punishments were more brutal; their poor and futile revolts, their strikes in Alexandria[31] and Asia Minor (unusual in the Roman world), their wholesale abandonment of villages and homes,[32] are scattered through the sadness of these centuries: their appeals to the emperor against his officials ring with a desperate sincerity: but they might have continued to suffer for a long time unnoticed and unheard if the frontier invasions of the second century and the fact that the peasants supplied the frontier armies had not made their happiness important to their governors. The Roman army in the second century gradually lost touch with its cities. It became once more an army of landowners and peasants, of country people who had not yet severed their connection with the country: the provincials and the soldiers groaned under the same burdens,[33] and the fear of still worse impending sank deep into the hearts of the soldiers now determined to remain rulers and masters of an empire which they held like a soft fruit with a hard fighting rind round the Mediterranean basin from the North Sea and Atlantic to the Caspian.

Diocletian's edict on prices in A.D. 301 (which was anyway a failure) was declared to be issued for the protection of the soldiers. Through them the voices of the villages continued to be heard; and the tones of a new age were in those voices. They represented the majority of the populations of the Empire[34] and regarded the cities and the hellenised ruling class, and Rome which frustrated all opposition, with estrangement. Like the barbarians, they looked upon towns as so many 'graves surrounded with nets'[35]; the deep division between town and country was then, as it is now and will probably continue to be, the

THE VILLES MORTES OF ANTIOCH:
BURJ HAIDAR CHURCH OF SIXTH CENTURY A.D.
REFADE VILLA OF SIXTH CENTURY A.D.

FROM THE WALLS OF ANTIOCH

problem of the East: Rostovtzeff looks upon it as the main driving force of the social revolution of the third century.[36] The Emperor Aurelian, when his troops wished to sack Tyana, was to say: 'We are carrying on war to free these cities; if we are to pillage them, they will trust us no more.'[37] It was not easy to convince the soldiers that the cities of the Empire were not their chief enemies.

*   *   *

We have followed a thread that led from cause to cause through the labyrinth of an empire based for its economy on expansion. When the expansion stopped, a decline in markets led to a weakening of the productive classes; to the government's effort to substitute their voluntary services with bureaucracy; and to the consequences of this desperate remedy, which nearly finished the well-to-do but dragged the now unsupported poor to an extremity of ruin.

Here and there extremely modern defences were tried – trade unions of artisans[38] or insurances among ship-owners; the donkey drivers in Palestine clubbed together among themselves. All was of no avail. Even Rhodes, that had once solved the problem, now suffered from 'the envy of the less towards the greater, the self-seeking of the great towards the less'.[39] Antagonism to the cities, even in the prosperous regions of Syria, is the theme of both Libanius and St John Chrysostom,[40] pagan and Christian.

The revolution was a social one. 'There were no victors in the terrible class war', and the peasants in the fourth century were much worse off than they had been in the second.[41] Their condition was one of increasing serfdom as one travelled towards the eastern provinces, though industry in Asia Minor depended mainly on free labour and there seems to have been little agricultural slavery.[42] Rents paid in kind still gave the Galatian nobles their vast stores of grain[43]; and barter, or some antiquated system of currency, would linger[44] in an empire whose silver values were reduced by half.[45] As conditions grew worse, the old-fashioned serfdom gradually spread westward[46]; peasant languages were continued or revived; 'Phrygian experienced a renascence . . . Gallic was still spoken in Galatia. . . . It is unlikely that Lycaonian ceased soon after St Paul's visit.'[47] In obscure and ancient places people clung to their outmoded traditions. Almost in our time, the Hon. Frederick Walpole found Astarte worshipped in the region of Killis, and wives and daughters offered to guests in 1851.[48] The women's red pad under the head-veil was pointed out to him as the dress worn by the Virgin.

Many village customs today continue as the Romans adopted or inspired them: the toga is worn in Libya, and the guest all over the East will stay for three days, and call for his slippers – *soleas poscit* – as a signal for departure as in Horace.[49] The Islamic covering of the head (for women of quality), the refraining from wine, the ritual meal from which our communion is taken, all existed in Palmyra[50] long before Muhammad: the word *pagan*, first met in the fourth century under Valentinian I, began by merely designating villagers among whom the old faiths lingered.

Christianity and the Revolution

Christianity came in on this flood and, linking itself with the *humiliores*, happened, at this particular crisis of history, to have chosen the winning side. The military necessity and the Christian teaching inspired the same practical outlook, until, under Constantine, subjection to the government became resignation to the will of God: the two currents coalesced – the one perhaps purified, the other unquestionably muddied – and each no doubt convinced that it alone had brought about the change.

As early as the second century, Pliny found the Bithynian temples[51] deserted, and there is no doubt that a widespread weariness and longing encouraged Christianity in Asia.[52] The standards of culture had dropped, and 'the books in the libraries rotted; Latin speech so far decayed that Plautus and Terence were read, if at all, as prose, and the correct pronunciation of Virgil could be found only in the commentaries of a few scholastics'[53]; the drama that had 'required a certain unity of education . . . among its vast audiences . . . succumbed',[54] and the mimes, which Plato had first brought from Sicily to Athens, alone survived[55] with the games of the arena. The preachers of the new gospel turned expressly to the lower classes.

A gradual increase in humanity was not exclusively Christian. The games had long ago been loathed by people like Marcus Aurelius, who gave blunted foils to the 'wild beast fighters that . . . beg to be kept till the next day, to be thrown again torn as they are.'[56] Dio Chrysostom speaks against the butchery in Corinth, the most Roman Greek city, and the only one in Greece proper where the games were held.

Slavery too was looked upon generally with increasing mercy; ' . . . and although the law allows anything in dealing with a slave, yet in dealing with a human being there is an extreme which the right common to all living creatures refuses to allow.'[57]

Seneca had popular opinion with him, and even in the time of Nero, when a murdered senator's slaves were all sentenced to death, it was only by lining the street with soldiers that the authorities could carry out the execution.[58] The slave's evidence was taken by torture, and it was not until Hadrian's reign that masters were forbidden to put him to death. Hadrian was easy in his ways: 'When he saw one of his slaves walk away from his presence between two senators, he sent someone to give him a box on the ear and say to him: "Do not walk between those whose slave you may some day be."'[59] As captives became more scarce their value increased; their breeding became profitable, and a slave woman could obtain freedom with a third child.[60] By the third century their numbers had diminished[61]; they and the poor held together, and voices began to be heard on their behalf. Epictetus was himself a slave; and Dio Chrysostom speaks for the equality of mankind, 'all alike made for an equal measure of honour, by God who gave it its being'.[62] He is anxious too to show 'that poverty is no hopeless impediment to a life . . . befitting free men who are willing to work with their hands'.[63]

Imperial Adoption of the Poor

In the reign of Marcus Aurelius it became abundantly clear that the Roman expansion was over and that the Flavian and Antonine city civilisation, with the support of the educated upper classes throughout the Roman world had failed. Nerva (A.D. 96–98) was the last of the emperors whose ashes were deposited in the mausoleum of Augustus, and the accidental terminus fits the historic facts: for the wars of Trajan that followed were the turning point of disaster.[64] The Roman offensive had to turn to defence; the need of troops to protect the vast and unarmed regions of the Empire grew urgent; and Hadrian's reversal of the tiller was insufficient to meet the tide. He indeed looked at the problem

squarely, and 'was the real foster-father of the policy . . . adopted by all
the emperors of the second century and even, or perhaps especially, of
the third – the policy of defending the weak against the strong, the poor
against the rich, the *humiliores* against the *honestiores*'.[65]

Forced to defend the peasant orders that produced their armies, no
emperor at this period could afford to increase the senate's power.[66]
The thread of the Roman history leads into a senatorial twilight and
long Imperial animosity against the 'cream of the educated classes of the
Empire.'[67] Dio, a senator himself, together with the Scriptores whose
poor authority is often all we have, grade their emperors according to
senatorial merit: apart from any prejudice of class, however, one need
not be much moved by the decline of a body whose habitual prudence
could punctuate itself with nothing better than suicide.

Dio says that: 'When the news [of the murder of the Emperor Pertinax
in A.D. 193] was brought to each of us individually and we ascertained
the truth, we were possessed by fear of Julianus. "I am here alone" is
what he said, though he had actually surrounded the entire senate-house
outside with heavy-armed troops and had a large number of soldiers in
the chamber itself; moreover he reminded us of our knowledge of the
kind of man he was, in consequence of which we both feared and hated
him.

'The next day we went to pay our respects to him, moulding our faces
so to speak, and posturing so that our grief should not be detected. The
populace however went about openly with sullen looks, spoke its mind
as much as it pleased, and was getting ready to do anything it could.'[68]

In 192, after the death of Commodus, 'the crowd called out to the
senators: "Huzza! Huzza! You are saved. You have won."'[69] 'I know that
my behaviour does not please you,' Caracalla wrote to the august body,
'but that is the very reason that I have arms and soldiers, so that I may
disregard what is said about me.'[70]

'Why, when you are a worm, do you claim that you are a man?'[71] had
already been said by Epictetus. 'At a meeting of the senate a man does
not say what he thinks, while within his breast his judgement shouts
loudly' – although, he adds truly enough, the senate's was a 'strong
and serviceable judgement, and familiar with its business by having
been trained in action.'[72] The activities of commerce, which might have
roused it, remained down to the last age of Empire forbidden to a senator.

One is inclined to sympathise with Epictetus, and wonder how history might have developed if the barons of Runnymede had been the Conscript Fathers: yet the emperors were themselves senators till A.D. 260, and the point of view of the senate, however feebly endorsed, was that of most supporters of law and order today. They were defending their caste against revolution, which a complete reorganising of society on a new foundation implies. They continued to be honoured in the abstract while fleeced in practice, and if the emperors had not needed the soldiers they might have won. As it was, every ruler, good or bad, from Hadrian onwards, was in desperate straits for men. Those sent to the east or south rarely returned to their homes: many were killed, and large numbers were utilised to colonise and urbanise the newly acquired provinces[73]; military deserters increased,[74] and 'Spain again refused to send soldiers to the army'. The emperors had to yield[75]: the Danube and the Rhine were pouring their tribes towards them, and the peasantry of the fighting provinces had the power to speak.

The Severi

The senate still chose a few emperors, who came to swift and disagreeable ends. So did most of the others for that matter. Septimius Severus at the beginning of the revolution was killed by nothing worse than gout in York after a reign of eighteen years; his consistent dislike of the senate has probably damaged his reputation unduly, for he held to one part of his course at any rate with a firm successful hand, 'strict, honourable and self-restrained', and was loved by the Gauls he governed.[76] His deep admiration for Marcus Aurelius may not have been mere dynastic or financial interest in the Imperial estates which he pocketed[77]; and he shared a certain amount[78] of the philosophy and the general culture[79] for which his Syrian Empress was more famous. He showed too, a taciturn generosity towards the ingratitude of a minister or a son. When the Egyptians built a statue to his defeated rival, he let it stand, for 'if indeed he was such a man, let all men learn how great was the man we vanquished; if such he was not, let all men deem that such was the man we vanquished; no, leave it as it is, for such he really was.'[80]

He left, he said when dying, an empire for his two sons 'strong if they prove good, feeble if . . . bad'.[81] Caracalla, having murdered his brother in the arms of his mother, and massacred the whole youth of Alexandria, proved definitely bad, but he continued in a brutal way to protect the peasant army and the *humiliores* who produced it. 'No one but myself ought to have money and that in order to give it to the soldiers,'[82] he is supposed to have said, and kept great numbers in attendance upon him, 'alleging one war after another; but he made it his happiness to strip, despoil and grind down all the rest of mankind, and the senators by no means last.'[83] It was a policy for military usurpers not yet dynastically established, and Septimius had inaugurated it by opening the army's honours to the private soldier, by giving many of them the Equestrian's golden ring,[84] and by never forgetting the interests of the humble and the poor. It is in the time of the Severi that we first hear of village elementary schoolteachers as a class.[85] It would be grudging to deny Septimius a genuine benevolence merely because it paid him; for 'the legislation of the Empire was never more humane . . . and the great jurists, Papinian, Ulpian and Paulus. . . were given a free hand to develop their favourite . . . ideas of equal law' under him and his successors.[86]

He too had been driven by forces greater than himself. In his reign of eighteen years, only six were free from war. Even Africa and Syria, favoured by Emperor and Empress as their homes, suffered in spite of the splendour of their buildings; and the enormous stores acquired at the expense of private fortunes did not enrich, as we have seen, but eventually helped to improverish the Empire.[87] Government agents penetrated everywhere; recruiting became compulsory – the earliest record seems to be under the Severi[88]; and the villages complain to the Emperor, whom they trust, against his men. Disastrous remedies were soon found for the perennial want of money. 'The great Roman Empire was on the brink of returning to a natural economy', and became, according to T. Frank, adept in the machinery of barter.[89] It could not rectify its currency[90] which had been deteriorating since the age of Nero,[91] so that, in the eastern provinces, the issue of Imperial coins came to be rejected[92] and payment became necessary by ingots, and one city after another ceased to coin its own.[93] The granting, in A.D. 199, of civic privileges – such as municipal councils for Egypt, or the levelling of classes in some of the Asiatic cities, or, eventually, in A.D. 212 under Caracalla, the general grant of the Roman citizenship itself – were but means to increase the scope of taxation[94] and to bring new sheep into the fold for shearing. The privileges of the army – increase of pay, exemptions, the legal permission to marry – were bound to undermine military discipline and did so: they were granted not from choice but from necessity,[95] and the days when Augustus, or Tiberius, could make one donation only to their legions were long past.[96]

The money was spent on the soldiers and on the mob, on gifts to the armies, on holidays and games and public works which gave employment, and on the *congiaria*[97] to the citizens of Rome, which must have exhausted the treasury over and over again. These too had a long history behind them, from the citizen dole of the Gracchi which Caesar tried to limit,[98] to the distributions of Trajan, who seems to have lavished over one-third of the booty of Dacia on the urban poor.[99] The whole problem of finance became cardinal from the second century onwards. Marcus Aurelius in his day had been in desperate straits, though 'he burdened no one by levies of money'.[100] The more his men received, 'the more would be wrung from the lifeblood of their parents and kindred' he told them[101]; yet he too scattered seven *congiaria* and on his return to Rome distributed to the people 'a larger sum than they had ever received before'.

After the extravagances of his son Commodus 'there was such a dearth of funds in the Imperial treasury that only one million sesterces could be found, and Pertinax raised money as best he could from the Imperial statues, arms, horses, furniture and favourites', and gave to the Praetorians 'all that he had promised and to the populace 100 denarii per man.'[102] Septimius found himself unable to repress, but appeased his army with a bounty,[103] and increased their pay by nearly one third.[104] Caracalla added another third in his turn, continued to depreciate the coinage, and turned his father's surplus, obtained by such desperate extortion, to a deficit.

It was now too late for any Roman to dream the dream of Alexander,[105] and by the time that Caracalla had been enrolled among the demi-gods ('the senate of course passing the decree'),[106] and his assassin Macrinus had declared it impossible either to give or not to give the troops their donatives,[107] and had been destroyed together with his 'delightful iambics' while the soldiers turned to Elagabalus[108]; and when that adolescent product of Syrian ease lay in a sewer forgetful of his rose-scented wines, and the senate, 'slaves in togas', expunged his name from the records (after he was dead)[109]; and even when his younger, but better, cousin Alexander, after eleven years of the Syrian mother's unofficial reign, had marched eastward with the senate's blessing – the effigy of his Macedonian namesake in his private sanctuary[110] weighing heavily upon him – and had underestimated the vacuum left by Parthia and failed in what he yet declared a victory against the conquering Iranians[111]; and found that neither the silver shields of his soldiers, nor the calling of them 'citizens' in the manner of the great commanders,[112] nor the visiting of their sick, nor the lightening of their packs,[113] helped to make of him a genuine Alexander – when all this had happened, and he and his mother had been obscurely murdered, the dynasty of the Severi in A.D. 235 came to an end.

By this time a return to the Seleucid system of military colonies appears.[114] It had begun with the housing of the legions in their own provinces by Hadrian, and had been progressively developed by Septimius and Alexander. The lands taken from the enemy were presented to leaders and soldiers of the frontier armies, for the emptying of the borderlands was gaining momentum, and Marcus Aurelius had already tried to populate even Italy round Ravenna with barbarians.[115]

Though a hellenised bourgeoisie of the Seleucid type still survived, it had become increasingly Asiatic in the old Greek cities of the East.[116] In its relapse towards feudalism the Levant was slipping back easily through a devastated hellenism into its original background of Asia.

Dio's history ends in Alexander Severus' reign, with the Persian Ardashir threatening 'not only Mesopotamia but also Syria . . . claiming that all this was his rightful inheritance . . . as far as the Grecian sea'. 'The danger lies', Dio writes of him, with senatorial blindness, 'not in the fact that he [Ardashir] seems to be of any particular consequence in himself, but . . . that our armies are in such a state that some of the troops are actually joining him. . . . Those in Mesopotamia even dared to kill their commander . . . and Alexander became afraid that they might kill me if they saw me in the insignia of my office, and so he made me spend the period of my consulship . . . somewhere outside of Rome.'

> *Hector anon did Zeus lead forth out of the ranks of the missiles,*
> *Out of the dust and the slaying of men and the blood and the uproar;*[117]

Dio leaves with these appropriate words, and the deaths of the emperors continue. *Morituri salutant.*

After the Severi

Emperors generally good but helpless followed the Severi, pressing one upon the other like Banquo's shadowy descendants: Maximinus the Thracian peasant 'beloved by the Getae of the Danube as if he were one of themselves', exchanging gifts with the Alani across the river[118] and hiding the names of his parents who came from their tribes[119]; 'prayers were made in the temples that he should never see the city of Rome'.[120] His Greek was too poor to follow verses spoken in the theatre against him,[121] but his son grew up cultured and singularly beautiful, more careful of his dress than a woman.[122] Their corpses were thrown into running water,[123] and the Gordians, as we have seen, followed during a brief senatorial interval with Pupienus and Balbinus drowned in blood and the youngest Gordian buried by Euphrates.

The Syrian Philip, when he made peace, was well aware that his countrymen had long regarded an occupation by the Parthians as a relief in comparison with a prolonged stay of Roman troops[124]; there is an unmistakeable lifting of tension in these regions when left to their own devices to bargain with both sides. This also happens with modern western efforts.

Before he too was killed in A.D. 249, Philip celebrated the thousandth anniversary of Rome[125] and there was still strength and splendour, and no decadence except possibly intellectual in the emperors themselves. Through these miserable years, while Decius dies with his son in battle and Gallus is killed, and Aemilianus murdered, and the plague continues, and the Goths take to plundering by sea: while the Persians march to join them overland,[126] and the Roman emperor is captured by Shapur, and echoes of Carrhae three centuries old beat on the Roman ear; while – in a short eight-year interval (A.D. 260–268) – Gallienus, a hellenist and a poet,[127] begins to reorganise the army and is murdered, and Claudius his successor dies (A.D. 270) of plague: with earthquakes endemic and Goths in Ephesus and Trebizond; with her own garrison plundering Byzantium[128] and armies reaching out for independent power – the most wretched of all Roman centuries declines towards its end.

Its emperors took arms against their troubles. They fought, and Claudius made Italy safe for over a century against the Goths.[129] We know little about them, and their times were short. Between Philip's death in 249 and Aurelian's accession in 270 – a span of twenty-one years – some thirty were proclaimed. Malaria among other things was spreading through lands that ran to waste. In vast tracts as far as the Maritime Alps along the Aurelian way Aurelian planned to settle families of slaves captured in war and to plant the hills with vines.[130] He tried to economise on all except the army, and to satisfy the populace with wheaten loaves instead of gold.[131] In the stormy sunset light it is pathetic to read that he 'was the first to give handkerchiefs to the Roman people, to be waved in showing approval,'[132] for the shows went on. He reconquered Gaul and Egypt, and destroyed Palmyra, and was murdered almost by accident by his soldiers after a five years' reign.

Tacitus, an old senator, succeeded him, still rich enough to offer 280 million sesterces to the state, and died in A.D. 275 within a year; and Probus (A.D. 276–282), fighting Germans and usurpers, provided 'farms and storehouses, homes and . . . grain' for garrisons beyond the Rhine, while the heads of barbarians were brought in to him daily, at the price of an aureus piece.[133] He also was murdered by his soldiers in the sixth year of his reign. There would soon be no need of soldiers, the authors of his dubious history make him say, and add the age's nostalgia: 'No rations would be furnished by any provincial, no pay for the troops taken out of the public largesses, the commonwealth of Rome would keep its treasures for ever . . . no tax required of the holders of land. . . . That throng of fighting men which now harries the commonwealth with civil wars, would be at the plough, busy with study, or learning the arts, or sailing the seas'.[134]

Such was the dream of that declining time. And then came Carus (282–283), successful against the Persians, and died a natural death, though his second son was murdered.[135] His eldest Carinus ruled the West (283–285) until Diocletian, who defeated and slew him, reigned contrary to all expectations for twenty-one years unopposed (A.D. 284–305). 'He was no worse and no better than his predecessors, and if he succeeded in the task in which they had failed it was because the time was ripe and the measure of suffering was full.'[136]

This was the period when Rome fell, if one can call her transformation by such a name. 'No recovery was possible except through the absolutism of Diocletian and that was not recovery.' The thread that can scarcely be followed through its obscure details brings the sombre and exhausted revolution to its end. The Severi — Afro-Syrians unfettered by the purely Roman tradition — had given the Antonine policy a twist mainly for dynastic or financial reasons. It did not intend to, but did in fact destroy a society which — given its essential lack of elasticity — was fated to be destroyed.[137] Most of the succeeding emperors in their short and bloody lives were faithful disciples of Septimius and tried as he did to make his principles work through a militarised bureaucracy with autocratic power, based as in the kingdoms of the Seleucids 'on the allegiance of the army and state officials and on the personal worship of the emperor'; (the few 'senatorial' emperors dismally failed). The old upper classes were gradually ousted and mostly replaced by common soldiers who had quite recently become members of the new equestrian class. The tradition of craftsmanship was almost broken until Constantine laboriously revived it.[138] The most important role in the administration was played by 'countless thousands of policemen . . . all of them personal military agents of the emperor'. Compulsion grew ever more stringent. 'Along with taxation, but much more oppressive . . . went the system of requisitioning foodstuffs, raw material, manufactured goods, money, ships, draught cattle and men.'[139]

These things pressed desperately on remote people who still — as in the time of Nero — 'neither knew what the Olympic festival was, nor what a contest nor an arena meant'.[140] With such a system every home, large and small, endeavoured to become as self-supporting as possible. No partial measures could counter this progressive decay. Measures were taken to make the cities responsible for waste land. Flight from one's place of residence was regarded as a crime. 'It was all in vain. . . . The productivity of the Empire steadily fell, and the government found itself forced to resort with increasing energy to violence and compulsion.'[141] The debased currency increased the value of material things, and a provincial governor in the time of Alexander Severus would be tempted with 'twenty pounds of silver, six she-mules, a pair of mules, a pair of horses, two garments for use in the forum, two for use at home, and one for the bath, one hundred aurei, one cook, one muleteer, and a concubine if a man had no wife and could not live without a woman.'[142]

The widening of a base of government is always a revolution, and, I think, peaceful only when operated from the top; and the paternal lines of a welfare state could possibly perhaps have been developed if converging invasions had not made the soldiers conscious of their strength. The struggle was not, in fact, between the old order and the new – 'the real fight was not between the emperor and the senate'[143] so much as between two powers, emperor and army, for the control of a change in which both were acquiescent.

Septimius kept his revolution, with difficulty, under control; and some among the stronger emperors – Galhenus, or Aurelian, or Probus – would hold it for short intervals: there was no wish, either in Septimius or his successors, to lose the old Antonine world. But the difficulties both military and financial were too great. Not even Gallienus could afford to patronise the senate, although he was one of them. After the senators, the bourgeoisie of the Empire in general had also been robbed as if they belonged to a conquered foreign state.[144] The accumu-lated capital of the Empire never recovered,[145] and 'even the soldiers were disgusted . . . for their relatives and fellow citizens complained that the emperor was acting solely for the benefit of the military'.[146]

With the Antonine society irreparably lost, and the evils of the Severan régime enormously increased,[147] and the revolution slipping through their hands, the later emperors began, reluctantly, to organise the militaristic state, which was supported by the army, the only real force in the Empire. Their efforts from Gallienus onwards were devoted to the task of reforming it so as to make it an efficient instrument, neutral in politics, as far as possible.[148] They did in fact guide what was essentially a class war into its new and reorganised world.[149] Rostovtzeff and T. Frank agree in thinking that Diocletian established peace and a firm government 'by denying all the ideas that had made Rome worthy of rule. . . . The state which he saved lived under such conditions that it is questionable whether it was worth saving.'[150]

In the eastern Mediterranean a reversion to the old feudal system of the Orient resulted from this chaos as the defence of the Empire broke down. The *liturgies* had destroyed the bourgeoisie, but the peasants and the great landowners survived. Large estates in the third century became increasingly numerous and a landed, self-contained gentry developed its villas on industrial lines.[151] New landowners, mostly ex-soldiers, inter-ested in the consolidation of peace and order, grew up, and the isolated south-eastern provinces which the harassed emperors on the Danube perforce neglected, began to look after themselves.

Meanwhile, as with Antiochus and as with Mithradates, the collapse of Parthia had left a vacuum behind it, with a young and unfleshed enemy beyond; and once more Rome prepared to destroy the only local power strong enough to fill this void – the remarkable merchant city of Palmyra.

XIII

The End of Palmyra

While the barbarians of the north increasingly drain the Empire's man-power and prepare the climate for revolution, the fighting emperors are held along the German rivers. The Asiatic provinces, overborne by calamity and not unforgetful of their past, break away into the last spurt of Palmyra. Many voices – a dying echo of Cleopatra, the Macedonian Antiochi, Mithradates and Parthians, are mingled in her fall. It marks the loss of Rome's last opportunity to construct a trading bulwark in the East. In strong contrast with her mercantile ineptitude, the Roman military capacity is unabated. Emperor after emperor displays it in the short years given him before he too is murdered; the genius of Gallienus is dimly inferred as it prepares a smoother run for Diocletian: the great change from the city state to the bureaucratic continues, buried in misery and oblivion.

> dum Capitolio
> regina dementis ruinas
> funus et imperio parabat[1]
> (Horace: *Odes*, I.37.)

Villes Mortes of Antioch

The dead cities of Antioch, the summer homes of northern Syria, are (apart from the Daphne mosaics) the only visible important fragments that remain of the great city's past.

Few now travel among the country villas and fourth- to sixth-century churches west and east of Aleppo, where Arab raids finally destroyed the pagan and Christian life of the first five centuries of our era.[2] The olive groves that must once have surrounded them[3] – for there are many oil presses about – have long ago vanished, destroyed by Arabs, or by the Antiochenes themselves when the lands grew unsafe or they needed timber for the roofing of their houses. Apart from the loss of the timber, these stand more or less as they left them, with doors and windows sharp and empty against the sky. The Byzantine ribbon-banding, the decorated lintels and colonnaded loggias once made a paradise of these small prosperous towns. Their stone has mellowed to a dove-colour with time, and is encrusted with lichens that fill the grooves and volutes of the carving. Their soil has washed to the plains below, and nothing now grows in the limestone pockets except a kaleidoscope of flowers through the spring. I spent a week in one of the villages, still active because it lay near the Antioch road. My friends were prosperous farmers, and the house they lived in was built on the model of the ancient Greek houses from which it came. A feeling of safety and seclusion enveloped it as one entered – by a door, not a gateway for cars – into its courtyard from the street. The men had a large room, and the women had a family room beyond it; and the many-windowed guest room, the 'upper room' of the Gospel, was reached by an open stair beyond the stables. The sanitation was simple enough: one followed an open terracotta conduit across the paved court to its origin in a corner of the stable separated by a four and a half foot wall from the rest: any woman of the household who saw the female guest going in this direction would come out to offer a copper ewer for the washing of one's hands.

The women would keep away till the guest room crowd departed, and come up chiefly in the evening, when the day's work was over. They lived in an atmosphere of sanctuary, in a private protected world, and from their guest-room terrace – which was the roof of the rest of the house – one could look into the next court belonging to a brother: and five or six children to each household grew up in a clan. The women did their tasks all together as they happened (which made everything accidental except an order given by the head of the house): this was the whole rule of their lives, an automatic discipline hammered into the art of living. Of all its labours, the pleasantest was the baking of bread in an earthenware oven whose hollow recess they filled with burning faggots.[4] When these died down, three of the younger women would stand by, the one to pat the dough to a round cake, the next to toss it from one braceleted wrist to the other till it stretched thin as cloth, which the third sister caught on a cushion and slapped against the oven's heated side: in a minute or so it was cooked and lifted away. The women prefer this ancient pattern to all others, and have a legend that Noah's flood came welling out of such an oven in Iraq; whereas the up-to-date telephone Effendi next door was surprised to see me photograph anything but the flour-grinding machine that had cost £1400. Into this mixed world a din of drums would pass along the streets under the waning moon to remind people to eat their breakfasts before dawn, in the fasting month of Ramadhan.

I rode on a little chestnut mare to a dozen or so of the ancient centres and reached many of the others with a donkey loaded onto the back of a lorry and taken as far as a track would go. Where it ended, the windswept limestone glittered in the sun so that the hillsides looked like half-obliterated carving. My donkey plodded or my young mare trod delicately along their treeless ridges, and the spring filled their pock-marked surfaces with flowers. Sometimes, sheltering under the ruins, a few hovels still lingered – Kurds from the eastern regions or one or two of the domed beehive huts that had wandered from the Aleppo landscape into this forgotten world. But mostly it was solitude, with no one in sight but a shepherd and his flock. Life had gone, ebbing like a wave, and the beauty of the built stone was its only memorial; one could enter porches and tumbled courts, and arcaded aisles and smooth apses of churches, and remember that these were but the rays of Antioch's sunken sun.

The Third Century in Asia Minor

Asia Minor, through the Antonine age, had been artistically and intellectually the most vital of all the Roman regions, and ruin spread here over a long time, with recoveries and destructions, through the Sassanian and later Arab wars.

After the middle of the third century, the Goths raided coastal towns like Pergamon, Nicaea, Ephesus, Miletus; and the military roads, so long maintained, declined. Antioch and Syria still kept a certain prosperity and much of the trade that remained.[5] Particularly cared for by the Severan empresses, their eastern trade indeed increased under Byzantium.[6] Antioch was advantageously placed, with Syria on one side of her and Asia Minor on the other, where, in numerous medium-sized towns, a small middle class of consumers still flourished. Cilicia and the highlands of Isauria were to become the Christian bulwarks of the eighth century, with ten of their seventeen bishoprics – Tarsus, Adana, Corycus, Pompeiopolis, Zephyrion, Anazarbus, Castabalus, Epiphania, Irenopolis[7] – small forgotten places that I love – still mentioned as existing, and still existing now. In Corycus, the loveliest of the Cilician bays, seven innkeepers, a writer, one wine and two oil merchants, a green-grocer, one fruit and two retail dealers, five goldsmiths and four coppersmiths, two instrument-makers and five potters, a clothes- and two linen-dealers, three weavers, a worker in wood and two shoe-makers, a skinner, a mariner, a midwife and two moneychangers were all included in one association.[8]

Their village properties still flourished. At Ankara, in the fourth century, the people adopted culture 'more zealously than the genuine Hellenes and, wherever the philosopher's cloak appears, they cling to it like iron to the magnet'.[9] A merchant could still send ships from Seleuceia to India, and own a library, and fit his house with modern windows – 'square panes of glass set in with pitch'; and a Hierapolis merchant could circumnavigate the Peloponnesus seventy times round Cape Malea in his lifetime.[10] Patrons of architecture were to be found in the first decades of the third century,[11] with such monuments as the Ephesus gymnasium and the propylaea of Baalbek to their credit: until, as the sombre age rolled over, the evils of the Severan century increased[12]; brigandage spread so that the care of the cities' own territories became impossible[13]; and many Syrians, Jews especially, emigrated eastward across the border.[14] 'Between 235 and 258, eighty-three cities of Asia Minor issued their last known coins; between 253 and 268, one hundred and seven more'[15]; and the ease and safety of travel, which had been so conspicuous a merit of Antonine rule, disappeared.

The Persian as well as the Gothic raiding became annual, and the emperors on the Danube could do nothing for the south. There had always been, as there still is, a great deal of coming and going across the border – and as early as Augustus there had been Parthian refugees[16] sufficient to build up a corps. But bitterness was now increasing and, from the third century, every house or church along the frontier became a place held for defence.[17] After Valerian's capture, Shapur marched home with an army so overloaded that he surrendered part of its treasure to the city of Edessa in exchange for permission to pass by. The borderlands that had once fed the hellenistic kingdoms became mere pathways for the coming and going of armies, and the emperors' thoughts and preparations would revert, in the short lulls that their northern frontiers left them, to the three-century-old preoccupation with the Mesopotamian wars. The very art of this time shows the brutalising of the Roman world. In their despair, the southern people began to fend for themselves, and generally repair their long-neglected walls.[18]

Asia Minor was saved from the worst misery by its basic dependence on its villages. 'When the opportunity for reconstruction arrived, the means of revival were not far away',[19] and the woollens and purple of Laodiceia and Miletus, and the linens of Tralles and Tarsus, are still in existence in the edict of Diocletian. Forty years later, in A.D. 345, six ounces of purple linen could be sold for over half a pound of gold.[20] 'It was not the strength of its cities, so much as its comparative freedom from invasion (for the Persians rarely got farther than Cappadocia), its self-sufficiency and the martial qualities of its peasants, that made Asia Minor for several centuries the mainstay of the later Roman Empire.'[21]

In Syria

In Syria too the country districts, pursuing a general trend towards feudalism, were 'ready to slaughter the men of the cities and return to the life of peasants and shepherds under the rule of ancient kings and sheiks'.[22] The cities themselves, although called by Greek names, still spoke their original Syriac,[23] and their Semitic populations had mostly been excluded for a long time from any share in administration by their ignorance of Greek – a language[24] which a Roman governor himself might not understand: 'During the period in which I lived in the Peloponnesus', says Apollonius, 'Hellas was governed by a man who knew as little of the Hellenes and their tongue as they of his. What was the result? He was in his mistakes as much sinned against as sinner, for his assessors, and those who shared with him judicial authority trafficked in justice . . . as if he had not been their governor but their slave.'[25]

It was a Syrian Christianity that spread eastward among the Aramaeans, and when Edessa (about A.D. 204) followed the example of its king and was converted, this was done in the Syriac language of the Nestorians, still in use today. In their monasteries, Greek and Syriac-speaking monks lived separately, meeting only for divine worship, celebrated in their own tongues.[26] In the West, the Romance languages were being born, changing their Latin vowels[27]; and in Asia and Africa the third-century development of native dialects, Syrian, Coptic, Punic, Neo-Phrygian (for inscriptions), is a symptom of the breaking Roman world.[28] Even in law, where Latin remained longest, judgment could be given and wills could be written in Greek by the end of the fourth century or immediately after.[29]

In its urban life, Syria was probably the most civilised of the Roman provinces.

There were schools everywhere and Syrian doctors were invited by Shapur to his medical school in Susiana. The great jurists, Ulpian and Papinian, were Syrians, and the law-school of Berytus (Beirut) drew scholars from all over the East. Antioch was renowned for philosophy and poetry, Emesa, Damascus and Chalcis for rhetoric, Apamea and Laodiceia (Latakia) for medicine, Palmyra for art, Sidon for astronomy; the list could be enriched and prolonged.[30] The best workers in bronze were in Sidon; a guild of gold- and silver-smiths in Palmyra; and Diocletian's armament factories in Antioch, Damascus and Emesa[31] were based on craftsmanship that came down to the Middle Ages in the damascened swords of the Crusades. Roman *negotiatores* had been settled in Antioch even in Caesar's day,[32] and Ascalon and Gaza wines continued to reach Gaul under the Merovingians[33]: the international span of Syrian commerce was very long indeed.

The spread of philosophy too was largely Syrian at this time. The greatness of Plotinus (A.D. 205–262) was preceded by Posidonius of Apamea, and followed by Porphyry of Tyre and Iamblichus of Chalcis; and after Origen – an Alexandrian settled in Acre – and the Greek Fathers, and the School of Cappadocia, Syrian theology reached the farthest west with a Syrian first archbishop of Canterbury, and produced a series of Syrian popes for Rome.

The divinity of kings was taken by Rome from Syria rather than from Egypt,[34] and Longinus, from Horns, gave its last gleam to Athenian philosophy in the pagan world. Educated in the Museum of Alexandria before the troops of Palmyra sacked it, he taught in Athens, and when the Goths pillaged that city in A.D. 268, sought shelter with the Palmyrene queen. *The Essay on the Sublime* is wrongly attributed to him and may indeed belong to an earlier age; it is one of the few clear notes credited to this decaying time – an unknown rhapsody still speaking in the rich common speech of the Greek *lingua franca* (*koine*) that comes across the ages. It too belongs to this late-flowering Syrian world that has nearly three hundred years of peace in its voice.

A long-standing desire for autonomy distinguished it then, as it does today. Places like Gerasa (Jerash) never forget that they had been Seleucid colonies. Avidius Cassius, at the head of his legions and of his country, was remembered[35]; so was Niger's cavalry so nearly successful against Severus; and the later effort of the bowmen who now ruled the desert warfare to force the purple on to a rival of Maximinus: their closed fraternity and high repute in the Roman armies had soon made them feel able to take on the legacy of Rome.

There was no actual wish for separation from the Empire among the eastern peoples, but the circumstances of the time forced the Syrian frontier to defend itself[36]: the Roman world was splitting and able men arose here and there in defence of one or another of its fragments; and while Valerian was growing old in a Persian prison and Gallienus was fighting in the north, the Arab Odenathus, Prince of Palmyra, gathered an army and restored the Roman power in all the marches of Palmyra and beyond them.

Alliance of Rome and Palmyra

The portrait of Odenathus is below even the dismal average of the Scriptores: 'fierce in warfare and, as most writers relate, ever famous for his memorable hunts . . . from his earliest years he expended his sweat, as is the duty of a man, in taking lions and panthers and bears. . . . Hardened by these, he was enabled to bear the sun and the dust in the wars with the Persians.' He rose with the suddenness of a mirage out of the desert. After A.D. 260 he was Corrector of the Orient, *Imperator* and King of Kings – a title which he shared with the kings of Bosporus, remaining, like them, a Roman vassal. He quelled two rivals for Gallienus and killed one of them, was consul and commander in the eastern provinces, defended Palmyra against the attacks of Shapur, prevented a Persian union with the Goths, and won for his harassed emperor the names of *Maximus* both *Persicus* and *Parthicus* (however obsolete). It was not until after his death that an irreparable clash with Rome occurred, when Palmyra's brief supremacy rose to its apex and fell.

He had good enough reasons to bind him to Rome, for the Palmyra trade which had increased with and after the Antonines had suffered from the Persian invasion. The loss of Charax, particularly felt until Odenathus re-opened the route during four years, meant the closure of the sea to the caravans. Odenathus having drawn near to Persia in the beginning and been rebuffed by Shapur, showed no later sign of disloyalty to the side to which his fortune drove him. He led the Persian war as *Dux Romanorum*, supplemented the Roman forces with his bowmen and heavy cavalry, regained Carrhae and Nisibis in A.D. 267, and a few years later marched with his son to the gates of Ctesiphon. He re-established the majesty of Rome in the East, and seems to have turned Armenia back to her allegiance; and he once more stationed a Roman-Palmyrene garrison in the strengthened walls of Dura. The virtual rule of Palmyra stretched from the Taurus to the Arabian gulf; Asia Minor and Egypt were added; and the Roman corn supply was seized from the usurpers whom Odenathus defeated and was sent to Gallienus in Rome.

The emperor Gallienus reigned alone after Valerian's capture, until A.D. 268. His features appear dimly through the senate's distorting rancour[37]: a poet, an orator, the patron of Plotinus, an aristocrat brave enough to cut loose from the senate, a re-organiser of the army in which he was a pioneer for the future, a fine general, a clear-sighted chooser of men, he alone among the emperors, if he had left a record, could have vied in vision with Julius Caesar. Of his character and compassion the same sort of stories are told.[38] He was tall, resolute and witty, with curling hair and thick beard, and well-dressed. He had become Augustus with his father at the age of thirty-five but, as soon as he could, cast off Valerian's vacillations. As his answer to the onslaughts of a breaking world, he tried to build up a personally devoted army and failed[39]; the whirlpool of his time was too strong, and his generals murdered him: but many of his measures survived.

In the intervals of warfare, his efforts to revive the classic age failed also. Yet his Hellenism too was, in a Greek way, undefeatable: he tolerated the Christians and collected the works of Plotinus, and the union of those two streams in the following decades was more radical than might appear. *Style is the shadow of a personality*,[40] and in dealing with the Levant the over-ruling strength of personal motives must always be remembered: Gallienus, generous and a hellenist, and desperate for help, showed consistent generosity to Odenathus and made him *Imperator*. His feeling for Syria and her philosophers, his power – like Caesar's – of concentrating on the moment, and the fact that he both owed and showed gratitude to Odenathus for liberating him from the two usurpers whom the rest of the south supported – his general character in fact, open and sympathetic – makes one surmise that the two remained friends.

It would however have been optimistic in a barbarian ruler as powerful as the prince of Palmyra to look with any confidence at his future under Rome. The alliance lasted till Odenathus' death: and the chance of peace, if there was one, then probably passed away with him. There is nothing to make one believe that Gallienus had really renounced the now basic Roman policy of the *weak periphery*, and 'there are many indications which suggest that he intended to make a thorough settlement with Palmyra'.[41]

Zenobia and the Weak Periphery

Odenathus' widow Zenobia too 'was inured to hardship . . . being indeed the noblest of all the women of the East . . . and the most beautiful'.[42]

If personal regard or friendship had, as I read it, largely helped to keep her husband and Gallienus together, his widow, a descendant of the Ptolemies,[43] had no such obligation; her father was called Antiochus[44]; Cleopatra was a living legend; the great names echo and re-echo down the history of the East: the Syrian examples of the Severan women were inspiring, for all that they had ended badly: and Shapur's capture of Valerian in A.D. 260 and the accumulation of disasters must have brought the feebleness of Rome home to the Orient. The Palmyrene army was the best in western Asia, and with it Odenathus had been victorious; and the attachments between Palmyra and Persia – rebuffed by the stupidity of Shapur – were many and intimate. There were troops actually drawn from east of Euphrates in the ranks of Palmyra, and their general way of life was the same[45]: and when the crisis came, Zenobia expected and perhaps obtained[46] help from Persia which Aurelian cut off.[47]

But there was a Roman side too in Palmyra – a long intermingling, the service of young Arabs in Africa and Europe, the now deeply-rooted Imperial prestige. The title not of Great King, but of Augustus was the final goal of the ambition of Vaballathus, Zenobia's son; and Zenobia herself, after the break with Rome, adopted the style of Pia and Augusta. She and her son both wore the laurel wreath of the *Imperator* instead of the Persian tiara; and the people who advised her, the Neoplatonist philosophers who fled from Rome on the murder of Gallienus, and particularly Longinus, were the most civilised products of the West.

That she was beautiful, is implicit in her behaviour, and the Scriptores for once give a likely portrait:

'She lived in regal pomp. It was rather in the manner of the Persians that she received worship and in the manner of the Persian kings that she banqueted; but it was in the manner of a Roman emperor that she came forth to public assemblies, wearing a helmet and girt with a purple fillet, which had gems hanging from the lower edge . . . and her arms were frequently bare. Her face was dark and of a swarthy hue, her eyes were black and powerful beyond the usual wont, her spirit divinely great. . . . So white were her teeth that many thought that she had pearls in place of teeth. Her voice was clear and like that of a man. She made use of a carriage and rarely of a woman's coach, but more often she rode a horse; it is said, moreover, that frequently she walked with her

foot-soldiers for three or four miles. She hunted with the eagerness of a
Spaniard. She often drank with her generals, though at other times she
refrained, and she drank too, with the Persians and the Armenians, but
only for the purpose of getting the better of them. At her banquets she
used vessels of gold and silver and [it is interesting to notice] even used
those that had been Cleopatra's. As servants she had eunuchs of advanced
age and but very few maidens. She ordered her sons to talk Latin, so
that, in fact, they spoke Greek but rarely and with difficulty. She herself
was not wholly conversant with the Latin tongue, but nevertheless,
mastering her timidity, she would speak it; Egyptian on the other hand
she spoke very well.'[48]

It is unlikely that the peace could have been kept. When Gallienus'
troops were ostensibly marching against Persia the Palmyrenians attacked
and defeated them; the intentions of a Roman army were clear enough
and Zenobia may have acted preventively like Mithradates before her:
the background is not clear. Gallienus anyway, though he continued
to refuse the title of Augustus to Vaballathus, was too hard-pressed
to retaliate,[49] and in 266 was murdered by his officers at the siege of
Milan.

His successor Claudius died two years later in A.D. 270. He must have
established some sort of *modus vivendi* with Zenobia since the Imperial
mint at Antioch, which she controlled, continued to produce coins with
his name.[50]

After him, Aurelian was a fighting, humbly-born Illyrian, deficient in
tact though fine in courage, according to the *Life*, and 'necessary rather
than good'.[51] Yet all the acts of his short reign appear resolute and
statesmanlike, and he pulled the Empire out of the worst of its crisis.
Hemmed in with enemies, he took the responsibility of evacuating
Dacia, whose cities had been terribly invaded, and gave that stretch
of the Danube frontier a century of peace. He defeated the Scythians
and Vandals, nursed his vineyards, did the best for the currency,[52] and
rebuilt the walls of Rome: and 'no sooner was he free in Italy than he
produced his own solution of the Palmyrene problem',[53] which brought
about – not through his fault – the destruction of Palmyra.

Zenobia's power stretched to Egypt at that time: 'the anti-Roman
party shouted in triumph as seventy thousand Palmyrene troops marched
in to Alexandria'[54]: yet she sent the Egyptian corn to Aurelian and –

while every other mint abandoned him – minted his head both in Syria and Asia Minor (on the reverse or inferior side, with her own son Vaballathus and his Roman titles on the other). It was a passing courtesy, 'a one-sided affair on the part of Palmyra alone, or, at most, a temporary concession by Aurelian'[55]: the joint coinage was struck at Alexandria from 269 to 271; early in that year the independent coinage of Zenobia and Vaballathus followed; before the end of August the mint was striking for Aurelian alone.

As he advanced from the Hellespont through Ankara, the Palmyrene army withdrew: at Tyana, near the Cilician Gates, the intercession of the venerated ghost of Apollonius is said to have saved the town.[56] Egypt had surrendered to the Romans; Zabdas, the best Palmyrene commander, was out-generalled on the Orontes; Antioch was spared and Daphne taken; and a decisive Imperial victory was won with Danube troops and eastern levies before Homs. Zenobia was left with nothing to hope for but Persian help, which disappointed her,[57] and a mirage of complications for Rome in the north – in that age a likely enough hope to entertain. The siege of Palmyra began.

There is an explorer's maxim that one should never go back through unsafe country through which one has come, and this might be said of Zenobia retracing the footsteps of Cleopatra when the omens were against her. Aurelian, wounded, and harried by the Bedouin, offered terms which she refused: she escaped to the Euphrates and was caught and brought back captive before crossing: and the peace party surrendered the city. Aurelian left it unharmed with a garrison of six hundred archers and a governor *totius Orientis* as praefect of Mesopotamia; and as Parthicus Maximus (for the Parthian name seems to have been applied to any enemy shooting arrows) he held a trial at Homs in which Zenobia saved herself by the sacrifice of her followers and advisers. Longinus died whom Gallienus would have spared. On the Danube, in the autumn of A.D. 272 as he moved north, the news of a second rising in Palmyra reached Aurelian; his six hundred archers had been butchered and an Antiochus placed at the city's head; and the swiftness of his march back caught the city unprepared. Zenobia could not save it, either with her charms or her walls, built and embellished with superb misguided confidence to the last.[58] Its treasure was carried off, its fortifications dismantled, to be reconstructed in part by Diocletian[59]; its fields vanished

until the aeroplane rediscovered them; and within a century the owl
had built her nest in the palaces and tombs. The re-enacting of the
Cleopatra drama worked itself out even to the abortive flicker of a revolt
in Egypt, where the spirit of nationalism smouldered from queen to
queen.[60]

The Queen herself walked in the victor's triumph, halting frequently,
complaining of the weight of her gems. 'Her feet were bound with
shackles of gold, and even on her neck she wore a chain of gold, the
weight of which was borne by a Persian buffoon.' No asp, as far as one
knows, had been sought for her, nor did the poets sing her end, for
Aurelian married her to a senator 'and she lived with her children in the
manner of a Roman matron on an estate that had been presented to her
at Tibur', near Hadrian's villa. 'Her descendants still remain among the
nobles of Rome.'[61]

Aurelian, *restitutor Orientis*, went on to subdue the West, with the
treasure of the East in his pocket like Augustus. 'Enough Palmyrenes
have been slaughtered. We have not spared the women, we have slain
the children', he is made to say in a letter, almost certainly faked.[62]
'We have butchered the old men, we have destroyed the peasants. To
whom, at this rate, shall we leave the land or the city? . . . the temple of
the Sun . . . pillaged by the eagle-bearers of the IIIrd Legion . . . I wish it
restored. . . . You have three hundred pounds of gold from Zenobia's
coffers, you have 1800 pounds of silver from the property of the
Palmyrenes, and you have the royal jewels': whatever the reliability
of the letter, the cash was there and fleetingly filled the Roman coffers
at the expense of the eastern trade; and Aurelian's severity towards the
senate was somewhat relaxed when he 'was able temporarily to fill his
treasury with the spoil of a part of the Empire'.[63]

Left to themselves, Palmyra and the Sassanians could soon have
come to an agreement, but the Roman adoption even in its early stages
had damaged the desert city: her caravan traffic was limited to the
export of Imperial products, while Parthia maintained her own exporting
caravans. After Zenobia, the caravan inscriptions cease altogether.[64] 'La
chute de Palmyre et la disparition de son armé posèrent à Rome un
problême redoutable,'[65] for the policing of the desert as well as the
re-establishment of the caravans now devolved upon Rome. There had
been an almost complete eclipse in commercial relations between India

and the Roman Empire[66] in the chaos of the preceding decades, and the fall of Palmyra dealt another heavy blow. No looting of accumulated treasure could compensate for the steady flow for which she had been the channel and which was now destroyed. The policy of the *weak periphery* had, as usual, created a void for the conqueror to fill.

The Drain of Man-Power

This occurred at a desperate time for man-power, when the wars in the north and west made it scarcely possible to bring up troops from other parts of the Empire. Yet Aurelian was a victor. He had silenced the Goths: *'per longa saecula siluerunt immobiles'*,[67] they kept quiet for many centuries. And on top of his victory he resolved to abandon Dacia. The Persian threat[68] made it impossible to feed the other fronts, and Zenobia's control of the corn fleet of Egypt had made the feeding of Rome itself precarious: the army of the Danube was alone available to subdue the East and secure the indispensable harvests; and this army could not be transferred while Dacia remained unsafe behind it. Such was the drain of these south-eastern unnecessary wars on armies which even in normal times were too small for their tasks.

The devastation in the northern Empire at this time can hardly be estimated. 'The terrors of those years are attested not only by coin hoards all over the Empire, but also by the burnt layers turned up everywhere by the archaeologist's spade as the hallmark of the epoch.' The Dacian withdrawal gave peace, but removed Roman civilisation from Dacian soil as completely as Trajan had driven out the earlier Dacian inhabitants. In ransom, or tribute, or subsidy to Goths or Germans, 'Rome's store of gold went as booty'.[69] As early as Caracalla the budget had been seriously burdened by the annual subsidies paid to barbarians; the movements of the Germans simply compelled the Empire to include the whole of the surrounding German world in this system, and, when the annual subsidies could not be paid, invasions followed. The disaster of the Euphrates war must therefore be measured in its absorption not only of available man-power, but also of the revenue lost along an otherwise prosperous and always potentially prosperous trade route – revenue which might have been spent on adding decades and perhaps centuries to the safety of the frontiers in the north. It must always be remembered that the nations who *did* keep the trade route open, were hardly ever short of money.

*   *   *

Palmyra sank into the sands that made it, and with some poor restored defences, and the Turkish fort on its hill, became the ruined beauty that we know. When I last went there, one could buy sandals, made by an old shoe-maker who had been minister to the Rashids of the Shammar of Hail. The great Abd-ul-Aziz Ibn Saud destroyed their power, and the old man worked for his living, sitting at the door of a one-storeyed shop in the silent dust of the oasis, plaiting delicate strands of green leather into sandals patterned like those of the Egyptian kings. When I once asked him if he minded the change in his fortune, he looked up with a smile and said 'No.'

The New Army

One would give a great deal for even a moderately good history to follow Dio Cassius from the Gordians to Diocletian. In that time of distress both state and army were remodelled; Christianity was on its way to become the voice of government: and the emperors – half carried, half swimming, and always drowned in the current of destruction – deserve more detail than the poor meed they get. 'When one remembers . . . that in these times of terrible pressure the whole organisation and tactics of the army were remodelled, and that a new class of professional commanders had to be trained to replace the dilettanti of the senate, the achievement, due above all to the soldier-sons of Illyricum and a few gifted personalities, must be rated very high indeed.'[70] Their new army was the product of this expensive holocaust and the instrument which operated the transformation from Rome to Byzantium.

A tax in kind, the *annona militaris*, was developed to supply the changing but usually exorbitant needs of Roman garrisons and administrations.[71] It increased throughout the third century, when Alexander Severus' favour had provided the legions with lands of their own.[72] The grants of such lands to foreign barbarians also had begun in A.D. 170 under Marcus with the Quadi, and was continued by most of the emperors with Alemanni, Marcomanni (Gallienus had married a

Marcoman wife), Vandals and Goths. This measure was made inevitable partly by the freezing of man-power in the vast Imperial estates confiscated by the Severi,[73] but chiefly by the new army – a personal, mobile, Imperial reserve and safeguard, distinct from the separatist armies of the frontiers with which it could either co-operate or cope. This second army, chiefly invented by Gallienus, was to win later victories when the frontier garrisons were beaten.[74] Withdrawn to a secure strategic distance from the borders, it left an empty unprotected space which the foreign mercenaries (*foederati*) tended increasingly to fill.[75]

Hadrian's single defence line, with the *numeri*[76] by which its gaps were supplemented, had proved hopelessly inadequate and disappeared altogether under Diocletian. The legion in any case was ho longer the sole decisive force in battle.[77] The Praetorian Guard had dwindled to no more than a garrison for Rome and was to die bravely and altogether in 312 at the Milvian bridge in the ranks of Licinius[78]; and its transformation, and the settling of the legions on the land continued gradually into the age of Constantine. The frontier troops drew their rations from near-by storehouses; but along a line like the Euphrates, in deserty regions surrounded by empty distances, the small detachments into which the legions were now broken up needed to have some cultivation within their reach in order to exist at all; and the frequent granting of frontier territories to settle the Arab nomads must also have been an example to influence the *vexillationes*[79] of Rome who were stationed beside them.[80]

The tendency towards a division between the civil and military continued to increase through the third century,[81] while the frontier girded itself for defence and built fortifications to make up for the want of men. Much of the old equipment was out of date and it was absurd to continue to dig the traditional camp every evening in the rock-like soils of Asia. Gallienus[82] seems to have been the originator of a constructive plan to deal with the barbarian waves of invasion. Two Greek architects built fortifications for him, and permanent Imperial residences grew up at or behind the front so that Rome gradually ceased to be the centre of political life; he also centralised the arms factories at Imperial headquarters, strengthening the bond with his soldiers and further divorcing them from Rome.

Diocletian (A.D. 284–305) completed the work. He concentrated on the borderlands, and ran his eastern outposts along the Khabur from Circesium to Nisibis,[83] where the trade was canalised and which he strengthened. The detailed geography towards the eastern river-frontiers of Nymphios and Tigris is lost; we only know that the number of troops was more than quadrupled[84] and the accent was placed on forts and garrisons. The diminished legions were multiplied to about sixty, and new and smaller ones with effectives of one thousand men were created. Early in the fourth century we find them still based on Melitene and Satala, on Trebizond for the Black Sea convoys, and in Armenia.

In the south, three legions were stretched between Tigris and Euphrates, at Cefa (Hasankeif on the Tigris gorges), Constantina (now Viranshehir), and Apadna[85] (on the Nisibis-Zeugma route); and a new camp was happily set, *feliciter condiderunt*, for Ist Illyrica at the western end of Palmyra. The XVIth Flavia, which had so long been stationed under the white downs of Samosata, was moved downstream to Sura, and the Xth Fretensis was kept at Aila (Akaba) on the Red Sea, a two days' ride from Petra by Lawrence's camp in the wadi Ram. The old life goes on, and a small police post now stands there, wrapped in barbed wire like a cocoon, and only vulnerable, I was told, 'if hand-grenades are lobbed in from above'.

From here the trans-Arabian route was reached, the *Strata Diocletiana*[86] that went by the emperor's name and led to Sura on the Euphrates by Resafa[87] – a desert city holy to St Sergius where a young Chosroes was to leave offerings during his flight.[88] Into its limestone cavities and cisterns the waters of the region settled. The road went by it,[89] keeping to the high ground with every cross-track guarded from well to well,[90] as the frontier became a zone in depth of increasing strength.[91] The cities inside it were so many fortresses ready for a siege[92]: the pattern of the feudal world began to appear, as Asia was to see it through her later invasions, walled towns protected by their local militias as if they were islands in a ravished countryside whose communications had broken down.

With the change-over to the defensive against Persian armies expert at sieges, independent provision of engines, armour and weapons had to be increased. Government arms factories are referred to as early as Cicero, and Vespasian manufactured arms in the important towns, but

Diocletian seems to have been the first to have provided adequately for the army service corps.[93]

The troops' personal protection too was now better cared for, and the cuirass and helmet which the Persians gave to all their better squadrons had been copied possibly as early as the reign of Hadrian.[94] Many of the barbarian inventions had been adopted and adapted, chiefly the use of cavalry: Mark Antony had known what he needed when he exchanged a legion for the cavalry corps of a Median king,[95] and Corbulo's victories, 'pace the vanity of the Roman historians, were given him by the foederati'.[96] Alexander Severus had instituted armoured cavalry on the Persian model, taking their breastplates from the enemy dead[97]: and Gallienus turned his horsemen into an independent international force, partly to control the frontier armies.[98] The bareback Moors with their javelins and small shields, the Dalmatian *equites*, the Illyrians, reorganised in A.D. 258 when he separated the western and eastern armies, were put by him on a par with the Praetorians. Aurelian separated them still further, under the name of *promoti* (*comitenses* later on); and their commander became the most powerful subject of the Empire: both Aurelian and Probus used this rank as a jumping-off post to the throne.[99]

Aurelian also developed the heavy cavalry which he had met and respected in the war with Zenobia: their scaled armour, conical helmets and Iranian dragon-standards can be seen on the arch of Galerius at Salonika. Mediaeval war with knights in armour was beginning in the centuries that now open, and was to be practised by Byzantines and Persians, Arabs and Mongolians, on the horse-breeding uplands of what was then Armenia and Kurdistan. When I was staying in Mardin, which is carved in white stone on a hill-top and overlooks the trade route and Nisibis and Dara, I was shown a shirt of chain mail just found in the earth of the citadel, with a triangular tear in the triple loops of metal where a javelin or spear had pierced some soldier's breast.

The Tendency to Mercenary Armies

Army recruiting, which had become compulsory under the Severi,[100] also changed with Diocletian and tended more and more to draw its strength from the frontiers of the Empire and Armenia. Conscription remained, and the sons of soldiers were still expected to serve, and

so were the able-bodied vagrants, *vacati* or *otiosi*, or the *vagi* attached
without a domicile to the land, or the *laeti*, prisoners of war settled within
the Empire. The obligation laid upon landowners to provide recruits
must have brought many abuses of the kind that Falstaff practised. But as
the need for men increased, the practice grew of accepting payment –
aurum Tironicum – instead of recruits, and using it to enlist free peasants
of the more warlike provinces, or German foreigners settled on Roman
land. 'The only classes on which the Empire may now rely are the
half civilised dwellers in direct contact with the countries of Rome's
enemies.'[101]

'He [Probus] took sixteen thousand recruits, all of whom he scattered
through the various provinces, incorporating bodies of fifty or sixty
among the soldiers along the frontier; for he said that the aid that Romans
received from barbarian auxiliaries must be felt but not seen.'[102] There
was a return to the fashion of mercenary armies. Their upper layers
formed the new aristocracy of the Empire, to be replaced, as they
became romanised, by the strongest and ablest of the foreign soldiers[103]
who were usually given a third of the Roman territory, wherever they
might be settled. (The Goths in the sixth century were to enjoy two
thirds, on particularly easy terms.)

By these methods the military revolution, the turn-over from offensive to defensive, was organised by the genius of Gallienus and carried on
by those who murdered and followed him, until the threads were firmly
gathered and put to use by Diocletian.[104] The third-century emperors,
wherever else they may have failed, brought the northern barbarians
into the Roman stream; and though Gallienus was misunderstood both
in his lifetime and after his death, Constantine bore his plans into the
daylight.[105]

Return to the Trade Route

The lesson of Mesopotamia, however, remained as little understood as
ever.

No government, Parthian or Persian, was going to relinquish the
trade route, and there was no getting round the fact that the sources of
the trade were beyond the Imperial sway. However many lands Rome
conquered, the origins of the luxuries she required would remain out of

her reach, and somewhere she would have to resign herself to meeting a customs' barrier.

The damage done to her by the drain of gold and silver has been over-estimated, according to T. Frank, although such illustrations as he gives – the effort to organise an exchange of goods by Vespasian, or the treasury's buying of gold in Alexandria – must imply a certain preoccupation in Rome.[106] One might think that the Empire could rectify the unfavourable balance by developing luxury sales in the opening worlds of North and West, and becoming a 'middleman' herself. Her richest cities lay on her great trade routes[107]; her internal tolls were low – two or two and a half per cent in the fourth century; her roads excellent[108]; her currency finally sailed into quiet waters in Byzantium under Constantine and Anastasius.[109] The realms she had defeated – now including Palmyra – had all been not only solvent but wealthy on the process of trade; the Italian republics in the mediaeval Mediterranean, and Holland and Portugal and England later in the Atlantic, were to be so in their turn; there was no reason for Rome not to be one in the long East–West chain of merchants. But her money had been collected by conquest in the first place, and neither land nor sea traffic were in her blood. It had taken Rome many laborious years in the past to pacify the Ligurian tribes for instance, so as to run a road along the north-west Italian coast instead of working out a coastal trade as any Greek would have done from the days of Odysseus onward; and in the future, Diocletian and Julian were both to try, and fail, to dragoon the economics of their day: 'The impossibility of enforcing cheapness by the hands of executioners was only recognised after fruitless attempts to terrorise tradesmen into submission.'[110] The destruction of all governments capable of trafficking round the Mediterranean seems to have been Rome's basic contribution to the economics of trade.

Gallienus however had gone so far as to accept the decentralised Syrian south and the bilingual statues of Odenathus[111] that show him holding the Euphrates. If these two could have escaped their murderers, a thin benefit of the doubt might have been given to the prospect of peace. The military oligarchy that killed Gallienus was probably antagonistic to the hellenising Levant which the north despised.[112] His successors, Claudius and Aurelian, belonged to the West, and the Syrian philosophers were scattered when Gallienus died.[113]

The Advent of Diocletian

Aurelian and then Probus were both murdered while their plans for a new Persian war were incomplete. But Carus succeeded (A.D. 282–3) and, taking his younger son Numerian with him and leaving his elder Carinus to govern, he found the Persians distracted by revolts in the east and ready at the frontier to negotiate. Hardly listening to them he passed on, and died near Ctesiphon, which brought ill-luck to all who took it. He was killed either by a stroke of lightning or by Aper, the captain of the guard; and Numerian retrieved Armenia and Mesopotamia without bloodshed, and retreated across Asia Minor – 'a young man of excellent character . . . notable, moreover, for his eloquence . . . and in verse he is said to have had such skill that he surpassed all the poets of his time. . . . After his father's death, when he had begun to suffer from a disease of the eyes [a very easy thing to catch in Iraq] and was being carried in a litter, he was slain by the treachery of his father-in-law Aper. . . . But the soldiers continued for several days to ask after the emperor's health, and Aper kept haranguing them, saying that he could not appear before them for the reason that he must protect his weakened eyes from the wind and the sun. At last at Nicomedia close upon Byzantium, the stench of his body [from the litter] revealed the facts. Then all fell upon Aper, whose treachery could no longer be hidden, and they dragged him before the standards in front of the general's tent. Then a huge assembly was held and a tribunal, too, was constructed. And when the question was asked who would be the most lawful avenger of Numerian and who could be given to the commonwealth as a good emperor, all, with a heaven-sent unanimity, conferred the title of Augustus on Diocletian, who, it was said, had already received many omens of future rule. He was at this time in command of the household troops, an outstanding man and wise, devoted to the commonwealth, devoted to his kindred, duly prepared to face whatever the occasion demanded, forming plans that were always deep though sometimes over-bold, and one who could by prudence and exceeding firmness hold in check the impulses of a restless spirit. This man, then, having ascended the tribunal was hailed as Augustus, and when someone asked how Numerian had been slain, he drew his sword and pointing to Aper, the prefect of the guard, he drove it through him, saying as he did so, "It is he who contrived Numerian's death." So Aper, a man who lived an evil life and in accordance with vicious counsels, met with the end that his ways deserved. My grandfather used to relate that he was present at this assembly when Aper was slain by the hand of Diocletian: and he used to say that Diocletian, after slaying him, shouted, *Well may you boast, Aper, 'tis by the hand of the mighty Aeneas you perish*." I do, indeed, wonder at this in a military man, although I know perfectly well that very many soldiers use sayings in both Greek and Latin taken from the writers of comedy and other such poets.'[114]

So Diodes Diocletian came to the throne, and in 285 killed Carinus in battle, and established the defensive frontier of the later Roman Empire, based between two towers on the river,[115] on the Euphrates at Circesium, since the bastion of Palmyra had gone.[116]

XIV

The Government of the Cross

After Actium, the Principate and Empire have held a more or less
steady course in their eastern expansion: one may describe it as a
geographic drifting of the Mediterranean world back towards its natural
centre, the knot of the great trade routes of the East whose wealth
dazzled the Imperial mind whenever there was an interval of leisure
from the days of Augustus onward. Unfortunately, except for a brief
spasm under Hadrian, the basic fact never penetrated – that transit is
more important than possession wherever a trade route is concerned, and
armies were constantly conducted to destroy what their governments
most wished to treasure. This process has been the history of the frontier
hitherto, and will continue to be so in monotonous squalor to my
book's end.

Many things have to be left out when a small canvas contains so
huge a picture – more particularly the steps by which an eastern capital
was chosen – first Nicomedia and then Byzantium; the gradual but inevitable separation of West and East which followed; the disintegration of
Diocletian's quartet of emperors and Caesars; and the final establishment
of the Christian Empire. The latter is the Mediaeval world we still know,
and had so profound an influence on the Asiatic frontier that there is no
irrelevance in trying to disentangle its complicated elements however
briefly.

See, the legend is laid bare. Leda is dead; the swan is dead; the eagle is dead. Search for your Zeus. Scour not heaven but earth. (Clement of Alexandria: *Exhortation to the Greeks*, II, p. 32.)

The Hellenistic Heritage

A Greek had once foretold that Cleopatra, having cast the Empire down and raised it up again, would then install the Golden Age in East and West; and the fear that her victory might shift Rome from its moorings had lain cold at the heart of the Augustans before Actium. Three centuries passed, and the queen could smile from whatever heaven she inhabits, as new dangers forced Rome back to the ancestral latitudes of Troy.

A day in a coasting steamer through the sea of Marmara takes one to Byzantium from Chanakkale. The snout of Gallipoli is opposite, and Troy is on one side and the Australian columns of Cape Hellas on the other. The liners of the nations go by as if the passage were a polished floor and the events of history crowded on either side to watch the dancers: and, where the Bosphorus narrows to the edge of Europe, the first Christian emperor established the Christian empire to shield the new weakness of Rome. Defence was the note: Byzantium looked both ways, towards the Danube and the Persian – and the Roman world, organised under four rulers by Diocletian and re-assembled under Constantine, was there to be tested.

Christianity, its main inspiration, poured through it in a mixed tide of detritus like any other ore; and among its foreign ingredients, apart from the Judaic substance, and the idiosyncrasies of every separate nation, and the general influence of Rome – two other elements must be mentioned that became identified with Christianity and helped to make the religion of the fourth century so different from its origins.

The first of these was the hellenistic heritage that persisted, visible and invisible. It entered into everything – into the rhetoric of the early Christian education; into the shape of the churches; into the state domains and the Ptolemaic style of their management: into the *panem et circenses* that were merely copied by Rome from later Hellenism[1]; into law, either local side by side with the Roman in places where Rome had neither wish nor power to enforce uniformity, or infiltrating through the Greek practice of 'putting everything into writing', into the Roman law itself.[2] It seeped through the Christian philanthropy, into which the civil beneficence of the pagans, the *alimenta* of the emperors, the private and municipal gifts and foundations, were easily transformed[3]; and entered with the Greek language that was gradually ousting Latin even from among the easternised Romans themselves, and even while their franchise and the use of the toga were spreading in the eastern provinces.[4]

Kingship

This Hellenism was by no means pure. Its kingship and all that belonged to it had in very early days become Iranian, and there were voices even as late as the fourth century pleading for the Macedonian freedom against the ceremonies of the East. 'Do you fare any better' Synesius asks the Emperor Arcadius, 'since this mystery surrounding kings was instituted, now that you are kept in your chamber like a lizard that hardly ever puts its head into the sunlight all in order that you should not be detected by men as being but a man yourself?'[5]

In the third century the royal divinity had been particularly useful to the house of Severus, and even Caracalla's devotees stole garlands from his busts to wear round their insecure necks as preventives of malaria.[6] The title of *dominus* which Augustus rejected and Domitian enjoyed was adopted by Septimius, and the Hellenism of his court was rooted in an oriental past.[7] A nimbus appeared round the Imperial head; his Syrian empress was portrayed as Cybele; and prostration (*proskynesis*), which had given so much trouble to Alexander, was taken by Dio Cassius for granted. The fashion developed. A gold coin of the mid-third century shows a representative of the people receiving an Imperial benefaction on his knees[8]; and the custom of standing in the royal presence appears under Diocletian or possibly before him. The 'philosophy' of the deified Antonines gradually changes into the monotheistic Byzantine 'theology', and the emperors try to stem their revolutions by becoming Imperial vicars of the Sun-god.

Oriental ceremonial, to which the Roman *gravitas* was anyway inclined, encouraged the regimentation of the hellenistic forms even in trifles: Alexander Severus permitted old men and matrons to wear cloaks on a journey,[9] and the deified Aurelian allowed these to be purple instead of bright pink as before[10] – a boon to some red-haired beauty no doubt. The purple cloak, the *paludamentum*, was a symbol of power when Gallienus at his death sent it to Claudius. The jewelled belts and ornamented harness which soldiers thought effeminate in Macrinus were soon to be recognised emblems of royalty. With Gallienus the hellenistic revival became self-conscious, and his friends, bound by a purely personal allegiance, remind one of those of the Seleucid kings.[11] Aurelian adopted the Sun-god: he was the vicar on earth, and the conception was taken over by early Christianity, even to the globe in his hand.[12] Diocletian, the next strong emperor, added the Jovian adjective to his name and adopted the Persian pageantry in the height of his prestige. Jove's long sceptre, since it indicated a divine investiture, was Christian enough to be retained by Constantine and his successors: the king as God's representative was no Christian invention.[13]

'We must practise ourselves by praising earthly kings and so habituate and train ourselves for adoration of the Deity'[14]: the pagans had said this already, and the royal theory and its practice slipped easily into a church where fear God and honour the King was St Peter's teaching. 'As God is to the universe, so is the King to the state'[15]: it was the old Seleucid claim of law incarnate; and Constantine as the divine vice-regent reverted to Aurelian, both as a pagan and when he became Christian.[16] Christendom had to be a rival or an ally, and he chose wisely; yet his son still said (possibly in a moment of pique): 'What I wish, that is law.'[17]

Tertullian (*c.* A.D. 160–240) says that 'the end of the age itself with its menace of hideous suffering is delayed by the respite which the Roman Empire means for us. We do not wish to experience all that: and when we pray for its postponement, we are helping forward the continuance of Rome . . . for when the Empire is troubled, we too are sure to be involved . . . and though we are counted aliens by the masses, we are none the less to be found in some corner of the calamity.'[18]

Tertullian, a vehement but reasonable man who admitted that Babylon came before Rome and Amazons before Vestal Virgins,[19] held, with a decent and unusual reluctance to blame the government for everything, that there were none more apt to shout for the death of the Christians than the common herd.[20] 'We are ever making intercession for all the emperors', he says. 'We pray for them long life, a secure rule, a safe

home, brave armies, a faithful senate, an honest people, a quiet world.'[21]
'It would have been a hindrance', Origen had already written, 'to the
spreading of the teaching of Jesus through all the world if there had
been many kingdoms.'[22] With the Augustus and Christ, according to
Eusebius, peace covered all the earth.[23]

When Tertullian and Origen wrote, the third century with all its
squalid horror was just beginning to sweep across the Roman world.
After it had passed, a less secure and more political sentiment is caught in
the Christian history, and Constantine, 'like the light of the sun . . . steers
and guides men on earth according to the pattern of his prototype . . . who
determines the establishment of a single authority for all men. . . . There
is one God . . . and there is one King.'[24] The Church, accepted by the
state, becomes increasingly useful to the emperors, until in the shock of
the barbarian invasions it embodies the national defence; and the voice
of Dante and all the mediaeval hierarchy follow Eusebius in their time.

*   *   *

In this process, many things beside the royal divinity came through,
and symbols hellenistic and older than hellenistic lived on: Isis worship,
fostered in Italy at Ostia, still echoes in Stella Maris; gladiators flourished,
brought by the Etruscans, substitutes for human sacrifices at the grave[25];
and the winged angel grew from the antique Victory. The classical nimbus
appeared round the heads of saints; and Orpheus became an allegory for
Christ. Tertullian describes the intimate original profanity of the circus
whose 'ornaments are in themselves so many temples – the eggs (that
marked each completed circuit) assigned to the honour of Castor and
Pollux . . . the dolphins in honour of Neptune . . . the triple gods, the
Great, the Potent, the Prevailing. . . . The huge obelisk . . . is set up for
the sun; its inscription is like its origin; the superstition is Egyptian. The
concourse of demons had been dull without their own Great Mother;
so she presides over the trench. Consus, as we said, is in hiding there
underground at the goals – the Murcian goals; and these also are made
by an idol. . . . When they harness the horses, the four-horse chariot is
consecrated to the sun, the two-horse to the moon. . . .[26] The path to the
theatre is from the temples and the altars, from that miserable mess of
incense and blood, to the tune of flutes and trumpets . . . till in the arena
you clamour for the bloodshed for which upon the stage you weep.'[27]

Even now, travelling in the East, one finds customs from ages before history was written. Along the modern boulevards in Turkey, in the time of his triumph when Menderes was returning from London, men with the sacrificial knife in their hands held sheep ready by the pavement for his arrival, as Newton from his consulate in Victorian Mitylene saw holes dug in the ground in Homeric fashion to receive the immolated blood. The most ancient things remain in the ceremonies of life and death, and I too have seen, like Newton, in Syria on a young girl's bier 'the face exposed, the head encircled by a chaplet of fresh flowers, after the manner of the Ancients'.[28]

Influence of the Pagan World

'Through the Middle Ages and from the Renaissance the line leads straight back to the Christian humanism of the Fathers of the fourth century A.D.; to their idea of man's dignity and of his reformation and rebirth through the spirit.' (W. Jaeger: *Early Christianity. Greek Paideia*, p. 100.)

A taste for dialogue inspired the controversial writing of the time and the Fathers of the Church continued to read Plato[29]: 'Origen is always consorting with Plato,' says Eusebius[30] – Origen most fruitful of the earliest teachers, the first to employ the forms of Greek scholarship in Christian literature[31] – whose amiable heresy destroyed him – for he thought the devil himself might have been saved had he been able to repent.

Origen and Plotinus attended the same courses in the current Greek of Alexandria. The Christian liturgy was Greek even in Rome to the middle of the third century[32] and there was no Roman pope with a Latin name until A.D. 198.[33] At a time when none except St Jerome and Origen had mastered Hebrew, and until the Africans established Latin, Greek was the language of the Church as far as Lyons in the West.[34] St Basil used it in his studies in the 'metropolis of eloquence', in Caesarea (Kaiseri of Cappadocia). 'You live', he said to his students, 'with the great men of the past, thanks to their works'; and when he complained of forgetting them, his old pagan teacher Libanius replied that 'those books that are ours and were once yours, their roots remain and will remain in you as long as you live. Time can never destroy them, even if

you cease to water them.'[35] Their millennial civilisation was a climate
rather than a teaching, an atmosphere breathed by all in the common
education of the Levant. Alexandria, Athens, Palestine, Byzantium: even
today the feeling of a common world beneath its variety assails one on
any little steamer east of Italy that coasts between the Aegean islands
and the Anatolian and African shores.

Libanius, born in A.D. 314, is the voice of this submerged world,
passionate with nostalgia and regret. Antioch, where his two uncles gave
games which he did not see 'because I was learning the ancient poets
by heart,'[36] he cherished and defended with a love that can be felt in
every sentence: the walls that embrace it, the countryside around it,
the waters, the breezes that refresh it – 'what land however remote,
has not heard of its fame?' He departed, turning to look once more on
the walls he was leaving, and wept till he reached the heights of Taurus
at Tyana; and when, loaded with fame and honours, he returned and
rejoiced under the pagan Emperor Julian, he saw 'the blood flow once
more across the deserted altars, and the smoke of the victims rise to
heaven, and the gods honoured with holidays which old men scarcely
remembered . . . and we were allowed to praise and admire . . . and the
Romans could again attempt great things'.

The old man describes his copy of Thucydides as if it were a string of
pearls – 'so finely written, so easy to hold that even if I took a slave, I
could carry it by myself'.[37]

Pursued by the pestilences and famines of his time, he wished to die
after his pupil Julian's death. He had taught St John Chrysostom also, as
his favourite pupil; the two ships had sailed out of the same harbour for
separate ports.

Christians and pagans stood together in the light of unity with Plato
and Pythagoras beside them; and even in Rome the chmate of mystery
and the constant oriental awareness of the unknown existed ever since
Scipio Africanus under the Republic first accompanied the black stone
of Cybele to its home on the Palatine. It was not in the awareness
of the Divine that the difference of the Christian lay: Pherecydes of
Syros, according to Cicero, first – in the sixth century B.C. – pro-
nounced the souls of men to be eternal,[38] and an oracle from the Apollo
of Claros in that Aegean dawn-land declared eternity to be the only

God.[39] 'When our souls are released', says Plutarch, 'into the region of the pure, invisible and changeless, this God will be their guide and king who depend . . . on the beauty which may not be spoken of by the lips of man.'[40] Marcus Aurelius surmises one living Being, possessed of a single substance, and a single soul,[41] and Dio in the second century finds that many people make of the gods 'one single force and power'.[42]

'When the space of life is over and men are on the very threshold of darkness . . . the might of the goddess is wont to choose them and by her providence to give them as it were a second birth'[43]: the priest of Isis is speaking, and 'thou shalt see Him fully', says Maximus of Tyre (about A.D. 155) 'only when He calls thee in age or death.'[44]

In the twilight before the Christian recognition, the scepticism of the Neronian age had almost disappeared: Christians felt themselves citizens or subjects of the Roman Empire; and pagans who, like Celsus in the second century, upheld a tolerant variety in gods and nations,[45] were yet eager for partnership and aware of unity behind the separate façades. Two hundred years later, when Julian was dead and the Emperor Jovian had issued his edict of toleration, it was the pagans who feared reprisals and Themistius (one of their scholars and statesmen) pleaded for that diversity which God has made 'a common attribute of the nature of men, so that they should be duly disposed to piety but has made the mode of their worship depend on the will of each. Bethink you, Sire, that the Author of the universe rejoices in this diversity. . . . This is a law against which no confiscation, no crucifixion, no death at the stake has ever yet availed: you may hale and kill the body . . . but the mind will escape you, taking with it freedom of thought and the right of the law as it goes, even if it is subjected to force in the language used by the tongue.'[46]

The ancient and civilised pagan world reached its climax in Plotinus who strove to give back the Divine in himself to the Divine in all. There was no uncertainty in this man who discovered that thought is action – the friend of Gallienus, who went to see life as a soldier, who lived in a house full of children of whom he was the guardian, who radiated benignity and 'when he was speaking, his intellect visibly illuminated his face'; who thought it unsound to deny the happiness of a good life to animals only because they do not appear to man to be of great account, and who was able, while engaged at the summit of thought, to describe some unsatisfactory person as 'shrivelled like a money-bag pulled tight'.[47]

His body, 'the thing bound up with him . . . he tends and bears with as the musician cares for his lyre, as long as it can serve him: when the lyre fails him, he will change it . . . as having another craft now, one that needs no lyre, and then he will let it rest unregarded . . . while he sings on. . . . But it was not idly that the instrument was given him in the beginning: he has found it useful until now, many a time.'[48]

'It is precisely to meet the undesired when it appears that man has the virtue which gives him, to confront it, his passionless and unshakeable soul,' and before this soul is set the greatest and uttermost struggle: 'It is for this', he says, 'that all men's toil is spent: that they may not be left without part in the best and highest vision, which if he gain it not a man is most unfortunate indeed. For the unfortunate man is . . . he who fails to find this one and only thing for the winning whereof a man must put aside empires and offices in all the earth, yea and in sea and sky, if only, by leaving aside and looking beyond such things, he can turn to it and behold it.'[49]

St Augustine says: 'Could this exaltation of spirit have ever continued, and all other visions of a far other kind been quite taken away, and that this one exaltation should ravish us, and swallow us up . . . as that his life might be for ever like to this very moment of understanding . . . were not this as much as "enter thou into thy Master's joy" ?'[50]

This is the positive voice, Christian and pagan, strophe and anti-strophe in the same chorus.[51]

It is more rarely found in the pagan world. Marcus Aurelius in his tolerant tentative uncertainty expresses the more usual negative – reducing to one unknown level Alexander of Macedon and his muleteer: 'For either they were taken back,' he says, 'into the same Seminal Reason of the Universe or scattered alike to the atoms.'[52] 'There cannot be only one way to so great a secret',[53] Symmachus pleads in the senate house when the pagan altar was to be removed; and it seems to me that the loss of his tolerant uncertainty is the outward and visible point of separation, the acute angle of the Christian divergence that will never join the ancient world again.

The Greek Fathers

Joy pure and pervasive, their gift from the Redeemer, differentiates the early Christian teachers from the pagan world which was still their nest – in whose warmth the origins have not withered and Plato and Moses walk with them, as if veiled in light. 'All things in Creation are listening to the new song, which is so ancient that it came before the morning star, and yet it is new: as word ancient, as Christ new . . . Christ is our hymn and our truth.'[54] The crucifixion was foreign to them, its (probably) earliest known representation on a third-century gem in the British Museum[55]: the fair shepherd was the favourite image, with angels 'receiving – if it is reverent to say so – all the beauty of the absolute goodness . . . and the secret silence'.[56] 'You will find the blessed vision', says Gregory of Nyssa, 'in the serenity of your heart.'[57]

By this time the early complaint, that Christians ignorant even of the meaner arts should come to conclusions on the universe,[58] had lost its sense in the presence of great speakers whom the fiercest places were producing – not Alexandria alone, but Pontus and Cappadocia, in whose capital city the walls were falling to ruin, 'like castles on the sands'[59] while man was being destined for perfection: – a creature of celestial origin, partaking with the God-head both in rank and name.[60] 'All life is a holy festival', said Clement, describing the Greek philosophers as a part of the divine education of man.[61]

Clement of Alexandria (died *c*. A.D. 220) comes almost at the beginning of this line, of Greek and Jewish descent, the first Christian writer to assert the doctrine of free will,[62] the first known to assume the divine ordination of clergy. 'He never shared the bigotry of the narrower-minded Christians who discouraged or even forbade the study of pagan literature. To his latest days he held it to be at once a duty and delight to utilise for the loftiest purposes the great poets and philosophers of the heathen world . . . and there are very few of the Christian Fathers whose fundamental conceptions are better suited to correct . . . the rigidity and the formalism of Latin theology.'[63] John of Damascus, five hundred years later, a Christian minister to an Arab Caliph, is almost the last. He believed that man 'becomes deified by merely inclining himself towards God'.[64] Between these two, in the short span of the fourth century, came Origen and Athanasius and Antony from Alexandria, John Chrysostom from Antioch, and Basil and the two Gregorys from the highlands of Cappadocia that had before been used only to breed horses and slaves. Through all the galaxy, in a time of sorrow, mortal uncertainty and struggle, with their world falling about them, they kept their assurance and delight, and, together with it, the easy urbanity, a fruit of their rhetorical training, that was so soon to disappear.

'I tossed to the winds all other things', says Gregory of Nazianzen, 'those who want them can have wealth and high birth, fame and the power to govern other men, all those earthly pleasures which pass like a dream. But there is one thing I cling to – my power of words, that alone, and so I do not grudge the vicissitudes by land and sea that gave me this [for he travelled to study in Athens]. May the power of words be mine, and may it belong to him who calls me friend. I cherish it deeply, and so I shall always, placing it first except for that which is the very first – I mean all holy things and the hopes which stretch beyond the tangible world.'[65]

Gregory is supposed to have had the parchments scraped on which the odes of Sappho were preserved, in favour of his own sermons: however this may be, neither he, nor St Jerome, nor St Augustine were free from the love of the craft of words in which they had been trained. 'I would not have people see me treading again an old and used-up track',[66] says Jerome, who has much of the journalist about him. 'A natural weakness easily beguiles us. We willingly smile on such flatterers, and although we may blush . . . the soul within us rejoices to hear their words'[67]; and the temptation which St Augustine found it most difficult to overcome was the loss of human praise. 'He not only guarded himself', says Dean Farrar, 'from every form of sinful passion, but scrutinised the working of all his senses, and if he sometimes felt curiosity in watching a dog chasing a hare, or lizards or spiders catching flies, he reproved himself if he did not immediately connect the incident with some religious meditation.'[68]

The Greek Fathers were free from so much reproval, and Basil delights in animal stories which I find it difficult to resist[69]: his letters, among their difficulties and trials, 'some ceased and some present and some expected', are full of charming fancies. 'My letters are rare,' he writes to the sophist Leontius, 'but not rarer than yours. Yet you have leisure and I have none. It is no trouble to a sophist to write. A tongue that is both sophistic and Attic will converse with itself . . . and will never be silent, any more than the nightingales.'[70]

There is asceticism, but with it a pleasant love of the world as God has made it, which comes surely from that old curiosity of the Asiatic-Grecian union long before?

'Let me take you', Basil writes, 'as people take foreigners by the hand to visit a strange town, through the hidden wonders of this great city of the Universe.'[71]

Out of his love for the world comes the beautiful gift of description. The sea reaches 'as if with hands' to earth and air, and among its waves 'one sinks, another rises, and a third is *already turning black with rippling*',[72] like our troubles; and 'light sprang up to the very ether of the heavens, and all the extent of the world was suddenly bathed in light, north, south, east and west. And the waters shone, glittering, sending forth quivering flashes of reflected light from their clear surfaces.'[73]

Gregory of Nyssa has an even more human touch. 'You are pleased', he says in one of his sermons, 'because you are handsome, because your hands move quickly, because your feet are nimble, because your curls are tossed by the wind and your cheeks show a downy beard. You are proud because your clothes are dyed a deep purple and on your silken robes there are embroideries of war and hunting. . . . And perhaps you look down at those black leather sandals you are wearing, with their elaborate needlework. You look at such things, but you do not look at yourself.'[74]

He first described the 'dark night of the soul'. He saw the river Halys, the Kizil Irmak, as we still see it 'gleaming like a river of gold through a deep purple robe, and scarlet sand is washed down from the bank to touch the river with redness. High up lie the oak-crowned ridges of the hills, all green, and worthy of some Homer to sing their praises; and as the oaks wander down the slopes they meet the saplings planted by man . . . and the sweet shade under the clusters of grapes, and the new wall where the roses climb and the vines trail and twist and form a kind of protecting fortress against invaders, and what about the pond which lies at the very top of the pathway and the fish that are bred there ?'[75]

Gregory Nazianzen describes the ships in spring unfurling their sails amid the songs of the sailors, with the dolphins around them, the shepherds underneath the trees, the bees in the blossom, the glory of the

fierce and lovely Aegean world praising God.[76] Nor were they above
some shrewd criticism of their time's wrangling: 'If you always live
alone, whose feet will you wash?' St Basil asks the anchorites;[77] and
Gregory of Nyssa after a pilgrimage and its endless controversies, reports that: 'If you wish to know whether your bath is hot enough, you
must be content with the assurance that "the Son has been educed out
of nothing",'[78] and ended by advising the brethren strongly against a
journey to Jerusalem. Clement takes the skit of a comic poet to criticise
his female congregation:

> Is the woman small ? She stitches cork to her shoe soles.
> Is she tall? Then she will wear the thinnest of slippers
> And hang her head low on her shoulder.
> Has she no buttocks ? She will sew them on,
> And the spectators will exclaim at the beautiful curves of her behind.
> Has she a big stomach ? Oh, there are ways to flatten it!
> Has she blonde eyebrows? She paints them with soot.
> Or are they black? She smears them with white lead.
> Is she white-skinned? She puts on rouge.
> Is part of her body worthy to be looked at? She strips it bare.
> Has she beautiful teeth? She laughs all the time,
> And if she is not in the humour for laughing, she spends the day indoors
> With a slender twig of myrtle between her lips,
> As the butchers put a sprig of myrtle between the lips of a dead goat.[79]

After its swift and dazzling blossoming, the Eastern Church declined
with equal suddenness, too mystical, too intellectual, and perhaps too
spiritual for its world. Its heaven is no longer 'the circumference of things
created, visible and invisible',[80] its theology 'a fuller recognition of the
freedom of conscience and the freedom of grace'[81]; and the sanity of a
Gregory departs, who can say in that age of wasteful talk that 'conduct is
the step to contemplation'.[82] His body lies buried in the Vatican, carried
there secretly after the Latin sack of Byzantium in A.D. 1204.[83]

The Western Fathers

The Fathers of the Western Church were drawn by an equally strong
but far less acquiescent magnetism to the classical tradition.

'We still remember Homer', says Tertullian, whose parents were second-century pagans and had given him a good education[84]; and Ambrose quotes Virgil and Thales, Pythagoras and Plato, Aristotle, Homer and Euripides as well as the Greek Fathers.[85] Augustine read Virgil with delight and Homer with difficulty[86]; and Jerome read everything there was to read and dreamed that he was no Christian but a Ciceronian. 'Even when I was on my way to Jerusalem . . . I could not bring myself to forego the library which with great care and labour I had got together in Rome. And so, miserable man that I was, I would fast, only to read Cicero afterwards. I would spend many nights in vigil, I would shed bitter tears called from my heart by the remembrances of my past sins; and then I would take up Plautus again . . . Oh Lord,' he cries, 'if I ever possess secular manuscripts, if I ever read them, I have denied Thee,' – a thing which, however, even after this episode, he frequently did.[87]

The West, and particularly the loveless soul of Jerome, was filled with such scruples and shadows. It was preoccupied with a future immortality, careless of the present in which the Greeks found their deification.[88]

Its asceticism too differed from that of the early Greek Fathers, who followed the prevalent fashion in mortification with no particular ideological animosity, and for whom, in spite of suffering and of the hardship of their lives in the midst of corruption, the beauty and splendour of the world were never denied as they soon came to be by both West and East. 'Glory be to God for all things' are the words of St John Chrysostom, exiled, persecuted and dying in Pontus near the ancient temple of Comana. How the gentle *normality* of Christ was reconciled with their passionate renunciations – whether St John, as he tore down the church ornaments of Byzantium,[89] ever reflected that it was Judas alone among the apostles who had wished to economise and sell the expensive box of ointment for the poor; whether, sleeping hard and eating little, they remembered how the miracle of Cana was performed for a human feast and its transitory pleasure – remains untold. They tormented themselves without bitterness, and one need only compare the diatribes of St Jerome (amusing as they are) with those clear voices to see how the barbarian night comes closing in.

St Jerome was a singularly arid and self-centred man, all guilt and escape from a world where 'those that are in the flesh cannot be pleasing to Christ'.[90] 'Nothing', he says, 'is so good for a young Christian as a diet of herbs.'[91] Infants 'lament that they are born as soon as they see the light of day'[92]; and 'do you expect peace on earth, which yields only thorns and thistles and is itself the serpents' food?'[93]

'Is your skin rough and scurfy without baths? He who has once washed in Christ needs not to wash again', and in fact Jerome disapproved altogether of baths for a full-grown virgin. 'She ought to blush at herself and be unable to look at her own nakedness. . . .[94] Never sit alone', he suggests, 'with a woman in a quiet place,'[95] for 'virginity can be lost even by a thought'.[96] One is relieved to learn that his treatise on virginity was greeted with showers of stones.[97] 'A man like ourselves', he says, 'whatever he suffers we may possibly suffer also. Let us regard his wounds as our own, and all our lack of sympathy for others will be overcome by pity for ourselves'[98]; nor does this nauseating bit of egocentrism stand alone; the monk Paphnutius[99] might have hesitated to admit, as Jerome does without even noticing, that home, parents, sister and relations were less missed by him than 'the dainty food to which I had been accustomed'.[100]

As a writer, his learning was vast, his skits and thumbnail sketches masterly: he watches the pseudo-devout as she 'sits in too lowly a place and pretends she is unworthy of a footstool, and covers up the face, all but the glimpse of one eye'[101]; or the young presbyters with fingers 'that glisten with rings; and if there is wet on the road, they walk across on tiptoe so as not to splash their feet'[102]: or the distributress of alms on the steps of St Peter's, slapping the woman who tried for a second penny.[103] One is constantly diverted and never moved; and not too surprised that Luther denies the teaching of hope, faith or charity to Jerome's 'inordinate vanity, his jealous envy and implacable wrath'.[104] He cannot be overlooked, for more than any other, more even than Athanasius who brought the monastic idea to Rome, his influence clung with its sad negations to the West. His sense of guilt has not yet departed, and many an unhappy life derives from Jerome. With him and his age and fashion we reach a stretch of Christianity involved not only in paganism, but in the 'ideology' of the Roman revolution; and it seems to me that a great deal of the fourth-century history, if disentangled, might be ascribed to this un-Christian ancestry. The proportions of the mixture interest us at a time when modern revolution is in various ways repeating the Roman experiment.

The same sort of social phenomena crept, then as now, into the Christian sphere and worked a change foreign to Christianity altogether – an infiltration of social and political discontent justified, no doubt, but no more divine than the revolutions of today which it resembles.

The Social Revolution

Divine unity implied the brotherhood of man and was part of the Christian message: but the unpopularity of the rich belonged to the social revolution, allied perhaps to the Jewish belief that alms win heaven. It was certainly a part of that perennial current which the third century emperors recognised when they needed the poor for their armies.

'Now the poor are blessed, and Lazarus is set before David in his purple.'[105]

Even when there is no rancour, in the nobility of Tertullian, the soul's social status so to say is stressed. 'Take thy stand, oh soul . . . not such as when moulded in schools, trained in libraries, fed in Attic academies . . . I address thee simple and rude, and uncultured and untaught, such as he possesses thee who possesses thee and nothing else: the bare soul, just as it is from the road, the street, the weaver's shop.'[106]

The 'man in the street' has appeared; and very early, even in the Epistle of St James, there is more politics than Christianity. So there is in Lactantius (A.D. 250–317), who was tutor to Constantine's son:

'God, who has created men and given them breath of life, has willed that they should all be equal – that is to say on a level. This is the reason why neither the Greeks nor the Romans could keep a hold on justice . . . separated from one another in a number of different classes [gradus], and from the private citizen to the . . . monarch.'[107] St John Chrysostom declares after an earthquake that 'the vices of the rich caused it and the prayers of the poor averted the worst consequences'.[108]

'The hungry He hath filled with good things. And the rich He hath sent empty away'[109]; there is a sting here foreign to the words of Christ who sat happily with his nondescript company at any kindly table rich or poor, and whose moderation the first age generally followed. Clement in particular walks on eggs delicately and advises not to abandon riches well-used: 'a tool . . . if you are a poor workman, suffers from your clumsiness; but it is not to be blamed for that'.[110]

A different essence distinguishes such practical considerations, moderate or otherwise, from those, for instance, of Gregory of Nyssa for whom man was formed out of the abundance of God's love 'for it was not right that light shall remain unseen, or glory unwitnessed, or goodness unenjoyed'. The human seed itself was sacramental to him and beautified the Incarnation: 'and should we think it strange that God was united with human life in the same way that nature wars on death?'[111]

Philanthropy also, of which there was almost an epidemic in the early centuries, came with a mixed parentage into the Christian stream. 'Nor again is it a new thing to renounce wealth and give it freely to the poor, or to one's fatherland, which many have done before the Saviour's coming.'[112]

The pagans in the past, as we have seen, had gone far beyond their legal obligations in a civic generosity that stretched unbroken from the earliest ages of the Greek city state; and the innovation brought by Christianity merely changed the municipal character of this generosity into a general climate of charity to the poor.[113] This too was an innovation that belonged in great measure to the social revolution. 'We build hospitals', says St Basil, 'for strangers . . . for those who require some care because of sickness. There must also be occupations to go with these men, both those necessary for earning a livelihood, and such as have been discovered for a decorous manner of living. And again, they need other buildings . . . all of which are an ornament to the locality, and a source of pride to our governor'[114]; the touch at the end is in perfect harmony with its pagan background, and indeed with the modern philanthropic conscience which has swung back to the pagan attitude, and looks upon philanthropy as an equivalent rather than a consequence of faith.

The Fourth-Century Christian World

If the mixture of its ingredients is borne in mind, the miserable religious picture of the third and fourth centuries A.D. falls into a reasonable perspective. The senate's ancient world was long ago forgotten, and the equestrians had also waned.[115] The army proletariat was on the crest of its wave with great and sudden rises, and, as far as they could, the emperors were keeping it in check. The common barbarian soldier, from the outskirts of the Empire or beyond it, could see greater careers of power opening out before him every day. It would be strange indeed if his religion had not reflected the coarsening and widening of the social stage.

With the foundation of Constantinople, Christianity was accepted as the root of Empire: it marked a complete change of direction and the shadow of its policies stretched more fateful and longer even than those of Augustan Rome to the Euphrates. The question of the single or double nature of Christ, which one would like to consider safe beyond the arrogance of a human horizon, became urgent enough to tilt the balance of the Arab invasions.

The social revolution was much as we now witness it. There was a decline in literature; by the end of the second century reading had already deteriorated and anthologies and digests had taken the place of original texts; and after Severus, and the *Pervigilium Veneris* with its nostalgic cadence, and *Drink to me only* written for Ben Jonson by Philostratus,[116] poetry itself had collapsed into the visual and the mime. In art as in literature, apart from a hellenistic echo like *Daphnis and Chloe*, it was the day of the documentary, from the reliefs of the Antonine columns to the arches of Severus and Galerius, to the third-century sarcophagi with their sculptured anecdotes, and to the mosaics and paintings of the churches, whose saints and patriarchs turn their full faces ever more hieratically towards their audiences as they advance towards the Byzantine age. Only the basilica, the last triumph of Roman architecture, continued to flourish through the general decay,[117] together with novelties such as the baths of Diocletian, which were influenced by the Sassanians.

The games flourished, reprobated by pagan and Christian alike: 'The most noteworthy event of the rule of Carus, Carinus and Numerian,' their historian relates, 'was the series of games they gave the Roman people; for there was exhibited a rope-walker who in his buskins seemed to be walking on the winds, also a wall-climber who, eluding a bear, ran up a wall, and some bears which acted a farce.'[118] The sporting mosaics of the villa Armerina were laid in Sicily while the Goths were crossing the Danube.

The Emperors Diocletian, Constantine and his successors had to face the three problems of poverty, depopulation and invasion in a state which was coming more and more to be based on the peasants and the countryside. 'Compared with the delicate and complicated system of the early Empire . . . in which stress was laid on the self-government of the cities . . . the system of the late Empire was much simpler . . . and infinitely more brutal.' A new bureaucratic aristocracy destroyed the germs of self-government, which had developed in the village communities.[119] If one thing rather than another is demonstrated by the late Roman Empire, it is the fact that revolutions help the proletariat only if organised from the top.

Augustus had been given time; Diocletian had a frontier pressing in on him. His economics, if he had any, had no chance to develop, and all he did was to stabilise the anarchy of the third century and collect the *annona*,[120] basing it freshly for every current year on the amount of land a man and his ox could tend: the peasants were once more exactly where they were in the days of their oriental and hellenistic kings. The darkness did not lift, nor did Diocletian change the conditions which he inherited. The *curiales*, or gentry, who were responsible for the collection of the taxes, were not free to move from their cities and in dying had to substitute for themselves a suitable heir. When Constantine exempted the clergy from certain taxes, the rush for holy orders was so great that taxpayers eligible to the *curia* had to be excluded from ordination. 'The state meant compulsion, and organisation meant organised violence.' The successful peasant knew that his fate was to be promoted to a *curialis*, which meant slavery, oppression and ruin. The same with soldiers and artisans.[121] A townsman could not travel without a permit from the governor; an heiress could only marry outside her curia on payment of one quarter of her wealth: the depth of servitude was touched when the curia came to be forced on its victims as a punishment for various misdemeanours (as if one were punished by being compelled to pay supertax).[122]

In the general impoverishment, the trade in luxuries prospered, together with bribery, by which large fortunes were made; and while the senators, politically inactive but immensely respected, lived in their fortified villas and became the forerunners of the mediaeval baron or Ottoman *derebey*, the islands of culture grew ever smaller: 'St Augustine was amazed when he saw St Ambrose reading to himself silently without moving his lips.'[123]

'Have we the right', Rostovtzeff asks, 'to accuse the emperors of the fourth century of having deliberately . . . built up such a state? . . . It is idle to ask such a question. The emperors of the fourth century, and particularly Diocletian, grew up in the atmosphere of violence and compulsion. They never saw anything else, they never came across any other method. Their education was moderate, and their training exclusively military. They took their duties seriously, and they were animated by the sincerest love of their country. Their aim was to save the Roman Empire, and they achieved it. To this end they used, with the best intentions, the means which were familiar to them, violence and compulsion. . . . They never asked whether it was worth while to save the Roman Empire in order to make it a vast prison for scores of millions of men.'[124] I like to quote an historian better qualified than I am to paint a picture of such extraordinarily modern implications.

A stream of this potency was bound to affect whatever came near it, and much of what was called Christianity in the third and fourth centuries was really the class revolution. 'Nothing within the Empire save the army could compare with the compact organisation of the Christian church.'[125] It acquired enormous strength. Religion, a demand for less intellect and more emotion as a different class came into power, was gradually felt to be paramount not only in the Roman-Christian world but in other faiths also, and the oriental civilisations, chiefly based on religions, showed a greater stability than the Greco-Roman because they were nearer to their peoples. The popular Cynic preachers whom no emperor had ever regarded, were taken up by Septimius Severus as part of his proletarian appeal; and H. Metzger notices already St Paul's preferences for centres as far removed as possible from the intellectual Athenian climate – commercial amorphous cities like Antioch or Ephesus,[126] in which the proletariat is ever more articulate and alive.[127]

But the identification of Christianity with the poorer and unintellectual classes was an extraneous, an accidental and not an intrinsic development. In the Gospels, the rich man's difficulties, the advice to dispense with his wealth, refer to his private good, and form no part of a political movement – the teaching is devoted to *individual* freedom: human nature and the change of the age twisted these two strands together, and faith and works, in spite of all the mystics, have never been basically separated since.

Emperor and Church

The emperors of the third century, faced with an army movement as momentous as that of the trade unions in industry in our own time, did what most governments do – they tried to crush the sources of trouble, while conciliating its effects. The Christians were an obvious source. Their theories of brotherhood were too near the political not to become involved; their gatherings of all sorts made the emperors abnormally suspicious[128]; their God, a crucified criminal, represented the personified poverty which was causing all the trouble; and though many Christians continued in military service until the Imperial decree forbade it and even after, their pacific religion tended to undermine those very armies for whose sake one Emperor after another was throwing the senators and all the upper classes to the dogs.

As for instance the Christian soldier: 'When he came outside the court Theotecnus, the bishop, approached and drew him aside in conversation, and taking him by the hand, led him forward to the church. Once inside, he placed him close to the altar itself, and raising his cloak a little, pointed to the sword with which he was girded; at the same time he brought and placed before him the book of the divine Gospels, and bade him choose which of the two he wished.

'Without hesitating he stretched forth his right hand and took the divine book. "Hold fast then," said Theotecnus to him, "hold fast to God; and strengthened by Him, mayest thou obtain that thou hast chosen. Go in peace." As he was returning thence, immediately a herald cried aloud, summoning him before the court of justice. For the appointed time was now over. Standing before the judge he displayed still greater zeal for the faith; and straightway, even as he was, was led away to death, and so was perfected.'[129]

In the welter of revolution, the one remaining bond of Empire was the emperor himself: his divinity was carefully tended, a dyke against the waves of chaos; when the Christians opposed it, however submissively, the cup of their iniquities was full: it was, on the whole, and with the exception of the tolerant Gallienus, the better later emperors who persecuted them – those who, like Septimius or Aurelian, were in other respects wholeheartedly on the side of the *humiliores*.

Meanwhile, united in a common philanthropy with the revolution, Christianity was coming in on the winning side. From being a cause of trouble, to be annihilated, it had become a result, to be reconciled; and just as we have reconciled the 'damned radicals' of my youth, and the trade unions, and Labour in the past, and the Russians no doubt in the future; and just as the reconcilement of the *humiliores* had become a manifest basis of Imperial policy since Severus, so the incorporation of Christianity became inevitable, quite apart from its divine implications. Even before Constantine, Diocletian opened the way. 'For twenty years a policy of toleration was maintained, and in his capital, Nicomedia, the Christian cathedral faced the Imperial palace.....'[130] There was a decade of persecution due to Galerius, and then Constantine as a Christian completed the work of his pagan predecessors: 'He gave orders that a memorial of the Saviour's Passion should be set up in the hand of his own statue; and indeed when they set him in the most pubhc place in Rome holding the Saviour's sign in his right hand, he bade them engrave this very inscription in these words in the Latin tongue: "By this salutary sign, the true proof of bravery, I saved and delivered your city from the yoke of the tyrant; and moreover I freed and restored to their ancient fame and splendour both the senate and the people of the Romans."'[131]

There is no need in these accommodations to suspect the motives of either Emperor or Church. Constantine dreamed that his legions carried the crucifix on their shields to battle, and the sub-conscious advice was probably sincere; that he was using Christianity as a means and not an end could easily be unknown even to himself, and the strange remark on his death bed – 'Let there be no ambiguity'[132] might have various interpretations. But that politics came first and that he regarded unity as 'the mother of order'[133] is nowhere shown more clearly than in his letter on the Arians to Alexandria – a city in which turbulence ever threatened the Roman corn supply: 'The subjects in dispute are trivial,' he writes; [The Arian cry on the Nature of Christ, *there was a time when the Son was not*, was to split the Church in two.] 'I offer myself as arbiter.... It is a pity that the question was ever raised. No Christianity requires the investigation of such subjects; they arise from the disputatious cavils of ill-employed leisure.'[134] The bishops sent him their complaints about each other and he 'received them in displeased silence, and sealed them with

his signet ring . . . and ordering a brazier . . . burnt them in the presence
of all'.[135] An earlier pro-consul, no doubt equally exasperated, had once
offered himself to arbitrate on philosophic divergences in Athens.[136]
Constantine felt equally sure of himself, and when he demanded the
adoption of a creed throughout the Empire, banished those bishops who
refused to accept it.[137]

*   *   *

Such was the Imperial attitude. That of the Church was equally legitimate, for there was no canon by which opposition to government was
advised. Subjection was preached from the days of Constantine onwards
and gave its religious patina to the economy of the Byzantines, and it
was soon only the individual – the golden nugget in an earthy stream –
who remembered like John Chrysostom that 'to be a Christian is to be
a hero'.[138]

   'And now henceforth a day bright and radiant with rays of heavenly
light, overshadowed by never a cloud, shone down upon the churches
of Christ throughout the whole world; nor were even those outside our
society grudged, if not the equal enjoyment of our divinely sent blessings,
at any rate a share in their effluence and a participation thereof.'[139] 'And
bishops constantly received even personal letters from the emperor, and
honours and gifts of money,' and 'everyone of the Church's rulers that
were present . . . delivered panegyrical orations.'[140]

   This dubious pleasure soon changed its tone, and Eusebius himself,
and far more so the Fathers, began to castigate prelates and congregations. Monks made it impossible even for Augustine's saintliness to keep
scandal from his doors.[141] 'They murdered Hypatia . . . worried and
vexed the episcopal life of Basil . . . attacked the refuge of Chrysostom,
troubled his sickness, and assailed his life.'[142] The bishops, often elected
by force and without any preparation, 'slaves often and sailors',[143] were
equally troublesome if less revolting. 'I am determined to avoid any
assembly of bishops', Gregory Nazianzen writes. 'I have never seen a
single instance in which a synod did any good.'[144] 'Make me bishop of
Rome', said the Roman prefect, 'and I will turn Christian at once.'[145]
'Especially in the larger towns', says Origen, 'may be found bishops
who would refuse to own even the best among the disciples of Jesus as
their equals.'[146]

St John Chrysostom told a bishop that he was no better than a brothel keeper,[147] and soon found himself in exile. Few were able, like St Ambrose, to justify the speed of their transit from baptism to episcopacy in the course of a week,[148] or to be, like Synesius, simultaneously baptised and ordained[149] while disbelieving such a basic tenet as the Resurrection. It is, however, hard to tell whether this splendid man belonged more to paganism or Christianity.

The church councils did what they could, while the bishop 'struts in the market places, reading and dictating letters as he walks in public, attended by a bodyguard',[150] and Jerome's priest 'starts out at daybreak to pay his respects to the wealthy, and . . . drives about with such spirited horses that you would take him for a Thracian prince'. Chrysostom goes so far as to advise the rich not to make the clergy their almoners.[151]

This was no Christianity, but a social revolution in a society where the hiatus between rich and poor had passed all limits. Those who had £81,000 a year fell (according to Dean Farrar's evaluation, which would be much higher today) only into the second senatorial class.[152] He attributes the whole trouble to the long atrophy of paganism,[153] a statement surely unreliable, since poverty and corruption continued under a deluge of indiscriminate charity when the Church, by the fifth century, was the greatest landowner in the Empire.[154] The old order had indeed been atrophied by an ancient city framework too inelastic to expand; but the revolution failed to do anything but destroy, and neither the vices nor the merits of religion were to blame: the genuine Christian voices in the East soon died with the Greek Fathers. What caused their quick and sudden extinction? One would like to discover whether the climate of revolution followed by its inevitable companion, bureaucracy, is not a climate incompatible with public Christianity, if such a thing exists?

Heresy and Schism

Apart from Hellenism and the proletarian revolution, the troubles with heretics were a third moulding influence of the time and a torment born to the Church within itself. They throve in that consciousness of absolute right which is perhaps the most prolific as well as the most insidious of all known factors of human misery. The Arians were let loose among their fellow Christians as if in a looted city; the bishops of Spain 'first reddened the axe of the executioner with Christian blood shed by Christians . . . for a difference of opinion'.[155] St Basil, of whose saintliness there can be no doubt, expressed the fear lest in addition to his other sins he might also experience a hatred of mankind.[156] He could be happy if the Macedonians admitted that the Holy Spirit was not created; if the Apollinarians would not press their error about the Incarnation; if the Sabellians would confess that there were three persons.[157] 'Ask as a grace from the Lord that He may send upon the churches some memories of peace',[158] he writes, and longs for the blessedness of a time when those who suffered from the malady of inquiry were few.[159]

The differences between West and East made themselves felt very soon. Jerome went so far as to say that in the Eastern Church there were only three orthodox bishops,[160] and St Cyprian in A.D. 256 summoned eighty-five North African bishops who unanimously decided to disregard the menaces of Rome.[161]

Basil refused to send his brother (Gregory of Nyssa) to visit the Pope. 'What benefit to the common interest would accrue from the society of a . . . man . . . entirely alien from servile flattery to a lofty . . . person who sits somewhere up on high . . . unable to hear those who speak the truth to him from the ground beneath him? . . . What help is there for us from the arrogance of the West?'[162] 'We fight about words,' St Hilary wrote; 'we dispute about novelties, we get up quarrels about uncertainties, and we mutually anathematise each other till scarcely anyone is of Christ.'[163]

They kept Christ's first commandment; the second might scarcely have been given, and things were forgotten that John Chrysostom with all his vehemence remembers – 'a tax gatherer transformed into an evangelist . . . a persecutor, and he was changed into an apostle . . . a robber, and he was led into Paradise . . . a prostitute, and she was made the equal of virgins . . . wise men, and they were taught the Gospels. Evil fled away, and gentleness took its place. Slavery was put away, and freedom came in its stead. And all debts were forgiven, and the grace of God conferred. Therefore Heaven became earth, and from repeating this again and again I shall not cease.'[164]

This Christian voice of gentleness was not often to be heard along the Euphrates frontier, where conflicts of rehgion become paramount from now on.

> Oh bridle of colts untamed,
> Wing of all hovering birds,
> Helm of the steady ships,
> Shepherd of royal lambs,
> Gather Thy children around,
> So they may sweetly sing
> From holy and innocent lips,
> Christ the Protector of children.
>   (Clement of Alexandria)

XV

The Last Offensive

J ulian's Babylonian invasion and expedition to Ctesiphon (A.D. 363) is a
remarkable instance, like that of the Athenians in Sicily seven hundred
years before it, of how human sympathy can be captured irrationally but
irresistibly by the aggressor. The Roman age had now become defensive,
even when it ventured on conquest; and Julian's was the last aggression
undertaken for its own sake in the manner of his forebears; the fact of
its failure stabilised the frontier for one hundred and forty years; yet
one follows it with anguish and contemplates its end with sorrow; and
honours discipline and courage in the gaunt hunger of the armies trapped
in Mesopotamia however sterile the cause.

'Here is the star of autumn. And he looks towards the rising sun, directing
his course, I suppose, against the Persians.' (Procopius: *Buildings*, I.2.10.)

The Desert War

The Romans, through the confused and echoing corridors of their history, tried to follow the Macedonian Alexander's footsteps in the East.
The ghost of the great Emathian led them on – republican generals,
emperors good and bad, Lucullus, Pompey, even Crassus, Caesar and
Antony, Nero, Trajan, Caracalla, the Severan Alexander, and young

men soon killed like Gordian or Numerianus whose dreams died with them. Julian in his campaign of A.D. 363 was, for the classic ages, the last.

It was the end of the Roman adventures of conquest, and we are lucky to have Ammianus Marcellinus, an eye-witness and a fair-minded man, to write its history.

By the middle of the fourth century the private crossing of the desert frontiers had become a feature of the Mesopotamian wars. Personal and religious ties cut across the military, and wove their unobtrusive background into the policies of empire. From the days of the Parthians there were Romans to the east of the fighting lines and Orientals to the west, and the bedouin ('a race whom it is never desirable to have either as friends or enemies'[1]) would take them to and fro as they do today. Fugitive usurpers or the defeated Zenobia were caught, but lesser men escaped across the border, like that Antoninus who 'had devoted his attention to the accounts' and was in fear of the treasury. Being acquainted with both languages, he bought a farm on the banks of the Tigris to elude the soldiers, and crossed with all his family at night. He persuaded his new Persian friends to waste no time over sieges on the boundary, but to press on towards Euphrates and the richer lands beyond; and, as he was guiding them, met the Roman army marching in the opposite direction. 'Taking off the tiara which he wore as a badge of honour, he ... saluted the Roman general, calling him patron and master; and, holding his hands behind his back, which among the Assyrians is a gesture of supplication', explained that his creditors alone had driven him to desert. 'Having said this he withdrew, ... retiring backwards in a respectful manner.'[2]

The Persians, like the Romans, kept local contingents for the frontier and a national army in the rear, and the actual fighting, before the main forces engaged, began with skirmishes often led by some local guide. Ammianus' history is full of the sudden glitter of arms as one marches from Samosata or Edessa in the moonlight across treeless bright expanses. 'We lit a lamp and fastened it tightly on a horse, which we turned loose without a rider ... in order that the Persians might fancy the light was a torch held before the general ... and so keep in that direction'[3] – as the British during the last world war illuminated the rocks of Little Aden to decoy the Italian raiders.

Ammianus – crossing into Corduene (Kurdistan) to spy along the Tigris – found a friendly satrap who had pursued liberal studies as a hostage in Syria and was anxious to return.[4] Corduene had been nominally Roman for sixty-two years, but had fallen back to Persia, as the eastern Tigris lands were apt to do,[5] and Ammianus was able to explain his errand in secret, and to see 'from some lofty rocks all the circuit which we call the horizon filled with countless hosts of men, and the Persian king marching before them glistening with the brilliance of his robes. Next to him on his left hand marched Grumbates, king of the Chionitae, a man of middle age and wrinkled limbs, but of a grand spirit, and already distinguished for many victories. On his right was the king of the Albani, of equal rank and splendour.' They offered a sacrifice on the middle of the bridge that crosses the Anzaba (Zab river), while Ammianus, returning through a deserted country, took back the news that the kings were across the Tigris by a bridge of boats and were making for the west.[6]

This was in A.D. 362, the opening of a war that outlasted the reigns both of Constantius and Julian, and wasted the frontiers of Mesopotamia to their familiar desolation; for Shapur the king, leaving Nisibis alone, marched westward, by 'grassy valleys at the foot of the mountains' where water can be dug for underground[7] along the trade route; and the Romans burnt the crops before him, while the duke of Nisibis ordered the inhabitants to retire with their families and flocks.

'And when these orders had been executed . . . and the fire was kindled, the violence of the raging element so completely destroyed all the corn, which was just beginning to swell and turn yellow, and all the young herbage, that from the Euphrates to the Tigris nothing green was to be seen. And many wild beasts were burnt, and especially lions, who . . . wander in countless droves among the beds of rushes along the banks of the rivers in Mesopotamia.'[8]

The country was fortified in depth, and there were castles – in rather poor repair – and pontoon bridges that could be cut. The merchants still made their way to Eski Seruj, Batnae's annual fair in September, for goods which India and China sent in spite of barriers and military stations. The country was 'accustomed to be continually disturbed'.[9] The atmosphere of intercourse and solitude, of privacy and danger, has always belonged to the desert and is part of its sphinxish allurement:

I remember waiting through a long summer day on Euphrates for the ferry whose box-like planks and pre-historic propulsion took five hours to get across, and bathing in the interval – held on a rope by my Arab companions, for the stream was in flood and would carry one away like a straw; and from this artificial safety in the tossing water I watched the train, crossing its metal bridge beside the mound of ancient Carchemish, in a security as temporary, historically speaking, as my own.

The Taurus express runs from Aleppo and Antioch to Mosul, clanking in Roman or Persian footsteps as it moves from west or east. Travelling there one day, also in September, when every desert station was stacked with sacks of corn, I found an Arab school-girl in my carriage: about fifteen years old, she was reading Victor Hugo in French, and presently showed me the poem that had attracted her growing mind:

> Le cœur de l'homme vierge est un gouffre profond:
> Lorsque la première eau qu'on y verse est impure
> L'Océan passerait sans laver la souillure,
> Car l'abime est immense et la tâche est au fond.

Her youth and modern sophistication, and the desert background beyond the spinning windows shimmering through its long-forgotten impurities unperturbed in the morning sun, have remained in my memory.

Ammianus found a runaway horse in this country between the rivers. A groom, riding bareback and without a bridle, had knotted it by a halter to his left hand, and presently, being thrown and unable to break the knot, had been torn to pieces as he was dragged over the rough ground. The weight of his dead body stopped the tired beast, and Ammianus caught and rode it, and with his small company made for 'the boat which long custom had stationed at the Euphrates'[10] exactly like today. Its slow manoeuvres were as slow then as now and a Persian division appeared before the party could embark; and they made for Melitene through thickets and over the Taurus, along the opposite bank to that where my godsons and I travelled in the present quiet remoteness of the Ottoman peace.

Ammianus was escaping from Amida, which fell at the opening of the war in the year A.D. 359. The Persians had surrounded it, from sunrise to sunset, 'immovable as if rooted to the ground . . . nor was even the neigh of a horse heard. . . . Opposite the western gate were the trains of elephants with their wrinkled skins, which marched on slowly, loaded with armed men, terrible beyond the savageness of any other sight',[11] for the Romans always hated and feared them: and Shapur the king, taller than the rest, led his army on horseback, wearing a golden ram's head instead of a crown; and would have been slain if the dust had not obscured him.

There were seven legions within the city, and a vast promiscuous crowd, 'and at the dawn of the next morning we saw from the citadel an innumerable multitude which, after the capture of the fort called Ziata, was being led to the enemy's camp . . . men and women enfeebled by age . . . hamstrung and left behind'.

' . . . day broke, and the dense lines advanced without any skirmishers in front, and not in an irregular manner as before, but to the regular and soft music of trumpets; protected by the roofs of the engines, and holding before them wicker shields.'

And when the city had fallen, 'Aelian the Count, and the tribunes by whose valour the town had been defended . . . were wickedly crucified . . . and the treasurers of the commander of the cavalry, and others, were led as prisoners with their hands bound behind their backs; and the people of the district beyond the Tigris, who were diligently sought for, were all slain,' since the Persians judged them to be traitors from a province which they considered as their own.[12]

But a man whose beautiful captive wife the king had admired 'mounted a horse (from Nisibis) and fled at full speed to a predatory troop of Persians . . . and recovered not only his wife, but his family and all his treasures', since life goes on, in spite of all the wars.

In the next year, Sinjar was taken and its inhabitants transported. (The Sinjar garrison was always lost with every capture; no help could reach it, for the whole country round was almost waterless as it is today.)

Shapur came next to Bezabde, now Jizre or Jazira below the Tigris gorges, where the road from Antioch by Edessa reached the river, and Xenophon and his ten thousand had once turned aside into the Kurdish hills. The road was used till 1918 and taken as a border line in 1927; its Roman paving stones and signal towers appear here and there,[13] and the bridge, where it ended, now stands at the meeting-place of three frontiers – Syria, Turkey and Iraq. Shapur besieged its three legions and

Kurdish archers, and took it and repaired it, soon carrying away nine thousand of its inhabitants[14]; he then crossed the width of Mesopotamia to try, but fail, against Zeugma on the Euphrates.

The Emperor Constantius now came down from the north. He stopped in Cappadocia to fortify the (probably shaken) devotion of the Armenian king; crossed to Edessa to collect divisions flocking from all quarters; and rode weeping through the cinders of Amida,[15] which he loved beyond all other towns. He then inflicted another siege on Bezabde with the vast battering-ram left by the Persians.

Little of his life remained to him. While the preparation for war went on he passed, conscientious, burdened, and suspicious, from the stage where his strong crooked legs and thick eyebrows and bright eyes were remembered, that 'turned neither to right nor left as if he had been a statue'. When he visited Rome for the first time, under the dragon-pennants of his barbarians,[16] he had never nodded, or moved his hands, as the carriage shook him. He died in Tarsus, and Julian, his only surviving nephew, took on the war. He was already marching through Thrace with the Gallic legions – 'a youth in the flower of his age, of slight body but renowned for great exploits . . . the unresisted master of the world'.[17]

The Emperor Julian

Ammianus' historical integrity gives the darker side of Julian's picture – a certain levity that came perhaps from an insecure desire to be praised. 'An "Asiatic Greek", a chattering mole, a purple-robed ape, a pedant [he possibly was], a fool pretending to be wise' – such was the clamour of rivals at court or on the Rhine when he was serving.[18] He was accused of ingratitude not only towards Constantius – who, although he spared and made him Caesar, had accepted (if he did not organise) the murder of nearly all his relations – but also towards Ursulus the treasurer who had helped him in the poverty of his youth.[19] Ammianus mentions his mediocre verse, his inadequate imitation of Marcus Aurelius, his praise of his own justice 'of which he was always speaking'.[20] His closing of the classic teaching to Christians was, the forthright pagan thought, 'a cruel action . . . deserving to be buried in everlasting silence'.[21]

An even less kind portrait is drawn with Christian harshness by St Gregory Nazianzen: 'The loosely jointed neck, the shoulders continually shrugging . . . the eye . . . with that insane glitter . . . his proud disdainful snorting . . . the violent guffaws of laughter . . . the disorderly unintelligent questions pouring out in an incoherent stream . . . :'[22] the great aristocrat's fastidiousness was clearly offended by such symptoms of strain.

But to Ammianus Julian remained a hero – a straight young man 'with soft hair, as if he had carefully dressed it; with a rough beard ending in a point; with beautiful brilliant eyes that displayed the subtlety of his mind . . . an incorruptible judge, a rigid censor . . . mild, a despiser of riches and indeed of all mortal things' – cherished for justice and economy in his province and followed by his soldiers. He describes his handsome eyebrows and straight nose, and rather large mouth with drooping lower lip, thick neck and broad shoulders.[23] He leaves him as he has remained, a controversial figure, inferior to Marcus Aurelius in that he was something of a prig,[24] intolerant of human nature's natural disorders: the streets of Antioch annoyed him, where donkeys and their drivers, 'incapable of following any rule', trespassed under the colonnades.[25] Alexander, the great ghost, who lured him across Euphrates, is sunlit even in death, and one can spend much thought over the causes that made the one so easily capture the admiration of his time, which the other so un-availingly pursued.

Haunted by deception and fear from his childhood, Julian had felt the sword of Damocles suspended. He was affectionate and enthusiastic, yet had to pretend to belong to a religion he had long since abandoned: 'on the day of the festival, . . . which the Christians call Epiphany, he went into their church, and offered solemn public prayer to their God.'[26] When he came to power, he had the looted pagan columns pulled out again from the houses of the citizens of Antioch and there is a rapture in the first flush of empire, a passion of liberation in all his anti-Christian dealings. 'We pray openly to the Gods,' he writes from Byzantium; 'and most of the troops that follow are full of piety'[27]; the desirable tolerance of the Emperor Arcadius was beyond him, who remarked of one of the cities that it was sadly devoted to idols, but loyally disposed in the matter of taxation.[28]

LADY OF URFA (ANCIENT EDESSA)

STREET BUILT BY THE EMPEROR ARCADIUS TO THE PORT OF EPHESUS

THE MIDDLE EUPHRATES

WALLS OF DYARBEKR

RUINS OF NISIBIS

'If one says the opposite of what one thinks on the most serious questions, what is one but a salesman?'[29] Yet the words Julian finds are rarely essentially his own. In death, in his tent by the Tigris, the touch of bitterness alone rings pitifully true: 'Nor am I oppressed by the recollection of any grave crime, either when I was kept in the shade, and as it were in a corner . . . or after I arrived at the Empire which . . . I have preserved, as I believe, unstained' and, in warfare, 'have always been under the influence of deliberate reason'.[30]

Always is no word for philosophers, and it is rather as a soldier that Julian is happily remembered, shaking off the pleasure-loving dust of Antioch in March (A.D. 363) 'when the coming of the swallows pushes us . . . towards the frontier'.[31] 'Weary of peace and dreaming of battles' and eager to add to his other glories the surname of Parthicus,[32] a century out of date, he led the whole army and the Scythian auxiliaries by a bridge of boats across Euphrates[33] for a double advance, like that of Trajan, down the rivers.[34] There was as little point in this invasion as in that of Crassus and in all those in between. The advances and retreats of the armies across the same stretches of sand during the intervening four centuries must look to the eye of history as purposeless and as temporary as the beating and retreating of the sea: and there were voices, possibly not only of inactive and malicious detractors as Ammianus supposes, that laboured with all their might to postpone the campaign.

The March to Ctesiphon

Julian had refused help to threatened Nisibis because of her Christianity, and had skirted Christian Edessa and its arsenal.[35] He now travelled through lands 'where the smoke of incense was rising', to the Moon Temple at Carrhae, where two 'royal roads' branched off and led to the East.

Libanius the orator accompanied him for the first stretch of the adventure, together with the unreconciled elders of Antioch, and complained almost in the suburbs of Antioch of the roads. Julian himself, writing from Hierapolis,[36] describes them as stones pressed in a bed of mortar, like Turkish roads still found in country places, pleasant with their wells and plane trees for the leisurely philosopher,[37] but hard on carts without springs that carried a bare fifth of their average today.[38] A chosen force of thirty thousand men[39] was detached along the northern road, and Julian himself followed the Balikh tributary to Callinicum, to keep the feast of Cybele 'in the manner of the ancients'. He is said to have had sixty-five thousand troops, the most numerous army ever led against Persia,[40] and he waited to watch his fleet sail down the main river – a thousand transports of various sorts and sizes and fifty ships of war.

Loaded with biscuit and vinegar, which the troops drank mixed with water, the fleet, keeping alongside, floated southward across the Khabur estuary at Circesium, and downstream for some ninety miles – past the tomb of the Emperor Gordian conspicuous in the emptiness at Zaitha[41]; past Dura, deserted and forgotten, where herds of gazelle were grazing; across the Persian frontier between 'Auqa and the high tower of al-Qayem[42]; past Anah which they burnt, sending the inmates of the fort unharmed to Syria. The foot marched in open formation spread out over nearly ten miles along the bank of gently rolling solidified sand, with the cavalry close in against surprises, and fifteen hundred skirmishers in front.

Some places on the river were fortified and promised to surrender if the Persian king's war went against him, 'and looked down on our boats as they passed under the very walls without attempting to molest them'; others that were weak had the few women left put to death and were burnt. They passed a tribunal of Trajan's and, some three hundred miles from the frontier, came to vestiges of walls half destroyed which had served, they thought, to protect Assyria from foreign invasion.[43]

About fifty miles from Ctesiphon, on the Euphrates and west-south-west of the present Baghdad, they reached the city of Perisabora or Sippar or Anbar,[44] whose double brick walls were bonded with bitumen in the ancient Babylonian way; and forcing it to surrender by assault, found a great store of arms and provisions, and burnt it; and came thence to sluggish canals and palm groves that lie between Euphrates and Tigris where they approach each other below the cornlands and the gravelly Fallujah plain. Here they first met organised resistance, and found an enemy 'covered from head to foot with thin plates of iron like a bird'[45]; and fought till the heat, increasing at midday, made fighting impossible.

They were reaching the hellenised lands of Seleuceia, and were so pleased to come upon a palace built in the Roman fashion, and so tired no doubt of the blind yellow walls of mud villages, that they left it unhurt; and the emperor, pushing on with the advance guard, reconnoitred a deserted city destroyed by the Emperor Verus. Through such old memories, *unhappy far-off things*, they came to the canal which Trajan and after him Severus had cleaned out to reach the Tigris; and crossed and fought their way up its bank in darkness.

The Persian regular army appeared here with squadrons of cavalry – their horses wrapped in leather – and infantry in reserve behind wicker shields described by Herodotus eight centuries before.[46] Behind them were elephants 'like so many walking hills',[47] which the Romans pursued to the walls of the royal city.

But Ctesiphon this time was not to be taken. Its later palace still spreads the half of a sophisticated Greco-Parthian-Sassanian façade[48] above the vanished ruin – a landmark among thin harvests, and the tallest arch in the world without a keystone; in its uneven vault the Muslim believer can see the crack that appeared when Muhammad was born. But the city in its circular walls, and the dynasty that built it, and the Roman armies that camped beside it, have been blown away like the smoke of the burning stubble with which the Persians soon surrounded their retreat.

*   *   *

It has never been ascertained why Julian left the conquest unfinished, except that Shapur was known to be gathering his army and that the Romans might have been caught with inadequate forces between his advance and the hostile city. They made for the tracks of Alexander and the 'royal road' that led through Kirkuk to Persia in the north-east. They must have hoped for a junction with their own thirty thousand as they marched towards Kurdistan.[49] The destructiveness of their coming had made a return by the Euphrates impossible, and now, with summer upon them and the country devastated, with the fleet – in that land of canals – unwisely destroyed and the rivers flooded from melting Armenian snows, they started in June from the Tigris' left bank and followed not the Tigris but the Diyala,[50] hurrying to catch Shapur and his army before he closed the mountain passes of the Jebel Hamrin.

When they saw dust, which they thought was made by wild asses of which there were great numbers in those regions, the trumpets sounded a halt near the Diyala[51] stream in a grassy valley; and there, in a circle of their shields, they camped, wakeful and ready, till dawn showed them the steel-fringed breastplates and glittering cuirasses of their enemies.

The Sassanians had altered the light-armed Parthian tactics and relied largely for their skirmishing on Arabs or Armenians.[52] Their own heavy horsemen moved, armed with long pikes, 'like statues of bronze' among their foemen, and are represented in the sculptured mountain friezes as carrying long straight swords or maces, with many varieties of headgear that ended in the necklet of chain-mail under a circular steel cap, worn by the Chosroes of Tak-i-Bustan and by the cavalry of the Middle Ages in Europe.

The chivalry of the Middle Ages as well as its armour began with the Persian wars, and flourished from Septimius Severus onward in numerous epics, perhaps fortunately lost.[53] It threw its picturesque veil over miseries unimaginable and mostly unrecorded – the riffraff of conscripted peasants dragged along and despised by the mounted Persian soldiers, the death penalty on the Tigris 'for anyone . . . who saved a twelve-year boy',[54] a possible fighter, in the general massacres that have left their emptiness along the trade routes of Asia.

Death came to the emperor after eleven days of rear-guard fighting through the burnt lands beyond Hucumbra (Baquba). The last battle is placed by Lane at Kifri.[55] 'The clashing of shields, the din of men, the doleful whistle of the javelins' were ended for Julian, and the intolerable heat and killing hunger, and the arrows of the Persians wide-armed as they drew their bows to the breast. The night before, as he wrote in his tent, Ammianus tells us, he had seen the genius of the Empire depart. He expired quietly in the dry oriental darkness, and was laid out hastily, like Sir John Moore at Corunna, with no respite for lamentation, while the march was resumed.[56] More than for most men, one feels pity for a spirit so disinterested and so frustrated, and recognises the magic that led his men with scarce a murmur to the borders of Media from their homes in Gaul.

There was no longer any thought, or indeed hope, of any advance in the steps of Alexander or any other. Before it marched back towards

Sumere (Samarra)[57] the army elected Jovian as emperor and accepted the Persian peace. The Tigris, sliding in summer flood, scarcely differentiated except by wetness from its earthy background and with spinning whirlpools like spider webs upon it, still lay between the troops and their safety; a makeshift bridge laid on inflated goatskins, and the twelve small boats that alone had been carried from Ctesiphon, ferried the men across. Six days starving on desert herbs through the waterless lands of Hatra, by the ruined *castella* that had guarded the road to Sinjar,[58] brought them to the frontier at Zagura ('Ain ash-Shahid)[59] and here the thirty thousand from the northern route, who seem never to have crossed into Kurdistan at all, offered such food as by 'living sparingly' they had saved. Here too messengers set out for Gaul to announce Julian's death, while the army, having killed all its animals, dragged on in famine till it saw the yellow barrier of Masius with summer-dry grass thin and shiny as a beetle's wing upon it, and the security of the walls of Nisibis below.

The Peace of A.D. 363

The frontier marches in this age were usually held by the citizens,[60] and Nisibis offered to defend herself as she had often done before.[61] But this chief bulwark of Mesopotamia had been abandoned at the signing of the peace, and the emperor camped outside the gates for shame. Three days later, the Persian standards floated from walls that are now a mere blur in the cultivation, far out beyond the knot of shabby streets that cling there like limpets to the drowned. Marble fragments, half smothered in their dust, lie beside the mud-built doors, and five columns alone remain standing as pedestals for storks' nests where the fields have swallowed the vanished town.

Southgate, in 1841,[62] declared that nowhere else in Turkey had he seen such dirt and ugliness as among the hundred and fifty houses of Nisibis, and I spent a night there in a hotel of peeling walls and sagging rafters whose floors were soggy with waste waters poured over them for coolness in the almost intolerable heat. Wakeful among the mosquitoes, I pondered on *the worst inn's worst room*; yet even here there was the usual kindness, and the hotel keeper came with thin shoulders and red eyes and tousled hair like some deteriorated Gaul of the *foederati* to sit and save me from the (imaginary) embarrassment of eating alone at the *lokanta*. This is probably all changed since 1954.

In the morning I found the *bekchi*, the guardian of the church where St Jacob lies buried after leading the defence of the last of the Nisibis sieges in A.D. 350, thirteen years before the surrender of the town. His tomb is in one of those domed interiors scooped in a square building in the Mesopotamian fashion, with dark and splendid friezes cut in honey-coloured stone; and a tall old woman in Byzantine blue, the 'last Christian left in Nisibis' the *bekchi* told me, watched with the sad, long face of the mosaics as I laid my offering on the grave. The anger is still hot in Ammianus when he tells the story of Nisibis and of Jovian's triumph, a ceremony 'never before celebrated by Rome for anything that had been lost'.[63]

*   *   *

Although Jovian's preoccupation was not patriotism so much as an anxiety to bring his army out intact and to consolidate his empire, the thirty-years' treaty which he signed, or at any rate the boundary there established, was an unobtrusive base for a comparatively stable peace of one hundred and forty years.[64]

Shapur got back sixteen fortresses, as well as Nisibis and Singara and the territories east of Tigris whose acquisition had been so cheerfully celebrated with games under Diocletian.[65] The Persians continuing the policy of the Parthians before them, all Roman interference in Armenia was forbidden; and indeed the Sassanian claim went further, for the king argued that 'after the death of Julian there was nothing that ought to hinder him from recovering those lands which he could prove to have belonged to his ancestors'.[66]

He seized and blinded the Armenian king, loaded him with silver chains 'which are looked upon as a solace for men of rank in that country', and remained on good terms with the Romans until they secretly sent the young crown prince Pap, or Para, to rule Armenia with a Roman general beside him, but without any of the insignia of royalty – 'a wise resolution, in order that we might not be accused of breaking the treaty of peace'.

Wise or not, Shapur, 'shutting as it were the gates of friendship', began to prepare his army and to entice Para away from allies whom he had indeed every reason to suspect: and the Romans on their side murdered him during one of those dinner parties which the Armenians in the course of their history should have learnt to avoid.[67] The Emperor Maurice, writing soon after to the king of Persia, advocated the destruction of Armenia altogether as a permanent source of trouble to them both.[68]

The Sassanian policy continued to be remarkably homogeneous in Armenia. However many centuries might intervene and however many invasions might be forgotten, the Romans were aggressors there as far as Persia was concerned. Anything is aggression that without absolute necessity puts a neighbour in danger of his livelihood or life: and this was the key to Shapur's so-called war of revenge. The intrinsic truculence of a Roman Mesopotamia and Armenia had been forgotten by the West with the passing of the centuries and so many campaigns along the eastern rivers: assault had become legitimate by repetition, not for the first time nor the last in human history; and Ammianus can, in perfect good faith, attribute to mere obstinacy and 'unbridled covetousness' the Persian king's resistance to such long-inflicted wrongs. Such clichés are too often repeated; and the evidence goes to show that both the Parthian and the Persian policies persisted through many centuries on basically defensive geographic lines.

The pattern was continually repeated as the fourth and fifth centuries moved through the reign of Theodosius (378–395) to that of Justinian (527–565), and on to Heraclius when the Arabs stepped in. With the eastern trade safe and their Armenian flank guarded, the Sassanians had no reason for war, and only sought it, when, in their later years, they began to look for an income from their raids, like the Romans before them: there was no wish to hold permanently anything west of the Syrian desert, so long as the trading cities of the Tigris remained in their hands. While the Byzantines kept within their borders, there was peace and even friendship, and the Jovian frontier remained more or less permanent: it ran from the Euphrates north up the Khabur river, east of Amida the new metropolis and of Cepha (Hasankeif) built by Constantius as a military centre: and followed the Tigris and its Nymphios (Batman Su) tributary east of Martyropolis, the ancient Tigranocerta,[69] through wooded headwaters and ragged passes a four days' journey into the Armenian lands of Mush.[70] In the last years of the fourth century, a friendly partition gave Rome the smaller, western share of this country, while the Armenian suzerainty remained to Persia over the rest.[71]

The death of Julian actually ended the Roman wars of aggression beyond the Euphrates, and the next two and a half centuries may be considered as a period of adjustment during which the transition from ancient to mediaeval, from Roman to Byzantine, was slowly and more or less blindly accomplished. Blindly, because the ghost of the unified Mediterranean Empire continued to reign in men's minds with unchallenged supremacy while in fact the Levantine world was returning from Roman to Greek.

XVI

The Age of Justinian

An eye for the *present* is rare in statesmen as in others, and it is usually the past that they hammer on their anvils of government with zealous strokes: the present flies as it is looked at, caught as the mountaineer catches the path before him, casting his eyes ahead. The sporadic wars that continued right up to the Arab conquest along the Persian border were no longer wars of aggression on either side – but they were based on the aggressions of the past, and were repeatedly set off by whatever was happening in Armenia: to Persia this continued to be aggression as it would have appeared to any king of Parthia in the days of Augustus; to Byzantium, the long passage of time and frequent conquests made it appear as a conservative protection of long-acquired rights.

Laboriously and with habitual bloodshed the facts of the situation made their way, and after the wars of Heraclius – which were defensive in spite of the brilliance of their advances – a chance for peaceful intercourse with Persia seems to have come – too late. Persia went down before the Saracen invaders, and Byzantium lost the richest of her possessions in the south. For this loss, the dream of the Western Empire, and the religious policy of Justinian so strenuously combated by Theodora, were largely responsible: and it is with Justinian that my thread, the Roman policy on the Euphrates frontier, comes, after a development of eight centuries, to its end.

> 'As the end of this world approaches, the state of human affairs is bound to change for the worse, owing to the growth of wickedness. . . . Wars will rage everywhere: all peoples will be in arms. . . . The cause of this devastation will be . . . the blotting out of the name of Rome, by which the world is now governed, and the return of empire to Asia, so that the East shall again be mistress and the West her slave. . . . Let no man think it strange that a realm founded by so much effort, augmented so long by so many and such great men, and consolidated by resources so vast, should nevertheless one day collapse. There is nothing built up by human effort which cannot equally be pulled down by that effort: all the works of mortal men are mortal too. . . . The prophets darkly announce the fall of Rome; the Sybils openly announce her destruction. . . . '(Lactantius: *c.* A.D. 250–317; *Divine Institutions*, VII.c.15.7 ff.)

The Barbarian Inroads

By the sixth century the Sassanians had long ago renewed the Parthian roads and bridges and built up their trade.[1] Carpets and jewels, textiles and Iranian rouge travelled to China[2]; polo and chess, from Afghanistan and India, reached the West.[3] New ports in the Persian Gulf were served by Arab seamen; new industries were founded by prisoners in exile; a new Antioch was built on the banks of the Euphrates; while the Byzantines continued the old boxing match (which Augustus might have recognised) with a left hook at the Black Sea and a right hook in Abyssinia, in the perennial effort to dodge the Persian customs and secure the eastern trade.[4]

Passing along the southern route, Byzantine coins circulated in India from the reign of Constantine onwards,[5] and Abyssinian merchants in the days of Justinian were encouraged to secure the Chinese trade at its distributing centre in Ceylon. They did indeed attempt to do so but failed.[6] In the north, the Turks first appeared, mentioned by name in A.D. 568,[7] and made an unsuccessful effort for direct communication with Rome similar to that which the Hyrcanians had made in the reign of Nero. The Persians on their side were straining their engineering resources to master the forests of Colchis and capture a way to the Black

Sea coast.[8] They too failed, but kept the more southerly overland routes in their hands.

The treaty signed with Persia in A.D. 562 shows the commercial nature of the struggle. 'Since the time when the Emperor Justinian took over the Empire, he has established a public custom house on each strait' (of Marmara and Bosphorus).[9] The drain of the silk trade was heavy on Byzantium; the fixing of prices merely ruined the merchants,[10] and it was finally the private enterprise of two monks who brought the silkworm eggs in hollow reeds from China that solved the problem and allowed the beautiful craft to have its way in Byzantium.[11]

Between wars which simmered half-heartedly after Julian's death and Jovian's peace, the love-hate natural to a frontier became habitual. In an interval of ease in A.D. 524 for instance, a mixed international committee was set up to deal with border tensions whose religious background was adding its quota to the general discomfort; even when relations deteriorated, the local populations were now treated as property to be transferred rather than to be killed: the terrible Chosroes gave orders to massacre Romans only; and the prosperity of the desert fringe waxed and waned as arbitrarily as we have watched it do today.[12]

'Our victories abroad have taught us to consume the goods of others', said the Emperor Tiberius.[13] Three centuries later the Sassanians also took to raiding for profit, and left a devastation which has never been healed. The Parthians had kept the peace as far as possible, trusting their hellenistic cities to manage the trade route; but the Sassanians accepted the fallacy that a government can live by plunder, and in A.D. 540 Antioch with its one hundred and twenty-seven bishoprics was taken and burnt.

'Everything', says Procopius, 'was everywhere reduced to ashes and levelled to the ground, and since many mounds of ruins was all that was left standing of the burned city, it became impossible for the people of Antioch to recognise the site of each person's house . . . and since there were no longer public stoas or colonnaded courts in existence anywhere, nor any market place remaining, and since the side streets no longer marked off the thoroughfares of the city, they did not any longer dare to build any house.'[14] One hundred and twenty-nine years after another and last destruction, the Arab historian Tabari describes the city of Antioch as an empty ruin-field.[15]

Apart from these raids, the East on the whole escaped the worst of the barbarian inroads of this age. Italy was a depopulated wilderness, and in Rome itself the temples were 'covered with soot and cobwebs, and the people hurry past the ruined shrines and pour out to visit the martyrs' graves'.[16] 'No settlement, no mountain, no cave – nothing in fact in the Roman domain – remained unplundered, and many places had the misfortune to be captured more than five times.'[17]

In Africa Synesius, in the fifth century, describes the weariness of life. 'I long to give to my eyes sleep uninterrupted by the sound of the trumpet. How much longer shall I mount guard upon the ramparts, how much longer shall I patrol the intervals between the turrets?[18] ... All is lost, all is destroyed. ... There is nothing left but the cities, nothing. What may befall tomorrow God alone knows. ...'[19]

The desert, and the Berbers, swallowed the landscape of Cyrene, that slips tier below tier into its Mediterranean luminous silence, where Hadrian's marble basin still lisps with water in the sunlight and the temple of Zeus is shuffled on its hill. In the city of Ptolemais on the coast which Synesius defended, his church stands within his threatened walls, and the Roman villas excavated by the transient spades of the Italians spin the shadows of their painted columns month after month, year after year, century after century, in the whiteness of the moon.

Yet at the end of the fourth century the Empire still spread from Clyde to Euphrates. The poet Claudian had no inkling of its approaching disruption:

> *nec terminus unquam*
> *Romance dicionis erit,*

nor had the image of Imperial Rome yet faded; and it would be a mistake to think of the picture drawn by Synesius or Procopius as true of every province all the time. In the reading of history the pace is inevitably forgotten, and long intervals are lost sight of as they lie in shadow between the waves of each succeeding climax: Sidonius Apollinaris, in the fifth century, has a rule-Britannia-penny sort of picture of the countries of the world still bringing their products to Rome the Imperial city – India, Chaldaea, Assyria, China and Arabia; Greece and Phoenicia, Epirus, Libya, Gaul and Spain.[20]

His is the best description I know of a provincial villa of the time (in Gaul), when wealthy senators lived on their estates more or less independently, with barbarian settlers around them and the modern world simmering slowly in its cauldron. He describes 'the house-wall faced with slabs of cut marble up to the gilded ceiling',[21] or the homes of friends side by side in a country of olives and vines, with a playground for 'opposing ball-players', and books – devotional near the ladies' seats, with Augustine, Varro, Horace, Prudentius and Origen provided for the men. Plumbing vanishes together with civilisation, but both his entertainers were building baths. 'In neither case were they in working order . . . a trench would be hastily dug close to the spring or the river, and a pile of heated stones poured into it. Then while the ditch was heating it was roofed over with a dome of pliant hazel twigs . . . rugs of hair cloth were thrown over . . . so as to keep in the rising steam, which is created by pouring boiling water on hot stones.'[22]

The barbarians at most times were an infiltration rather than an invasion. There was a constant flow seeking military service,[23] or to be settled, according to the old Roman system of quartering, on owners of land from whom they received one third of the produce and sometimes more. In this gradual way Western Europe changed hands. Many people seem to have preferred to live in the barbarian regions altogether, in a more tax-free world than that of Rome[24]; and the mercenary armies had mostly served the Empire before greed or hunger led them to attack it: 'Every band has at some time caused Rome to tremble.'[25] From Diocletian onwards, the divisions in the army from being functional had become racial, and the non-citizen became the more privileged soldier[26] as the good recruiting grounds diminished[27]: the first Germanic king to become a Roman general was a Teuton who supported Constantine in his election.[28]

Our own time has been violently shaken, yet it is hard to picture the brutality of contrast which at any moment could break into the later life of Rome. When, in A.D. 414, the brother of Alaric the Goth married the emperor's sister, he offered as his wedding gift part of the treasure which Alaric had taken from the sack of the city in 410.[29] Nor was it the Empire alone that suffered: the treatment of the Goths as they crossed the Imperial border of the Danube was as unjust as anything in the long catalogue of Roman officialdom,[30] and Synesius from Africa writes that 'there is scarcely one of our families that has not a Goth in service: in our villas the mason, water-carrier, porter are Goths'.[31]

Sidonius Apollinaris describes the Teutonic settlers, their eyes faint and pale, with a glimmer of greyish blue, their faces shaven all round, 'and instead of beards they have thin moustaches which they run through with a comb'. Close-fitting garments confine the tall limbs of the men; they are drawn up high so as to expose the knees, and a broad belt supports their narrow middle. ' . . . a reek of garlic at early morn from ten breakfasts', he writes from Gaul to a friend in Rome: 'You are not invaded even before dawn . . . by a crowd of giants so many and so big that not even the kitchen of Alcinous could support them.'[32]

Byzantium resented, but suffered comparatively little from the invaders and liberated herself from the Gothic power once for all in the late fifth century with the help of her own mountaineers.[33] Yet Procopius still complains of the discomfort of their presence; 'since we have made mention of rooms for billeting, we must not pass over the fact that the owners of the houses in Byzantium, having to turn over their dwellings there as lodgings for the barbarians to the number of about seventy thousand, could derive no benefit from their own property.'[34] The emperor's politeness to the barbarian, the lavish subsidies and entertainments, are a continual source of complaint to the historian, who is unaware that a new order is slowly forming. Byzantine emperors were to succeed each other for close upon nine centuries, with short and stormy interludes, but able and hard-working and peacefully on the whole, and with never a change in the pattern of their rule.[35] When the decline eventually came, it 'was due to no marked decadence in the national character, but to the loss of both the military and maritime Themes of Asia Minor', the recruiting ground of army and navy.

Byzantium

In A.D. 476 the last emperor of the West was allowed to retire to a villa built by Marius and Lucullus five centuries before.[36] The clock had come full circle, and the hellenistic civilisation, defeated on the battlefield of Magnesia[37] and transformed in Italy, blossomed once more untrammelled in the lands of its birth.

ne vetus indigenos nomen mutare Latinos
neu Troas fieri iubeas Teucrosque vocari
aut vocem mutare viros aut vertere vestem . . .
occidit, occideritque sinas cum nomine Troia.

'Command not the native Latins to change their ancient name, nor to become Trojans . . . to change their tongue and alter their attire . . . Fallen is Troy, and fallen let her be.'

So Virgil had spoken for the Augustan age, whose hopes and fears both came to pass:

commixti corpore tantum
subsident Teucri . . .
omnis uno ore Latinos.

'Ausonia's sons shall keep their fathers' speech and ways and their name shall remain – the Teucrians shall but sink down, merged in the mass . . . all Latins of one tongue.'[38]

The admixture came and went, and an *Italian* renascence began with the removal of the Court from Rome: but the dominant in Byzantium was Greek.

'The civilisation of the later Empire . . . was simply the last phase of Hellenic culture. Alexandria . . . yielded the first place to Byzantium in the course of the fifth century. There was no breach of continuity, there was only a change of centre', and the change was gentle and continuous. The code of Theodosius in A.D. 43 8 was in Latin; the novels of Justinian a century later were nearly all in Greek.[39]

Constantinople was a Greek city, with arts which she developed chiefly from her Syrian and oriental past.[40] Her manuscripts written on purple parchment in letters of gold and silver belonged to the age of Justinian; her religious poetry – the only literary form in which she achieved greatness – reached its peak with the Beirut Jew, Romanos, and with John of Damascus, and the Patriarch Sergius' Acathistus hymn. Her patterns of brocade came from Persia, but cloisonné was an invention of Byzantine craftsmen,[41] as were the golden backgrounds that spread through the western world. The oriental love of detail for its own sake, the Greek longing to reach the meaning of things beyond the concrete shape of their façade, distinguish this civilisation essentially from that of

Rome: and the difference shows, in buildings, in books, in every sort of object,[42] in the fact that gladiators were forbidden by Anastasius, and that education, not birth, gave the entrée to society.[43]

Latin declined in the army; a Greek inscription was issued by the mint of Heraclius; and the Roman Pope complained of the want of interpreters in Constantinople. As late as the eleventh century, the century of the first Crusade, Psellus knew the whole Iliad by heart; and in the fourteenth century, when the sack of the Latins had done its worst, the dwindling city still spoke pure Greek to the eve of its fall.[44]

All this is beyond my perspective, which ends with Justinian's last attempted insertion of the traditional policy of Rome into the already established, profoundly different, Byzantine stream.

The Persian War

The long truce after Jovian lasted with only two short interruptions, of which the second (A.D. 420–424) was closed by a so-called hundred-years' peace, partly inspired by White Huns beating against the Persians in the Caucasus: but the war started again in A.D. 440 after Theodosius II had founded Erzerum (Theodosiopolis) in Armenia, on the bleak highlands where many decisive frontier battles have been fought.[45] It is not known that this was the occasion for the war's renewal, but a clause in the ensuing peace treaty forbade the building of new fortifications near the border on either side.[46] Sixty years later, when Qawad was king of Persia and war had again broken out, and Amida after hideous massacre had been sold back to the Byzantines – when the loss of Nisibis had been ever more bitterly felt and peace was restored – the Emperor Anastasius selected a 'hitherto insignificant village close to the Persian boundary, Daras by name, enclosing it with a wall. . . . But since it was forbidden in the treaty . . . the Persians, citing the terms of the peace, tried with all their might to obstruct the work, though they were hard pressed. . . . The Romans built all the more keenly, being anxious to get ahead of the enemy before they should finish their struggle with the Huns.'[47]

The Emperor Anastasius paid compensation for the infringement of the treaty, but the fortress of Dara remained, 'thrown out like an earthwork before the whole Roman Empire',[48] confronting Nisibis and

THE RUINS OF DARA

UKHAIDR IN THE DESERT

SASSANIAN CHIVALRY

THE SELJUK SCHOOL OF MARDIN

the Tigris crossings,[49] and screening the Euphrates road for the next hundred years. Its hasty building, no less than that of Erzerum, rankled in the Persian mind. They saw both perpetually pointed against them,[50] while they alone were left to hold the Caucasian gate against the Hun; and Qawad wrote to Justinian explaining how Anastasius had refused to join him in the common defence, how he himself had stationed a great army alone, and supported it, 'giving you the privilege of inhabiting the land unplundered . . . But as if this were not sufficient for you, you have also made . . . Daras as a stronghold against the Persians . . . and as a result . . . it is necessary for the Persian state to be afflicted with . . . two armies, the one in order that the Massagetae may not fearlessly plunder the land of both of us, and the other in order that we may check your inroads. . . . And even now the Romans may choose peace or they may elect war . . . ' and with these words Qawad dismissed the ambassadors, with the hint that a payment in money might solve the problem.[51]

Justinian was in the full tide of his western conquests and anxious for peace in the East. He paid the gold for the Caucasus defence in two heavy contributions, and withdrew the headquarters of Mesopotamia from Dara to Constantina along the Euphrates road. The Persian ambassador was allowed to move freely with his retinue about Constantinople,[52] and the popular disapproval of this liberal policy probably deepened the bitterness of Procopius.

Dara however remained, and lies where the lands of Nisibis curve upward to the Taurus, and is surrounded on three sides by heights that overlook it, so that except for the hardness of its rock against the Persian sappers in an otherwise alluvial plain,[53] one would think it singularly unsuited for defence. Justinian improved it with high walls and towers[54] which in 540, eight years after the signing of another 'endless peace', resisted the attack of Qawad's successor, Chosroes I.

Something of the great work is left, with rock-cut cemeteries around it, slanting down slopes of cornland. The far hills float in air there like islands, and villages squat on their imperceptible rises as if flattened under the dome of the sky. The women walk out with amphorae on their shoulders, dressed in purple and magenta, to draw water from the padlocked wells of the plain. Their faces are framed in red and black

cotton with dark turbans wound above, and their velvet sleeves hang
open from the elbow. Their bright tin buckets flash from far away. The
Arab speech comes up here from the south: 'May Allah make it pleasant
to you', they will say, tilting the water to your lips. 'May He give you
health and rest; may He help you in all your journeys.' Their goats and
sheep drift home in the last level shafts of sunlight that flows like a rich
and bleeding river, perpetually renewed; and catches and envelops in its
descent to darkness some square village wall or corner tower, unchanged
since the Persian cavalry came riding through the corn.

*   *   *

The character of the Mesopotamian wars had altered.[55] The im-
pulse of six hundred years had died away, and the sweeping plans of
Julian, Severus, Trajan, were out of date. Except in the Black Sea area
which was apt to be excluded from the peace treaties, trivial and often accidental incidents took the place of the over-riding objects of
invasion, and the Morte d'Arthur rather than the Ancient World appears in personal challenges and duels under the walls of Dara. A young
Persian, beaten by a wrestler from a training school in Byzantium –
'the Persians, deeply vexed ... sent forth another ... a manly fellow
and well-favoured ... but not a youth, for some of the hair of his head
already showed grey': he brandished his riding whip and summoned to
battle whoever among the Romans was willing, and the trainer again
came forward; 'the spears driven against their corselets were turned
aside with mighty force, and the horses fell and threw their riders'.[56] It
is the mediaeval chivalry as Europe came to know it.

The Jovian boundary now remained practically stationary, and when
Chosroes at last took Dara after a long siege in A.D. 573, he gave it back[57]:
the Romans too, whose object was no longer conquest but defence, gave
back the east Tigris lands after a victory.

Chosroes' countrymen remember him kindly as Anushirvan the Just.
A muleteer one day in Persia, walking beside me, told me the legend
of his palace, where all who desired a judgement could ring a bell and
be heard. In the fairness of his reign it was never rung, and its very
existence was forgotten; until one day an old thin horse, turned out to
starve, came shambling down the road, and pulled at a creeper that had
twined itself round the forgotten metal. A rusty tinkle caught the king's

ear, and he sent his servants to see; and they brought the old horse in and found the owner, who was made to feed it to the end of its days.

The picture of the 'vicious Chosroes', who was not, however, given too bad a press by Procopius,[58] was naturally different on the other side of the border, for he exploited the system of plunder with appalling thoroughness: the cities, during his yearly campaigns, bought safety or were burnt. In A.D. 540, Chalcis and Edessa each gave two hundred pounds of gold; Dara, a thousand of silver. Edessa collected all it had left to ransom the captives of Antioch, 'for there was not a person who did not bring ransom according to the measure of his possessions . . . for the harlots took off all the adornment which they wore on their persons . . . and any farmer . . . who had an ass or a sheep brought this to the sanctuary': but it was all seized by the general in command of the citadel, and Chosroes therefore took the captives away with him, and built them a city one day's journey from Ctesiphon, 'constructing for them a bath and a hippodrome'.[59]

Year after year the raids continued. The Persian siege of Edessa failed in 544, but the city paid five hundred pounds of gold notwithstanding; and in 545 and again in 551 Justinian purchased a five-year truce (from which the Pontic war was excluded).[60] Peace then lasted from 562 to the end of his reign in A.D. 578.

These wars made the stretch between the rivers, the main line of the caravans, almost uninhabitable, and turned their ancient resting places into dusty heaps that hardly keep a name. For many generations the citizens had repaired them. Under the Emperor Arcadius it had been decreed that bridges, roads, aqueducts and walls could be mended with the débris of fallen temples,[61] and every house in Edessa was taxed ten pounds of iron. But decay had set in before Justinian. Dura was forgotten and the routes were lost that had been familiar to Palmyra, and Procopius' account itself has a vagueness of hearsay about it: 'in the territory anciently called Commagene but now known as Euphratesia . . . a land altogether bare and unproductive separates the Roman and the Persian territory . . . and contains nothing worth fighting for. Both however have built forts carelessly of unbaked bricks in the desert which chances to lie nearest . . . these forts never suffered attack from their neighbours since they possessed nothing which their adversaries might desire.'[62] Until Justinian provided more solid defences, a slight wall only surrounded them, sufficient for cavalry that never contemplated a siege,[63] 'for these walls', says Procopius, 'were utterly unguarded from early times even to my day, and some peasants from the neighbourhood, when the enemy came down, would suddenly change their mode of life . . . and keep guard'.

Here Zenobia once founded a small city, the present ruin of Halebiya, 'and gave her name to it . . . but the long period of time . . . had reduced its circuit wall to a ruin . . . and it had come to be altogether destitute of inhabitants',[64] as indeed it is today – a triangular corner which the Euphrates hits with great swiftness as it makes for Deir-ez-Zor. There are many such, with nothing but hovels or the sandy desert beside them – palimpsests of old fortifications that sprang up or died with the desert seasons.[65] And when Justinian and his transient repairs were over, even the *Strata Diocletiana* was abandoned,[66] leaving the Khabur river more or less open to raiders, while Palmyra is referred to as a city 'in Phoenicia by Lebanon . . . built in a neighbourless region by men of former times . . . by lapse of time . . . almost completely deserted'.[67]

Justinian's Army

But Justinian, Procopius wrote, 'has made impregnable . . . all the places which previously lay exposed to the assailants. And as a result . . . Mesopotamia is manifestly inaccessible to the Persians'.[68]

By this time, in the mid-sixth century, the Roman and Persian armies had grown very much to resemble each other.[69] The Parthians had been too pacific to develop the art of sieges,[70] but the Persians had become good engineers[71]; while, on the other hand, the heavily armoured horseman copied from them by Constantius[72] had become the mainstay of battle,[73] and was to remain so till the invention of gunpowder. In 378 the Roman infantry were swept away at Adrianople by the Gothic horsemen; a century and a half later Belisarius was winning with cavalry alone.[74] The infantry was no longer supreme, yet the Byzantine army would still be drawn up, in three main bodies, mail-cuirassed under linen surcoats,[75] with a tuft of their regimental colours in their caps, with their best in the van[76] mixed with the *foederati*[77] and the *bucellari* – privately engaged followers of whom Belisarius kept some seven thousand of his own.[78] The very name of *legion* had disappeared.[79]

The horse-archers too were trained in the tactics of Persia through Palmyra, and Narses in Italy forestalled the experiment of Crécy and Agincourt by breaking a cavalry charge with their arrows.[80] They wore corselets and greaves; 'from the right side hang the arrows, from the other the sword'; and Procopius describes them drawing the bow to the right ear to pierce any armour – unlike the Homeric bowstring drawn only to the breast.[81] When, a hundred years after Justinian, these archers fought at the battle of the Yarmuk in Palestine, many of the Muslim dead were found pierced through the eye by the Byzantine skill.[82]

These armies, on either side, took a long time to collect,[83] and the defence tended to become immobilised in cities as the main forces on both sides grew weaker. Fortified towns would be linked to fortresses and supported by larger forts in their rear, and the summer fighting season would go by before they could be escaladed. It was the natural desert defence[84]; and behind the desert, with increasing difficulty yet for longer than one would have thought possible, the more protected cities continued to be rich within their walls. Two generations before Antioch was destroyed, a single citizen there was still able to free eight thousand of his slaves[85]; and Ammianus in Alexandria found teachers of various sects, and many kinds of secret knowledge 'explained by geometrical science. Nor is music dead among them, nor harmony. And by a few, observations of the motions of the world and of the stars are still cultivated; while of the learned arithmeticians the number is considerable. . . . The study of medicine is carried on with daily increasing eagerness, so that . . . it is sufficient for any medical man to say that he was educated in Alexandria.'[86]

Society in the Sixth Century

In his palace on Marmara, far away from these desert frontiers and their troubles, the Byzantine emperor, the 'equal of the Apostles'[87] lived in a mediaeval and oriental world.

The East had been pouring into Constantinople[88] for two centuries since Constantine had worn the oriental diadem.[89] Heraclius a hundred years later was to adopt the Iranian title (Basileus) derived from hellenistic kings.[90] By the reign of Justinian, clothing, headgear, ornaments for horses were modelled on the Persian, and the discarded toga had given place to long coats of stiff brocade copied from the Huns.[91] In the hippodrome, the factions wore their beards 'long as the Persians do': their hair was long behind and shaved over the forehead (as I still saw it in the Elburz mountains in 1931) – a 'senseless fashion they call the Hunnic'.[92] The emperor, wearing white at Easter in memory of the resurrection and seated with his twelve apostolic guests at table,[93] did not interfere with the oriental tradition and Asiatic ritual of the eunuchs of his court.[94]

In general structure the two great empires grew closer together, more intelligible to each other than to the increasingly distant West. The pattern of their monarchy – a despotism controlled by revolution or murder, with an elective streak inserted into the dynastic – was understandable to both[95]; and a respect for law – more abstract in the Roman, more individual in Persia – was shared on each side of the border.[96] The Sassanian king's religious supremacy – one of the chief changes introduced into the easy-going tolerance of the Parthians – was very near the royal Byzantine interference in church matters[97]; and both rulers remained at the head of their own carefully organised bureaucracy, that lasted practically unaltered in Constantinople to the Crusaders' sack in A.D. 1204.[98] The military administration of the Themes[99] was to correspond to the Marzbans' areas of defence into which Persia was quartered,[100] and the aristocrats in both countries – ancient in Persia but recent in Byzantium,[101] were too few in number to hold actual power. The middle people in Persia were the dekkans, a lesser nobility who officered the armies or lived on their lands, and collected the royal taxes more leniently and efficiently than any later foreigner was able to do[102]; whereas the administration of the Byzantine Empire was basically that of a professional middle class that had come to depend on office and not on birth.

'I went back into the hall,' writes an official at the end of his career, 'having served in all forty years and four months. I had received the recognition which it is customary that the emperor should give to those who serve their time; and I returned to my books.'[103] In Persia on the contrary there was at court a privileged hereditary caste with prerogatives not unlike those of feudal England.[104] As in England too, they immediately broke the realm up into feudal districts if a weak ruler was crowned.

During such intervals of disintegration a fundamental difference showed in spite of all between the Iranian East and the Byzantine West whose still unforgotten traditions had been forged in a city life more ancient than Rome. The atmosphere of Greek popular government continued to tinge the royal spendour of Byzantium; the embers of democracy flared up in the hippodrome; the Theodosian code gave its structure of law to many barbarian states beyond the borders[105]; 'the bureaucracy of functionaries trained in the Roman tradition', says Byron,[106] 'precluded the pursuit of a purely arbitrary rule.'

The senate, swollen to an enormous size,[107] and unofficially extremely influential, still flickered in Byzantium, strangely transformed.[108] 'In ancient times', says Procopius, 'the senate, as it came into the emperor's presence, was accustomed to do obeisance in the following manner: any man of patrician rank saluted him on the right breast; and the emperor would kiss him on the head and then dismiss him. . . . The empress however it was not at all customary to salute. But in the case of Justinian and Theodora, all the other members of the senate . . . would prostrate themselves on the floor . . . and holding their hands and feet stretched far out they would touch with their lips one foot of each before rising.'[109]

The Macedonian, or even the Achaemenian simplicity had wandered far away. St John Chrysostom saw the emperor 'like some marvellous animal'[110] with his gilded beard, while the Persian king in his hall of Ctesiphon, when the Arabs first met him, was hidden by a curtain[111] twenty cubits away from the first of his nobles.

The external Iranian formality was easily assimilated by the *gravitas* of the Roman, that old Augustan and pre-Augustan façade. Even in Antioch, a governor could prevent 'people of respectable rank' from eating in public.[112] Ammianus remarks that a senator of the old days 'would have been branded with infamy' for kissing his wife in the presence of his daughter.[113] The Persian rigidity went farther, and sent minor sinners, 'who take hot baths or eat with their mouths full', to hell, together with sodomites and assassins.[114]

The freer life of women in an aristocratic society,[115] the Renaissance quahty of courtesy and cruelty combined, belong to the general landscape of this hellenistic-oriental world which finally built up the Ottoman refinement. When the Dark Ages had intervened, and distance and the barbarian chaos had done their work, Byzantine and oriental were scarcely to be distinguished in the West. The bath that was a Roman institution belonged to the same foreign climate of sophistication as the habits of the royal Byzantine bride who first brought forks to Venice, or the saffron-tinted paper dipped in rose-water on which Chosroes liked to study his accounts.[116]

Diplomacy was born in this atmosphere and came perhaps to its culmination in Byzantium. Viziers and secretariats were Persian institutions, and transmitted later to Islam[117]; a network of well-connected brides was flung out from the capital in the hellenistic manner[118] to encourage intercourse in a more personal way[119]; and a mediaeval politeness inspired such acts as the adoption of helpless royal children by king or emperor of the other side. The Emperor Arcadius (395–408) appointed, as guardian over his son, the Persian King Isdigerdes (Yezdegeird), who 'did then display a virtue at once amazing and remarkable. For loyally observing the behests of Arcadius, he adopted and continued without interruption a policy of profound peace with the Romans, and thus preserved the Empire for Theodosius.'[120]

Such royal solidarity,[121] like that which for years prevented Elizabeth of England from signing the death warrant of the Queen of Scots, came through into the Middle Ages, not only between rulers across the frontiers of Mesopotamia, but among the armies in Syria and Palestine also, when the Arabs had taken the place of Persia. During the Crusades, the lord of Sheizar on the Orontes noticed the surprise of new arrivals over the sort of friendly enmity, of the kind recorded in border ballads, among adversaries to whom war had become a habit, with its interludes of pleasure, like anything else.

Byzantine Trade

As the generations passed, the merchandise of the East was to feed the coffers of Constantinople as it had once fed Persia and Parthia and the hellenistic kings. Two thirds of the world's riches were said by the Greeks to be within the city walls[122] and not once in nine centuries was their government to be bankrupt[123]; their budgets remained 'without precedent until the present age'.[124] Their strength was economic as the Roman never had been,[125] and the idea that it was undignified to make money never entered their heads.[126] In the Baghdad of the Caliphs, the ambassador from Constantinople was able to distribute *bakhshish* 'like the sands of the sea',[127] and when, in 1204, Constantinople was sacked by the Crusaders, the French share of booty alone amounted to seven times the annual revenue of England.[128]

Echoes of Mithradates are awakened when the Empire at last succeeds in exploiting the Caucasian shores.[129] In the thirteenth century, when Constantinople had been ruined, Trebizond became the great port of the East,[130] and sustained the Comneni as Sinope and Amisus had sustained Mithradates before them; and the northern shores, that had once dealt with Athens and enriched the Bosporan kingdoms, became outposts of a commerce on which the whole existence of early Russia came to depend.[131]

Justinian's flash back to Rome and the West was no more than an interruption, though it embodied the ideas of his day. It influenced and damaged the building of an Empire that finally showed itself to be Christian-Greek-Oriental, based less on rapine than on commerce and defence.

This character had already shown itself by the sixth century in spite of the frequency of war; and trade – chiefly in luxuries – had returned to the ports of Asia Minor, Syria and Egypt. Eastern commerce, with all its handicaps, revived,[132] and Justinian's gold was paid to Persia to keep the Black Sea clear. The Mesopotamian customs were less profitable, since the Persian dues out-balanced them; but here also traffic was regulated, and the trade which Diocletian had tried to canalise through Nisibis was centred by treaty during the fifth century on Artaxata, Nisibis and Callinicum on the Euphrates. (This was partly intended as a measure against espionage, since 'many men from ancient times are maintained by the state ... either on the pretext of selling something or by some other device, and ... would report all the secrets of the enemy to the magistrates.'[133])

The Frontier Christianity

The desert edges had been growing increasingly Arab, and indeed the lands between Euphrates and Tigris have always been easy of access to people who knew their ways. They should not, strictly speaking, be called desert at all: in a year of good rain, I have seen camels in June browsing from Baghdad to Damascus; and in the days of the Parthians – when the Seleucid trade was maintained in its old grooves – the Scenites, as we have seen,[134] took merchants from cistern to cistern or well to well. In such a country the Arab, if he wished to live at all, was forced either to guide or to loot the caravans, and the latter alternative was the only one left him when war took the place of peaceful trading.

The traffic of the Scenites had long since been disorganised and in Justinian's day two rival Arab tribes were destroying each other under the respective flags of Persia and of Rome. The Saracens, says Procopius, were over-running the Romans of the East from Egypt to the frontiers of Persia throughout this whole period without interruption[135]; and the only fragile network of restraint among them was cast by Christian missionaries who travelled there or found a refuge from persecution.

Christianity in general was far from inspiring peace, but it was an influential instrument for making the discords of the age international, and the historian has no choice except to venture back into the disheartening dogmatic tangle of the churches, if he wishes to understand how Byzantium lost all except the peninsula of Anatolia to the Saracens of the south.

Until the edict of Theodosius the Great in A.D. 383,[136] paganism remained the Roman state religion. The pagan and Christian faiths inhabited the Empire side by side while the last oracle of Delphi was said to be given to Julian, and the last Olympic games were celebrated in 393; Christian emperors found no difficulty in accepting the title of Pontifex Maximus in Rome.[137] It was only after Christianity had become recognised by government that the effective consequences of theology could be felt.

Until this happened the Christians were tolerated in Persia with very few exceptions, and a letter from Constantine to Shapur (of doubtful authenticity but probably embodying a current tradition), congratulates him on the prosperity of his churches.[138] This atmosphere of mildness disappeared when the emperor took his bishops with him to his wars not in spirit only but in fact (with a portable church-tent for their prayers[139]), and when Shapur turned the church of the martyred bishop of Seleuceia into a synagogue. The purely spiritual atmosphere, if it had indeed ever been usual, was lost.

'You will arrest Simon, chief of the Christians,' Shapur writes to his generals. 'You will keep him till he signs this document and consents to collect for us a double tax and a double tribute from the Christians . . . for we Gods have all the trials of war and they have nothing but repose and pleasure. They inhabit our territory and agree with Caesar, our enemy.'[140] And the persecution went on, from A.D. 343 almost uninterruptedly in all the north and centre of what is now Iraq and across the Tigris also, where the Roman war extended. The White Huns, pressing the rival empires into a common defence along the Caucasus, and interrupting the persecution through two reigns, must have been contemplated with thankfulness by the Persian Christians. During such intervals the bishops of both countries could be employed on embassies as interpreters, and were useful, to the Byzantines in particular, for information.[141]

One of them, Maruta, bishop of Martyropolis, was sent, with the added accomplishment of being a doctor, to Yezdegeird the king, and through his influence a council of Persian churches was held in Seleuceia in A.D. 410. It founded five metropolitan sees from the Persian Gulf to Kurdistan, and accepted the Nicaean creed, which seems until that moment to have remained unnoticed by the Persian church.[142]

This was as far as its compliance with the West would go, and when the bishops met again fourteen years later, from dioceses not only in Mesopotamia and Iran, but as far distant as Herat, Oman and Isfahan, they declared that the Western Fathers, 'now that persecution and anguish were heavy upon them, were unable to care for them as they formerly did', and affirmed the independent authority of the catholicus of Seleuceia: 'Any case that cannot be brought before him', they added, 'will be reserved for the tribunal of Christ.'[143] The immediate result of this important decision was that a war with Byzantium no longer necessarily entailed a Christian persecution,[144] for the king of Persia had become as theocratic east of the border as the Emperor was in the west: he could choose his catholicus as he pleased,[145] and had it in his actual if not theoretic power to inspire the nomination of either a Monophysite or a Nestorian.

The controversy between these two sects, over the single or double nature of Christ, need not be detailed here. Of its three main branches the Nicaean, which has remained orthodox in the West, held the two natures, human and divine, to be 'without division or separation'; it was supported by Rome and frequently by Byzantium, and was able, at intervals, to fraternise with the Nestorians, who also believed in the two natures, 'conjoined but separate'. But neither of these two faiths could for one moment tolerate the Alexandrian and Syrian Monophysites, who believed in one single divine nature only, and were repudiated by the Patriarch of Constantinople and the Pope of Rome, as well as by the Persian Nestorians.[146]

$$*\qquad*\qquad*$$

There had been 'Parthians and Medes and Elamites and dwellers in Mesopotamia' in the Pentecost of the *Acts*,[147] and an old unsponsored legend makes St Thomas evangelise Parthia.[148] That the religion travelled through Edessa to Nisibis seems likely, and also that there may have been an early Jewish wave whose record was lost after the destruction of Jerusalem in A.D. 70.[149] By A.D. 225 a church with twenty bishops had developed, with a literature[150] that produced good things, such as the works of Tatian, an epic on the lines of *The Pilgrim's Progress*[151] and the Discourses of Aphratcs. These disclose complete unawareness of the Council of Nicaea, which, in fact, no Persian bishop had attended,[152] and choose for reprobation an almost completely different set of errors – Chaldaean magic, poetry, the forbidden sciences, the seduction of sweet language, fornication, blasphemy, adultery and falsehood.[153]

About a hundred years later, after the Roman loss of Nisibis in A.D. 363, a school of theology was founded by St Ephraim at Edessa[154] and became the cradle of the Nestorian faith. With the passing of another century, by A.D. 489, that faith itself had been anathematised as a heresy, the school was closed, and a number of the 'Persian' teachers, who were mostly Syrian, were expelled and took refuge in Nisibis across the border.[155] The disciple Barsama, or Barsauma, who was already on good terms with the Persian king, then 'devoted himself to the task of freeing the Persian church from the western yoke'.[156]

He was made bishop of Nisibis, was induced by the king to marry, and made by the king's favour inspector of Persian frontier troops and member of a commission for the pacification of the border – together with a Byzantine *Dux*, a Persian *Marzban* and an Arab king; and he used his court favour to convince the King of Kings that the Monophysite Christians were bad.[157] Nestorianism, prosely-tising India and China in its brief and fertile race, was to have seven metropolitan provinces and over eighty bishoprics at the time of the Muslim invasion, with Nisibis as its chief centre after Seleuceia.[158]

Its almost miraculously swift spread had, like the Mithra worship,[159] a geographic explanation in the caravan routes that crossed all the frontiers[160]: compared with the slowness of the West, the range and speed of the eastern diffusion give a measure of the hellenistic frame, in which ideas as well as merchandise still travelled along the ancient roads.

The background of Mesopotamia in which this church was cradled must be remembered. Inspired by Theodore of Mopsuestia and Nestorius (who came from Germanicia, i.e. Marash or near it) the faith or heresy bore marks of its origin on the spiritual and physical watershed that runs between the Mediterranean and the East. Its strong characteristics pervade all the religions of these regions with a black-and-white Manichaean duality Mesopotamian rather than Iranian. Mani had preached in Seleuceia and his inspiration too came from Edessa, from heretics like Bardaisan or Marcian.[161] In recondite placcs, like the mountains of the north Syrian Nosairi or of the Yezidis in Iraq, the pagans to this day worship in their groves[162]; the ancient faiths of the East gave their living tinge to a Christianity different in essence from that of the Mediterranean or the West.

When in A.D. 489, the Nestorian school was driven from Edessa, Barsama set it up again in Nisibis under Narses, a famous teacher known as the Leper to his enemies, but as the Harp of the Holy Ghost to his admirers.[163] Barsama himself died peacefully, between 492 and 495; the Monophysite Christians continued to be persecuted at Nestorian instigation; the Persian wars devastated Mesopotamia; but the school of Nisibis persisted, forging the ancient unrecognised hellenistic bond.[164] Narses the great doctor died, probably early in the sixth century, and a nephew and then two other disciples succeeded him, while the school was said to number as many as eight hundred pupils. They lived almost monastically, and above all were forbidden to cross the Roman border close by – either to traffic or even to visit the holy places – nor were they allowed to leave Nisibis except during the summer vacation or when sent to the surrounding villages to teach.[165]

The tradition of this first important theological Christian university continued when Nisibis had long forgotten it. The Muslims built a school in Mardin near by, with two eleventh-century mosques for two different congregations,[166] under white fluted domes; in the hills some four miles to the east, an even closer tradition survives in the Chaldaean-Catholic, once Monophysite, school of Mar Zafaran. With ten monks or so, over-housed in their precarious poverty, among the still-splendid friezes of Justinian's Byzantium – tendrils and birds and vine-wreaths – it seems to have outlasted its own history. It was still living ten years ago went I went there, in a military area closed to travelling, in its solitude of the rocks.

The Nestorians grew in power, and they were able to visit the Roman lands when the Monophysites under Justin and Justinian fell out of favour. As soon as the emperor became their friend, however, the Persian kindness lessened, and in the sixth century, when Chosroes was destroying Syria, the Nestorians suffered with the rest.[167] Maraba, their greatest catholicus (A.D. 540–552), remained the king's friend until it was discovered that he had once been a Zoroastrian; he was then shut up near the sacred fire of Phraaspa,[168] whither the whole of Christian Persia climbed to visit him during seven years until he was forgiven[169]: the church seemed to have grown too strong to be attacked.

Its strength had begun and chiefly remained in the riverlands of ancient Assyria,[170] and its enemies were the Magian priests and the nobles of the plateau who had ever been against the cities from the days of Alexander and of Antiochus; the church relied against these on her riches and on the protection of the king. When her downfall came with oriental suddenness, it was not due to the pagans but to the long-persecuted Monophysites, and to a twist of fortune which threw the younger Chosroes into Byzantine arms.

Justinian had long been dead, and Maurice was emperor (582–602) when the young king, defeated by a rebellion in his own country, crossed by the raiders' way to Antioch and asked for help. Maurice reinstated him on his throne, and the Nestorian catholicus, who had taken the wrong side in this crisis, fled and died among the newly converted Arabs of the middle Euphrates.[171]

The Monophysites were now in the ascendant. Their monks spread in every direction from monasteries on the banks of the Tigris or from

Armenia; they comforted and inspired the captive exiles of their sect where they lived in camps in great numbers and whence the doctrine spread; and it was to these monasteries, of which there were about sixty, that the long Persian Christian resistance to Islam was eventually chiefly due.[172] King Chosroes, apart from gratitude to Byzantium, had a Monophysite Christian wife to persuade him, and in A.D. 605, when an over-zealous Nestorian bishop had stirred up a rising and been crucified, the election of a new Nestorian catholicus was forbidden. The king and his queen countered the flock's plaintive petitions with three theological questions, and took the representatives of both sects along with them to the Persian highlands for the summer season.[173] Chosroes considered himself head of the Christian churches in his realm, and it is never indeed safe to forget politics in an oriental religion: the see of Seleuceia remained vacant till his death.

The Monophysites

The Monophysite monks had asked Antioch to ordain their bishops, but the prudent patriarch refused, because, with a supreme head resident in Roman territory, their enemies could easily have denounced them to the Sassanian prince as spies for Byzantium.[174] A political feeling for autonomy soon came to strengthen their doctrinal deviations. By the seventh century it had become so strong that when a Persian patriarch visited the Emperor Heraclius in Aleppo and conformed to the Imperial ritual of the double nature out of politeness, his own bishops erased his name from the records: 'the Greeks,' they said, would never have let him celebrate the holy mysteries on their altars 'unless he had called Mary the Mother of God'.[175]

A different but even more passionately autonomous slant appeared in Syria and Egypt, where long-lost liberties – revived during the Empire's distresses in the north – had flared their brief spurt under Palmyra. Arianism had flourished, fed by influences surviving from older ages, under a hellenistic-pagan surface, and welcomed as natural allies by the Christians. The bishops, who came from the people and whose services soon came to be held in the native spoken languages, were the natural leaders of these flocks: the foreign Byzantines were Melkites or King's

382 of Rome on the Euphrates

men,[176] aliens to the Monophysites in all the regions that lay east of Alexandria.

If the western and eastern halves of the Empire had been sooner divided, Byzantium would probably have solved its dogmatic tangle in such a way as not to alienate the south-eastern Mediterranean provinces, of whose importance the Byzantine emperors were naturally more realistically conscious than the western. The heart of civilisation was in them. Most of the writers were Asiatic or African in the age of Justinian: the jurists of Beirut, the rhetoricians of Caesarea and Gaza, the continued productivity of Alexandria persisted through this time. Not only did the Syriac literature now reach its apogee in what had become a national language, but the writers of Greek like Procopius of Caesarea or Malalas of Antioch were Syrians too. In law, in religion, in art, in oratory, philosophy, and letters, the glow that had been encouraged by the Severans and had become self-conscious for a moment in Palmyra, still remained.[177]

The emperors tried to reconcile, but were helpless; while the Church of Rome, continuing to carry on without recognising it the traditional policy of the weak periphery,[178] was largely responsible for the weakening of the Roman border before its final submersion in Islam.

Trouble had been given some time before the reign of Justinian by Roman claims of ecclesiastical precedence.[179] They had no theological basis, since Antioch had been St Peter's earliest foundation, and they aroused what would now be called a strong nationalistic resistance. The council of Chalcedon, in A.D. 451, admitted the old supremacy 'for the Fathers rightly granted privileges to the throne of old Rome, because it was the Imperial city'; but 'the one hundred and fifty most religious bishops . . . gave equal privileges to the most holy throne of new Rome, justly judging that the city which is honoured with the sovereignty and the senate, and enjoys equal privileges with the old Imperial Rome, should in ecclesiastical matters also be magnified as she is, and rank next after her', and should have the ordaining of the bishops of her own provinces – a decision which the old Rome never thought of recognising for a moment.[180]

The south-eastern provinces were unimpressed not only by Rome but by Constantinople also, and the unlucky council of Chalcedon alienated them altogether. The emperors, trying to compromise between incompatibles, met predestined failure. Zeno (474–491) produced a schism of thirty-five years with Rome and forced the Persian Christians into the arms of the Persian king. Anastasius (491–518), who favoured the provinces, had to promise to introduce no new doctrine before the Patriarch in Constantinople would crown him, and – accused on religious grounds – had to apologise to the crowd in the hippodrome.[181] Any agreement between Rome and the emperor provoked instant antagonism in Syria and Egypt; while any Monophysite leanings in Constantinople brought down the anger of the Pope. The church services became patriotic, translated into Coptic in Egypt, while in 536 two bishops of the Euphrates sign their names in Syriac[182]: nationalism, as we might say today, filled the streets of Alexandria with bloodshed and riot.

Justinian and Theodora (527–565)

What line Justinian would have followed if the magnet of Italy had not held him, is uncertain.[183] He and Theodora 'did nothing separately in the course of their life together',[184] and he may have known more of her policies than appeared. He was not unwilling to use Monophysite missionaries like John of Ephesus, 'destroyer of idols and hammer of the pagans', when abolishing the worship of Isis or of Ammon.[185] But a friendly Papacy was necessary for his campaigns, and he declared Rome 'head of all holy churches'. Right belief, according to Malalas,[186] 'was made a condition for admission to the service of the state'; an attestation of orthodoxy from three witnesses was required, and heretics were debarred from the professorial chairs. Unable to make wills, to receive bequests, or to testify in court, fifty thousand are said to have fled to Persia.

The great Empress on the other hand favoured the oriental provinces throughout. Slight and small, with ivory skin and pale contracted brows, she saw farther than Justinian.[187] She hid the deposed bishop Anthemius for years in the labyrinth of her Marmara palace while the Pope's persecution raged against his flock,[188] and – pressing the eastern claims on the undecided emperor – died with the Monophysites seemingly triumphant. Justinian, 'anxious to carry out the policy of his dead wife',[189] published another long and bloody effort at compromise,[190] which antagonised the Nestorians, embittered the Papacy, and failed to conciliate the Monophysites: the policy of appeasement is only useful in a crisis before the crisis has occurred.

Theodora made a permanent contribution to history before she died by protecting Jacob Baradaeus, the most remarkable of the Monophysite missionaries, who was ordained clandestine bishop of Edessa in 543 by the other bishops hidden in the Marmara palace. Disguised as a beggar, and dressed in the saddle-cloths of asses from which he got his name,[191] he spent years of lonely preaching, pursued and ever threatened; and the name of Jacobite, which is (incorrectly)[192] given to the Syriac church, bears witness to his memory.

With him, the break with the West became absolute. The bishops of Euphratesia, Edessa, Mesopotamia, turned their backs on Antioch, and the desert quality became intensified along the Mesopotamian border. The tribal chief of the Ghassan, Harith, the protector of Baradaeus, was sent a Monophysite desert bishop by Theodora,[193] and the episcopal nomad hierarchy continued long into Muslim times.[194]

The Desert Christianity

In 1901, when Chapot travelled there, this desert border was a dangerous district and travellers passed rapidly by in a countryside alight with insurrection[195]; and Edessa (Urfa) is still at the end of journeys, and so is Hierapolis the capital of Euphratesia, and Carrhae and Samosata, and Constantina-Viranshehir, city of ruin, so often fought for on the Nisibis road: they scarcely tick over, as if time itself had grown slow with the vanishing of their trade. The drying lands blow their dust, and the half-settled bedouin, ploughing under solitary horizons, find some slab of tombstone Greek or Arab to build the lintels of their houses in the treeless fields; and when they come on market days to Edessa, the police feel them all over for hidden weapons, while they change their desert head-dress for the modern peaked cap of civilisation in the town.

Ideas and heresies have ceased to flourish in that once teeming ground, where pantheists like Stephen Bar Sudaili were forced to leave 'because of advanced opinions',[196] or Paul of Samosata, the friend of Zenobia in Palmyra, thought to put himself on an equality with Christ.[197] Two centuries after his death he still influenced Nestorius. The later, seventh century, Paulician heresy began in Samosata, took refuge in the desert,[198] and reached the Black Sea by the help of Saracen emirs in Tarsus and Melitene; the Paulicians, to Mas'udi who must have known them, 'stood half way between Christians and Zoroastrians'[199] – a position which tallies with their geography as well.

The dualism of Mesopotamia, the hellenism of Syria, the Semitic monotheism, were tossed about in these fierce little towns as the trade passed east or west. On a forgotten day, when the Emperor Anastasius remitted some tax to Edessa, 'the whole city rejoiced, and they all put on white garments . . . and carried lighted tapers and censers full of burning incense', and, praising the emperor and celebrating the eucharist, resolved in their optimism to keep their festival for ever.[200] The confidence in durability has long since vanished, yet Urfa still smoulders, though the churches that made it famous are destroyed; it has gone to older memories; the fat and sacred carp of Abraham jostle each other in his pool; and the Christians have changed their names and live uneasily beside the Kurds who so recently killed them, whose white-cloaked women walk about under their enormous headgear in the shadow of the Ottoman peace.

Beyond the traders' fringe, the two rival tribes of Ghassan and Hira fought respectively for Byzantium and Persia and chiefly for themselves, while the desert Christianity spread quietly among them. As early as the fourth century, Mawia, a chieftainess of the Arabs of Palestine, refused to lay down her arms unless the emperor agreed to let her have a bishop of her choice.[201] In A.D. 431 a Mesopotamian bedu is said (in a rather doubtful account) to have been made phylarch of the Saracens under Byzantium, and to have reached the Council of Ephesus as a Palestine bishop after turning Christian with all his tribe.[202] A more normal Arab seized an island with the Red Sea customs in the gulf of Akaba about A.D. 470, and sent a bishop afterwards to regularise his position at court.[203]

At Ukhaidr in the steppe of Kerbela the palace of the kings of Hira still stands, sterile and magnificent, and the Lakhmids there were said to have had a bishop as early as A.D. 410.[204] Their religion however remained sketchy and Mundhir their prince, who helped the sixth century Persians to beat Belisarius back across Euphrates and to sack Edessa,[205] is said to have sacrificed four hundred nuns to the Arabian idols[206] as well as an Armenian prince to Aphrodite[207]: both he and his Ghassanid rival on the Palestine border would easily change sides, and one may say that during the time of their activity (A.D. 528–582) they 'brought nothing but deceptions to their suzerains'.[208] But they formed a background into which the disaffected, and the Monophysites in particular as time went on, could disappear into the safety of the desert. An ever-increasing intercourse preceded the Islamic invasion, which opened some eighty years after A.D. 582 when both small desert kingdoms had been dissolved.[209]

Justinian to Heraclius

Justinian died in A.D. 565 and already his work lay in ruins.

'We have good hopes', he had proclaimed, 'that God will grant us to restore our authority over the remaining countries which the ancient Romans possessed to the limits of both Oceans.'[210] If one has to be conquered, it is better to have it happen once only: Justinian's hopes almost succeeded, and no Roman victories can have cost quite so dear: in Italy the continuous tradition of government and promise of stability under the Goths was disrupted and the emptiness for a Lombard invasion prepared; in Africa the last hope against the encroaching Berbers disappeared with the Vandals; Monophysite Armenia was estranged[211]; and the already insecure loyalty of the south-eastern Mediterranean coast was so shattered that the Arab invasion found welcome instead of resistance in many places when it came.

Justinian's revenue amounted to nearly a third of the gross yield of the land,[212] yet even so the shrunken periphery of Rome was too expensive to be restored, and even before the emperor's death, during his sad old age deprived of Theodora, the fortresses he had repaired or built were beginning to decay. There were eighty or more along the Danube,[213] and a continuous line from Trebizond through the newly constituted county of Armenia,[214] across Chorzianene where the inhabitants refused to recognise a frontier and continued to intermarry,[215] and through the two *clisurae*[216] clefts into the delightful wooded tangle between Ilidja and the upper Nymphios, where Pheison and Citharizon and Aphumon[217] stood above precipices of grey rock. The fortresses then reached the Tigris gorges through the shallow cups of Masius, and forts and watch towers crowded each other closer than ten to a mile. At their back was

Amida, with the walls that modern progress has only partially destroyed; and from it a multitude of *castella* descended to cover the trade route and Dara.

In the west, Euphrates castles as far south as Circesium were also crumbling into their sandy dust. The frontier garrisons had lost their prestige since Constantine had reorganised the army, had come to be settled with lands or business of their own in the hellenistic tradition,[218] and were – according to the possibly over-darkened picture of Procopius – 'so casually and meanly treated that their pay musters were four or five years behind'.[219] After the peace of 545, the army was reduced and their five-yearly donative (the soldier's chief financial hope)[220] was stopped. 'The names of the dead remained on the lists and there was no promotion.'[221]

Recruiting, which seems to have been partly voluntary in the time of Justinian,[222] had naturally become difficult, and the powerful landed senatorial families blocked conscription which drew the peasants from the landlords' fields. In the fifth century, in the days of Theodosius, a recruit who amputated his thumb to escape conscription (our word poltroon comes from the Roman *pollex*) was liable to be burnt alive; by the sixth, it was sufficient to present two mutilated recruits in place of one sound one. They could take up some profession in the stations where they were settled – such as the soldier of the regiment of Elephantine 'by profession a boatman', or the basket weaver from Alexandria who would put on his uniform and go on parade when his day's work was over.[223] These poor people came to depend on private charity if they were moved from the small businesses they had found for themselves in the places where they were settled, and a bishop of Antioch is described as having acquired great influence among them by distributing money and food as they marched across his lands.[224]

The picture drawn by Procopius is a nightmare of ruin, and probably true though not due solely to Justinian. After 543 the plague added its dead[225]; the cities, impoverished ever since Constantine had appropriated their lands,[226] had to economise on physicians and teachers, 'nor were the public lamps kept burning ... nor was there any other consolation ... for the theatres and hippodromes and circuses were closed ... and there was no laughter in life'.[227] The postal services – except the main line to the Persian frontier[228] – were cut off or reduced; the farmers could only export their grain to the ports at their own expense[229]; and the land continued to fall out of cultivation. Tenants and their children after them remained attached to the soil, and those that ran away 'stole their own person'.[230] It is however not fair to attribute all this to the sixth century only: Diocletian's finance had been largely responsible, and as early as the fourth century a workman in a government factory was branded so as to be recognised and arrested if he fled.[231]

Such, as Procopius saw it in the blackness of his disillusion, was the end of the golden age of Justinian, that has yet left us, among many lesser beauties, the church of St Sophia.[232] An even deeper blackness followed it, and when that clears away nearly a century later under Heraclius, the corner that separates the Mediaeval from the Ancient world is turned.[233]

Heraclius and Islam

Near the end of the sixth century, in the interval of friendship with Persia, the young refugee King Chosroes gratefully handed back Dara to the Emperor Maurice who had helped him to his throne, and in A.D. 591 he also ceded the greater part of Armenia. This had been growing in importance as a recruiting ground. Its excellent troops were always reviewed by the Great King in person in Ctesiphon,[234] and the Byzantines – who had shaken off their foreign mercenaries and had lost the Balkans to Slav invaders – were increasingly in need of men from these neighbouring highlands. But now, with the gaining of the fatal country, the perennial occasion of war was renewed. The Byzantines held all the north, to Lake Urmiah and Van, and nearly to Tiflis; and sooner or later the menace to Persia was bound to operate as usual. The moment came when the Emperor Maurice, threatened by rebellion, asked Persia for help in his turn. The young Chosroes was too late to save him, but marched to avenge his murder. Dara was retaken (A.D. 604) and Mesopotamia, Syria and Palestine were ravaged; by 609 the Persians were on the Bosphorus. In 610 Heraclius sailed from Africa to deal with the usurping Phocas in Constantinople and to offer Persia a peace which she rejected.[235] The Empire touched its nadir of danger: the whole of Syria was overrun and Jerusalem captured after a twenty-days' siege; the Monophysites were lukewarm and the Jews sided with the invaders. Sixty thousand Christians were said to have perished; the Holy Cross, the most venerated relic, was carried away; and the corn supply of Constantinople was lost with Egypt.

Little information has come through from the darkness of those days.

Heraclius, slowly organising with insufficient men or means, fought probably three campaigns between 622 and 628, and beat the Persians with the help of the Caucasian tribes and the people of the steppes beyond them,[236] as Mithradates had done the Romans long before. In October 627 he marched south along the western shore of Lake Urmiah, and was making for Ctesiphon when the Persian general threatened to cut him off. Forced to battle, the emperor turned and won a brilliant victory near the ruins of Nineveh in December. The road to Ctesiphon and the unplundered Sassanian provinces lay open.[237] In the fortress of Dastgerd, as they marched down the left bank of the Tigris beyond Julian's lost grave, they came upon three hundred Roman eagles[238] captured in the past. Chosroes was dethroned and killed and his successor asked for peace; and on March 21st, A.D. 630, the emperor reinstated the Holy Cross in Jerusalem. 'None could sing the hymns because of the deep and poignant emotion of the King (he adopted the title of *Basileus* since Persia was vanquished)[239] and of all the crowd.'[240]

The queen of Persia, Borane, who had restored the cross, made a formal peace and, if fortune had favoured them after the exhaustion of the Heraclian wars, there was perhaps a chance for the two powers to stumble into a lasting friendship: Chosroes, once writing to Maurice, had compared themselves to the two eyes in the front of the world, and they had already come far together.[241] But the time had passed; the names of eight Persian kings flash by between A.D. 629 and 632[242]; and the Church and the desert settle the Eastern destiny between them.

All 'Greeks' were now looked upon as enemies by the provinces of the south-east.[243] The attempts of Heraclius to reconcile them failed, and so did those of their leader, Baradaeus himself, whose efforts were annulled by the monks of his own party.[244] The arrival of Islam was looked upon in remote Byzantium as a new sort of Arianism, to be bracketed with other Christian sects,[245] while the small Islamic armies when they came – never more than twenty-seven thousand if so many in Syria or Palestine[246] – were welcomed by a people that had grown accustomed to the desert infiltration, and felt more kinship with it than with the Byzantine strangers of the north. 'It was no small advantage to us to be delivered', Michael the Syrian wrote when the Arabs came.[247] When their invasion reached Damascus, the citizens welcomed it, and their bishop arranged the surrender with the treasurer Mansur[248]; some cities held out for a short time or had to be twice taken, but others – like Ma'arret-en-Nu'man near Aleppo – came out in procession[249]: the desert Arabs and the Monophysites were on the side of the invaders.

Conclusion

The earlier dynasties that Rome defeated, the Seleucids, the Pontic and Palmyrene traders, and the un-political Parthians, all tried to realise a river-economy that fed its peoples along or across its safe and (as far as possible) peaceful course. They succeeded in a moderate and interrupted degree, until the Sassanians, unlike the Parthians, took the commerce into their own hands, and acted as the Romans had acted for centuries, on the basic principle that the holes in an exchequer can be patched with plunder. When they too had gone, and the Arabs consolidated themselves in their conquered provinces, the caravans once again travelled for a short time without a frontier from Damascus to Khorasan, and a cheque written on the banks of the Oxus could be cashed on Tigris or Euphrates as it had been in the days of the hellenistic kings. Hellenism had transcended the frontiers of the Roman Empire, and Aurelian or any other *Restitutor Orbis* was cutting an artery when he claimed his Roman part-world as the whole – an artery furthermore that had demonstrated its possibilities by actually existing. After the early Caliphs, when the Abbasids followed, the value of the trade routes was clearly recognised and the Arabian Nights' world of the Baghdad merchant came into its own. The great Abbasid bridges are mostly washed away; there is one stranded in sand between Baghdad and Mosul, another, almost obliterated, at Hasankief and another (badly restored) over the Nymphios near the battlefield of Lucullus; but the beautiful *khans* left by the Seljuks, who carried on when the Abbasids had departed, still mark the roads that led from Istanbul to Mesopotamia.

Byzantium reverted to Greek (Maurice, born in Cappadocia, was its first Greek emperor); and trade and diplomacy were honoured from the very founding of the Imperial city as never in Rome before. The golden *solidus* of Constantine became the currency of international commerce for centuries,[250] and Greek architects, artists, statesmen and accountants ran the administrative part not only of their own empire but of that of the early Caliphs as well: the Syrian accounts till the eighth century were kept in Greek.[251] The 'power and prestige of Byzantium were founded on her gold,'[252] and this was given her by her position on the trade routes[253]; and when the end came, 'the tragedy of Byzantium was above all a financial tragedy,' when Venice and the Genoese had snatched her sea-borne traffic.[254]

Yet the earlier Imperial Rome, whose exchequer was so chronically depleted, had enjoyed the same, or indeed greater geographic advantages for trading, when she held all the frontier cities of Syria which were lost to Byzantium.

* * *

A better historian than I am may be able to assess the amount of damage done to Rome in her decline by the frontier blindness which I have tried to describe. There are plenty of witnesses – less noticeable in the early centuries when Rome was the aggressor, but ever stronger as the oriental world took its revenge. 'The absence of the emperor in Asia' is ever an excuse for plunder. The Goths, says Bury, 'argued with truth that Justinian would not have embarked on his enterprises in the West if he had not been secured in the East by the peace he had concluded with Chosroes. If they could succeed in embroiling him in a war with Persia, it would be impossible for him to continue the war in Italy.'[255]

And after the defeat of the Vandals, Chosroes 'sent envoys to Byzantium, and said that he rejoiced with the Emperor Justinian, and he asked with a laugh to receive his share of the spoils of Libya, on the ground that the emperor would never have been able to conquer . . . if the Persians had not been at peace with him'.[256]

Through all the generations when armies were being collected to send against Parthians or Sassanians, the Roman Empire was suffering from a desperate shortage of fighting men; and the barbarians who settled in it or invaded it, and then transformed it, had mostly once been recruited to hold a frontier which, along all the desert and Euphrates reaches, could have been at peace. It should not be forgotten that not one of Rome's adversaries, or such as had access to the eastern trade routes, was ever except very temporarily short of cash, on which the payment of the mercenaries depended.[257] The frontier from the Black Sea to the Indian Ocean could be an asset instead of a liability. Nor is the study of these unhappy far-off things by any means academic today. The lorry follows the tracks of the caravans, and trade moves across the world's waistline from east to west or vice versa: and the choice on the map is still open and indeed urgent – between the vertical closed line of defence and aggression (from either side) or the horizontal open line of commerce with all that it entails.

Rome, that old Phoenix, never died. She still flourishes in west and north, and in the east was born again out of her ashes. Sacked by Alaric or Vandal, tossing in her embers, she watched in temporary darkness while the eastern lands of her Empire crumbled to rebirth. Her antagonists cast great shadows – Antiochus riding through the night from the stricken field of Magnesia; Cleopatra with purple sails making for the south; the Pontic invincible ghost of Mithradates; Palmyra rising like a desert flower and Parthian riders flitting through the dust. Her own sons too are there – Sulla and Pompey and Lucullus; Crassus wrapped in his cloak; the hawk-eyed Caesar and the flashing gaze of Augustus; young emperors twisted by power; and the long fighting trail of the Illyrians on the steadfast road – all, with immortal longings, for the dark.

Lists of Kings, Emperors and Dynasties

ROMAN PRINCIPLES AND EMPERORS
(from *The Cambridge Ancient History*)

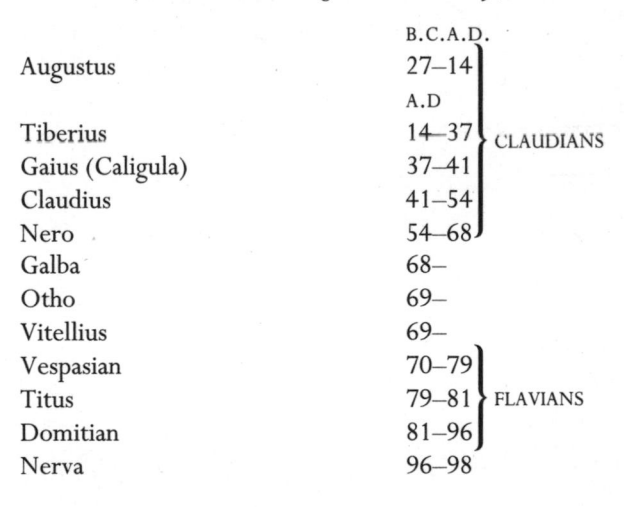

	B.C.A.D.	
Augustus	27–14	CLAUDIANS
	A.D	
Tiberius	14–37	
Gaius (Caligula)	37–41	
Claudius	41–54	
Nero	54–68	
Galba	68–	
Otho	69–	
Vitellius	69–	
Vespasian	70–79	FLAVIANS
Titus	79–81	
Domitian	81–96	
Nerva	96–98	

Trajan	98–117	
Hadrian	117–138	
Antoninus Pius	138–161	ANTONINES
Marcus Aurelius	161–180	
Lucius Verus	161–169	
Commodus	180–192	
Pertinax	192–193	
Julianus	193	
Septimius Severus	193–211	
Bassianus (Caracalla)	211–217	SEVERANS
Geta	211–212	
Macrinus	217–218	
Elagabalus	218–222	SEVERANS *cont'd*
Severus Alexander	222–235	
Maximinus	235–238	
2 Gordians	238	
Pupienus and Balbinus	238	
Gordianus junior	238–244	
Philip the Arabian	244–249	
Decius	249–251	
Valerian	253–260	
Gallienus	253–268	
Claudius	268–270	
Aurelian	270–275	
Tacitus	275–276	
Probus	276–282	
Carus	282–283	
Numerian	283–284	
Carinus	–285	
Diocletian	285–305	
Maximian	286–305	
Constantius	305–306	
Galerius	305–311	

BYZANTIUM
(from Ostrogorsky)

Constantine	324–337
Constantius	337–361
Julian	361–363
Jovian	363–364
(Valentinian I West)	
Valens	364–378
Theodosius I	379–395
Arcadius	395–408
Theodosius II	408–450
Marcian	450–457
Leo I	457–474
Leo II	474
Zeno	474–475
Basiliscus	475–476
Zeno	476–491
Anastasius I	491–518
Justin I	518–527
Justinian I	527–565
Justin II	565–578
Tiberus I Constantine	578–582
Maurice	582–602
Phocas	602–610
Heraclius	610–641
Arab invasions	

SELEUCID KINGS (*selection*)
(from Von der Osten)

	B.C.
Seleucus I Nicator	305–280
Antiochus I Soter	280–261
Antiochus II Theos	261–246
Seleucus II Callinicus	246–226
Seleucus III Soter	226–223

Antiochus III the Great	223–187
Seleucus IV Philopater	187–175
Antiochus IV Epiphanes	175–164
Antiochus V Eupator	164–162
Antiochus VII Sidetes	137–128

A confused tangle of short and violent reigns followed, to Antiochus XIII Asiaticus 69–65 when Pompey annexed the Kingdom.

PARTHIAN KINGS
(From Neilson C. Debevoise: *A Political History of Parthia*)

	B.C.		B.C.
Arsaces	ca. 250–248	Mithradates III	58/57–55
Tiridates I	ca. 248–211	Orodes II	ca. 57–37/36
Artabanus I	ca. 211–191	Pacorus I	died in 38
Priapatius	ca. 191–176	Phraates IV	ca. 38–2
Phraates I	ca. 176–171	Tiridates II	ca. 30–25
Mithradates I	ca. 171–138/37	Phraataces	
		(Phraates V)	
Phraates II	138/37–ca. 128		2 B.C.–A.D. 4
Artabanus II	ca. 128–124/23		
Mithradates II	ca. 123–88/87		A.D.
Gotarzes I	91–81/80	Orodes III	4–ca. 6/7
Orodes I	80–76/75	Vonones I	7/8–12
Sinatruces	76/75–70 or 69	Artabanus III	12–ca. 38
Phraates III	70 or 69–58/57	Tiridates III	ca. 36
	A.D.		
Cinnamus	ca. 37	Parthamaspates	ca. 117
Gotarzes II	ca. 38–51	Vologaeses II	105/6?–147
Vardanes	ca. 39–47/48	Mithradates IV	128/29?–147?
Vonones II	ca. 51	Vologaeses III	148–192
Vologaeses I	51/52–79/8o	Vologaeses IV	191–207/8
Pacorus II	78–115/16?	Vologaeses V	207/8–222/23
Artabanus IV	80–81	Artabanus V	ca. 213–227
Osroes	ca. 109/10–128/29	Artavasdes	ca. 227–228/29?

PERSIAN KINGS – SASSANIAN
(from Von der Osten: *Welt der Perser*)

A.D.

	A.D.		A.D.
Ardashir	224–240	Peroz	479–483
Shapur I	241–272	Qawad	483–531
Bahram I	271–276	Chosroes I Anushirvan	531–579
Bahram II	276–293	Ormuzd	579–590
Narses	293–303	Chosroes II Parviz	590–627
Shapur II	310–379	Shiroz	627
Yezdegerd I	399–422	Yezdegerd III	632–657
Bahrain V	422–439	Arab invasion	634
Yezdegerd II	439–459		

Notes

Full titles are given once and then abbreviated, and are to be found in the Bibliography. Where the author's name is given but no title, the work referred to is the only one mentioned in the Bibliography. *The Cambridge Ancient History* and *The Cambridge Mediaeval History* are referred to throughout as *C.A.H.*, and *C.M.H.* respectively.

Preface

1. See Pliny: *Natural History*, XV.24.89.

Chapter I. The Battle of Magnesia

1. Modern Gedik Su.
2. Polybius; *Histories*, XVIII.32.13. It had already been defeated at Cyno-scephalae eight years before.
3. Plutarch: *Eumenes*. Everyman 1948, Vol. II.344.
4. *Ibid., Aemilius Paulus*, I.414.
5. *Maccabees* (Apocrypha) I.6.39.
6. E. Bikerman: *Institutions des Séleucides*, 90.
7. *Ibid.*, 60–2, for elephants and chariots.
8. Polybius: *Histories*, III.14.6; 42.11; 74.11.
9. *Ibid.*, I.39.12.
10. Ammianus Marcellinus: *Roman History*, XIX.7.6.

11. Bikerman: 61.
12. Livy: XXXVII.59.3–6.
13. Polybius: V.84.3–6.
14. Frontinus: *The Stratagems*, II.4.4; Herodotus, VII.211–13 (transl. J. E. Powell).
15. Polybius: XV.15.8; XVIII.29.1 ff.; H. M. D. Parker: *Roman Legions*, 12–16.
16. Polybius: XXIX.17.1.
17. *Ibid.*, XVIII.29.1 ff.
18. Appian: *Syrian Wars*, VI.35.7.
19. Frontinus: *Stratagems*, IV.7.30.
20. Polybius: XXIX.24.16.
21. Herodotus: I.192.
22. Polybius: xviii.49.1 ff. for all this meeting.
23. Bikerman for the structure of Seleucid royalty, Ch. I.
24. Appian: *Syrian Wars*, XI.1.1.
25. Livy: XXXV.16.1–6.
26. Livy: XXXVI.8.3–5; Appian, *Syrian Wars*, XI.3.16.
27. *C.A.H., VII.26.10*, p. 857.
28. *Ibid.*, VIII.6.3, p. 152.
29. Livy: XXXVI.41.1.
30. Polybius: VII.9.
31. *Ibid.*, IX.22.1–5.
32. Horace: *Odes*, III.6.
33. Livy: XXXVI.7.16.
34. Polybius: XXI.4.5.
35. *Ibid.*, XXXI.2.2.
36. Livy: XXXVII.51.9.
37. *C.M.H.*, Vol. I, Ch. 1, p. 17.
38. Livy; XXXVII, ff. 27–31. Possibly an almost inevitable result of the extraordinary *centralisation* of monarchy in the person of the king.
39. Livy: XXXVII.3.5.
40. When treating for peace after his defeat at Raphia 'the chief difficulty . . . was the matter of Achaeus; for Ptolemy wished him to be included in the treaty, but Antiochus absolutely refused to listen to this, thinking it scandalous that Ptolemy should venture to take rebels under his protection or even allude to such persons'. (Polybius: V.67.12.)
41. Polybius: V.54.8–12.
42. Livy: XXXVI.12.6.
43. *Ibid.*, XXXVII.34.7.

44. Livy: XXXVIII.39.2 ff. for the treaty.
45. *Ibid.*, XXXVII.52, for Eumenes' speech; Polybius: XXI.18 ff.
46. Sequel to above.
47. Polybius: XXX.19.7.
48. *Ibid.*, XI.5.6.
49. *Ibid.*, V.104.1–11.
50. *Ibid.*, XXXI.27.9–11.
51. *Ibid.*, VI.56.1 ff.
52. *Ibid.*, IX.10.2.
53. *Ibid.*, XXXI.10.7.
54. *Ibid.*, XXIV.10.4.
55. *Ibid.*, XXIII.17.4.
56. *Ibid.*, XXXVIII.1.1.
57. *Ibid.*, XXX.18.7.
58. *C.A.H.*, IX.14.1, p. 577; V. Rostovtzeff: *Social and Economic History of the Hellenistic World*, I.72–3.
59. Polybius: XXIV.12.1–13.2.
60. Appian: XI.8.49.

Chapter II. The Tax Collectors

1. T. Frank: *An Economic Survey of Ancient Rome*, I.146; 202; 134 ff.
2. *Ibid.*, I.227.
3. *Livy.* XXXIV.52.2.
4. *Ibid.*, XXXVII.46.3–4; 58.4; 59.3–6.
5. Polybius: XXI.40.2.
6. Livy: XXXVIII.45.4 ff.
7. Cicero: *Ad Atticum*, II.6 and note.
8. T. Frank, IV.858–9.
9. *Ibid.*, I.274.
10. Rostovtzeff: *Hell. World*, 680.
11. Athenaeus: XII.527e.
12. See T. Frank on the temporary set-back to the Levant currency through the Roman invasions. He does not include the Seleucids whose income continued to pour in from the east (1.147).
13. Markets.
14. T. Frank, V.195; IV.189.
15. See for purple: Pliny; *Nat. Hist.*, IX.60.124 ff. It was £4 to the lb in the youth of Augustus.
16. But see Polybius: II.62.4.

17. T. Frank: I.203; V.242; V.21.

18. Polybius: XXXI.24.7.

19. T. Frank: I.206; IV.224.

20. *Ibid.*, I.276; 278.

21. *Ibid.*, I.204; 282; 288; 178.

22. Rostovtzeff: *Hell. World*, 763.

23. T. Frank: IV.553–4.

24. *Ibid.*, I.275.

25. T. Frank: IV.505.

26. *Ibid.*, I.126; 181 (from Plutarch: *Tib. Gracchus*, 8.7); 188.

27. Pliny: *Nat. Hist.*, XV.21.82.

28. For an idea of money values see the table of values in the Preface.

29. T. Frank: I.167; 376.

30. *C.A.H.* for this war.

31. Rostovtzeff: *Hell. World*, II.1105–6; T. Frank: IV.506.

32. Rostovtzeff: *Hell. World*, II.942.

33. *Ibid.*, for Egypt, where we have more documents than elsewhere.

34. T. Frank: I.240 from Livy: Epit. 58 and Plutarch: *Tib. Gracchus*, 14; IV.511; Pliny: *Nat. Hist.*, XXXIII.53.149.

35. T. Frank: I.244.

36. *Ibid.*, I.245.

37. *Ibid.*, I.254; 262.

38. Cicero: *Ad Quintum Fratrem*, I.1.32.

39. Cicero: *Ad Attic*, V.14.

40. *Ibid.*, V.15.

41. *Ibid.*, VI. 1.

42. *Ibid.*, V.16.

43. *Ibid.*, VI. 1–2.

44. Cicero: *Verrine Orations*, I.14.41.

45. Syme, *The Roman Revolution* pages 183–4, says what there is to say in Brutus' favour.

46. *Ibid.*, II.1.25 ff.

47. *Ibid.*, II.1.87.

48. *Ibid.*, II.1.22.

49. Pliny: *Nat. Hist.*, XXXIV.24.82–3.

50. Rostovtzeff: *Hell. World*, passim.

51. Seneca: *De Ira*, 1.2.2. 'See, over many miles, the uninhabited solitudes; these anger has drained'.

52. Cicero: *Verrine Orat.*, II.3.18.

53. *Ibid.*, II.3.56.

54. *Ibid.*, II.3.43.103.
55. *Ibid.*, II.3.21.53.
56. *Ibid.*, II.3.32.75.
57. *Ibid.*, II.3.73.173.
58. *Ibid.*, II.3.51.120.
59. *Ibid.*, II.3.52–3; 3.17–18.
60. T. Frank: V.294; IV.878.
61. Rostovtzeff: *C.A.H.*, VIII.18.5, p. 584.
62. Strabo's *Geography*, XI.12.17.
63. *Ibid.*, XI.7.3.
64. *Ibid.*, XI.5.8.
65. *Ibid.*, VII.4.6.
66. Mahaffy: *The Silver Age*, 143.
67. Strabo, VII.3–4.
68. *C.A.H.*, IX.5.3.

Chapter III. Mithradates

1. Strabo: XI.2.16–17.
2.   How oft shall he
   Lament that faith can fail, that gods can change,
   Viewing the rough black sea
   With eyes to tempest strange,
   Who now is basking in your golden smile,
   And dreams of you still fancy-free, still kind,
   Poor fool, nor knows the guile
   Of the deceitful wind.
   (Horace, Bk. I, *Ode* 5 Conington's translation)
3. *C.A.H.*, VIII, Ch. 18.4 for earlier Bosporan history.
4. V.55.7–10.
5. T. Frank: I.138; 230.
6. *Ibid.*, I.296.
7. Livy: XXXVIII.12 ff.
8. Cicero: *Ad Attic.*, IV.17.
9. Appian: *Mithridatica*, II.11.
10. *Ibid.*
11. Appian: *Mithradates*, IV.22–3; Plutarch, 'Sulla', p. 150, says 150,000.
    See Cicero: *Pro Flacco*, XXV.60.1.
12. Dio Cassius: XXXIII.8–9.
13. Plutarch: *Aemilius Paulus*, I.423.

14. T. Frank: IV.515.
15. Appian: *Mithr.*, IX.62 (my italics).
16. *Ibid.*, XXXV.3.
17. *Ibid.*, IX.62.
18. Rostovtseff: *Hell. World*, II.808. Cicero: *Pro Sestio*, XLIV.95 ff. describes the general Roman attitude towards democracy.
19. Cicero: *Pro Flacco*, VII–VIII.17–19.
20. Appian: *Mithr.*, IX.63.
21. *The sword of Sulla drank deep and the spiked earth lifted his blood-fed harvest to the sun* – the verdict of the civilised Petronius.
22. Appian: *Mithr.*, III.20.
23. T. Frank: I.297.
24. The 'Walwal Incident' of December 5th, 1934 was 'called a frontier squabble, but in reality, as even Italian maps showed at the time (they have been hurriedly changed) Walwal is about one hundred miles from the Somaliland border, well inside Abyssinian territory. The fight began when a joint Anglo-Abyssinian frontier commission discovered an Italian military detachment encamped at Walwal'(J. Gunther's *Inside Europe*, p. 222).
25. Strabo: XII.3.36; 3.15–16.
26. Pliny's *Nat. Hist.*, I think, but cannot find it.
27. Appian: *Mithr.*, XI.75.
28. Strabo: XII.3.31
29. See *C.A.H.*, IX, note p. 897–8.
30. Magie: *Roman Rule in Asia Minor*. The exact site of Talaura is a point of controversy.
31. Frontinus: *Stratagems*, II.5.33.
32. There must always have been obvious water at Purk, and as it is on the neck of one of the long snout-peninsulas that line the Lycus valley, it could not easily be encircled. Eski Shehir east of Purk, is suggested by J. G. C. Anderson (*J.R.S.*, XII, 1922) who seems to give the best account of the geography. The hill above the present Kelkit (Lycus) bridge, which closes the valley, fifteen minutes by lorry from Su-Shehri, might also, though less probably, be considered.
33. Tacitus describes a similar episode in the year of the Four Emperors, in Italy. *Histories,* XXIII.
34. Sinoria – tentatively identified as Baiburt – still crowned with splendid Byzantine and Seljuk walls.
35. Plutarch: *Pompey*, II.414–15.
36. Strabo: XII.3.28.

37. Cicero: *Pro Murena*, XVI.34.
38. *Ibid.*, XV.33.
39. Dio Cassius: XLIX.39.3.
40. Pliny: XXV.3.6.
41. Appian: *Mithr.*, XVI.112.
42. *Ibid.*, XVI.109.
43. *C.A.H.*, VIII.7.11.
44. *Ibid.*, VIII.56.
45. Tarn and Griffith: *Hellenistic Civilisation*, pp. 38 ff. on the Achaeans against Rome. 'It is not the business of history', they remark, 'to cheer for the big battalions', p. 5.

Chapter IV. Across the Euphrates

1. And Medus' flood, 'mid conquered tribes
   Rolling a less presumptuous tide,
   And Scythians taught, as Rome prescribes,
   Henceforth o'er narrower steppes to ride.
   (Conington's translation.)
2. Plutarch: *Sulla*, II.114.
3. Cicero: *Ad Attic*, II.7.
4. *Ibid.*, II.8.
5. *C.A.H.*, IX.8.5, p. 366 note 1.
6. Kinnear: *Journey through Asia Minor*, p. 508, says 'the only blood horse I ever met with in Asia was bred in Ooscat, in the plains of Cappadocia'.
7. Strabo: XII.2.1; and *C.A.H.* above.
8. Strabo, XI.14.1; L. Dilleman: *Haute Mésop. Orient.*, 33–4; 124.
9. Strabo (11.12.4; 16.1.23; 11.14.2) has: 'Masius, the mountain which is situate above Nisibis and Tigranocerta' (the two towns might of course be on opposite sides of the same mountain). Tacitus (*Annals*, XV. 5) has: 'Nisibis, 37 miles from Tigranocerta', and (XV.4) 'a city with a considerable river protecting part of its walls and a large fosse round the remaining circumference.' Pliny (*Nat. Hist.*, VI.31.129), describes this river – Nicephorion – as coming from *Armenia into the Tigris*, i.e. as coming from east or north, since western streams flow into Euphrates. He also describes the city as *in excelso* (VI.10.26) which applies to the appearance of Silvan from the Tigris. Plutarch (*Life of Lucullus*, Everyman edition, p. 223) says: 'Hastening his march and passing the Tigris, he came into Armenia' obviously west to east or south to north. Ptolemy, Sallust, Livy and Eutropius also place the city east of

the Tigris in Arzanene. The matter is further complicated by the fact that another Nicephorius river flows from the southern range (Masius), not into Tigris, but into Euphrates; and that the Tigris has had two sources attributed to it, and sometimes even the Bitlis river which makes a third (see Dilleman, *Haute Mesopotamie*, p. 45). Strabo himself, it is evident, had never been near any of them (XI.12.13). L. Haupt and Dilleman give the location in greatest detail, though no certainty can be expected until the site – or one of them at least – is excavated.

10. See p. 67.
11. Plutarch: *Lucullus*, II.222.
12. *Ibid.*, 223.
13. Strabo: XI.4.3.
14. Lehmann-Haupt: *Armenien einst u. jetzt*, 409, from Moses of Chorene, III.26.8.
15. *Ibid.*, 422 from El Wakidi.
16. See my note on Tigranocerta, p. 65.
17. Appian: *Mithr.*, XII.84.
18. Plutarch: *Lucullus*, II.224.
19. Appian, see above.
20. *C.A.H.*, IX.8.5 p. 366 and note; see K. Eckhart, 'Die Armenischen Feldzüge des Lukullus', for quotations: *Klio*, X.1910.
21. Plutarch: *Lucullus*. II.225.
22. *Ibid.*, 226; Frontinus: *Strat.*, II.1.14; II.2.4.
23. Appian: *Mithr.*, XII.86.
24. T. Frank, IV.529–30 for detail of loot; Plutarch *Lucullus:* II.227–8.
25. Plutarch: *Lucullus*, II.228.
26. Cicero: *Tusc. Disput.*, IV.13.22.
27. Plutarch: *Lucullus*, II.218; T. Frank, IV.545 and note; I.305; 343.
28. Plutarch: *Lucullus*, II.228.
29. T. Frank: I.368.
30. *C.M.H.*, I. p. 434.
31. T. Frank: IV.529–30.
32. Cicero: *Ad Attic.*, I.19.
33. Plutarch: *Lucullus*, II.237.
34. *Ibid.*, II.240.
35. *Ibid.*, II.222.
36. Appian: *Mithr.*, XVII.119.
37. Cicero: *Pro Sestio*, XXXI.67.
38. Plutarch: *Lucullus*, II.228–9.

39. Lucan: *Pharsalia*, II.589–627.
40. Dilleman: *Haute Mésop.*, 38.
41. According to Lehmann-Haupt, *Armenien Einst u. Jetzt*; see Dilleman 236 *Haute Mésop.*
42. Appian: *Mithr.*, XII.87.
43. Plutarch: *Lucullus*, II.229.
44. *Ibid.*, II.233.
45. *Ibid.*, II.230.
46. *Ibid., Pompey*, II. 35 (quoted by V. Chapot: La *Frontière de L'Euphrate*, 217.)
47. *Ibid., Lucullus*, II.221.
48. *C.A.H.*, IX.8, p. 380.
49. T. Frank: I.231 (from Appian.)
50. *Ibid.*, IV.529.
51. Plutarch: *Lucullus*, II.234–5.

Chapter V. The Seleucid Kings and the Empire of Trade

1. Cicero: *Ad Attic.*, VI.1.
2. T. Frank: IV.132 from Pliny.
3. *Ibid.*, IV.134.
4. Bithynia's reply to a Roman demand for troops: that the majority of his subjects had been kidnapped as slaves by the publicans.
5. *Epistle*, I.6.39.
6. Strabo: XII.2.11.
7. *Ibid.*, XII.2.7.
8. Duggan: *He Died Old*, 33.
9. Cicero: *Verrine Oral.*, II.4.27.62.
10. T. Frank: IV.545; 555; 628; Rostovtseff: *Hell. World*, II.1245.
11. T. Frank: IV.721.
12. *Ibid.*, I.305; IV.726–7; Rostovtseff: *Hell. World*, II.829.
13. T. Frank: IV.533; I.228–9; 305–6; 322; IV.508; 530.
14. *Ibid.*, I.344; IV.537.
15. *Ibid.*, I.310.
16. Cicero: *Ad Quintum Fratrem*, I.1.25.
17. See the exchange rate table in Preface.
18. *Ibid., Ad Attic*, V.20.
19. Pliny: *Nat. Hist.*, XXXVII.6.12; XXXIV.6.12.
20. *Ibid.*, XXXIV.8.14.
21. T. Frank: I.333; 324.

22. *Ibid.*, I.393.

23. *Ibid.*, I.325; 396.

24. *Ibid.*, I.324.

25. Cicero: *Ad Familiares: Ad Brutum*, II.(II.3.)5.

26. Appian: *Civil Wars*, IV.8.64. T. Frank: I.341.

27. Appian: *Civil Wars*, IV.9.67–68.

28. *Ibid.*, 68–74.

29. T. Frank: IV.555.

30. See Chapters I and VI.

31. Strabo: XIV.1.39.

32. See Ch. VI.

33. Philostratus: *Life of Appollonius of Tyana*, III.32.

34. Appian: IV.9.72.

35. Cicero: *Ad Fam.*, I.II; *Ad Quintum Fratrem*, III.2.2; *Pro Sestio*, XXVI.57.

36. Cicero: *Pro Sestio*, XLIII.93.

37. Cicero: *Verrine Orations*, II.1.32.

38. Cicero: *Ad Attic*, VII.18.

39. Cicero: *Pro Flacco*, V.II–VII.16.

40. Cicero: *Ad Quintum Fratrem*, I.1.16.

41. Cicero: I.2.4. (Mahaffy's translation, p. 159). See also Cicero: *Pro Flacco*, XXV.61 ff.; XXVII.65.

42. Cicero: *Ad. Fam.*, XV.1.5.

43. *Ibid.*, XV.1.5.

44. W. W. Tarn and G. T. Griffith: *Hell. Civ.*, p. 5.

45. T. Frank: I.389.

46. *Ibid.*, I.346; 317.

47. Rostovtzeff: *Hell. World*, 1.70–73.

48. A. H. M. Jones: *Cities of East Rom. Prov.*, 23–4.

49. Ghirshman: *Iran*, 220.

50. This dynastic loyalty continued through the Parthian and Sassanian dynasties. There is a legend recounted by Sir Percy Sykes of an old woman who, not recognising Bahram in his flight, in the sixth century, spoke to the king of himself as 'a silly fool who claims the kingdom not being a member of the Royal House'.

51. Magie: *Roman Rule*, 97.

52. M. Gough: *The Early Christians*, 36.

53. Cicero: *Pro Deiotaro*, XIII.36.

54. Bikerman, *passim*, for the Seleucid kingship.

55. Rostovtzeff: *Rom. Emp.*, I.3.

56. Rostovtzeff: *Hell. World*, I.459.

57. According to Mahaffy, 36–38.
58. After 217 B.C. See *C.A.H.*, IX.14.1, pp. 576 ff.
59. Pliny: *Nat. Hist.*, XVIII.43.144.
60. Appian: *Syrian Wars*, VIII.46.
61. Tarn and Griffith, 37.
62. Tarn and Griffith, 33.
63. Appian: *Mithr.*, XVI.106.
64. R. Campbell-Thompson: *Ignatius.*
65. Plutarch: *Moralia*, I., p. 263 records a dinner with him.
66. Cicero: *Ad Attic.*, I.4–7.
67. Rostovtzeff: *Hell. World*, I.78.
68. Tarn and Griffith: 2–3.
69. T. Frank: IV.125.
70. Rostovtzeff in *C.A.H.*, IX.14 for Parthia.
71. Rostovtzeff: *Rom. Emp.*, I.3.
72. Ghirshman, 239.
73. Tarn and Griffith: chapter on the Greek Cities, pp. 79 ff.
74. Rostovtzeff: *Hell. World*, II.1060.
75. *Ibid.*, II.1085.
76. T. Frank: IV.167 ff.
77. Rostovtzeff: *Hell. World*, I.483.
78. Bevan: *House of Seleucus*, 281.
79. T. Frank: IV.192; 204.
80. Bikerman: 145; 205.
81. Tarn and Griffith: 128.
82. L.-Haupt: *Ar. E. & J.*, 193.
83. Philostratus: *L. of A.*, III.43.
84. Rostovtzeff: *Hell. World*, II.1097–8.
85. Ghirshman: *Iran*, 267.
86. Bikerman: 208.
87. Bikerman: 159; 199 for general variety; also Rostovtzeff: *Hell. World*, II.1057–8; Tarn and Griffith: 87–9.
88. See Ammianus Marcellinus: XIV.8.6.
89. Bikerman: 177.
90. T. Frank: IV.630.
91. *Ibid.*, IV, 634–7; 639.
92. Strabo: XI.13.1.
93. T. Frank: IV.159.
94. Ghirshman: *Iran*, 225.
95. T. Frank: IV.159; Pliny: *Nat. Hist.*, VI.30.122.

96. Rostovtzeff: *Hell. World*, II.1044.
97. Ghirshman: *Iran*, 237.
98. Rostovtzeff: *Hell. World*, I.186.
99. *Ibid.*, I.459–61.
100. Not quite clear if Antiochus III or II: the habit of always giving the same names complicates the records.
101. J. C. Macurdy: *Hell. Queens*, 92 (from *O.G.I.*, 224, Oxford 1932).
102. Plutarch's *Agis* (7), quoted by Rostovtzeff: *Hell. World*, I.205.
103. Rostovtzeff (Hell. *World*, II.1155) considers this a reasonable estimate.
104. Rostovtzeff: *Hell. World*, II.1155.
105. Philostratus: *L. of A*, I.20.
106. T. Frank: I.230; IV.565–6; Cicero: *Lex Manilia*, 14.
107. Ghirshman: *Iran*, 245.
108. Rostovtzeff: *Hell. World*, II.705.
109. *Ibid.*, I.68–9.
110. *Ibid.*, I.69.
111. Mommsen: *Prov. Rom. Emp.*, II.20–1.
112. Ghirshman: *Iran*, 248.

Chapter VI. The Parthians and the Trade Route

1. E. Meyer: *Blüte u. Niedergang*, 69.
2. Seleucis and Antiochis. Pliny: *Natural History*, II.67.167.
3. Rostovtzeff: *Hell. World*, II.927.
4. T. Frank: IV.143.
5. *Ibid.*, IV.126; 138; 152.
6. Ghirshman: *Iran*, 286.
7. *C.A.H.*, IX.14.4, p. 596.
8. Chang-K'ien: born about A.D. 96 (see Isidore of Charax: *Parthian Stations* for quotations; also Hirth: *China and the Roman Orient; C.A.H.*, IX.14.4, p. 590.
9. Ghirshman: 237; also Dilleman: *Haute Mésop.*, 134.
10. Ghirshman: 284–5.
11. Rostovtzeff: *Hell. World*, II.103 7–40.
12. Dilleman: *Haute Mésop.*, 175.
13. There is a controversy as to whether the 'royal road' crossed at Melitene or Zeugma: I have adopted Dilleman's itinerary.
14. Pliny: *Nat. Hist.*, V.21.87; Isidore of Charax: *Parthian Stations*, 1.
15. Pliny: VI.30.119.
16. *Ibid.*, XII.40.80.

17. Dilleman: *Haute Mésop.*, 167–8.
18. These secret cut water-ways are still seen, as they were seen by Ammianus Marcellinus 'in all the fortresses in that district which are situated on any river'. Ammianus Marcellinus: XIX.5.4; Lehmann H. Haupt: *Armenien einst und jetzt*, 1.102–3.
19. Chapot: 273.
20. Hermann and Puchstein: *Rom in Kleinasien und Nordsyrien*, 175.
21. F. Walpole: *The Ansayrii*, 269.
22. Dilleman: *Haute Mésop.*, 131.
23. Isidore of Charax: *Parthian Stations, C.A.H.*, IX.4.4, p. 599.
24. Dilleman: *Haute Mésop.* (maps), esp. Figs, XVII and XVIII.
25. *C.A.H.*, IX.4.4, p. 599.
26. Poidebard: *Rome dans le Désert de Syrie*, 84; 89.
27. Strabo, XVI.1.28.
28. Pliny: *Nat. Hist.*, VI.XXXII.144.
29. T. Frank: 1.299, fr. Plutarch. Unspecified quotations following are from Plutarch's *Crassus*.
30. Pliny: *Nat. Hist.*, XXXIII.47.134; T. Frank, I.371 (50 million denarii).
31. P. Green: *The Sword of Pleasure*, 264: 'untouched by imagination, a butcher organising the slaughter house'.
32. Cicero: *Tusc. Disp.*, V.40.116.
33. Pliny: *Nat. Hist.*, XXI.4.6.
34. Cicero: *De Officiis*, III.19.75.
35. R. Syme: *Rom. Rev.*, 351.
36. Cicero *Ad Attic*, IV.13.
37. Cicero: *Pro Sestio*, XLIII.93.
38. *Ibid.*, XXIII.51.
39. T. Frank: I.291; Parker: 24; 45–6.
40. *Ibid.*, I.333.
41. Suetonius: *Lives of the Caesars*, I.26.3.
42. Dio Cassius: XL.15.4.
43. Dilleman: *Haute Mésop.*, 165.
44. Duval: *Histoire d'Edesse*, 4 ff.
45. Seton Lloyd: *The Listener*, April 24th, 1952.
46. *C.A.H.*, IX.14.6, p. 608.
47. Dilleman: *Haute Mésop.*, 188; 131.
48. E. Bevan: *The House of Seleucus*, 1.307.
49. Dilleman: *Haute Mésop.*, 65 and *passim*.
50. Plutarch: *Crassus*, 290.
51. Dio Cassius: XL.12.2.

52. *C.A.H.*, IX.14.4, p. 609.
53. Dio Cassius: XL.19.4.
54. Chapot: 44.
55. Dio Cassius; XL.23.4.
56. *Ibid.*, XL.24.3.
57. Polybius: IX.3.9.
58. Plutarch: *Crassus*, 290.
59. Tabari (trans, by Nöldeke); 437.
60. *C.A.H.*, IX.14.5–6.
61. Plutarch: *Crassus*, 297.
62. Lucan: *Pharsalia* (R. Graves' transl.), VIII.364–84.
63. Dio Cassius: XXXVII.5.5.
64. Plutarch: *Crassus*, 300.
65. If there were any hidden bay beyond, or land producing the yellow gold – that became Rome's enemy, and armed to the teeth the search for riches went on. (Petronius, *Satyricon* 119)
66. *C.A.H.*, IX.14.5, p. 604; D. Magie: I.361.
67. *Ibid.*, XLII.32.6.
68. *Cambridge Ancient History*, IX.8.10, p. 396.
69. Appian: *Mithr.*, XVII.117.
70. Dio Cassius: XXXVII.21.2.
71. Cicero: *Ad. Attic*, V.i8 ff.
72. Dio Cassius: XLVII.24.6 ff; see Frontinus: *Stratagems*, II.5.36; Rice Holmes: *The Archit. of the Rom. Emp.*, 120–2.
73. Lucan: *Pharsalia*, VIII.420–30.
74. Seneca: *To Helvia*, X.3.
75. *C.A.H.*, IX.17.5, and *passim*.
76. Dio Cassius: XLII.6.3; T. Frank: IV.538.
77. R. Syme: 290.
78. Rice Holmes: 125 and 223 for the route.
79. Florus: XIX and XX.
80. Cicero: *Ad Attic*, V.20.
81. Dio Cassius: XLIX.25.3 ff.; Plutarch: *Antony, passim*. I was indebted to the kindness of Mr Hillier in Teheran for the location of Taht-i-Sulaiman and how to get there.
82. See E. Honigmann and A. Maricq: *Res Gest. Div. Sap.*, pp. 56(note 2)–60.
83. Polybius: X.27.2.
84. Rostovtzeff: *Hell. World*, I.549.
85. Plutarch: *Antony*, 296.

86. Rice Holmes: 127.
87. Suetonius: *On Rhetoricians*, V.
88. Pliny: *Nat. Hist.*, VIII.21.55.
89. Plutarch: *Antony*, 270.
90. *Ibid.*, 300.
91. Plutarch possibly overstates here (Plutarch: *Lives*, 'Antony', p. 316 Everyman ed.).

Chapter VII. The Rome of Augustus

1. Pliny: *Nat. Hist*, XVIII.28.107.
2. *Ibid.*, XIX.6.23.
3. *Ibid.*, XXXVI.64.189.
4. *Ibid.*, XXXVI.60.184.
5. T. Frank: I.287; 352; Pliny: *Nat. Hist.*, XXXVI.7.48–9.
6. T. Frank: I.356.
7. *Ibid.*, I.286.
8. For money values see the exchange rate quoted in the preface.
9. Velleius Paterculus: II.10.1.
10. T. Frank: I.393.
11. Pliny: *Nat. Hist.*, XII.6.13.
12. *Ibid.*, XVI.60.140a.
13. *Ibid.*, XIII.29.91–2.
14. *Ibid.*, XXI.10.14.
15. *Ibid.*, IX.58.123.
16. *Satire*, II.3.239; T. Frank: I.353.
17. Pliny: *Nat. Hist.*, IX.81.172.
18. Germanicus.
19. Pliny: *Nat. Hist.*, IX.58.117–8.
20. *On Benefits*, VII.9.5.
21. Pliny: *Nat. Hist.*, XXXIII.13.42.
22. *Ibid.*, XXXIII.4.11.
23. *Ibid.*, XXXIII.12.41.
24. *Ibid.*, XXXIII.18.57.
25. *Ibid.*, XXIV.38.59.
26. *Ibid.*, XXIV.102.164.
27. *Ibid.*, XII.26.44.
28. *Ibid.*, IX.63.137; T. Frank: I.354.
29. Suetonius: *On Grammarians*, III.
30. *Ibid.*, XVII, XXIII.

31. Pliny: *Nat. Hist.*, VII.39.129.
32. *Ibid.*, X.72.141.
33. *Ibid.*, X.71.140.
34. *Ibid.*, X.27.52–4.
35. *Ibid.*, XI.70.183.
36. *Ibid.*, XXXVI.2.4.
37. See Cicero in *Verrine Orations*.
38. Velleius Paterculus: I.13.5; see T. Frank: I.353.
39. Pliny: *Nat. Hist.*, XXXV.36.70.
40. Petronius.
41. Pliny: *Nat. Hist.*, XXXV.1.3 ff.
42. *Ibid.*, XXXV.1.3.
43. *Ibid.*, XXXV.9.26.
44. *Ibid.*, XXXV.36.94.
45. *Ibid.*, XXXV.37.116.
46. *Ibid.*, XXXV. 40.126.
47. *Ibid.*, XXXIV.18.47.
48. *Satire*, II.7.95–101.
49. Pliny: *Nat. Hist.*, XIII.4.20–5.
50. *Ibid.*, XXIII.20.33.
51. *Ibid.*, XIV.13.87.
52. *Ibid.*, XIV.17.96.
53. *Ibid.*, XV.1.3.
54. *Ibid.*, XXXVI.66.194.
55. *Ibid.*, XXXIII.53.148–50.
56. *Ibid.*, XXXIII.50.141.
57. *Ibid.*, XXXIII.17.56.
58. Bikerman: 126.
59. Magie: I.366; T. Frank: I.338.
60. Pliny: *Nat. Hist.*, XXXIII.47.134.
61. T. Frank: I.401.
62. Pliny: *Nat. Hist.*, II.3.8.
63. *Ibid.*, VII.1.8.
64. *Ibid.*, XV.5.19.
65. *Ibid.*, II.24.95.
66. *Ibid.*, XXXVII.11.41.
67. *Ibid.*, X.2.5.
68. *Ibid.*, XXIV.29.44.
69. *Ibid.*, XXI.19.42.
70. *Ibid.*, XV.40.134–5.

71.   *Ibid.*, II.40.107.
72.   *Ibid.*, X.33.69.
73.   *Ibid.*, II.13.66.
74.   *Ibid.*, XI.30.86.
75.   *Ibid.*, VIII.26.68.
76.   *Ibid.*, VIII.50.114.
77.   *Ibid.*, X.59.120.
78.   *Ibid.*, XI.8.19.
79.   *Ibid.*, XI.10.26.
80.   *Ibid.*, XI.10.26.
81.   *Ibid.*, X.93.199.
82.   *Ibid.*, VIII.84.229.
83.   *Ibid.*, VII.3.33.
84.   *Ibid.*, XI.56.154.
85.   *Ibid.*, VII.7.43.
86.   *Ibid.*, X.34.71.
87.   *Ibid.*, XVIII.89.365.
88.   *Ibid.*, XX.69.178.
89.   *Ibid.*, IX.4.9.
90.   *Ibid.*, VII.1.6.
91.   *Ibid.*, XVIII.63.233 and 64.235–6.
92.   *Ibid.*, XVIII.1.5.
93.   *Ibid.*, XVIII.56.206.
94.   *Ibid.*, XVIII.57.209.
95.   *Ibid.*, XL.11.30.
96.   *Ibid.*, II.37.101.
97.   *Ibid.*, II.4.12; 67.70.
98.   *Ibid.*, XVII.3.39.
99.   *Ibid.*, II.63.154.
100. *Ibid.*, VII.30.116.
101. *Ibid.*, VII.40.130.
102. *Ibid.*, XIX.1.6.
103. *Ibid.*, XXXVI.1.2.
104. *Ibid.*, XIX.1.5.
105. He died in the A.D. 79 eruption of Vesuvius.
106. *C.A.H.*, X.16.4, p. 526.
107. Virgil: *Georgics*, II. 136–9.
108. Horace: *Epistles*, II.1.32–3.
109. Suetonius: *Lives of the Caesars*, II.29.3.
110. Seneca: *Moral Essays* (On Tranquillity of Mind), IX.7.

111. Dio Cassius: LIX.7.8.
112. See *C.A.H.*, X.17.6.
113. T. Frank: I.187.
114. Dio Cassius: IV. 10.9.
115. *C.A.H.*, VIII.11.7, p. 346.
116. T. Frank: V.278.
117. T. Frank: IV.544; 1.275.
118. Mahaffy: 76.
119. Dio Cassius: LIV.8.4.
120. Suetonius: II.XXX.2; Dio Cassius: LII.22.1.
121. *C.A.H.*, IX.19.6, pp. 795–6.
122. *C.A.H.*, IX.19.6, p. 796.
123. T. Frank: I.357 from Cicero: *Ad Earn.*, 16.21.
124. J. Buchan: *Augustus*, 296.
125. Charlesworth: *Trade Routes.*
126. Warmington: *The Commerce between the Roman Empire and India*, 57.
127. Strabo: III.5.3.
128. Lebedos; see my *Lycian Shore*, 21.
129. Horace: *Epistles*, I.11.6–10.
130. P. Green: *Essays in Antiquity*, 86.
131. E. Barker: *From Alexander to Constantine*, 45.
132. Tacitus: *Agricola*, 4.
133. See P. Green's Essay: 'The Garden and the Porch', in *Essays in Antiquity*, 74 ff.
134. *Ibid.*, 90; also Barker: *Alex., to Const.*, 205–6; Cicero: *Pro Murena*, XXX–XXXI.
135. Barker: 48.
136. Luke, VII.47.
137. P. Green: *Essays in Antiquity*, 75.
138. *Ibid.*, 85, and Barker above.
139. Syme: *Rom. Rev.*, 286.
140. T. Frank: I.360, quoted from Varro: *De Re Rustica*, I.17.2.
141. Rostovtzeff: *Rom.Emp.*, 18.
142. T. Frank: I.378.
143. *Ibid.*, I.383.
144. *C.A.H.*, X.13.6, p. 422; 14.9, p. 458.
145. See Rostovtzeff: *Rom. Emp.*, Ch. I, *passim.*
146. Syme: 513.
147. *Ibid.*, 502; 328.
148. *Ibid.*, 350–1.

149. Rostotvzeff: *Rom. Emp.* 21.
150. *Ibid.*, 103.
151. *Ibid.*, 47.
152. Dio Cassius: LV.22.5.
153. *C.A.H.*, X.20.6, p. 693.
154. P. Green: 148–9.
155. *Ibid.*, 150.
156. Syme: 323.
157. Cicero: *Tuscan Disputations*, I.27.98.
158. *Ibid.*, I.40.145.
159. Tacitus: *Histories*, II.20.
160. *Sic* – in Loeb translation Dio Cassius: LV.9.1.
161. Martial: *Epigrams*, III.68.
162. *C.A.H.*, X.18.2, p. 591.
163. Val. Maximus: 6.2.8 quoted by Syme, 317.
164. Caesar had adopted him as a son.
165. Suetonius: *Caesars*, II.67.2.
166. *Ibid.*, III.11.5; 12.1.
167. Dio Cassius: LV.13.1.
168. *Ibid.*, LVI.32.4.
169. Suetonius: *Caesars*, II.65.2.
170. *C.A.H.*, X.14.9, p. 456.
171. Buchan: *Augustus*, 135 and T. Frank: I.322.
172. 'To spare the submissive and disarm the proud.'
173. Rice Holmes: 12; 65; T. Frank: I.334.
174. Syme, 284.
175. T. Frank: V.12; see T. Frank: V, Ch. 1, pp. 1–14 for Augustus' budget.
176. Dio Cassius: LI.8.5–6; Rice Holmes: 160–74.
177. Dio Cassius: 21.3.
178. *Ibid.*, LI.22.3.
179. *Ibid.*, LII.6.1.
180. T. Frank: V.14.
181. Rostovtzeff: *Rom. Emp.*, 80.
182. Syme, 380.
183. 'Not even herself is so like herself,' Martial: I.109.
184. Rostovtzeff: *Rom. Emp.*, 30.
185. *Ibid.*, 36.
186. Rice Holmes: 158.
187. *C.A.H.*, X.7.2, p. 193.
188. *Res Gestae*, III.16 in Loeb edition of Velleius Paterculus, also in V.8–9.

189. Dio Cassius: LI.10.3.
190. Rostovtzeff: *Rom. Emp.*, 82.
191. *C.A.H.*, X.17.1–2.
192. *Ibid.*, X.15.4, p. 480.
193. Syme: 481.
194. Suetonius: *Caesars*, II.43.3; II.75.
195. Julius Caesar compelled a Roman knight to act in his own mimes. Horace: *Satires*, X.5–6, note c.
196. *C.A.H.*, X.16.4, p. 524.
197. Mahaffy: 147.
198. *C.A.H.*, X.15.5, p. 492.
199. Suetonius: *Caesars*, II.18.1.
200. *Ibid.*, I.77.
201. *Ibid.*, III.2.2.
202. Buchan: *Augustus*, 338–9; Syme: 317.
203. Buchan: *Augustus*, 205.
204. *Ibid.*, 82.
205. *Ibid.*, 20.
206. *Ibid.*, 234.
207. Martial: *Epigrams*, XII.8.
208. Buchan: *Augustus*, 283.
209. Dio Cassius: LIII.33.1.
210. P. Green: *Essays in Antiquity*, 124 from Suetonius.
211. Horace: *Satire*, I.10.
212. P. Green: *Essays in Antiquity*, 164.
213. *Ibid.*, 116 quoted from Prof. Highet.
214. Petronius: *Satyricon*, 115.
215. W. Y. Sellar: *The Roman Poets, passim*.
216. *Tristia*, V.10.51–2.
217. Martial: V.1; XII.6; X.72.
218. Seneca: *Thyestes*, 34, 86.
219. Seneca: *Moral Essays*, 'On Mercy', I.25.2.
220. Seneca: *Thyestes*, 312 ff.
221. Tacitus: *Annab*, XIV.37.
222. Velleius Paterculus: II.76.1–2.
223. Dio Cassius: LX.16.7.
224. P. Green: *Essays in Antiquity*, 161.
225. Aeschylus: *Agamemnon*, G. Murray's trans.
226. Menander: *The Brothers*, act I.
227. Martial: III.58.
228. Seneca: *Moral Essays*, 'On Tranquillity of Mind', 1.5–10.
229. Velleius Paterculus: I.11.7.

Chapter VIII. Nero's Armenian Wars

1.   the Capitol may stand
      All bright, and Rome in warlike pride
      O'er Media stretch a conqueror's hand.
                  (Conington's translation)
2. Rostovtzeff: *Rom. Emp.*, I.35.
3. See Ch. VI.
4. In the battle against Arminius.
5. Ace. to Parker, 78–90.
6. *Ibid.*, 45–6.
7. *Ibid.*, 77.
8. T. Frank: I.327.
9. Chapot: 92.
10. Rostovtzeff: *Rom. Emp.*, I.23.
11. Parker: 169.
12. *Ibid.*, 170.
13. Rostovtzeff: *Rom. Emp.*, I.29.
14. Dio Cassius: LIII.33.2.
15. Velleius Paterculus: II.101.1.
16. T. Frank: V.21; 49; 267.
17. *Ibid.*, I.217.
18. *Ibid.*, IV.883: V.267; 51–2; 295 for too absolute a view?
19. *The Periplus of the Erythraean Sea* (Schoff), 19.
20. Warmington: 260.
21. Charlesworth: 59.
22. Strabo: II.3.4 ff.; Philostratus: *L. of A.*, VI.25.
23. Warmington: 52; Charlesworth: 77.
24. Tarn and Griffith, Hellenistic Civilisation p. 214 ff. There is some controversy as to the date of the monsoon discovery.
25. Pliny: *Nat. Hist.*, XII.42.94.
26. Warmington: 66.
27. Strabo: XVI.4.23 ff. A friend of Aelius and well-informed.
28. A.D. 23–87.
29. *Ibid.*, 62.
30. *The Periplus of the Erythraean Sea*, 39; 49; 59.
31. Charlesworth: 69.
32. Buchan: *Augustus*, 292.
33. Warmington.
34. *The Periplus of the Erythraean Sea*: 10.

35. T. Frank: V.230–31. See Pliny, *Nat. Hist.*, For details on spices.

36. *Ibid.*, V.282 ff.; Pliny, *Nat. Hist*, XII.32.63 ff.; 41, 84.

37. See W. Schur and Kornemann (*Janus*, 1, 1921, 55 ff.) for the theory of Nero's plan to save this route from the Abyssinians; and *C.A.H.*, X, p. 881 for the refutation. It seems to me that a policy of annexation – a very obvious one – going back to the Augustan expedition, would again recommend itself naturally at any moment of financial stringency, provided the conquest of Arabia was not too difficult – aggression, straight and naked, though probably with no general policy beyond immediate finance behind it.

38. T. Frank: IV.593–5.

39. Syme, 265.

40. *Ibid.*, 272.

41. T. Frank: IV.593 ff.; Magie: I.457 ff.

42. Rostovtzeff: *Rom. Emp.*, I.259–61.

43. Dio Cassius: LIV.24.4 ff.

44. Strabo: XII.3.29.

45. He writes from Tomi (Constantia in the Dobrudja).

46. Ovid: *Tristia*, III.14.41.

47. *Ibid.*, III.10.30.

48. *Ibid.*, V.7.13 ff.

49. *Ibid.*, V.10.17 ff.

50. *Ibid., Ex Ponto*, I.8.31 ff

51. *C.A.H.*, X.22.3, p. 751.

52. Magie: I.195.

53. *C.A.H.*, X.4.1, p. 114.

54. Suetonius: *Caesars*, II.48.

55. *C.A.H.*, X.9.3, p. 258.

56. T. Frank: IV.651.

57. See Dio Cassius: XLIX.20.4.

58. *Ibid.*, illustrations in Ghirshman, *Iran, Persians and Sassanians*.

59. Malik Mansur. See The Earl Percy: *Highlands of Asiatic Turkey*, 100–7.

60. Pliny: *Nat. Hist.*, V.20.85.

61. *Ibid.*, XVIII.27.105.

62. In 1901: *R.G.S.J.*, August 1902.

63. von Moltke: 307; 519 ff.

64. Salmanassar I in the ninth century B.C. first reached Malatya-Melitene (Lehmann-Haupt: *Armenien einst und jetzt*, II.117).

65. Lehmann-Haupt: *Ar. E. & J.*, *passim*; also *Armenien u. Nord Mesopotamien* Lecture March 6th, 1900 (Berlin).

66. Chapot, 248: 'Sur les sommets de l'Arménie la frontière était purement idéale et la seule mesure avantageuse et praticable consistait à établir des forts d'arrêt dans les étranglements des vallées.'

67. Dilleman (p. 117–121) following Strabo (XI.14.2), makes Sophene reach Mt Masius in the south and identifies its capital, Carcathiocerta, with Egil, near Nisibis.

68. See above, p. 158.

69. *C.A.H.*, X.9.3, p. 257.

70. Dio Cassius: XL.15.6.

71. *Res Gest. Diu. August*: IV.32 (in Loeb: *Velleius Paterculus*).

72. Pliny: *Nat. Hist.*, XI.115.278.

73. Henderson: *Nero*, 96.

74. Seneca: *Moral Essays*, 'On the Shortness of Life', IV.5.

75. Kings II.5, 18.

76. Seneca: *Moral Essays*, 'Benefits', I.10.3.

77. *Ibid.*, 'On Leisure', III.3.3.

78. *Ibid.*, 'On Firmness', XIV.2.

79. Henderson: *Nero*, 104.

80. Seneca: *Moral Essays*, 'On the Happy Life', XXII.I.

81. *Ibid.*, XXII.5.

82. *Ibid.*, 'On Mercy', I.11.3.

83. *Ibid.*, I.1.5–8.

84. Seneca: *Tragedies*, 'Hercules Oetaeus', I.1700–4.

85. Seneca: *Moral Essays*, 'On Benefits', VII.27.1.

86. *Ibid.*, 'On Firmness', XIX.3.

87. *Ibid.*, 'On Mercy', II.6.4.

88. *Ibid.*, 'On Benefits', VI.29.2–30.4.

89. *Ibid.*, 'On Anger', II.5.3.

90. *Ibid.*, 'On Firmness', V.4.

91. Tacitus: *Annals*, XI.18.

92. *Ibid.*, XI.19–20.

93. Seneca: *Moral Essays*, 'On Firmness', XVII.1.

94. Tacitus: *Annals*, XIII.8.

95. *Ibid.*, XIII.7.

96. *C.A.H.*, X.9.9, pp. 279 ff.

97. Pliny: *Nat. Hist.*, XX.16.

98. Tacitus: *Annals*, XIII.35.

99. Tacitus: *Hist.*, II.8o.

100. Tacitus: *Annals*, XIII.35.

101. Kinnear: *Journey through Asia Minor*, 395.

102. R. Curzon: *Armenia*, 193.

103. *Ibid.*, 162.

104. Kinnear: 240.

105. *Ibid.*, 536.

106. Bryce: *Transcaucasia and Ararat*, 93.

107. Burnaby: *On Horseback through Asia Minor*, II.130.

108. R. Curzon: 147.

109. *Ibid.*, 115.

110. E. Honigmann: *Die Ostgrenze des Byzantischen Reiches*, 183.

111. *C.A.H.*, X.22.5, p. 759.

112. See Lucullus' campaign also, Ch. IV.

113. Pp. 268 ff.; see also Schur: 'Die Orient-Politik des Kaiser Nero' in *Klio*, (XV, 1923), p. 12; and Lehmann-Haupt's journey in *Armenien Einst u.Jetzt.*

114. Tacitus: *Annals*, XIV.25; Schur, *loc. cit.* ff.

115. Adopted by them as the Tigris source when the territory of the higher, actual source had been lost to them.

116. Tacitus: *Annals*, XIV.26.

117. *Ibid.*, XV.i ff.

118. *C.A.H.*, X.9.9, p. 280.

119. Charlesworth: 13.

120. Tacitus: *Annals*, XV.3. *Bellum habere quamgerere malebat.*

121. *Ibid.*, XV.5.

122. Kinnear: 374 ff.

123. Polybius: VIII.23.1.

124. Henderson: *Nero*, 187.

125. Tacitus: *Annals*, XIV–XV for all the story.

126. Dio Cassius: LXII.19.2.

127. Tacitus: *Annals*, XV.27–8.

128. *Ibid.*, XV.28–31.

129. Dio Cassius: LXII.17.6.

130. Suetonius: *Caesars*, VI.57.

131. Dio Chrysostom: *Discourses*, XXI.

132. Henderson: 195.

Chapter IX. The Trade Routes and Trajan's Wars

1. The sons of Danube shall not scorn
    The Julian edicts; no, nor they
    By Tanais' distant river born,

Nor Persia, Scythia, nor Cathay.
    (Conington's translation)

2. A. Berthelot: *L'Asie Ancienne*, 86; T. Talbot Rice: *The Scythians*, 43.
3. Warmington: 175.
4. Berthelot: *L'Asie Ancienne*, 89, 156.
5. *Ibid.*, 89.
6. *Ibid.*, 249; A. Herrmann: *Die Alten Seidenstrassen*, 79.
7. See main pull-out map.
8. Herrmann: 57.
9. *Ibid.*, 120.
10. Discovered in the Lop Desert by Sven Hedin.
11. Sir Aurel Stein is the chief explorer of this region: see his *Ancient Khotan*.
12. Herrmann: *Die Alten Seidenstrassen*, 98, 96. Marco Polo's route.
13. *Ibid.*, no.
14. *Ibid.*, 118–19.
15. *Ibid.*, 121.
16. Described by Ptolemy (c. A.D. 150) from Marinus of Tyre: Berthelot *L'Asie Ancienne*, 151, etc.; Warmington: 23, 108, 133; Ammianus Marcellinus: XXIII.6.60.
17. Berthelot: *L'Asie Ancienne*, 243.
18. Ghirshman: *Iran*, 250.
19. Written about 91 B.C. (C. Hirth: *China and the Roman Orient*, Schi-Chi, Ch. 123).
20. Herrmann: *Die Alten Seidenstrassen*, 48; 36; Berthelot: *L'Asie Ancienne*, 247.
21. The stadium is taken to be equivalent to 200 metres: the *farsakh*= *parasang*= 1 hour's transport, i.e. about 4 miles in Persia with horses or 3 in Arabia with camels.
22. *Ibid.*, 6.
23. Warmington, 261–72.
24. Herrmann: *Die Alten Seidenstrassen*, 125, quotes Pan-Tschau's letter to the Chinese Emperor (76–88 A.D.).
25. *Ibid.*, 8–9.
26. *Ibid.*, 126 quoted from Chavannes' translation of the Hou-han-Schu.
27. *Ibid.*, 9–10.
28. Lucian: *Octogenarians*.
29. Berthelot: *L'Asie Ancienne*, 238.
30. *Ibid.*, 413; Warmington: 130.
31. Strabo: XI.1.73.
32. H. H. von der Osten: *Die Welt der Perser*, 117.

33. Inhabitants of the Scythian steppes.

34. Berthelot: 85.

35. Philostratus: *L. of A.*, II.17 and 20.

36. *Hou-han-shu*, Ch. 88, quoted by Isidore of Charax in *Parthian Stations.*

37. Warmington: 130–5.

38. Charlesworth: 11.

39. Magie: *Rom. Rule*, I.370.

40. Polybius: IV.38.4.

41. Pliny: *Nat. Hist.*, XII.28.49.

42. Magie: *Rom. Rule*, I.182.

43. Farrar: *Lives of the Fathers*, I.688–90.

44. T. Talbot Rice: *The Scythians*, 152.

45. Plutarch: *Lucullus*, 224.

46. Strabo: XI.5.6.

47. J. Bryce: *Transcaucasia and Ararat*, 45.

48. Strabo: XI.2.17; 3.5.

49. Arrian: *Periplus*, 89.11.

50. Strabo: XI.3.3.

51. Schur: *Die Orient Politik*, 84.

52. Strabo: XI.4.3.

53. See Honigmann: *Res Gest. Div. Sap.*, 89.

54. *Ibid.*, 88–90, for the geography of the two passes.

55. Dio Cassius: XXXVII 1–3, the Caspian Gates are primarily the pass.

56. Tarn: *The Greeks in Bactria and India*, 363 ff., 90; 112–13 and Appendix 4; Berthelot: 197.

57. Tarn: *Gr. in B. & I.*, p. 109.

58. Pliny: *Nat. Hist.*, VI.24.88.

59.   'Bactrian and Serian haunt your dreams,
     And Tanais, toss'd by inward feud.' (Conington's translation.)

60. Berthelot: 239; from Orosius.

61. Strabo: XI.7.3; II.1.15.

62. Warmington: 27.

63. Pliny: *Nat. Hist.*, IV.12.89–91.

64. Berthelot: 198.

65. *C.M.H.*, I.324–6.

66. Berthelot: 202.

67. *Ibid.*, 219; 'Toute cette description des monts de la Scythie occidentale indique que les traffiquants . . . parcouraient la steppe turque (ou Kirghise) et la connaissaient. Leurs informations s'arrêtent . . . à notre 54ème degré de latitude et ne disaient rien des grandes rivières sibériennes. . . . On

peut conclure que ce n'étaient pas des marchands de fourrures et qu'ils n'ont pas pénétré l'immense forêt sibérienne. Ils devaient faire route vers la Mongolie, portant des marchandises grecques du genre de celles que Kozlov a exhumés.' Berthelot: 225.

68. Berthelot: 160.
69. *Ibid.*, 179.
70. 'Les itinéraires consultés s'étendaient beaucoup plus au nord que ne l'ont supposé la plupart des commentateurs; ils prolongeaient sans doute ceux tracés au travers de la Scythie occidentale, la grande steppe Turco-sibérienne . . . ' Berthelot: 254.
71. Berthelot: 230; Tarn: 105–9.
72. *Ibid.*, 234.
73. Amm. Marcellinus: XXII.8.42.
74. Talbot Rice, *Scythians*, 140, 128, 121, 142.
75. Tarn: *Gr. in B. & I.*, 109.
76. *Ibid.*, 105.
77. Talbot Rice: *Scythians*, 194.
78. *Ibid.*, 69.
79. Tarn: *Gr. in B. & I.*, 109.
80. *Ibid.*, 109.
81. See Talbot Rice: *Scythians*, 39–44.
82. von der Osten: 42.
83. M Kishimoto: 'Indo-Europeans and horses'; *Journal of Classical Studies*, IX, 1961.
84. Talbot Rice, *Scythians*, 70.
85. Strabo: XI.5.8.
86. See p. 191, above.
87. Tarn: *Parthian Studies*, 15–16.
88. Ghirshman: *Iran*, 263.
89. Talbot Rice: *Scythians*, 49.
90. Tacitus: *Histories*, I.79.
91. *C.M.H.*, I.332.
92. Pliny: *Nat. Hist.*, VI.12.31.
93. Charlesworth: 106–7; Procopius: I.10; 3 ff.
94. T. Frank: IV. 862–5.
95. Henderson: *Nero*, 170; T. Frank: IV.745.
96. Arrian: *Periplus*, 24; 2.
97. Tacitus: *Histories*, III.47.
98. Mommsen: *Prou. of Rom. Emp.*, II.33; see Schur, 63–4.
99. T. Frank: V.295; 269. I think the objections here are overstated.

100. *C.A.H.*, X.21.2, p. 714, 2 *passim* for Seneca's policy.
101. Seneca: *Phoenissae*, I.599–601.
102. Buchan: *Augustus*, 222.
103. *Scriptores Historiae Augustae*, 'Marcus Aurelius', XVII.4–5.
104. *Ibid.*, 'Commodus', VII.8.
105. Dill: *Rom. Soc.*, 36.
106. Suetonius: *Caesars*, V.10.4.
107. T. Frank: V.45; Suetonius: *Vespasian*, XVI.3.
108. *Ibid.*, V.39; Suetonius: *Caligula*, XVI.3.
109. Tacitus, *Hist.*, I.20.1.
110. Rostovtzeff: *Rom. Emp.*, I.103.
111. T. Frank: V.35. Frank attributes this to the mismanagement of Tiberius rather than to Nero.
112. *C.A.H.*, X.21.4, p. 724.
113. Ammianus Marcellinus: XXXI.2.21. The Sarmatians and the Alani – first known to be mentioned by Lucan in A.D. 64–5 – became interchangeable terms from now on. See *C.A.H.*, XI.3.1–2.
114. Dio Chrysostom: *Discourses*, XXXVI.5
115. *C.A.H.*, XI.3.2, p. 96.
116. Dio Cassius: LXV.15.3.
117. Chapot: 219–20.
118. Markwart: 2.
119. Syme: 54.
120. Suetonius: *Caesars*, IV.52.
121. Tacitus: *Hist.*, III.47–8.
122. Rostovtzeff: *Rom. Emp.*, 154.
123. *Ibid.*, 81.
124. T. Frank: IV.597.
125. Chapot: 349–51.
126. T. Frank: IV.866.
127. *Ibid.*
128. Frontier system.
129. Lepper: *Trajan's Parthian War*, 106–9.
130. Tacitus: *Hist.*, I.50.
131. Rostovtzeff: *Rom. Emp.*, 106.
132. D. Nock: *Conversion*, 125.
133. T. Frank: V.45.
134. *Ibid.*, V.47.
135. *C.A.H.*, XI.1.3, p. 17.
136. T. Frank: IV.745.

137. Syme: 502 ff.
138. T. Frank: V.60.
139. Syme: 508.
140. Dio Cassius: LX.17.4.
141. Magie: *Rom. Rule*, I.536.
142. Pliny: *Nat. Hist.*, XXXIV.17.36.
143. Mahaffy: 215.
144. Dio Chrysostom: *Discourses*, XXXI.67 and 100. Titus restored the Rhodian freedom.
145. T. Frank: IV.740.
146. Magie: *Rom. Rule*, I.573; Tacitus, *Hist.*, II.81 ff.
147. Lepper: *Trajan's Parth. War*, III.
148. Syme: 303.
149. Dio Cassius: LXVIII.17.2.
150. See Longden: Notes on 'the Parthian Campaign of Trajan', *J.R.S.*, XXI, 1931, p.25.
151. Dio Cassius: LXVIII.19.3–20.4.
152. *Ibid.*, LXII.7.1a, p. 147.
153. Fronto: 14 and 15; (Loeb: II, p. 213).
154. *Paradiso*: XX.44–5; 112 ff.; *Purgat*, X.74 ff.
155. Dio Cassius: LXVII.7.5.
156. Dio Chrysostom: *Discourses*, III.I.
157. *C.A.H.*, XI.5.2 *passim*.
158. Tacitus: *Hist.*, I.1.
159. Carcopino: *La Vie quotidienne à Rome*.
160. F. G. Teggart, *Rome and China*, VII–IX.
161. Henderson: *Nero*, 158.
162. Dio Cassius: LXVIII.29.1.
163. Dilleman: *Haute Mésop.*, 282–5. I have followed his routes and dates where they disagree with Lepper.
164. Dilleman: *Haute Mésop.*, 112.
165. Chapot: 141 note 1; 21 note 7.
166. Dio Cassius: LXVIII.21.2.
167. *Ibid.*, 26.1.
168. Chapot, 183.
169. Acc. to Lepper: *Traj. Parth. War*, 210.
170. Strabo: XVI.1.16.
171. Dio Cassius: LXVIII.28.3.
172. Isidore of Charax: *Parthian Stations*, 17.
173. Pliny: VI.31.138 ff.

174. Milton: *Paradise Lost*, II.1.2.
175. Rostovtzeff: *Rom. Emp.*, I.155.
176. See Dilleman: *Haute Mésop.*, 289 in favour of glory rather than profit; T. Frank: IV.239 and Fronto, Loeb Vol. II, p. 219 (17).
177. Longden: *Parthian Campaign*, pp. 27–8.
178. Lepper: *Traj. Parth. War*, 154.
179. Beazley: III.56.
180. Chapot: 23 for their anti-Roman feeling.
181. Dilleman: *Haute Mésop.*, 100; Lepper: *Traj. Parth. War*, 154.
182. Lepper: *Traj. Parth. War*, 154.
183. *C.A.H.*, XI.6.2, p. 248.
184. Dilleman: *Haute Mésop.*, 129 from Hami south-west of Sinjar.
185. Ghirshman: *Iran*, 35.
186. Dio Cassius: LXVIII.31.1–4.
187. *J.R.A.S.*, 1941: 'The Ancient Trade Route past Hatra and its Roman Posts', 310–11.
188. Excavated by Mr and Mrs David Oates, whose kind hospitality I gratefully remember. See *Iraq*, XXI, Pt. 2, Autumn 1959, p. 207.
189. A. Stein: 'Hatra Trade Route', *J.R.A.S.*, 1941.
190. Dilleman: *Haute Mésop.*, 69; 100–101.
191. *C.A.H.*, XII.12.2, p. 416.
192. Dio Cassius: LXIX.2.3.
193. Martial: XII.8.

Chapter X. The Antonine Climax

1. Trajan, Hadrian and Marcus Aurelius.
2. Rostovtzeff: *Rom. Emp.*, 150.
3. Seneca: *Epist. Mor.*, 90.25.
4. *C.A.H.*, VIII.12.6, p. 377.
5. Magie: I.655.
6. Philostratus: *L. of A.*, I.16.
7. Buchan: *Augustus*, 207 from Sidonkis Apollinaris.
8. *C.A.H.*, XI.11.4, pp. 450–1.
9. Jones: *The Later Roman Empire*, II.7.14.
10. *Ibid.*, II.748.752.
11. All through the second century A.D.
12. Magie: I.583, from Aelius Aristides: *Orat.* XXIII.245, Keil.
13. Philostratus: *L. of A.:* IV.2.
14. Magie: I.626–7.

15. Jones: II.721.
16. T. Frank: IV.750 from Aelius Aristides.
17. Magie: I.585.
18. *Ibid.*, I.593.
19. T. Frank: IV.733.
20. Epictetus: IV.1.14.
21. T. Frank: IV.712.
22. *Ibid.*, IV.884; V.62; 66; 75, etc.
23. *Ibid.*, IV.745.
24. *Ibid.*, V.55.
25. Magie: I.162.
26. *C.A.H.*, XI.5.4; T. Frank: IV.740–4; 810.
27. Pliny: *Letters*, X.40.
28. Magie: I.657.
29. Marcus Aurelius' adopted colleague.
30. *C.A.H.*, XI.19.2, p. 750.
31. *Script. Hist. August.*, 'Verus', V.6–7.
32. Magie: I.627–8.
33. T. Frank; V.76.
34. Rostovtzeff, *Rom. Emp.*, I.173.
35. *Ibid.*, I.172.
36. *C.A.H.*, XI.11.4, p. 449.
37. C.AH, XI.12.3, p. 499.
38. Pliny: *Letters*, IX. 11.
39. Dill: 148.
40. Rostovtzeff: *Rom. Emp.*, I.147.
41. Suetonius: *On Grammarians*, XXIV.
42. Dio Chrysostom: *Discourses*, XXXVI.9.
43. *C.A.H.*, XII.17.2 from Apuleius: *Apol.*, 64.
44. Dio Chrysostom: *Discourses*, IV.13.
45. *Ibid.*, I.51.
46. *Ibid.*, VII.38.
47. *Ibid.*, VII.138.
48. Plutarch: *Moralia*, 'On How to Study Poetry', 29.F.
49. *Ibid.*, 32.F.
50. Philostratus: *L. of A.*: XI.4.
51. Lucian: *Alexander, or the False Prophet*.
52. Philostratus: *L. of A.*, I.2.
53. Dio Chrysostom: *Discourses*, VII.121.
54. Lucian: *Dialogues of the Dead*.

55. Plutarch quoted by Mahaffy: *The Silver Age*, 351–2.
56. Dio Chrysostom: *Discourses*, XXXIV.48.
57. Fronto: I, p. 175.
58. *Ibid.*, II, p. 79.
59. *Ibid.*, II, p. 139.
60. Philostratus, *L. of A.*, IV.30.
61. Epictetus: III.10, 2–3.
62. *Ibid.*, III.13.9–11.
63. *Ibid.*, IV.I.108–9.
64. *Ibid.*, III.1.26.
65. *C.A.H.*, XI.18.11, p. 742.
66. Marcus Aurelius: *Meditations*, II.17.
67. *Ibid.*, III.5.
68. *Ibid.*, XII.2.
69. *Ibid.*, I.7.
70. *Ibid.*, XI.1–2.
71. Philostratus, *L. of A.*, VII.15.
72. Lucian: *The Ship*.
73. Philostratus: *L. of A.*, IV.32.
74. Dio Chrysostom: *Discourses*, VII.117 ff.
75. Cicero: *De Off.*, I.42.150.
76. Pliilostratus: *L. of A.*, VII.23.
77. T. Frank: IV.549.
78. *Ibid.*, I.313.
79. *C.A.H.*, XI.18.11, p. 742.
80. *Ibid.*, XI.20.1, *passim*.
81. Dill: 169.
82. Tarn and Griffith: *Hell. Civilisation*, 50.
83. *C.A.H.*, VIII.19.2, p. 593.
84. Epictetus: II.19.27.
85. Tarn and Griffith: *Hell. Civilisation*, 55.
86. Cicero: *Ad Attic*, XII.36.
87. *C.A.H.*, IX.7.8.
88. *Res Gestae*, IV.24.
89. Lucian: *Death of Peregrinus*.
90. Mid whom Augustus, couch'd at ease,
    Dyes his red lips with nectar deep.
                              (Horace: *Odes*, III.3.)
91. Tacitus: *Annals*, XV.74.
92. *C.A.H.*, XI.1.6, pp. 23 ff.

93. See Charlesworth: 'Fear of the Orient in the Roman Empire', *Cambridge Hist. Journal*, II, 1926.

94. ne nimium pii rebusque fidentes avitae recta, velint reparare Troiae. (Horace: *Odes*, III.3.)

95. Buchan: *Augustus*, 165.

96. *C.A.H.*, X.7.1, p. 183.

97. *Ibid.*, 21.1, pp. 706–7.

98. Bikerman: 246.

99. *C.A.H.*, XI.10.6, p. 425; 19.2, p. 745.

100. Pliny:*Letters*, IV.11; Mahaffy: 306; Hahn: *Rome u. Romanismus*, 71.

101. *Pro Rabirio Postumo*, 25 ff.

102. Syme: 440.

103. Magie: I.618–19.

104. Fronto: II, p. 9.

105. Magie: I.623.

106. *Ibid.*, I.612.

107. Fronto: I, p. 113.

108. Marcus Aurelius: *Meditations*, I.3.

109. *C.A.H.*, XI.9.1, p. 334.

110. *Script. Hist. August.*, 'M. Antoninus', V.2.

111. Marcus Aurelius: *Meditations*, VII.70–1.

112. *Ibid.*, V.10.

113. *Ibid.*, VII.69.

114. Parker: *Rom. Leg.*, 179.

115. Tacitus: *Hist*, I.46.

116. *Ibid.*, I.4.

117. Syme: 70.

118. T. Frank: I.385.

119. *C.A.H.*, X.7.4, p. 206; Magie: I.415.

120. Parker, *Rom. Leg.*, 104; 212–14.

121. *Ibid.*, 245.

122. Tacitus: *Annals*, I.17.

123. See Parker, *Rom. Leg.*, 179.

124. Rostovtzeff, *Rom.Emp.*, 112.

125. *Ibid.*, 107.

126. T. Frank: V.56, note 54; V.25.

127. Dio Cassius: LXXV, 5–6.

128. Rostovtzeff: *Rom. Emp.*, 127.

129. Parker: 164.

130. Bikerman: 97.

131. Rostovtzeff: *Rom. Emp.*, 271–2.

132. Parker: *Rom. Leg.*, 225; Dill, 208.

133. *C.A.H.*, XI.2.6, p. 82.

134. *Script. Hist. August.*, 'Hadrian', XXI.6.

135. *Ibid.*, 'M. Antoninus', VIII.6.

136. Dio Cassius: LXXI.2.

137. The incident of Walwal in 1934 (see note 24 in Chapter 3).

138. *Ibid.*, LXXI.4.

139. Fronto, II.149.

140. *Ibid.*, II.209.

141. *Script. Hist. August.*, 'Avidius Cassius', V.6.

142. P. Lambrechts: 'L. Verus', *Revue Classique*, 1934.

143. Ammianus Marcellinus: XXIII.6.24.

144. Dio Cassius: LXXIII.14.3–4.

145. Tarn and Griffith: *Hell. Civilisation*, 163.

146. T. Frank: IV.159.

147. Warmington: 104.

148. *C.A.H.*, XI.9.3.

149. T. Frank: V.76.

150. Script. *Hist. August.*, 'Verus', X.6–9.

151. Dio Cassius: LXXII.14.2.

152. Fronto: II.197.

153. Dio Cassius: LXXII.4.2.

154. *Ibid.*, LXXII.27.1a.

155. *Script. Hist. August.*, 'M. Antoninus', XXV.12–XXVI.3.

156. *C.A.H.*, XI.9.4, p. 362.

157. *Ibid.*, p. 356.

Chapter XI. The Lower Euphrates and the end of Parthia

1. Von der Osten: 92.

2. H. Seyrig: *Syria*, XIII.1932, pp. 266–8.

3. See *C.A.H.*, XI.3.4, p. 116.

4. R. Dussaud: *Pénétration des Arabes en Syrie*, 73.

5. It was first seen by the Romans at the siege of Cyzicus according to Ammianus Marcellinus (XXIII.6.56). See also C. P. Grant, *The Syrian Desert*, pp. 52–3.

6. Dussaud: 73; *C.A.H.*, XI.15.1, p. 607.

7. Rostovtzeff: *Caravan Cities*, 92–5.

8. T. Frank: IV.191–3.

9. Dussaud, 96.
10. Rostovtzeff: *Car. Cities*, 104.
11. Dussaud: 72.
12. *Ibid.*, 75–6.
13. Seyrig: *Syria*, XIII.1932, p. 271.
14. Dussaud, 75–6; Seyrig, 270.
15. *C.A.H.*, XI, p. 859, note 2.
16. *Ibid.*, XII.6.6.
17. *Ibid.*, XII.6.4, p. 199; Rostovtzeff: *Car. Cities*, 109.
18. Mommsen: *Prov. of Rotn.Emp.*, 93; T. Frank: IV.253.
19. 62 miles S and SSE of Babylon (Rostovtzeff: *Mélanges Glotz*, 799; Seyrig, *Syria*, XIII.1932, p. 272).
20. Ghirshman: *Iran, P. and Sass.*, 69.
21. T. Frank: IV.200–1.
22. *Ibid.*, IV.239–41; 257.
23. Seyrig: *'Inscrip. rél. au commerce maritime de Palmyra'*, *Mélanges Cumont*, 399.
24. Rostovtzeff: *Car. Cities*, 172; 132.
25. *Ibid.*, 142; 129.
26. *C.A.H.*, XII.1.2, p. 18.
27. Warmington: 138.
28. From A. T. Clay: *Babylonian Records II*, No 53 (*C.A.H.*, IX.14.4, p. 596).
29. *C.A.H.*, XI.3.5, p. 123, note 3.
30. Warmington: 135.
31. Philostratus: *L. of A.*, I.20.
32. Poidebard: 173.
33. *Ibid.*, 194.
34. Glubb Pasha: *War in the Desert*.
35. See Isidore of Charax: *Parthian Stations*; Dilleman: *Amm. Marcel, et les pays de l'Euphrate*, 153 and map ff.; Pliny: *Nat. Hist.*, VI.30.122–32; Chapot: 255 ff.
36. Dilleman: *Haute Mésop.*, 203; Grant: *The Syrian Desert*, 42; but see *C.A.H.*, XI, note 3, p. 860; Chapot; 297.
37. Bikerman: 161.
38. *C.A.H.*, XI, note 2, p. 860.
39. Rostovtzeff: *Rom. Emp.*, 267–9.
40. Posting house.
41. *C.A.H.*, XI, note 3, p. 860; Chapot, 256, note 1.
42. Fronto: I.11; also Herodian: *Hist, of the Rom. Empire*, IV.15.3.
43. Chapot: 255 ff.

44. *Ibid.*, 251, note 1.
45. *Ibid.*, 250.
46. *Ibid.*, 338, note 1 from J. Czernik; p. 26.
47. *Ibid.*, 297.
48. Grant: *The Syrian Desert*, 42.
49. Chapot: 329.
50. From Lucian, *The Syrian Goddess.*
51. Chapot: 299, note 1.
52. 'Viros habent optimos et in negotio valde acutos et bene nandes et prae-cipue divites', Dilleman: *Haute Mésop.* (from 'Liber Junioris Philosophi', *G.G.M.*, II, p. 517, par. 22).
53. Philostratus: *L. of A.*, 1.37.
54. Altheim: *Die Soldaten Kaiser*, 112.
55. *C.A.H.*, XI.15.3, pp. 634–5; Rostovtzeff, *Rom. Emp.*, 169.
56. W. Heyd: *Le Commerce du Levant*, 1.168, see also Wm. of Tyre, XVI.4.
57. A. Stein: 'Hatra Trade Route', *J.R.A.S.*, 1941, 307–9.
58. Dilleman: *Haute Mésop.*, 104.
59. Tacitus: *Annals*, II.57; Chapot: 327, note 1.
60. Zeus Oromazdes in Tarn and Griffith: *Hell. Civilisation*, 343; M. Gough: *The Early Christians*, 35.
61. T. Frank: V.85.
62. Chapot: 337.
63. Bevan: 210 (until the Crusades).
64. T. Frank: IV.904.
65. 'A Persis ipsi in omnem terram Romanorum vendentes et ementes interim tradunt'. Dilleman: *Haute Mésop.*, 191.
66. Homo: *Siècle d'Or de l'Empire Romain*, 438.
67. D. Oates: 'Ain Sinu', in *Iraq*, Vol. XXI, part 2, p. 217; T. Frank: V.85.
68. Chapot: 378.
69. Quoted by Homo: *Siécle d'Or*, 218–23.
70. Josephus: *Wars of the Jews*, III.5.1 ff.
71. *Ibid.*, quoted by Chapot, 82, note 4.
72. Parker: 250–2.
73. *C.A.H.*, X.8.2, pp. 226–7.
74. Parker: 160; *C.A.H.*, XI.4.10; 8.4.
75. Warmington: 231.
76. See Chapter VII.
77. T. Frank: IV. 199 and note.
78. *Ibid.*, V.274.

79. Chapot: 109.
80. Rostovtzeff: *Rom. Emp.*, I.169.
81. *C.A.H.*, XI.3.5, p. 123.
82. Rostovtzeff, *Rom. Emp.*, 157.
83. T. Frank: V.282–3.
84. Clermont-Ganneau: *Odeinat et Vaballat*, 404.
85. Homo: *Siècle d'Or*, 224.
86. Mommsen: *Prov. of Rom. Emp.*, II.236.
87. Rostovtzeff: *Car. Cities*, 144.
88. *Script. Hist. Aug:* 'Hadrian', XXI.10.
89. Dio Cassius: LXXIII.1.1.
90. *Ibid.*, LXXV.7.4; and my account of the battle of Issus in *Alexander's Path; C.A.H.*, XII.1.2, pp. 7–8.
91. Herodian: III.4.7; II.8.8.
92. Dio Cassius: LXXVI.9.2–5; Herodian, III.9.12, suggests that it was taken by surprise.
93. *Ibid.*, LXXV.3.3.
94. *Ibid.*, LXXV.2.3.
95. Dilleman: *Haute Mésop.*, 71–2 (quoting Amm. Marcellinus: XX.6.9 and Th. Simocatta: I.13.)
96. Dio Cassius: LXXVI.9.4, ff.
97. Dilleman: *Haute Mésop.*, 63.
98. Dio Cassius: LXXVI.11.12.
99. Herodian: III.9.12.
100. Dio Cassius: LXXIX.1.4.
101. *Script. Hist. Aug.:* 'Caracalla', II.2.
102. Dio Cassius: LXXVIII.7.2.
103. *Script. Hist. Aug.:* 'Caracalla', VII.1.
104. *Ibid.*, 'The Thirty Pretenders', XIV.6.
105. *Ibid.*, 'Severus Alexander', L.4–5.
106. *Ibid.*, XXXIX.1–2.
107. Ghirshman: *Iran*, 231; 290.
108. E. Honigmann: *Res Gest. Div., Sap.*, 3–4.
109. Ghirshman: *Iran*, 291.
110. *Ibid.*, 264.
111. *C.A.H.*, XII.3.6.
112. Ghirshman: *Iran*, 273.
113. Altheim: *Die Soldaten Kaiser*, 172.
114. Ghirshman: *Iran, Parth., Sass.*, 137.
115. Upham Pope: *A Survey of Persian Art*, 419; 423.

116. Ace. to Strabo: XVI.1.5 (*c.* 739).

117. Ghirshman: *Iran, Parth., Sass.*, 36; Von der Osten, 120.

118. Rostovtzeff: *Car. Cities*, 140; Ghirshman: *Iran, Parthia, Sass.*, 102.

119. Upham Pope: 423; 419.

120. Ghirshman: *Iran, Parth., Sass.*, 116; 148–9; Gough, 105–6.

121. Bevan: *H. of Seleucus*, II.265.

122. Ghirshman: *Iran, Parth., Sass.*, 36–7.

123. *Ibid.*, 41; 182.

124. *Ibid.*, 102 and 140 ff.; 76 ff.; Rostovtzeff: *Car. Cities*, 147.

125. Mommsen: *Prov. of Rom. Emp.*, II.86.

126. Christensen, A: *Empire des Sassanides*, 10; 27.

127. *Ibid.*, 13.

128. *Ibid.*, 7–8.

129. *Ibid.*, 17; 77.

130. Ghirshman: *Iran*, 288.

131. *Ibid.*, 249.

132. *C.A.H.*, XI.3.4, pp. 119–20.

133. Chapot: 188.

134. Herodian: III.4.9.

135. Ghirshman: *Iran*, 263.

136. *Ibid.*, 261; Honigmann: *Res Gest. Div. Sap.*, 100.

137. Ghirshman: *Iran*, 260–2; see also Honigmann.

138. See Ch. VIII.

139. Ghirshman: *Iran, Parth., Sass.*, 122.

140. Christensen, 92.

141. *Script. Hist. Aug:* 'Severus Alex'. L.2.

142. Magie: I.700, from an inscript. in Ephesus.

143. Dilleman: *Haute Mésop.*, 208.

144. Tabari (Nöldeke transl.): 37; 150.

145. A. Stein: 'Hatra Trade Route', *J.R.A.S.*, 1941, 307.

146. At Dura, acc. to Zosimus, or Zaitha acc. to Ammianus: quoted by Dilleman: *Ammien Mar. et les pays de l'Euphr.*, 135. Honigmann quotes Shapur's inscrip. for Perisabora, *Res Gest. Div. Sap.*, 122.

147. A.D. 244 and 254.

148. *Script. Hist. Aug:* 'The Two Valerians', VIII.2.

149. *C.A.H.*, XII.4.6, p. 132.

150. *Script. Hist. Aug.:* 'The Two Valerians', V.6.

151. T. Frank: IV.904.

152. Controversial dates differ in *C.A.H.*, XII.4.6. and *C.A.H.*, XII.6.2. I follow Honigmann: *Res. Gest. Div. Sap.*, 131–3.

153. Ditto for Dura.
154. See Honigmann, *Res Gest. Div. Sap.*, for the Shapur invasion, pp. 131 and 136 ff.
155. Circa 1200 B.C.
156. Ghirshman: *Iran, Parth. and Sass.*, 149; 159.

Chapter XII. The Revolt of The Poor

1. Rostovtzeff: *Rom. Emp.*, I.XII.
2. Epictetus: II.14.28.
3. Rostovtzeff: *Rom. Emp.*, I.350–2.
4. T. Frank: V.297; IV.877.
5. Rostovtzeff: *Rom. Emp.*, I.173.
6. Aelius Aristides: 58 (quoted by Barker: *Alex. to Const.*, 325).
7. Mommsen: *Prov. of Rom. Emp.*, I.355.
8. T. Frank: IV.795; 803–8.
9. Rostovtzeff": *Rom. Emp.*, I.358.
10. *Ibid.*, I.359; T. Frank: V.62; 66; 75.
11. St Basil: Letter, LXXXIV.
12. *Ibid.*, Letter, C; See Jones: *Later Rom. Emp.*, II.748–52.
13. Rostovtzeff": *Rom. Emp.*, I.407.
14. T. Frank: V.301.
15. *Ibid.*, V.87.
16. *Ibid.*, V.80; IV.745; 905.
17. *Ibid.*, IV.656; Dio Cassius: LXXV.8.4.
18. T. Frank: V.85; 300.
19. *Ibid.*, I.232.
20. *Ibid.*, I.314.
21. *Ibid.*, V.56.
22. *C.M.H.*, I.19, p. 551.
23. Rostovtzeff: *Rom. Emp.*, I.408–10.
24. Rostovtzeff: *Rom. Emp.*, I.379, *passim*.
25. *Ibid.*, XIV–XV; T. Frank: IV.811–12; *C.A.H.*, XII.7.4, p. 252.
26. E. Stein: *Geschichte d. Spätröm. Reiches*, I.3.
27. Dill: 102.
28. Rostovtzeff: *Rom. Emp.*, 385 for slowness of transport; T. Frank: IV.210.
29. T. Frank: IV.66o.
30. *Ibid.*, IV.910.
31. *Ibid.*, IV.197; 847–9; J. Bury: *Later Roman Emp.*, II.413–14; Jones, *Later Rom. Emp.*, I.17.

32. T. Frank: IV.241.
33. Ammianus Marcellinus: XXVI.6.9.
34. Rostovtzeff: *Rom. Emp.*, I.422.
35. Rostovtzeff: *Rom. Emp.*, I.496.
36. Ammianus Marcellinus: XVI.2.12.
37. Rostovtzeff: *Rom. Emp.*, I.497.
38. *Ibid.*, 499.
39. T. Frank: IV.848.
40. *Ibid.*, IV.757; fr. Ael. Aristides: XXIV.32 ff.
41. Rostovtzeff: *Rom. Emp.*, I.499.
42. *Ibid.*, I.501.
43. T. Frank: IV.841; 690.
44. *Ibid.*, IV.693.
45. *Ibid.*, IV.887.
46. *Ibid.*, IV.897.
47. *Ibid.*, IV.906.
48. *Ibid.*, IV.738.
49. F. Walpole: *The Ansayrii.*
50. *Satire*, II.8.77.
51. Dussaud: 117; 109; 105.
52. Pliny: *Letters*, X.96.
53. Mommsen: *Prov. of Rom. Emp.*, 348.
54. T. Frank: V.303.
55. *C.A.H.*, XII.17.1.
56. Hahn: *Rom und Romanismus*, 7.
57. *Meditations*, X.8; Dio Cassius: LXXII.29.3.
58. Seneca: *Mor. Essays*, 'On Mercy', I.18.2.
59. Tacitus: *Annals*, XIV.42–5.
60. *Script. Hist. Aug.*, 'Hadrian', XXI.5.
61. T. Frank: V.181; Jones: *Later Rom. Emp.*, II.794.
62. *Ibid.*, IV.846.
63. *Discourses*, VII.103.
64. *Ibid.*, VII.138.
65. Rostovtzeff: *Rom. Emp.*, I.358.
66. *Ibid.*, I.370.
67. Crees, J. H. E.: *Reign of Emp. Probus*, 98.
68. Rostovtzeff: *Rom. Emp.*, I.393; already perceptible under the Flavians.
69. Dio Cassius: LXXIV.12.2–13.3.
70. *Ibid.*, LXXIV.2.3.
71. *Ibid.*, LXXVIII.20.2.

72. Epictetus: IV.I.143.
73. *Ibid.*, IV.I.139–41.
74. Rostovtzeff: *Rom. Emp.*, I.355.
75. *Ibid.*, I.412.
76. *Ibid.*, I.373–4.
77. *Script. Hist. Aug.*, 'Severus', IV.i.
78. T. Frank: V.78 and note 39 For opposite view.
79. *Script. Hist. Aug.*, 'Geta', II.2.
80. *Ibid.*, 'Severus', XVIII.5.
81. *Ibid.*, 'P. Niger', XII.6–7; Dio Cassius: LXXVIII.4.2–3.
82. *Ibid.*, 'Severus', XXIII.3.
83. Rostovtzeff: *Rom. Emp.*, I.417; Dio Cassius: LXXVIII.3.2.
84. Dio Cassius: LXXVIII.9.1.
85. Rostovtzeff: *Rom. Emp.*, I.402–3.
86. *Ibid.*, 425; 409.
87. *Ibid.*, 405.
88. *Ibid.*, 423; T. Frank: V.85.
89. *Ibid.*, 412–13.
90. T. Frank: V.299.
91. Rostovtzeff: *Rom. Emp.*, I.423.
92. *Ibid.*, 413.
93. T. Frank: IV.223.
94. *Ibid.*, IV.746.
95. Dio Cassius: LXXVIII.9.5; T. Frank: V.87.
96. Rostovtzeff: *Rom. Emp.*, I.403.
97. Donations given by the emperors to the citizens and soldiers.
98. Parker: 222.
99. T. Frank: I.242; 312.
100. *Ibid.*, V.68.
101. Dio Cassius: LXXII.32.3.
102. Dio Cassius: LXXIV.5.4.
103. M. Aurelius: *Sayings*, 10, 17
104. *Script. Hist. Aug.*: 'Severus', VII.6–7.
105. T. Frank: V.86 and note 51.
106. Rostovtzeff: *Rom. Emp.*, I.422.
107. Dio Cassius: LXXIX.9.3.
108. *Ibid.*, LXXIX.36.2.
109. *Script. Hist. Aug.*, 'Macrinus', XIV.4.
110. *Ibid.*, 'Elagabalus', XVIII.2, ff.
111. *Ibid.*, 'Sev. Alexander', XXXI.5; VIII.4.

112. *Ibid.*, LVI.2.
113. *Ibid*, LII.3.
114. *Ibid.*, XLVII.I–2.
115. Bikerman: 53; Rostovtzeff: *Rom. Emp.*, I.425–6.
116. Rostovtzeff: *Rom. Emp.*, I.423; Dio Cassius: LXXII.11.4.
117. Rostovtzeff: *Rom. Emp.*, I.187.
118. *Iliad*, XI.163–4.
119. *Script. Hist. Aug:* 'The Two Maximini', IV.4.
120. *Ibid.*, I.7.
121. *Ibid.*, VIII.6.
122. *Ibid.*, IX.5.
123. *Ibid.*, XXVIII.5.
124. *Ibid.*, XXXI.5.
125. A.D. 248.
126. Rostovtzeff: *Rom. Emp.*, I.424.
127. *Ibid.*, 443.
128. *Script. Hist. Aug.:* 'The Two Gallieni', XI.9.
129. T. Frank: IV.908.
130. Rostovtzeff: *Rom. Emp.*, I.445.
131. *Script. Hist. Aug.:* 'Aurelianus', XLVIII.2.
132. *Ibid.*, XXXV.1.
133. *Ibid.*, XLVIII.5.
134. *Ibid.*, 'Probus', XIV.1–2.
135. *Ibid.*, XXIII.1–3.
136. *Ibid.*, 'Carus', etc., IX–XI.
137. Rostovtzeff: *Rom. Emp.*, I.448.
138. T. Frank: V.302–3.
139. Jones: *Later Rom. Emp.*, II.1014.
140. Rostovtzeff: *Rom. Emp.*, I.448; 452.
141. Philostratus: *L. of A.*, V.8.
142. Rostovtzeff: *Rom. Emp.*, I.477.
143. *Script. Hist. Aug.:* 'Sev. Alexander', XLII.3–4; also Jones: *Later Rom. Emp.*, I.6.
144. Rostovtzeff: *Rom. Emp.*, I.493.
145. *Ibid.*, I.452.
146. *Ibid.*, I.454.
147. Herodian: VII.3.6.
148. T. Frank: IV.907.
149. Rostovtzeff: *Rom. Emp.*, I.465–6; 459.
150. *Ibid.*, I.495 ff.
151. T. Frank: V.303.
152. *C.A.H.*, XII.7.7, pp. 274–5.

Chapter XIII. The End of Palmyra

1. While Egypt's dame
   Threatened our power in dust to lay
   And wrap the Capitol in flame.
   (Conington's translation.)
2. Devreesse: *Le Patriarcat d'Antioche*, 160.
3. Jones: *Later Rom. Emp.*, II.823.
4. A representation of this oven can be seen on the bas-relief of the tomb of Eurysaces the baker in Rome: reproduced in Rostovtzeff: I.32, Fig. 2.
5. 'The cities in which the most opulent men in the Roman world resided . . . lay on the sea near great trade routes or were centres of a lively river traffic'. (Rostovtzeff: I.172.)
6. Warmington: 139.
7. Devreesse: *Patr. d'Antioche*, 151.
8. T. Frank: IV.867–9.
9. Mommsen: *Prov. of Rom.Emp.*, I.342; also Magie: I.715.
10. Mommsen: *Prov. of Rom. Emp.*, I.360.
11. Magie: I.657; 712, etc.
12. T. Frank: IV.907.
13. *Ibid.*, IV.909; 904.
14. *Ibid.*, IV.159.
15. *Ibid.*, IV.912.
16. Chapot: 134, note.
17. *Ibid.*, 261.
18. T. Frank: IV.909.
19. *Ibid.*, IV.913; Jones: *Later Rom. Emp.*, II.861.
20. *C.M.H.*, I.549.
21. T. Frank: IV.916.
22. Rostovtzeff: *Rom. Emp.*, I.273.
23. Amm. Marcellinus: XIV.8.6.
24. *C.A.H.*, XI.15.2, p. 617.
25. Philostratus: *L. of A.*, V.36.
26. Jones: *Later Rom. Emp.*, II.994.
27. *C.M.H.*, I, p. 545.
28. *C.A.H.*, XII.12.3.
29. Jones: *Later Rom. Emp.*, II.989.
30. T. Frank: IV.172; 193.
31. *Ibid.*, IV.195.
32. *Ibid.*, IV.201 quoting Caesar: *B. Civ.*, III.102.

33. *Ibid.*, IV.204.
34. Barker: *Alex. to Const.*, 89.
35. See Dill: 552.
36. T. Frank: IV.910 and note.
37. *C.A.H.*, XII.6.7, pp. 229 ff.
38. L. Homo: *L'Empereur Gallien*, 10;25(fr. Zonaras; XII).
39. Altheim: 117 ff.
40. Cardinal Newman.
41. *C.A.H.*, XII.6.2, p. 177.
42. *Scrip. Hist. Aug.:* 'The Thirty Pretenders', XV.6–8.
43. Altheim: 242.
44. Clermont-Ganneau: *Odeinat et Vaballet*, 390.
45. *Ibid.*, 385.
46. Ace. to Rostovtzeff.
47. *Script. Hist. Aug.:* 'Aurelian', XXVIII.2.
48. *Ibid.*, 'The Thirty Pret.,' XXX.13–23.
49. L. Homo: 'Flarnininus', *Revue Historique*, 1913; 247–8.
50. *C.A.H.*, XII.6.2.
51. *Script. Hist. Aug.:* 'Aurelian', XXXVII.I.
52. *C.A.H.*, XII.7.6, p. 268.
53. *Ibid.*, 9.1, *passim.*
54. *Ibid.*, 6.2, p. 180.
55. *Ibid.*, 9.1.
56. *Script. Hist. Aug.:* 'Aurelian', XXXIV.3–6.
57. But see Rostovtzeff: *Rom. Emp.*, I.446.
58. The walls now existing belong to Zenobia and to a later time. Rostovtzeff: *Caravan Cities*, p. 125; Dussaud, p. 74.
59. Dussaud: 74, note 4.
60. *C.A.H.*, XII.9.1.
61. *Script. Hist. Aug.:* 'The Thirty Pretenders', XXX.24–27; XXVII.2.
62. *Ibid.*, 'Aurelian', XXXI.5–10.
63. Rostovtzeff: *Rom. Emp.*, I.461.
64. *Ibid., Mél. Glotz*, 811.
65. Dussaud: 80.
66. Rostovtzeff: *Rom. Emp.*, I.473.
67. Amm. Marcellinus: XXXI.5.17.
68. *C.A.H.*, XII.5.7, p. 164; 2.4, p. 85.
69. *Ibid.*, XII.5.4, p. 160.
70. *Ibid*, XII, *loc. cit.*
71. T. Frank: I.V.241–2.

72. Altheim: 199 ff.; *C.A.H.*, XII.6, pp. 208 ff.; 2.1, p. 66.
73. T. Frank: V.300–1.
74. Chapot: 89–90, note 10.
75. Jones: *Later Rom. Emp.*, II, Ch. XVII, on the army.
76. Detachments of Auxiliaries.
77. Chapot: 91.
78. *C.M.H.*, I.4.
79. Detachments instituted by Hadrian.
80. Chapot: 86.
81. T. Frank: IV.598.
82. Altheim: 199.
83. Chapot: 318, refers to Amm. Marcellinus: XXV.7.9.
84. Jones: *Later Rom. Emp.*, I, 52 ff. and II, Ch. XVII.
85. Dilleman for these routes.
86. Chapot: 328.
87. *Isaiah* XXXVII.12; and *Kings*, II.19: Rezeph.
88. Dussaud: 89; Devreesse: *Patr. d'Antioche*, note, 99.
89. Poidebard: 172; Dussaud: 76–7; Seyrig: *Syria*, XIII, 1932, p. 270.
90. Poidebard: *passim*; Altheim: 121.
91. Altheim: 197.
92. Synesius: *Letters*, 40 (introduction); Rostovtzeff: *Rom. Emp.*, I.425.
93. Chapot: 215.
94. *Ibid.*, 137, and note 3.
95. Dio Cassius: XLIX.44.1.
96. Tacitus: *Annals*, XV.26.
97. Chapot: 138.
98. *Ibid.*, 110; Altheim: 153 ff.
99. *C.A.H.*, XII.6.6, p. 217.
100. Rostovtzeff: *Rom. Emp.*, I.412.
101. *Ibid.*, I.429.
102. *Script. Hist. Aug.*: 'Piobus', XIV.7.
103. Rostovtzeff: *Rom. Emp.*, I.468.
104. Jones: *Later Rom. Emp.*, I.55–60.
105. *C.A.H.*, XII.6.7, p. 231.
106. T. Frank: V.298.
107. Rostovtzeff: *Rom. Emp.*, I.172.
108. Jones: *Later Rom. Emp.*, II.825–34; Vasiliev: I.216–17.
109. *Ibid.*, II.824–5.
110. *C.M.H.*, I.549–50.

111. Clermont-Ganneau: pp. 398 ff.; p. 383; Altheim: p. 242. The statues omitted 'Clarissimus' after A.D. 271.
112. Altheim: 290.
113. *Ibid.*, 276.
114. *Scrip. Hist. Aug.:* 'Carus', etc.: XI–XIII.
115. Chapot: 295.
116. Mommsen: *Prov. of Rom. Emp.*, 94–5.

Chapter XIV. The Government of the Cross

1. Tarn and Griffith: *Hell. Civilisation*, 108.
2. *C.A.H.*, XI.21.5, p. 837.
3. T. Frank: IV.713 ff.; V.68 ff.
4. Hahn: *Rom und Romanismus*, 110.
5. Letter 16D (Krabinger) quoted by Barker: *Alex. to Const.*, 3 83.
6. *Script. Hist. Aug.:* 'Caracalla', V.7.
7. Barker: *Alex. to Const.*, 347.
8. *C.A.H.*, XII.10.3 *passim* for King-worship; Barker: 353 ff.
9. *Scrip. Hist. Aug.:* 'Severus Alex.', XXVII.4.
10. *Ibid.*, 'Aurelian', XLVI.4.
11. *C.A.H.*, XII.6, 6, p. 219; Rostovtzeff: *Rom. Emp.*, I.467. The King's Friends had been slowly developing from the time of Augustus (*C.A.H.*, X.10.6, p. 425).
12. *C.A.H.*, XII.10.3.
13. Barker: *Alex. to Const.*, chapter on Kingship for the pagan parallels: esp. 474–8, 159, etc.
14. Barker: 375 (from the Corpus Hermeticum, 9: *c.* 300 A.D.).
15. *Ibid.*, 364 (from Diogenes the Pythagorean).
16. *Ibid.*, 356.
17. R. Payne: *The Holy Fire*, 122; Jones: *Later Rom. Emp.*, II.935.
18. *Apologeticus*, XXXII.I; XXXI.3 (Barker: 455).
19. *Ibid.*, XXVI.2.
20. *Ibid.*, XXXV.8.
21. *Ibid.*, XXX.1–4.
22. Quoted by Barker: *Alex. to Const.*, 439.
23. *Ibid.*, 477 fr. *Dem. Evang.*, VII.C2.
24. Eusebius: *De Laude Constantini:* C3, 4–5 (Barker: 478).
25. *Script. Hist. Aug.:* 'Maximus et Balbinus', VIII.7, note 1.
26. Tertullian: *De Spectaculis*, VIII–X.
27. Minutius Felix Octavianus: XXXVII.12 (in *Tertullian*, Loeb).

28. Newton: *Travels and Discoveries in the Levant*, I.275; 247.
29. Barker: *Alex. to Const.*, 278–80.
30. Eusebius: *Eccles. History*, VI.19.7.
31. Jaeger: *Early Christianity in Greek Paideia* 57.
32. See Barker, above.
33. Payne: *The Holy Fire*, 12.
34. See Barker, above.
35. Y. Courtonne: *St Basile et l'Hellénisme*, II, letter CCCXL.
36. L. Petit: *Essai sur la vie et la correspondance du Sophiste Libanius* (my trans, fr. French), pp. 173–4.
37. *Ibid.*, 170; 177; 220; 231; 253–84.
38. *Tuscan Disputations*, I.16.38.
39. A. D. Nock: *Conversion*, 231.
40. Plutarch: 'Isis et Osiris' (*Moralia*), e.LXXIX.
41. *Meditations:* IV.40.
42. Dio Chrysostom: *Discourses*, XXI.II.
43. Lucian: quoted by Nock: *Conversions*, 143.
44. *Dissertation*, XVII.II (quoted by Dill: 421).
45. Barker: *Alex. to Const.*, 430 ff, and 331 for Celsus.
46. *Ibid.*, 378–80.
47. Plotinus: *Enneads*, trans. S. MacKenna: I.4,16; 6.2; 4.8. *Ibid.*, I.91; 13; 4.1.
48. *Ibid.*, VII.4.6
49. Barker: *Alex. to Const.*, 335 (quoting Plotinus).
50. *Confessions*, IX.10.
51. See W. Jaeger: *Early Christianity in Greek Paideia:* 'In the intellectual history of the Church philosophy it was one of the basic factors', p. 80.
52. *Meditations*, VI.24.
53. Nock: 260.
54. Clement: *Exhortation* (Payne, 51).
55. *C.M.H.*, I.602.
56. Dionysius the Areopagite: *De Div. Nominibus*, IV (Payne: 275).
57. *De Beatitudinibus*: 6 (Payne: 15).
58. Minutius Felix: V.4.
59. T. Frank: IV.814 for Cappad. population; Payne: 138; Dean Farrar: *Lives of the Fathers*, II.5.
60. Gregory of Nyssa: *De Nominis Opificio*, IV.136 (Payne: 15).
61. Clement: *Stromata*, VII.7.49 (Payne: 62–66). See Nock: 248, who seems to leave the Eastern Fathers out. See also Byron: *The Byzantine Achievement*, 179.

62. Barker: *Alex. to Const.*, 424 ff.; Payne: 48 ff.
63. Farrar: *Lives*, I.7.388; 310.
64. *De Fide Orthodoxa*, II.12 (Payne: 289).
65. Gregory Nazianzen: Orat., IV.10 (Payne: 200).
66. Jerome: Letter LX.6.
67. *Ibid.*, XXII.24.
68. Farrar: II.488.
69. Basil: *Howily*, VIII, Ch. 6; *De Natura Animalium*, II.46 (Courtonne: 120).
70. Basil: Ep. XXIII and XX.
71. 117C (Courtonne: 186).
72. Basil: Ep. CXXIII.
73. Basil: *Hexae:* II.7 (Payne: 159).
74. Basil: *De Beatitudinibus*, I (Payne: 185–6).
75. Basil: Ep. 15 (Payne: 168).
76. Gregory Nazianzen: Orat. XLIV.10 (Farrar, I.747).
77. Payne: 147.
78. Gregory of Nyssa: *Orat. de Deit. Fil. et Spir. Sanct.* (Farrar: XII, p. 734; Payne: 190–1).
79. Payne: 58.
80. St John Damascene (Payne: 288).
81. Farrar: I.311.
82. Gregory Nazianzen: Orat. XX.12.
83. Payne: 221.
84. Tertullian: *Ad. Nat.* : I.10 (Farrar: 159).
85. Farrar: II.117; 189.
86. *Ibid.*, II.411.
87. Jerome: Letter XXII.30; Farrar: II.393; see also Letter, LII.3.
88. Farrar: II.699; also Epictetus: II.8.12 for the divinity of men.
89. *Ibid.*, II.662; Payne: 244.
90. Jerome: Letter XXVII.3.
91. *Ibid.*, LIV.io.
92. *Ibid.*, XXII.19.
93. *Ibid.*, XXII.3.
94. *Ibid.*, XIV.10; CVII.11.
95. *Ibid.*, LII.5.
96. *Ibid.*, XXII.5.
97. *Ibid.*, LII.17.
98. *Ibid.*, LXXVII.6.
99. In Anatole France: *Thais*.
100. Jerome: Letter XXII.30.

101. *Ibid.*, XXII.27.
102. *Ibid.*, XXII.27.
103. *Ibid.*, XXII.32.
104. Farrar: II.398; 347.
105. Quoted by St Jerome: Letter XXII.21; *C.M.H.*, I.591.
106. *De Testim. Animae*, I (Farrar: I.164).
107. *De Justitia:* Ch. 14, 16–19 (Barker: *Alex. to Constant.*, 462).
108. Bury: *Later Rom. Emp.*, I.142.
109. *Luke:* I.53.
110. Clement of Alexandria: *Quis Dives Salvetur*, D14.
111. Payne: 175.
112. Clement: *op. cit.*, 11.
113. T. Frank: IV.803–10; 912.
114. Basil: Letter XCIV.
115. Jones: *Later Rom. Emp.*, II.550.
116. Barker: 328.
117. M. Gough: *Early Christians*, Ch. V.
118. *Script. Hist. Aug.:* 'Carus', etc., XIX.
119. Rostovtzeff: *Rom. Emp.*, I.512–14.
120. Land tax.
121. *Ibid.*, I.521–23; also Jones: II.737–61 *passim*.
122. *C.M.H.*, I.556–7.
123. Buchan: *Augustus*, 264.
124. Rostovtzeff: *Rom. Emp.*, I.531–2.
125. *Ibid.*, I.509; *C.M.H.*, I.96.
126. Metzger: *Les Routes de St Paul*, 28 and 44.
127. Lucian: *Fugitives*, for the Cynic popular movement, Ch. 12; Dill: 340 ff.
128. Dill: 254 for these associations.
129. Eusebius: VII.15.4–5.
130. *C.A.H.*, XII.19.4, p. 668.
131. Eusebius: IX.9.11.
132. 'The Latin prayer he imposed on the army is quite indeterminate between Christ and Jupiter.' (*C.M.H.*, I.10.)
133. Payne: 101; Basil: Letter CXL.
134. Farrar: I.470.
135. *Ibid.*, I.484.
136. Hahn: *Rom und Romanismus*, 58.
137. Farrar: I.695.
138. Payne: 237.
139. Eusebius: X.1.8.

140. *Ibid.*, X.2.2–3.4.
141. Farrar: II.481.
142. *Ibid.*, II.232.
143. Gregory Nazianzen (Farrar: II.47).
144. Ep. CXXX; Farrar: I.768.
145. Farrar: II.254 from Jerome: *Joann. Hierosol.*
146. *Ibid.*
147. Payne: 244.
148. *C.M.H.*, I.152.
149. Synesius: Letter 105 and notes.
150. Eusebius: VII.30.8.
151. Farrar: II.281.
152. *Ibid.*, 389.
153. *Ibid.*, 198.
154. *C.M.H.*, I.594.
155. Farrar: I.650.
156. Basil: Letter CXXXI.
157. Farrar: II.41.
158. Basil: Letter CLXXII.
159. *Ibid.*, LXVI.
160. Farrar: II.68.
161. *Ibid.*, I.318 ff.
162. *Ibid.*, II.68–9.
163. *Ibid.*, I.599–10.
164. Homily in *Acts*: 2.1 (Payne: 239).

Chapter XV. The Last Offensive

1. Amm. Marcellinus: XIV.4.1.
2. *Ibid.*, XVIII.5.1–8.5.
3. *Ibid.*, XVIII.6.14.
4. *Ibid.*, XVIII.6.19 ff.
5. See Dilleman: *Haute Mésop*; 218 ff. for Tigris provinces.
6. Amm. Marcellinus: XVIII.7.2.
7. See Chap. VI for this route: Dilleman: 62 (for water); and 295.
8. Amm. Marcellinus: XVIII.7.4.
9. *Ibid.*, XIV.3.2.
10. *Ibid.*, XIX.8.7–12.
11. *Ibid.*, XIX.2.5.
12. See above for lands E. of Tigris.

13. Poidebard: 166; 163.
14. Labourt: *Le Christianisme dans l'Emp. Perse:* 78; Amm. Marcellinus: XX, Ch. 7 for this war.
15. Amm. Marcellinus: XX.11.4–11.
16. *Ibid.*, XVI.10.7–10.
17. *Ibid.*, XXII.2.5.
18. *Ibid.*, XVII.9.3; 11.1.
19. *Ibid.*, XXII.3.7.
20. *Ibid.*, XVI.1.4; XXII.5.4.
21. *Ibid.*, XXII.10.7.
22. Orat. V.23 (Payne: 199).
23. Amm. Marcellinus: XXV, Ch. 4.
24. 'Il avait fait entrer son érudition dans sa vie': *Lettres*, Julien, trans. J. Bidez p. 203 (editor's comment).
25. Quoted in Devreesse: *Patr. d'Antioche*, 112.
26. Amm. Marcellinus: XXI.2.4–5.
27. Julien: *Lettres:* N° 8o, p. 88; N° 26, p. 54.
28. Bury: *Later Rom. Emp.*, I.144.
29. Julien: *Lettres*, N° 42, p. 73.
30. Amm. Marcellinus: XXV.3.17.
31. Julien: *Lettres*, N° 40, p. 64.
32. Amm. Marcellinus: XXII.12.12.
33. *Ibid.*, XXIII. Ch. 2.
34. Dilleman: *Haute Mésop*, 300.
35. Julien: *Lettres:* N° 115, p. 196; 127.
36. *Ibid.*, N° 98, p. 180.
37. *Ibid.*, N° 36, p. 63, from Eustathius the Philosopher.
38. Rostovtzeff: *Rom. Emp.*, I.385.
39. Sixteen thousand according to Malalas; see Dilleman: *Les Pays de L'Euphrate*, 127.
40. Gibbon: XXIV, p. 417, Everyman edition.
41. Dura ace. to Zosimus; see Dilleman: *Amm. Marcelin et les pays de l'Euphrate*, 135.
42. Honigmann: *Res. Gestae Div. Sap.:* 112–15 for controversy. I follow the itinerary reconstructed by Col. H. Lane: *Babylonian Problems*, Ch. VI. See Honigmann for Pari-Sabora, etc. Also A. Sprenger: *Post u. Reiserouten des Orients*, XIII, p. 91 for Anbar.
43. Amm. Marcellinus: XXIV for whole march.
44. Chapot: 53.
45. See also Chapot: 48–51.

46. They were still recently used in Kurdistan. Col. J. Shiel in *R.G.S.J.*, 1838, p. 74.

47. Ammianus Marcellinus.

48. Date discussed by Otto Kurz: *J.R.A.S.*, 1941, p. 37.

49. Dilleman: *Haute Mésop.*: Ch. V, *passim*: p. 302 in particular.

50. Lane: 118 ff.

51. Dilleman: 306, quotes Zosimus: III.26.4 against Ammian.

52. Chapot: 47–8.

53. Herodian: II.15.6.

54. Chapot: 226, and see Procop: *Pers. Wars, passim*.

55. Lane: 124.

56. Amm. Marcellinus: XXV, Chs. 2 and 3.

57. Lane: 126.

58. Dilleman: 304–12, for the route: also, same author: *Amm. Marc, et les pays de l'Euphr.*, p. 109; A. Stein: *Hatra Trade Route*, 308.

59. Herzfeld in *Arch. Reise*, II, p. 307, makes Zagura 'ain Sinu. A. Stein (*Hatra Trade Route*, pp. 314–15), gives six days from the crossing above Samarra to Hatra; six more to Tel Afar or Singara by Ur (Jaddalah). Also see Dilleman's *Haute Mésopotamie*, p. 171.

60. Chapot: 376; 125; Bury: *Later Rom. Emp.*, II.14.

61. Amm. Marcellinus: XXV.8.14.

62. H. Southgate: *Narrative of a Visit to the Syrian Church of Mesopotamia in 1841*.

63. Amm. Marcellinus: XXV.9.

64. Bury: 1.96; Honigmann: *Die Ostgrenze*, 3.

65. Dilleman: 217–21 for the Tigris geography.

66. Amm. Marcellinus: XXVI.4.6.

67. For the Roman slant on this history see Amm. Marc.: XXVII, Ch. 12, and XXX, Ch. 1–2; and *C.M.H.*, 1.225 ff.; 231 ff.

68. Chapot: 19, from Sébéos.

69. See Ch. IV above for controversy on the site.

70. Chapot: 384; Honigmann: *Die Ostgrenze*, 3–6.

71. *C.M.H.*, I.240.

Chapter XVI. The Age of Justinian

1. Von der Osten: *Die Welt der Perser*, 126.

2. Christensen: 47–8; *C.A.H.*, XII.4.3; T. Frank: IV.200.

3. Von der Osten: 144.

4. Runciman: *Byz. Civ.*, 164 ff.; Bury: *Later Rom. Emp.*, II.113 ff.; 121; 314 for the Lazic war.

5. Vasiliev: 216 (from Cosmas: *Topog. Christiana*, XX).

6. *Ibid.*, 218; Bury: *Later Rom. Emp.*, 321.

7. Vasiliev: 221; Bury, *Later Rom. Emp.*, 314; Diehl and Marçais: 128.

8. Vasiliev: 181–2; Bury: II.123.

9. Procopius: *Anecdota*, XXV.5.

10. Bury: *Later Rom. Emp.*, II.331–2; Jones: *Later Rom. Emp.*, II.826.

11. It was still flickering when I first travelled out to Syria and Lebanon and Iraq in 1927–29.

12. See the rapid growth of Dunaisir on the Mesopotamian route in Yakut; Dilleman: *Haute Mésop.*, 79.

13. Tacitus: *Annals.*, III.54.

14. Procopius: *Buildings*, II.10.20.

15. P. 299.

16. Jerome: Letter CVII.1.

17. Procopius: *Anecdota*, XI.9.

18. Synesius: *Letters*, Introduction, p. 54.

19. *Ibid.*, 69, p. 160.

20. Sidonius Apollinaris: V, Panegyric on Maiorianus, 14–53.

21. *Ibid.*, XXII (Castle of Pontius Leontius.), 146–7.

22. *Ibid.*, V, To Donidius, II.9.4 ff.

23. Bury: *Later Rom. Emp.*, I.297; 206.

24. *C.M.H.*, I.53; 366.

25. Sidonius Apollinaris: V, to Maiorianus, 480.

26. Jones, *Later Rom. Emp.*, I.244.

27. Chapot: 117; Jones: I.157; 159 for the foederati.

28. Crocus, the Alemannic king.

29. *C.M.H.*, I.402.

30. Amm. Marcellinus: XXXI.4.6–11.

31. Quoted by Diehl and Marçais: 13.

32. Sidonius Apollinaris: Letter to Catullinus, XII.12–19.

33. Under Leo.

34. Procopius: *Anecdota*, XXIII.24; Bury: *Constit. of Later Rom. Emp.*, 43.

35. Byron: *The Byzantine Achievement*, 36–7, and *passim*.

36. *C.M.H.*, I.434.

37. See Ch. I.

38. *Aeneid*, XII.822 ff.

39. Bury: *Later Rom. Emp.*, I.4; II.399; Diehl and Marçais, 118–19.

40. Runciman: *Byz. Civ.*, 27; Ostrogorsky, 25–8; 42; 95.

41. Runciman: *Byz. Civ.*, 275.
42. *Ibid.*, 221.
43. *Ibid.*, 220.
44. *Ibid.*, 223–30.
45. Henderson: *Nero*, Ch. V, note 2, p. 472.
46. Bury: *Later Rom. Emp.*, II.6; *passim*.
47. Procopius: *Buildings*, II.1.4 ff.; *Persian Wars*: I.10.13 ff.
48. Procopius: *Buildings*, II.1.13; Bury: II.15; *C.M.H.*, 1.481–3.
49. Honigmann: *Ostgrenze*, 10.
50. Procopius: *Persian Wars*, I.10.19.
51. *Ibid.*, I.16.4 ff.
52. Bury: II.117–18.
53. Dilleman: *Haute Mésop*, 82.
54. Procopius: *Persian Wars*, II.13.17.
55. Diehl and Marçais, 66–7; Chapot: 166; Amm. Marcel.: XXIX, I.2–4; Jones: II.1030–1; Bury: *Later Roman Empire* II.14.
56. Procopius: *Persian Wars*, II.13.29.
57. Honigmann: *Ostgrenze*, Ch. 1.
58. Procopius: *Persian Wars*, I.7.34.
59. *Ibid.*, II *passim*.
60. Bury: *Later Rom. Emp.*, II.122 ff.
61. Chapot: 232.
62. Procopius: *Buildings*, II.8.4–7.
63. Dilleman: *Haute Mésop.*, 224; see Poidebard.
64. Procopius: *Buildings*, II.8.8.
65. Dilleman: *Haute Mésop.*, 79.
66. Devreesse: *Patriarc. d'Antioche*, 249.
67. Procopius: *Buildings*, II.11.10 ff.
68. Procopius: *Buildings*, II.4.21.
69. Bury: *Later Rom. Emp.*, II.78; Chapot: 59–60.
70. Chapot: 188.
71. *Ibid.*, 52.
72. *Ibid.*, 139, note 2.
73. Ever since the battle of Murcia in A.D. 351.
74. Bury: I.41–2; II.84.
75. Runciman: *Byz. Civ.*, 145.
76. Chapot: 54–5 (from the Emp. Maurice: *Strategicon*, XI.2, ed. Scheffer)
77. Jones: *Later Rom. Emp.*, II.612.
78. Bury: II, Ch. XVI for army in general.
79. Chapot: 91.

80. At the battle of Busta Gallorum.
81. Procopius: *Persian Wars*, I.1.13.
82. Chapot: 141, note 4.
83. *Ibid.*, 49.
84. Dilleman: *Haute Mésop.*, 195.
85. T. Frank: IV.165.
86. Amm. Marcellinus: XXII.16.17.
87. Runciman: *Byz. Civ.*, 26.
88. The *city* of Byzantium is referred to as Constantinople from now onwards. Byzantium refers to the Byzantine Empire.
89. Farrar: I.481 (opening of Nicaea Council); *C.A.H.*, XII.10.3, p. 365.
90. Bikerman: 14.
91. Runciman: *Byz. Civ.*, 188.
92. Procopius: *Anecdota*, VII.8.11.
93. Byron: *The Byzantine Achievement*, 115.
94. Runciman: *Byz. Civ.*, 85.
95. Christensen: 80.
96. *Ibid.*, 74; Bury: *Later Rom. Emp.*, I.12–14.
97. *Ibid.*, 79; Ostrogorsky: 71.
98. Runciman: 93.
99. Territorial divisions of the Byzantine Empire.
100. Christensen: 42.
101. Jones: *Later Rom. Emp.*, I.180.
102. Christensen: 44–5.
103. Barker: *Science and Politics*, 80 (quotes fr. Johan. Lydus de Magistratibus; see also Jones: I.106).
104. Christensen: 78; 27; 29; 110 (quotes Mas'udi and Ibn Haukal in tenth century A.D.).
105. Vasiliev: *Hist, de l'Empire Byzantin*, 130.
106. p. 115.
107. Jones: *Later Rom. Emp.*, I.144; *C.M.H.*, I.396.
108. Runciman: 73; Bury: I.18.19; *C.M.H.*, I.396.
109. Procopius: *Anecdota*, XXX.21.
110. Christensen: 89.
111. *Ibid.*, 97.
112. Amm. Marcellinus: XXVIII.4.4.
113. *Ibid.*, XXVIII.4.9.
114. Christensen: 67.
115. *Ibid.*, 109; Bury: I.214; Runciman: 198; Diehl and Marçais: 86.
116. *Ibid.*, 55.

117. *Ibid.*, 33; 39.
118. Tarn and Griffith: 130.
119. Runciman: *Byz. Civ.*, 161; compare Bikerman: 28 for the same policy under the Seleucids.
120. Procop: *Persian Wars*, I.2.7–9.
121. Christensen: 80–1.
122. Byron: *The Byzantine Achievement*, 134.
123. *Ibid.*, 133; Jones: I.108; 468.
124. *Ibid.*, 132.
125. Runciman: *Byz. Civ.*, 204.
126. *Ibid.*
127. Byron: *The Byzantine Achievement*, 143.
128. *Ibid.*, 256 (from Gibbon).
129. Ostrogorsky: 68.
130. Byron: 301.
131. *Ibid.*, 309; Bury: II.313–14.
132. Runciman: 164; 167.
133. Procopius: *Anecdota*, XXX.12; XXV.4.
134. In Chapter VI.
135. *Ibid.*, XVIII.22.
136. Bury: *Later Rom. Emp.*, I.368–9.
137. Ostrogorsky: 43; Bury: 1.370; *C.M.H.*, I.114.
138. Labourt: 44.
139. *Ibid.*, 44.
140. *Ibid.*, 45–6; Procopius: *Persian Wars*, II.24.6–10.
141. *Ibid.*, 87.
142. *Ibid.*, 94–8; 32.
143. *Ibid.*, 121–4.
144. *Ibid.*, 125.
145. *Ibid.*, 92; 192; 100; 196.
146. Bury: *Constit. of the Later Rom. Emp.* (for a concise definition); Diehl and Marçais: 31.
147. II.9.
148. See *C.A.H.*, XII.14.11, pp. 493 ff. for Addai legend and literature.
149. Labourt: 16–7.
150. *C.A.H.*, XII, pp. 492 ff.
151. *The Search for the Lost Rohe.*
152. Labourt: 32.
153. *Ibid.*, 35.

154. Close to the present Mosque of Abraham according to tradition. Duval: *Hist. d'Edesse*, 7.145.
155. *Ibid.*, 132–3.
156. *C.M.H.*, 1.514–16.
157. Labourt: 149; 147; 139.
158. *Ibid.*, 83; XIII.
159. Dill: 594.
160. Gough: *Early Christians*, 23.
161. Duval: *Histoire d'Edesse*, 114–15; *C.A.H.*, XII.14.3, pp. 509 ff.
162. Devreesse: *Patr. d'Antioche* for strength of Syrian paganism.
163. Labourt: 141; 291.
164. *Ibid.*, 152–7; 292–3.
165. *Ibid.*, 295.
166. Hanafi and Shafe'i.
167. *Ibid.*, 177 ff.
168. See Chapter VI for Antony and Phraaspa.
169. *Ibid.*, Ch. 7.
170. *Ibid.*, 6.
171. *Ibid.*, 204–6.
172. *Ibid.*, 218; 199; 320–4.
173. *Ibid.*, 228–31.
174. Labourt: 240.
175. *Ibid.*, 243.
176. *C.M.H.*, I.170.
177. Diehl and Marçais: 115.
178. *Ibid.*, 105–7.
179. Farrar: I.320 for Cyprian; *C.A.H.*, XII.15.3 for the Easter controversy.
180. *C.M.H.*, I.169.4; 510–11.
181. Bury: *Later Rom. Emp.*, I.439; Vasiliev: 139; 143.
182. Devreesse: *Patr. d'Antioche*, 96 and note 4; Vasiliev: 157.
183. Bury: *Later Rom. Emp.*, II.378.
184. Procopius: *Anecdota*, X.13.
185. Diehl and Marçais: 104.
186. Bury: II.364; see also Jones: II.938–9.
187. Procopius: *Anecdota*, X.11; Runciman: *Byz. Civ.*, 37.
188. Runciman: *Byz. Civ.*, 191.
189. Diehl and Marçais 112 from John of Ephesus: *Hist. Eccl.*, 248.
190. The Three Chapters.
191. Bury: *Later Rom. Emp.*, II.391; Devreesse: *Patr. d'Antioche*, 292–3.

192. Sir Harry Luke, *K.C.M.G.*, pointed out to me how much the Syriac church dislikes to be derived from an individual however much venerated.

193. Devreesse: *Patr. d'Antioche*, 75; 88; 96.

194. *Ibid.*, 75, note 4.

195. Chapot: 312–3, note 4.

196. Bury: II.381.

197. Runciman: *The Mediaeval Manichee*, 19 ff.

198. *Ibid.*, 35–41.

199. *Ibid.*, 58–9.

· 200. Bury: *Later Rom. Emp.* I.441 (from Joseph Stylites, XXX.1.22).

201. Devreesse: *Patr. d'Antioche*, 245–6.

202. *Ibid.*, 247.

203. *Ibid.*, 248.

204. Labourt: 206, note 4.

205. Devreesse: *Patr. d'Antioche*, 261.

206. *Ibid.*, 259.

207. Procopius: *Persian Wars*, II.28.13.

208. Devreesse: *Patr. d'Antioche*, 264–77 *passim*; Procop: *Pers. Wars*, II.1 *passim*; Jones: II.611.

209. Devreesse: *Patr. d'Antioche*, 97; 282.

210. Bury: *Later Rom.Emp.*, II.26 (from Novel: 30.11, 536 A.D.).

211. *Ibid.*, II.88–9.

212. Jones: *Later Rom. Emp.* I.469.

213. Procopius: *Buildings*, IV.5.1 ff; Diehl and Marçais, 77–8.

214. Mostly single towers: Procopius: *Buildings*, IV.5.

215. Procopius: *Buildings*, III.3.10; Chapot: note 361,7 (from George of Cyprus: 963).

216. Byzantine fortified gorges or natural gateways.

217. Procopius: *Persian Wars*, II.24.14.

218. Bikerman: 85; 88.

219. Procopius: *Anecdota*, XXIV.8.12.

220. *Ibid.*, XXIV.27–30; Jones: *Later Rom. Emp.*, II.670.

221. *Ibid.*, 2–5.

222. Jones: *Later Rom. Emp.*, II.668–70.

223. Jones: *Later Rom. Emp.*, II.662–3.

224. Devreesse: *Patr. d'Antioche* (ref. vanished).

225. Procopius: *Anecd.*, XXIII.20.

226. Jones: I.131; 136; 146.

227. Procopius: *Anecd:* XXVI.7.10; Bury: *Later Rom. Emp.*, II.352–3.

228. Dilleman: *Haute Mésop.*, 192 (from *Menander Protector*, p. 360).

229. Bury: *Later Rom. Emp.*, II.38.
230. *Ibid.*, I.56.
231. *Ibid.*, I.56–8.
232. Gough: *Early Christians*, 158.
233. Runciman: *Byz. Civ.*, 40; Diehl and Marçais: 142.
234. Procopius: *Anecd.*, XXIV.15.16; Christensen: 61–2; Diehl and Marçais, 131.
235. Devreesse: *Pair. d'Antioche*, 100.
236. Diehl and Marçais: 146.
237. *Ibid.*, 149; Honigmann: *R. Gestae*, 60.
238. Christensen: 104.
239. Bury: *Const, of Later Rom. Emp.*, 18–19.
240. Vasiliev: 262 (from the Armenian of Sébéos), note 1.
241. Th. Simocatta: IV.11.2 quoted by Chapot: 385, note 1.
242. Diehl and Marçais: 187.
243. Devreesse: *Patr. d'Antioche*, 96 ff.
244. *Ibid.*, 84; 90–1.
245. Vasiliev: 274.
246. *Ibid.*, 279.
247. Diehl and Marçais: 157.
248. Devreesse: *Patr. d'Antioche*, 104.
249. *Ibid.*, 106.
250. Ostrogorsky: 38–9.
251. Runciman: *Byz. Civ.*, 291 (from Theophanes, 375–6).
252. Ostrogorsky: 30.
253. Runciman. *Byz. Civ.*, 170.
254. *Ibid.*, 178.
255. Bury: *Later Rom. Emp.*, II.205.
256. Procopius: *Pers. Wars*, I.26.1–4.
257. Bikerman: 122; 69; 96 for mercenaries.

Bibliography

Sources Per Chapter

Chapter I
The most useful general works quoted are:

The Cambridge Ancient History, Vols. VII and VIII.
M. Rostovtzeff: *Social & Economic History of the Roman Empire*.
M. Rostovtzeff: *Social & Economic History of the Hellenistic World*.
T. Frank: *Economic Survey of Ancient Rome*, Vol. 1.
E. Bikerman: *Institutions des Séleucides*.
H. M. D. Parker: *Roman Legions*.

The sources (available in translation which is always in the Loeb Classics unless otherwise stated):

Polybius: *Histories*.
Livy: History Books XXX–XXXVIII.
Appian: *Syrian Wars*.
Plutarch's *Lives* of Aemilius Paulus, Flamininus, Aratus, Eumenes, Philopo-
    emon: Everyman edition.
Frontinus: *The Stratagems*.
Herodotus: History translated by J. E. Powell.
Maccabees I & II: (Apocrypha).

Other useful works consulted:

E. R. Bevan: *The House of Seleucus*.

H. A. Bouché Leclerc: *Histoire des Lagides*.

H. A. Bouché Leclerc: *Histoire des Séleucides*.

L. Homo: 'Flamininus', *Revue Historique*, CXXI and CXXII, 1916.

E. Meyer: *Blüte und Niedergang des Hellenismus in Asien*.

W. W. Tarn: *The Greeks in Bactria and India*.

W. W. Tarn and G. T. Griffith: *Hellenistic Civilisation*.

M. Cary: *A History of the Greek World*.

H. A. Ormerod: *Piracy in the Ancient World*.

Chapter II

The most useful general works quoted are those referred to for Chapter I with the addition of:

D. Magie: *Roman Rule in Asia Minor to the end of the Third Century after Christ*.

J. P. Mahaffy: *The Silver Age of the Greek World*.

Sources:

Cicero: *Ad Atticum, Ad Quintum Fratrem, Verrine Orations, Lex Manilia*, etc.

Livy: Bks. XXXIV–XXXIX.

Strabo: *Geography*, Bks. VII, XI.

Polybius: *Histories*, II, XXI, XXXI.

Athenaeus: *Deipnosophists*, Bk. XII.

Pliny: *Natural History*, IX, XXXIII.

Juvenal: *Satires*, trans. by S. H. Jeyes.

Other useful works:

A. H. M. Jones: *The Cities of the East Roman Provinces*.

E. H. Minns: *Scythians and Greeks*.

V. Rostovtzeff: *Iranians and Greeks in South Russia* (for the Black Sea northern coast background).

Chapter III

Apart from the general histories already mentioned:

T. Reinach: *Mithridate Eupator* is still useful.

A. Duggan: *He Died Old*, is both popular and careful.

Sources:

Plutarch: *Lives* (of Lucullus, Pompey and Sulla).

Strabo: excellent for the geography and everything to do with his own country of Pontus. Bks. 11 and 12.

Appian: *Mithridatica.*

Dio Cassius: *Roman History.*

Caesar: *Alexandrine Wars*, for the later expedition against Pharnaces.

Other works:

W. M. Calder and George E. Bean's indispensable *Classical Map of Asia Minor.*

J. A. R. Munro: 'Roads in Pontus', *J.H.S.*, XXI.

J. G. C. Anderson: 'Pompey and Mithradates', *J.R.S.*, XII for the geography and particularly for the Lycus campaigns.

Peter Green: *The Sword of Pleasure* (a reconstruction of the life of Sulla).

Chapter IV

The general histories are as before.

Sources:

Plutarch: *Lives* (of Sulla, Lucullus and Pompey).

Appian: *Mithridatica.*

Cicero: *Pro Sestio*; *Ad Atticum*, etc.

Horace: *Odes.*

Dio Cassius: *Roman History.*

Frontinus: *Stratagems.*

Sallust: (for Mithradates' letter).

For the geography, especially for Tigranocerta:

Strabo, Pliny (*Natural History*) and Tacitus are handled by modern experts like Dilleman, Rice Holmes, Lehmann Haupt (*Armenien Einst und Jetzt*, Berlin, 1926), K. Eckhart; *Klio*, X, 1910, 'Die Armenischen Feldzüge des Lukullus'; and F. Guse: 'Die Feldzüge des dritten Mithridatischen Krieges', *Klio*, XX, 1926.

Other works:

A series of modern travellers such as Kinnear (*Journey through Asia Minor*); Mark Sykes, Robert Curzon and Tozer, may be consulted for the character of the country where so many Roman wars are to be fought.

Chapter V

The general histories continue as before, with the addition of:

Bikerman: *Institutions des Séleucides.*

Bevan: *The House of Seleucus.*

H. A. Bouché Leclercq: *Histoire des Séleucides.*

Tarn and Griffith: *Hellenistic Civilisation.*

Rostovtzeff: *Social and Economic History of the Roman Empire* (which now begins to become indispensable).

Von der Osten: *Die Welt der Perser.*

Ghirshman: *Iran* (for the Iranian background).

Mommsen: *Provinces of the Roman Empire*, is still interesting.

Macurdy: *Hellenistic Queens* takes alluring byeways.

Sources:

Cicero chiefly: *Letters*; *Verrine Orations*; *Pro Sestio, Pro Flacco, De Lege Manilia, pro Deiataro*, etc.

Appian: *Civil Wars, Syrian Wars, Mithradatica.*

Pliny: *Natural History.*

Strabo: *Geography* (of Parthia and Media).

Other works:

For the eastern trade, both Charlesworth and Warmington should be consulted from now on.

Chapter VI

The general histories continue as before, with the addition of:

T. Rice Holmes: *The Architect of the Roman Empire*, which continues to be indispensable for the Augustan age.

Sources:

Plutarch: *Lives* (of Crassus and Mark Antony from which all quotations are taken unless otherwise marked): Everyman edition.

Dio Cassius: *Roman History*, indispensable from now on.

Cicero: *Ad Atticum*; and Appian: *Bellum Civ.*; and Lucan: *Pharsalia*, for the background of the Civil Wars.

History:

Karl-Heinz Ziegler: *Die Beziehungen zwischen Rom und dem Parther-reich.* From now to the end of the Parthian wars this book gives a lucid history of the Roman-Parthian tangles. Its interpretations insufficiently, I think, recognise the aggressiveness implicit in the Roman policy in Armenia, but as a documentation of references it is invaluable.

For the geography:

> Isidore of Charax: *The Parthian Stations.*
> Chapot: *La Frontiére de l'Euphrate.*
> Poidebard: *La Trace de Rome dans le Désert de Syrie.*
> Dilleman: *passim.*
> Duval: *Histoire d'Edesse.*
> Seton Lloyd: *The Listener*, April 24, 1952 for Carrhae.
> Strabo, Pliny and Ghirshman for Iran.
> Calder and Bean: *Classical Map of Asia Minor.*

Chapter VII

The general histories:

> The *C.A.H.*, Vols. ix and x.
> Rostovtzeff: *Social and Economic History of the Roman Empire.*
> Rice Holmes: *The Architect of the Roman Empire.*
> Syme: *The Roman Revolution.*
> Buchan: *Augustus.*
> Mahaffy: *The Silver Age of the Greek World.*
> Green: *Essays in Antiquity*, for the literature.
> Sellar: *The Roman Poets of the Republic.*
> T. Frank: *Economic Survey of Ancient Rome.*

The sources, apart from Augustus' own *Res Gestae* (added to the Loeb edition of Vell. Paterculus), could include practically all the Augustan authors. The following have been chiefly used:

> Virgil, Horace, Catullus, Ovid, Pliny the Elder, Tacitus, Suetonius, Dio Cassius, Velleius Paterculus.
> The satirists, Martial and Juvenal and Seneca, are all later, but relevant; as is the contrast of the earlier Terence.

Chapter VIII

The general histories continue to be:

> The *C.A.H.*
> T. Frank.
> Rostovtzeff.
> Magie, Kornemann, and Schur, and such useful surveys as E. Meyer: *Blüte u. Niedergang des Hellenismus in Asien.*
> Henderson: *Life and Principate of the Emperor Nero.*
> Charlesworth: article on Tiridates in *J.R.S.*, 1950.

The sources:

> Tacitus mainly, Dio Cassius, Seneca (essential for sidelights on Nero), *Res Gestae Divi Augusti* and Velleius Paterculus for the background to this reign.

For the Armenian geography:

> Chapot and Dilleman are indispensable.
> Vasiliev has useful detail; and a whole series of modern travellers from Von Moltke onward are available for the permanent features of what was once Armenia.

For the Indian–South Arabian trade route:

> Pliny: *Natural History.*
> *The Periplus of the Erythrean Sea.*
> Strabo (particularly on Aelius Gallus).
> Tarn and Griffith: *Hellenistic Civilisation.*
> Charlesworth: *Trade Routes and Commerce of the Roman Empire.*
> Warmington: *The Commerce between the Roman Empire and India.*

For the North of the Black Sea:

> Strabo.
> Ovid: *Tristia*; and *Ex Ponto.*
> Rostovtzeff: *The Iranians and Greeks in South Russia.*

For details of the Legions:

> Josephus, Parker, Chapot.

Chapter IX

The general histories continue to be:

> *C.A.H.*, Vols. IX, X and XI.
> Rostovtzeff.
> T. Frank.
> Magie: *Roman Rule in Asia Minor.*
> W. W. Tarn,: 'Seleucid-Parthian Studies'.
> Lepper: *Trajan's Parthian War.*
> Dilleman: Chapter on Trajan's War in Mesopotamia.
> Chapot: for the geography.

Sources:

Dio Cassius.
Strabo.
Arrian: *Periplus of the Euxine.*
Isidore of Charax: *Parthian Stations.*
Dio Chrysostom: *Orations.*
Pliny the Younger: *Letters.*
Tacitus: *Histories.*

For the northern trade route:

Herrmann: Die *alten Seidenstrassen zwischen China und Syrien.*
Talbot Rice: *The Scythians.*
A. Berthelot: *L'Asie Ancienne d'Après Ptolomée.*
Charlesworth.
Warmington.
Ghirshman: *Iran.*
Von der Osten: *Die Welt der Perser.*
Pierre Teilhard de Chardin: *Letters from a Traveller*, and Georges Le Fèvre,
La Croisière jaune, as well as the works of Owen Lattimore give the most
modern versions of the silk road journey at its eastern end.

Chapter X

The general histories continue to be:

C.A.H., vols. VIII–XI.
Magie: *Roman Rule in Asia Minor.*
Dill: *Roman Society from Nero to Marcus Aurelius.*
Rostovtzeff.
Barker: *From Alexander to Constantine.*
Parker: *Roman Legions* (for the army).
T. Frank.
L. Homo.
Altheim: *Die Soldaten Kaiser.*
Hahn: *Rom und Romanismus in Gr.-Rom. Osten.*
Meyer.

The sources are chiefly:

Dio Cassius, Suetonius and the *Scriptores Historiae Augustae* (Hadrian, Pius,
M. Aurelius, Verus, Av. Cassius and Commodus).
Marcus Aurelius: *Meditations.*

Fronto: *Letters.*
Dio Chrysostom: *Orations.*
Plutarch: *Moralia.*
Lucian.
Epictetus.
Aelius Aristides.
Philostratus: *Life of Apollonius of Tyana.*

Chapter XI

The fundamental general history from now on is:

A. H. M. Jones: *The Later Roman Empire* – so excellent and detailed a work that very little else is needed. Apart from this, the general histories already quoted continue to be relevant.
Altheim: *Die Soldaten Kaiser*, is useful.

The literary sources are very meagre:

Dio Cassius comes to an end with Alexander Severus and is replaced by Herodian and the *Scriptores Historiae Augustae*, inadequate as they are.

For the description of lower Euphrates:

Isidore of Charax: *The Parthian Stations.*
Philostratus: *Life of Apollonius of Tyana.*
Lucian (for Hierapolis).
Tabari (for the Arab description of Hatra) are all useful.

The modern works chiefly consulted are:

Chapot: *La Frontière de l'Euphrate.*
Poidebard: *La Trace de Rome dans le Désert de Syrie.*
Dussaud: *Pénétration des Arabes en Syrie.*
Rostovtzeff: *Caravan Cities.*
Rostovtzeff: 'Les Inscriptions Caravanières de Palmyre' in *Mélange Glotz.*
Grant: *The Syrian Desert.*
Seyrig: Article in *Syria*, XXII; and *Mélanges Cumont:* 'Inscriptions Rélatives au Commerce de Palmyre'.
Mommsen: *Provinces of the Roman Empire.*
Dilleman: *Haute Mésopotamie Orientale et Pays Adjacents.*
Warmington: *Commerce between the Roman Empire and India.*
Charlesworth: *Trade Routes and Commerce of the Roman Empire.*

For the Sassanians and the Kushans:

    Von der Osten: *Die Welt der Perser*.
    Sir Aurel Stein for Hatra.
    Ghirshman: *Iran*.
    Ghirshman: *Iran, Parthians and Sassanians*.
    Christensen: *Empire des Sassanides*.
    Honigmann and Maricq: *Recherches sur les Res Gestae Divi Saporis* – excellent for topography.

Chapter XII

General:

    C.A.H., Vol. XII.
    Rostovtzeff: *Social and General History of the Roman Empire*.
    T. Frank: *Economic Survey of Ancient Rome*.
    A. M. Jones: *The Later Roman Empire*.
    E. Barker.
    Hahn: *Rom und Romanismus in Gr. Rom. Osten*.
    Altheim: *Die Soldaten Kaiser*.

Sources:

    Herodian.
    Dio Cassius.
    Scriptores Historiae Augustae.
    Philostratus.

Chapter XIII

The general histories are useful as ever:

    C.A.H., Vol. XII.
    Magie: *Roman Rule in Asia Minor*.
    Rostovtzeff.
    T. Frank.
    A. H. M. Jones: *The Later Roman Empire:* indispensable, particularly useful for its detailed study of the legal documents of the period.
    Mommsen: *Provinces of the Roman Empire*.

Particular histories:

    Altheim: *Die Soldaten Kaiser*.
    L. Homo: *l'Empereur Gallien*.
    Clermont-Ganneau: *Odeinat et Vaballat* for the reign of Gallienus.

J. H. E. Crees,: *The Reign of the Emperor Probus.*
L. Homo: *Essai sur le Règne de l'Empereur Aurelien.*

The sources are mostly scattered beyond my reach, and the Lives of the *Scriptores Historiae Augustae* from Valerian to Diocletian are my only originals (and poor ones) apart from Longinus.

Rostovtzeff's *Caravan Cities*, Dilleman, Chapot, Poidebard, and Dussaud: *Pénetration des Arabes en Syrie* are all indispensable for the geography.
The Villes Mortes can best be studied in the works of the Princeton Expedition and in Tchalenko's exhaustive description.

Chapter XIV

General Histories:

We lose our two general guides — *The Cambridge Ancient History* and David Magie, though Rostovtzeff continues to be indispensable, and T. Frank, and particularly A. M. Jones' *Later Roman Empire*, and *The Cambridge Mediaeval History* cover the ground.
Runciman's introduction to the Byzantine Civilisation is an excellent short summing up: other general authorities on the Byzantine age will be given for the next chapter.

Sources:
My reading here is very inadequate in a vast field —

Clement of Alexandria.
The Apostolic Fathers.
St Basil.
St Gregory of Nyssa (trans. by Jean Daniélou).
Tertullian.
St Augustine.
St Jerome.
Eusebius.
Longinus.
Synesius.
Libanius.
Plotinus.
Various excerpts collected by E. Barker in his *Alexander to Constantine*.

For the Ecclesiastical History:

Dean Farrar's *Lives of the Fathers* is still a solid background.
Y. Courtonne: *St Basile et l'Hellenisme.*

D. Nock: *Conversion*.

R. Payne: *The Holy Fire*, an excellently careful bit of history made easy.

W. Jaeger: *Early Christianity in Greek Paideia* for its relation to the Greek humanism.

Chapter XV

The author followed in this chapter is Ammianus Marcellinus, helped by Julian's own letters and writings, with a background of the Fathers already listed for Chapter XIV, and of Libanius, whose friendship with Julian and intimacy with the life of Antioch make him particularly useful.

A helpful commentary and map on the itinerary is given by Lieutenant Colonel W. H. Lane in *Babylonian Problems* to be studied together with Honigmann and Maricq, *Recherches sur les Res Gestae Divi Saporis*: Dilleman – both *Haute Mésopotamie* and *Pays de l'Euphrate*; and Sprenger, *Post und Reiserouten des Orients* for the later Arab geography.

Chapter XVI

Apart from Procopius, who is indispensable, I have not been able to read the direct sources for this chapter which are chiefly written in Syriac, Armenian or Greek and not always translated.

The modern histories, however, mostly excellent for references and quotations, are also singularly homogeneous in their outlook, and when taken together give a varied but concordant picture of the age.

The general histories consulted are:

J. Bury: *The Later Roman Empire*.

J. Bury: *The Constitution of the Later Roman Empire*.

S. Runciman: *Byzantine Civilisation*.

A. Vasiliev: *Histoire de l'Empire Byzantin*.

G. Ostrogorsky: *History of the Byzantine State*.

A. H. M. Jones: *The Later Roman Empire*.

R. Byron: *The Byzantine Achievement*.

The Cambridge Mediaeval History, Vol. I.

E. Barker: *Social and Political Thought in Byzantium*.

Diehl and Marçais: *Le Monde Oriental de* 395 à 1081.

For the Persian: Christensen's *Sassanians* and Von der Osten as before.

For the geography: Honigmann, Dilleman and Chapot as before.

I have quoted Synesius (although he is a little earlier than the Justinian age) and Sidonius Apollinaris (although he belongs to the West) because they are both particularly vivid in their descriptions of daily life under the impact of the barbarians.

R. Devreesse: *Le Patriarcat d'Antioche*, and – particularly –
J. Labourt: *Le Christianisme dans l'Empire Perse* are indispensable for the tangled, largely legendary web of Christianity across the Euphrates border.

General Sources

Abbreviations: *J.H.S.* – *The Journal of Hellenic Studies.*
                         J.R.A.S. – *The Journal of the Royal Asiatic Society.*
                         J.R.S. – *The Journal of Roman Studies.*
                         R.G.S.J. – *Royal Geographical Society Journal.*
                         Loeb – The Loeb Classical Library published by Heinemann.

Aeschylus: *Agamemnon*, G. Murray's translation, London 1924, Allen & Unwin.
Ainsworth, W. F.: *Travels and Researches in Asia Minor*, London 1842, Parker & Son.
Altheim: *Die Soldaten Kaiser*, Frankfurt 1938.
Ammianus Marcellinus: *Roman History*, trans. C. D. Yonge, London 1862, Bell.
Anderson, J. G. C: 'Pompey and Mithradates', *J.R.S.*, XII, 1922.
Apostolic Fathers, The: Loeb, 2 vols.
Appian: *Roman History*, Loeb, 4 vols.
Arrian: *Periplus of the Euxine* (J. Baschmakoff: *La Synthèse des Periples Pontiques*, Paris 1948).
Athenaeus: *Deipsophists*, Loeb, 7 vols.
Augustine, St.: *Confessions*, Loeb, 2 vols.
Augustus: *Res Gestae Divi Augusti* (in Loeb edition of Velleius Paterculus).
Bachmann, W.: *Kirchen und Moscheen in Armenien und Kurdistan*, Leipzig 1913.
Barker, E.: *From Alexander to Constantine*, Oxford 1959.
––––––––– *Social and Political Thought in Byzantium*, Oxford 1957.
Barrow, R. H.: *Slavery in the Roman Empire*, London 1928, Methuen.
Basil, St: *The Letters*, Loeb, 4 vols.
Berthelot, A.: *L'Asie Ancienne d'après Ptolemée*, Paris 1930.
Bevan, E. R.: *The House of Seleucus*, London 1902, E. Arnold.
Bikerman, E.: *Institutions des Séleucides*, Paris 1937.
Bouché Leclerc, H. A.: *Histoire des Lagides*, Paris 1903–4, 2 vols.
––––––––– *Histoire des Séleucides*, Paris 1913.
Bryce, J.: *Transcaucasia and Ararat*, London 1877, Macmillan.
Buchan, J.: *Augustus*, London 1937, Hodder & Stoughton.
Burnaby, Capt. F.: *On Horseback through Asia Minor*, London 1887, S. Low.

Bury, J.: *The Later Roman Empire*, New York 1958.
———— *The Constitution of the Later Roman Empire*, Cambridge 1910, C.U.P.
Byron, R.: *The Byzantine Achievement*, London 1929, Routledge.

Caesar: *Alexandrian, African and Spanish Wars*, Loeb.
Calder, W. M. and Bean, George E.: *Classical Map of Asia Minor*, British Institute of Archaeology at Ankara, 1957.
Cambridge Ancient History (C.A.H.), C.U.P. ed. J. B. Bury, S. A. Cook, F. E. Adcock, 1923.
Cambridge Medieval History (C.M.H.), C.U.P., Vol. I (1957), *The Christian Roman Empire and Foundation of Teutonic Kingdoms*.
Cary, M.: *A History of the Greek World from 323–146 B.C.*, London 1951, Methuen.
Czernik, J.: 'Studienexpedition durch die Gebiete d. Euphrat und Tigris, nebst Ein- und Ausgangsrouten durch Nordsyrien', in: *geographischc Mitteilungen*, Erg. Heft 44, Gotha: 1871–76, J. Perthes.
Chanler, B.: *Cleopatra's Daughter*, London 1936, Putnam.
Chapot, V.: *La Frontière de l'Euphrate*, Paris 1908.
Charlesworth, M. P.: 'Fear of the Orient in the Roman Empire', *Cambridge Historical Journal II*, C.U.P.
———— *Trade Routes and Commerce of the Roman Empire*, Cambridge 1924, C.U.P.
Christensen, A.: *Empire des Sassanides*, Copenhagen 1907.
Cicero: *Ad Atticus*, Loeb, 3 vols.
———— *Ad Familiares*, Loeb, 3 vols.
———— *Verrine Orations*, Loeb, 2 vols.
———— *The Speeches*, Loeb.
———— *Lex Manilia* (Pro Lege Manilia) Loeb.
———— *Tuscan Disputations*, Loeb
Claudian: Loeb, 2 vols.
Clement of Alexandria: Loeb.
Clermont–Ganneau, C.: *Odeinat et Vaballat*.
Courtonne, Y.: *St. Basile et l'Hellenisme*, Paris 1935.
Crees.J. H.E.: *The Reign of the Emperor Probus*, London 1912, University of London Press.
Curzon, Robert: *Armenia*, London 1854, John Murray.
Devreesse, R.: *Le Patriarcat d'Antioche*, Paris 1945.
Diehl, C. and Marçais, G.: *Le Monde Oriental de 395 à 1081*, Paris 1936.
Dill, S.: *Roman Society from Nero to Marcus Aurelius*, London 1904, Macmillan.
Dilleman, L.: *Ammien Marcellin et Les Pays de l'Euphrate et du Tigre*, Paris, 1962.
———— *Haute Mésopotamie Orientale et Pays Adjacents*, Paris 1963.

Dio Cassius: *Roman History*, Loeb, 9 vols.

Dio Chrysostom: *Discourses*, Loeb, 5 vols.

Duggan, A.: *He Died Old*, London 1958, Faber.

Dussaud, R.: *Pénétration des Arabes en Syrie*, Paris 1955.

Duval, R.: *Histoire d'Edesse*, Paris 1892.

Eckhart, K.: 'Die Armenischen Feldzüge des Lukullus', *Klio*, X, 1910.

Epictetus: *The Discources*, etc. Loeb, 2 vols.

Eusebius: *Ecclesiastical History*, Loeb, 2 vols.

Farrar, Dean F. W.: *Lives of the Fathers*, Edinburgh 1889, Longmans Green.

France, Anatole: *Thaïs*.

Frank, Tenney: *Economic Survey of Ancient Rome*, 6 vols. Pageant Books, New Jersey 1959.

Frontinus: *The Stratagems*, Loeb.

Fronto, The Correspondence of: Loeb, 2 vols.

Fuller, J. F. C.: *Decisive Battles: Their influence on history and civilisation*, Eyre & Spottiswoode, London, 2 vols. 1939.

Ghirshman, R.: *Iran*, London, Penguin 1954.

————— *Iran, Parthians and Sassanians*, London 1962, Thames & Hudson.

Gibbon, Edward.: *The Decline and Fall of the Roman Empire*, Everyman edition, 6 vols, 1954, Dent.

Glubb Pasha: *War in the Desert*, London 1960, Hodder & Stoughton.

Gough, M.: *The Early Christians*, London 1961, Thames & Hudson.

Grant, C. P.: *The Syrian Desert*, London 1937, A. & C. Black.

Green, P.: *Essays in Antiquity*, London 1950, John Murray.

————— *The Sword of Pleasure*, London 1957, John Murray.

Gregory of Nyssa, St.: *Selections: From Glory to Glory* by Jean Daniélou, Trans. Herbert Musurillo, London 1962, John Murray.

Guse, F.: 'Die Feldzüge des dritten Mithridatischen Krieges,' *Klio*, XX, 1926.

————— 'Mithridates', *Klio*, XX, 1926.

Hahn, L.: *Rom und Romanismus in Gr.-Rom. Osten*, Leipzig 1906, Dieterich.

Henderson, B. W.: *Life and Principate of the Emperor Nero*, London 1903, Methuen.

————— 'Rhandeia', *Journal of Philology*, 1901, XXVIII.

Herodian: *History of the Roman Empire*, Trans. Echols, Cambridge 1961, C.U.P.

Hcrodotus: Trans. J. E. Powell, Oxford 1949, O.U.P.

Herrmann, A.: *Die alten Seidenstrassen zwischen China und Syrien*, Berlin 1910.

Herrmann and Puchstein: *Rom in Kleinasien und Nordsyrien*, Berlin 1890.

Heyd, W.: *Commerce du Levant*, 2 vols. Oxford 1885–86.

Hinks, R.: *Greek and Roman Portrait Sculpture*, London 1935, British Museum.

Hirth, C.: *China and the Roman Orient*, K. Paul and Luzac 1939.

Holleaux, M.: 'Sur l'Histoire des Négotiations d'Antioche III avec les Romains', *Revue des Études Anciennes*, XV Bordeaux 1913, Feret et Fils.

Holmes, T. Rice: *The Architect of the Roman Empire*, 2 vols., Oxford 1928–1931, O.U.P.

Homo, Léon: *Le Siècle d'or de L'Empire Romain*, Paris 1947.

————— *Essai sur le Règne de l'Empéreur Aurelien*, Paris 1904.

————— *L'Empéreur Gallien. Revue Historique* CXXXVII (1921) 182–199; CXXXVIII (1921) 1–32.

————— 'Flamininus', *Revue Historique*, CXXI and CXXII, 1916, Presses Universitaires de France.

Honigmann, E.: *Die Ostgrenze des Byzantinischen Reiches 363–1071*, Corpus Bruxell. Hist. Byz. 3, Brussels 1935.

Honigmann, E. and Maricq, A.: *Recherches sur les Res Gestae Divi Saporis*, Acad. Roy. de Belgique. Memoires XLVII, fasc. 4, Brussels 1953.

Horace: Loeb.

Huntington, E.: 'Through the Great Canyon of the Euphrates', *R.G.S.J.* August 1962.

Isidore of Charax: *The Parthian Stations*, Trans. W. H. Schoff, Philadelphia 1914.

Jaeger, W.: *Early Christianity in Greek Paideia*.

Jerome, St.: *Select Letters*, Loeb.

Jones, A. H. M.: *The Greek City*, Oxford 1940, O.U.P.

————— *The Cities of the East Roman Provinces*, Oxford 1937, O.U.P.

————— *The Later Roman Empire*, Oxford 1964, Blackwell.

Josephus: *Wars of the Jews*, Everyman edition, Dent.

————— *Antiquities of the Jews*, Loeb.

Julien: *Lettres*, translated by J. Bidez, Paris 1924,

Juvenal: *Satires*, translated by S. H. Jeyes, Oxford 1885, Simpkin.

Kinnear: *Journey through Asia Minor*, London 1818, John Murray.

Kornemann, E.: *Staaten, Völker, Männer, aus der Geschichte des Altertums*, Leipzig, 1934, Dieterich.

Labourt, J.: *Le Christianisme dans l'Empire Perse*, Paris 1904.

Lambrechts, P.: 'Lucian Verus' *Antiquité Classique*, Louvain 1934.

Lane, Col. W. H.: *Babylonian Problems*, London 1923, John Murray.

Lattimore, O.; *Studies in Frontier History*, Oxford, 1962.

Leake, W. M.: *Journal of a Tour in Asia Minor*, London 1824, John Murray.

Le Fèvre, G.: *La Croisière Jaune*, Paris 1933.

Lehmann-Haupt, K. F.: *Armenien einst und jetzt*, Berlin 1926, B. Behrsverlag.

————— *Armenien und Nord Mesopotamien*, Lecture in Berlin, 6.3.1900.

————— *Materialen zur aeltesten Geschichte Armeniens und Mesopotamiens*, Berlin, 1907.

Lepper, F. A.: *Trajan's Parthian War*, 1948, O.U.P.

Libanius: Trans. L. Petit (*Essai sur la Vie et la Correspondence du Sophiste Libanius*) Paris 1866.

Livy: Loeb, 14 vols.

Lloyd, Seton: *The Listener*, 'The Moon Temple of Harran' April 24th 1952, B.B.C.

Longden: 'Parthian Campaigns of Trajan', *J.R.S.*, XXI, 1931.

Longinus: *On The Sublime* (with Aristotle: *Poetics*), Loeb.

Lucan: *Pharsalia*, Trans. R. Graves, London 1956, Penguin.

Lucian: Loeb, 8 vols.

Lynch, H. F. B.: *Armenia*, 1901, Longmans Green.

Maccabees, Apocrypha.

Macurdy, J. G.: *Hellenistic Queens*, Baltimore 1932, Johns Hopkins U.P.

Magie, D.: *Roman Rule in Asia Minor to the end of the Third Century after Christ*, Princeton 1950, O.U.P. 1951.

Mahaffy, J. P.: *The Silver Age of the Greek World*, Chicago 1906, University of Chicago Press.

Marcus Aurelius: Loeb.

Markwart, J.: *Studien zur Armenischen Geschichte 1915–30* IV parts. Part 4: *Sudarmenien und die Tigris Quellen nach Griechischen und Arabischen Geographen.*

Martial: *Epigrams*, Loeb, 2 vols.

Maunsell, T. R.: 'Erzerum and Cizra', *R.G.S.J.*, III, 1894.

Metzger, H.: *Les Routes de S. Paul*, Paris 1954.

Meyer, E.: *Blüte und Niedergang des Hellenismus in Asien*, Berlin 1925, K. Curtius.

Minns, E. H.: *Scythians and Greeks*, Cambridge 1913, C.U.P.

Minucius Felix, Octavius (with Tertullian, *Apology de Spectaculis*), Loeb.

Moltke, Baron H. von: *Briefe*, Berlin 1893.

Mommsen, T.: *Provinces of the Roman Empire*, 1886, Macmillan.

Munro, J. A. R.: 'Roads in Pontus', *J.H.S.*, XXI, 1901.

Newton, C. T.: *Travels and Discoveries in the Levant*, London 1865, Day.

Nock, A. D.: *Conversion*, Oxford 1961, O.U.P.

Oates, D. and J.: 'Ain Sinu in Iraq' from *Iraq*, Vol. XXI, Part 2 (published by the British School of Archaeology in Iraq).

Oppenheim, M. von: *Tell Halaf*, 1933 Putnam.

Ormerod, H. A.: *Piracy in the Ancient World*, London 1924, Hodder & Stoughton.

Osten, H. H. von der: *Die Welt der Perser*, Stuttgart 1956.

Ostrogorsky, G.: *History of the Byzantine State*, Trans, by Joan Hussey, Oxford 1956, Blackwell.

Ovid: *Tristia, Ex Ponto*, Loeb.

Parker, H. M. D.: *Roman Legions*, Cambridge 1961, Heffer.

Payne, R.: *The Holy Fire*, London 1958, Skeffington.

Percy, The Earl: *Highlands of Asiatic Turkey*, London 1901, E. Arnold.

The Periplus of the Erythraean Sea, Trans. W. H. Schoff, Philadelphia and London 1912, Longmans.

Petit, L.: See under Libanius.

Petronius: Loeb.

Philostratus: *Life of Apollonius of Tyana*, Loeb, 2 vols.

Pindar: *Extant Odes*, Trans. Myers, London 1884, Macmillan.

Platnauer, M.: *The Life and Reign of Septimius Severus*, Oxford 1918, O.U.P.

Plautus: Loeb, 5 vols.

Pliny the Elder: *Natural History*, Loeb, 11 vols.

Pliny the Younger: *Letters*, Loeb, 2 vols.

Plotinus: Trans. S. MacKenna, 1917, Medici Society.

Plutarch: *Lives*, Everyman edition, Dent.

_____ *Moralia*, Loeb, 15 vols.

Poidebard, A.: *La Trace de Rome dans le Désert de Syrie*, Paris 1934.

Polybius: *Histories*, Loeb, 6 vols.

Pope, A. Upham: *A Survey of Persian Art*, Oxford 1938, O.U.P.

Procopius: *History of the Wars; Anecdota; Buildings*, Loeb, 7 vols.

Reinach, T.: *Mithridate Eupator, Rot de Pont*, Paris 1890.

Rostovtzeff, M.: *Caravan Cities*, Oxford 1932, O.U.P.

_____ *Dura and the Problem of Parthian Art*, Yale Classical Studies, V, 1935, O.U.P.

_____ *Iranians and Greeks in South Russia*, Oxford 1922, O.U.P.

_____ *Social and Economic History of the Hellenistic World*, Oxford 1953.

_____ *Social and Economic History of the Roman Empire*, Oxford 1958 O.U.P.

_____ 'Les Inscriptions Caravanières de Palmyre' in *Mélanges Glotz*, Paris 1932.

Runciman, S.: *Byzantine Civilisation*, London 1948, E. Arnold.

_____ *The Medieval Manichee*, Cambridge 1947, C.U.P.

Sallust: Loeb.

Schur, W.: *Die Orient-Politik des Kaiser Nero* Leipzig 1923 Dieterich.

_____ *Orient Frage im Römischen Reich*, N.J. für Wiss II, 1925.

Scriptores Historiae Augustae, Loeb, 3 vols.

Sellar, W. Y.: *The Roman Poets of the Republic*, Edinburgh 1863, Hamilton.

_____ *The Roman Poets of the Augustan Age*, Oxford 1899, Clarendon Press O.U.P.

Seneca: *Moral Essays*, Loeb, 3 vols.; *Tragedies*, Loeb, 2 vols.

Seyrig, H.: 'Antiquités Syriennes' in *Syria*, XIII, Paris 1932.

———— *Mélanges Cumont*, 'Inscriptions Relatives au Commerce de Palmyre', Bruxelles 1936.

Sidonius Apollinaris: *Poems and Letters*, Loeb.

Southgate, H.: *Narrative of a Visit to the Syrian Church of Mesopotamia in 1841*, New York 1844.

Sprenger, A.: *Die Post und Reiserouten des Orients*, Leipzig 1864.

Stein, Sir M. Aurel: *Ancient Khotan*, 2 vols., Oxford 1907 (Clarendon Press).

———— 'Hatra Trade Route', *J.R.A.S.*, 1941.

Stein, E.: *Geschichte des Spätrömischen Reiches*, Vienna 1928.

Strabo: *Geography*, Loeb, 8 vols.

Strategicon (Emperor Maurice), Edited by Scheffer, Uppsala 1664.

Suetonius: *Lives of the Caesars*, etc., Loeb, 2 vols.

Sykes, M.: *Dar-ul-Islam*, London 1904, Bickers.

Syme, R.: *The Roman Revolution*, Oxford 1939, O.U.P.

Synesius: *Letters*, Trans. A. Fitzgerald, Oxford 1926, Clarendon Press.

Tabari: Trans. Nöldeke.

Tacitus: *Histories; Annals*, Loeb.

Talbot Rice. T.: *The Scythians*, London 1957, Thames and Hudson.

Tarn, W. W.: *The Greeks in Bactria and India*, Cambridge 1951.

———— *Hellenistic Naval and Military Developments*, Cambridge 1930, C.U.P.

———— 'Seleucid-Parthian Studies' Oxford, from Proceedings of the British Academy XVI, 1865, O.U.P. 1930.

Tarn, W. W. and Griffith, G. T.: *Hellenistic Civilisation*, London 1952, E. Arnold.

Tchalenko, G.: *Villages Antique de la Syrie du Nord*, 2 vols, Paris, 1953.

Taggart, F. G.: *Rome and China*, Oxford 1939, O.U.P.

Teilhard de Chardin, P.: *Letters from a Traveller*, London 1962, Collins.

Terence: Loeb, 2 vols.

Tertullian: *Apology: de Spectaculis*, Loeb.

Thompson, R. Campbell: *Ignatius*, London 1933. Luzac.

Tozer, H. F.: *Turkish Armenia and Eastern Asia Minor*, London 1881, Longmans Green.

Vasiliev, A. A.: *Histoire de l'Empire Byzantin*, Trans. Brodin et Bourguina, 2 vols. Paris 1932.

Velleius Paterculus; Loeb, see Augustus: *Res Gestae*.

Virgil: Loeb, 2 vols.

Walpole, The Hon. F., R.N.: *The Ansayrii*, London 1851, Bentley.

Warmington, E. H.: *The Commerce between the Roman Empire and India*, Cambridge 1928, C.U.P.

Wheeler, M.: *Rome beyond the Imperial Frontier*, Bell 1954.

William of Tyre (Guillaume de Tyr): edited by Paulin Paris, Paris 1879.

Yorke: 'Euphrates', *J.H.S.*, 1898.

———— 'Euphrates' *R.G.S.J.* II

———— 'Upper Euphrates', *R.G.S.J.*, VIII, 1896.

Ziegler, Karl-Heinz: *Die Beziehungen zwischen Rom und dem Partherreich*, Wiesbaden 1964.

Index

Rome on the Euphrates

Dyarbekr (Amida), on upper Tigris, 140;
plain of, 67; road to, 172, 173
Dynamis, granddaughter of Mithradates
VI, 168, 169
Dzungaria, 196, 199

East and West, opposition of:
Roman-barbarian, 233, 241; division
within empire: (Latin-Greek), 253,
312, 336, 371–372;
(European-Syrian), 258;
Byzantine-Iranian, 373
Edessa (Urfa), 99, 106, 109, 114, 238,
241, 255, 339, 343, 348; kingdom of,
113, 117, 119, 211, 216, 243, 295;
sack of, under Trajan, 216; again
independent, 257, 267, 294; in
Byzantine times, 369, 385;
Christianity in, 378, 379, 384, 385;
modern city, 385
Ecbatana (Hamadan), in Persia, 98, 106,
126, 214
education, 270, 278, 363
Egnatia, Via, 27, 140, 205
Egnatius, with Crassus at Carrhae, 117,
118
Egypt: Ptolemaic, 8, 15, 17, 28, 29, 37,
40, 86, 97, 96, 100, 112; under
Roman empire, 151–152, 162, 165,
166, 184, 195, 206, 222, 231, 234,
240, 243, 253, 271, 281, 282, 286,
302, 303; under Palmyra, 297, 300,
301; under Byzantine empire, 375,
381, 383, 389; modern, 103
Egyptians, 206, 243, 281
Eknai (Skenai), in Mesopotamia, 117
Elagabalus (emperor A.D. 218–22), 259,
263, 283
Elazig, plain of, 67
Elegeia (Erzerum), 209, 238
Elephantine, in Egypt, 387
elephants, 4, 5, 7, 20, 165, 342, 350
Emesa (Homs), in Syria, 295

Ephesus, city of province of Asia, 2, 10,
16, 40, 207, 222, 267, 285, 293, 331;
Council of (A.D. 431), 385
Ephraim (Syrus), St. (ca. A.D. 306–73),
378
Epictetus, philosopher, 227, 270, 279,
280, 281
Epicurus and Epicureanism, 141, 142
Epiphania, in Cilicia, 293
equestrian order: see knights
Erbil (Arbela), 106
Eriza, 209
Ermenek, Tell (Tigranocerta?), 67
Erzerum (Elegeia), 124, 180, 209, 238;
refounded A.D. 440 (Theodosiopolis),
363
Eski Seruj, 340
Eski Shehir, 404n32
Ethiopians, 137
Euboea, Antiochus's wife named, 12, 17
Eudoxus of Cyzicus, explorer, 103
Eumenes I, king of Pergamon (reigned
197–159 B.C), 7, 18, 20, 21
Euphrates, R., 40, 58, 59, 65–66, 171,
180, 194, 209, 218, 370, 405n9;
trade across, 8, 98, 99, 192, 251;
crossing-places, 106–108, 179, 190,
248, 248–249, 301, 341; route along,
243, 248, 367; estuary of, 243, 246,
247
Roman frontier on, 44, 55, 76, 79, 110,
118–119, 160, 162, 175, 184, 185,
189, 205, 208, 250, 391; Antony and,
124; Trajan on, 212, 239; Hadrian
and, 219, 238, 246, 255; Lucius Verus
and, 239; under later emperors, 303,
305, 339; Julian crosses, 344; under
Justinian, 356–357, 387
Euphratesia (formerly Commagene),
369, 384
Euripides, 325
Eusebius, Church historian, 316, 317,
334

legions: number of, 161, 174, 254, 306; stations of, 237–238, 250, 284, 304–305; recruitment of, 253; disappearance of, in Byzantine age, 370. *See also* army, Roman; infantry, Roman

Lepanto (Naupactus), in Greece, 21

Lepper, F. A., 208

Leuke Kome, on Red Sea, 165, 167

Lex: *see under name of law, e.g.* Sempronia

li (Chinese measure), 192

Libanius, orator, 277, 317, 318, 348

Libya, 278, 359, 391

Licinius (emperor A.D. 308–324), 18, 305

Lije (Ilidja, Legerda), 183

limes, the eastern, 253–254

liturgies (public service), 271, 272, 288

Livia, wife of Augustus, 166

Livy (Titus Livius), historian, 19, 50, 73, 119, 154

Lombards, 386

Longinus, writer, 296, 299, 301

Lop Nor, in central Asia, 191

Lou-Ian, in central Asia, 191

Lo-yang (Ho-nan-fu), 191

Lucan, poet, 117, 155, 224

Lucian, prose writer, 171, 193, 225, 226, 227, 230, 232, 249

Lucullus, Lucius Licinius (115–47 B.C.), consul 73 B.C., and commander in war against Mithradates, 34, 54, 58–59, 65, 84; his dealings with Armenia, 66–77, 111, 116, 118, 185, 186, 390; superseded in the east by Pompey (67 B.C.), 77–78,79; character, 75, 78–79, 130,132, 134

Luristan, 199

Lycaonia, in Asia Minor, language of, 277

Lycia, in Asia Minor, 206, 221

Lycus (Kelkit) valley and R., in Pontus, 53, 54, 56, 57–59, 201, 209

Lydians, the, 1

Lysimacheia, in Thrace, 8, 9, 10, 11, 15, 18

Ma'arret en-Nu'man, near Aleppo, 390

Macedon, kingdom of, 8, 226. *See also* Alexander the Great

Macedonia, 1, 20, 91; annexed by Rome, 84

Macedonians, 214, 226, 240, 290; character of, 19, 24, 96, 314, 373; in eastern cities, 117, 218, 243, 243, 264; Caracalla's phalanx of, 259

Macedonians (heretics, followers of Macedonius), 336

Macrinus (emperor A.D. 217–18), 256, 259, 283, 315

Maecenas, Gaius Cilnius, Augustus's minister, 151, 152

Magians, 380

Magnesia on the Hermus (Manisa), 2; battle of (189 B.C.), 2–7, 18, 116; its results, 20–23, 99,129,134, 361

Magnesia on the Macander, 28

Malalas, John, Byzantine chronicler, 382, 383

Mani, 379

Manichaeanism, 379

Manlius Vulso, Gnaeus, consul 189 B.C., sent to Asia to conclude peace with Antiochus III, 27, 48

Mansur, the treasurer, 390

Malacca, straits of, 194

Malatya (Melitene), 66, 124

Maraba (catholicus A.D. 540–542), 380

Marcian, Christian heretic (2nd cent. A.D.), 379

Marcomanni, Germanic people, 304

Marcus Aurelius (emperor A.D. 161–180), 193, 194, 203, 210, 220, 224, 226, 230, 235, 238, 240, 241, 247, 256, 270, 278, 279, 281, 283, 284, 319, 320, 343, 344; his eastern policy, 220, 238, 240, 247;